David L. Petersen

HAGGAI AND ZECHARIAH 1–8

David L. Petersen

HAGGAI AND ZECHARIAH 1-8

A Commentary

The Westminster Press
Philadelphia

Book design by Gene Harris

First edition

Published by The Westminster Press®
Philadelphia, Pennsylvania

PRINTED IN THE UNITED STATES OF AMERICA
2 4 6 8 9 7 5 3 1

Library of Congress Cataloging in Publication Data

Petersen, David L.
  Haggai and Zechariah 1–8.

  (The Old Testament Library)
  Bibliography: p.
  1. Bible. O.T. Haggai—Commentaries. 2. Bible.
O.T. Zechariah I–VIII—Commentaries. I. Bible. O.T.
Haggai. English. 1984. II. Bible. O.T. Zechariah,
I–VIII. English. 1984. III. Title. IV. Title: Haggai
and Zechariah one–eight. V. Series.
BS1655.3.P48 1984   224'.97077   84-7477
ISBN 0-664-21830-X

CONTENTS

ZECHARIAH 1–8

PREFACE

This commentary grows out of my long-standing interest in and work on the formative period in ancient Israelite history known as the restoration and the character of Israelite prophecy during that period. The restoration followed the fall of the nation in 587 B.C.E. and preceded the development of the form of Judaism which we associate with the names of Ezra and Nehemiah. Since the appearance of the last comprehensive commentary in English on Haggai-Zechariah 1–8, much has been learned about this period, especially about the last decades of the sixth century, which provide the immediate historical context for the work of Haggai and Zechariah. In this regard, I owe a considerable debt to those who have focused their scholarly efforts on this era and on the roles which Haggai and Zechariah played in it, especially to the work of Peter Ackroyd. Moreover, I have benefited from the incisive studies of these two prophetic books which have appeared during the past several decades, particularly the monographs of W. Beuken, A. Petitjean, and C. Jeremias, as well as to the commentaries of W. Rudolph and S. Amsler.

No commentary can hope to be truly exhaustive and at the same time coherent. This volume includes text-critical and philological notes when these appear necessary for the elucidation of the biblical text under discussion. Similarly, I have introduced notes which represent the dialogue between my own work and that of my predecessors. However, my primary goal has been to provide a fresh interpretation of the oracles and visions included in these two prophetic collections rather than to create a systematic report on my research.

I am beholden to several individuals—Mary Crawford, Patricia Shelly, Judith Smith, and Sandy Smith—for their help in the preparation of the book manuscript. Also, I wish to thank the editors and publishers of *Vetus Testamentum* and the *Catholic Biblical Quarterly* for allowing me to use portions of earlier articles relevant to this commentary project.

The drawings in Chapter 4 were adapted by Nola Melcher from the following photographs: Figure 1—*Bulletin of the American Schools of Oriental Research* (No. 160, 1960, p. 14); Figure 2—*Biblica* (Vol. 51, 1970, p. 192).

The translation of Haggai and Zechariah 1–8 is my own. For other biblical quotations the text of the Revised Standard Version has generally been followed with slight adaptations, in particular the reading of "Yahweh" for RSV "the LORD."

This book is dedicated to my family.

ABBREVIATIONS

ANEP	*The Ancient Near East in Pictures Relating to the Old Testament*, ed. J. Pritchard. Princeton University Press, 1954
ANET	*Ancient Near Eastern Texts Relating to the Old Testament*, ed. J. Pritchard. Princeton University Press, 1955², 1969³
BASOR	*Bulletin of the American Schools of Oriental Research*
BDB	F. Brown, S. Driver, and C. Briggs, *Hebrew and English Lexicon of the Old Testament*. Oxford: Clarendon Press, 1906
BHK	*Biblia Hebraica³*, ed. R. Kittel, Stuttgart, 1937
BHS	*Biblica Hebraica Stuttgartensia*, Stuttgart, 1977
Bib	*Biblica*, Rome
Bib Or	*Biblica et Orientalia*, Rome
CBQ	*Catholic Biblical Quarterly*, Washington, D.C.
CTA	*Corpus des tablettes en cunéiformes alphabétiques*, ed. A. Herdner
Dt. Isa.	Deutero-Isaiah (Isaiah 40–55)
Dtr.	The Deuteronomistic history (Deuteronomy–II Kings)
dtr.	deuteronomistic
E	English (where numbering differs from the Hebrew)
ET	English translation
EI	*Eretz Israel*, Jerusalem
EThL	*Ephemerides Theologicae Lovanienses*, Louvain
EvTh	Evangelische Theologie, *Munich*
GK	*Gesenius' Hebrew Grammar*, ed. E. Kautzsch. Oxford: Clarendon Press, 1910
IDB	*The Interpreter's Dictionary of the Bible*. 4 vols., ed. G. Buttrick et al. Nashville: Abingdon Press, 1962
IDB Supp	*The Interpreter's Dictionary of the Bible, Supplementary Volume*, ed. K. Crim. Nashville: Abingdon Press, 1976
IEJ	*Israel Exploration Journal*, Jerusalem

IR	*The Iliff Review*, Denver
JAOS	*Journal of the American Oriental Society*, New Haven
JB	Jerusalem Bible
JBL	*Journal of Biblical Literature*
JJS	*Journal of Jewish Studies*, Oxford
JPS	*The Prophets: A New Translation of the Holy Scriptures According to the Masoretic Text*. Philadelphia: Jewish Publication Society of America, 1978
JSOT	*Journal for the Study of the Old Testament*, Sheffield
JSS	*Journal of Semitic Studies*, Manchester
JTS	*Journal of Theological Studies*, Oxford
LXX	Septuagint
MT	Massoretic Text
Mur	Scrolls of the twelve Minor Prophets, published in Discoveries in the Judaean Desert, Vol. 2, *Les grottes de Murabba'ât*. 2 vols., ed. P. Benoit et al. Oxford: Clarendon Press, 1961
NAB	New American Bible
NEB	New English Bible
Or	*Orientalia*, Rome
OTL	The Old Testament Library
OTS	*Oudtestamentische Studiën*, Leiden
P	The priestly work
QMIA	Qedem, Monographs of the Institute of Archaeology, Hebrew University
RSV	Revised Standard Version
S	Syriac
Sefîre	J. Fitzmyer, *The Aramaic Inscriptions of Sefîre*, 1967
ST	*Studia Theologica*, Oslo
T	Targum
TD	*Theology Digest*, St. Louis
TDOT	*Theological Dictionary of the Old Testament*, ed. G. Botterweck and H. Ringgren, 1974–. ET of *TWAT*
TWAT	*Theologisches Wörterbuch zum Alten Testament*, ed. G. Botterweck and H. Ringgren, 1972–
TZ	*Theologische Zeitschrift*, Basel
V	Vulgate
VT	*Vetus Testamentum*, Leiden
VT Supp	*Vetus Testamentum, Supplements*
ZAW	*Zeitschrift für die alttestamentliche Wissenschaft*
ZDPV	*Zeitschrift des deutschen Palästina-Vereins*
ZThK	*Zeitschrift für Theologie und Kirche*, Tübingen

SELECT BIBLIOGRAPHY

I. *Commentaries in Series*

Amsler, S. *Aggée, Zacharie, Malachie,* 1981. Commentaire de l'Ancien Testament XIc.

Baldwin, J. *Haggai, Zechariah, Malachi,* 1972. Tyndale Old Testament Commentaries.

Chary, T. *Aggée, Zacharie, Malachie,* 1969. Sources Bibliques.

Elliger, K. *Das Buch der zwölf kleinen Propheten,* 1967[6]. Das Alte Testament Deutsch 25.

Horst, F. *Die Zwölf kleinen Propheten Nahum bis Maleachi,* 1964[3]. Handbuch zum Alten Testament 14.

Mason, R. *The Books of Haggai, Zechariah and Malachi,* 1977. Cambridge Bible Commentary, Old Testament.

Mitchell, H., et al. *Haggai, Zechariah, Malachi, Jonah,* 1912. International Critical Commentary.

Nowack, W. *Die kleinen Propheten,* 1922. Göttinger Handkommentar zum Alten Testament III/4.

Rudolph, W. *Haggai—Sacharja 1–8/9–14—Maleachi,* 1976. Kommentar zum Alten Testament XIII/4.

Sellin, E. *Das Zwölfprophetenbuch.* Kommentar zum Alten Testament XII.

Thomas, D. W. "The Book of Haggai"; "The Book of Zechariah, Chapters 1–8." *The Interpreter's Bible* 6.

van der Woude, A. S. *Haggai, Maleachi,* 1982. De Prediking van het Oude Testament.

II. *Monographs*

Ackroyd, P. *Exile and Restoration: A Study of Hebrew Thought in the Sixth Century B.C.,* 1968.

Beuken, W. *Haggai—Sacharja 1–8. Studien zur Überlieferungsgeschichte der frühnachexilischen Prophetie,* 1967.

Beyse, K.-M. *Serubbabel und die Königserwartungen der Propheten*

Haggai und Sacharja. Eine historische und traditionsgeschichtliche Untersuchung, 1972.

Bič, M. *Die Nachtgesichte des Sacharja*, 1964.

Dandamaev, M. *Persien unter den ersten Achämeniden (6 Jahrhundert v. Chr.)*, 1963 (German tr. 1976).

Ehrlich, A. *Randglossen zur hebräischen Bibel*. 7 vols., 1908–1914.

Fitzmyer, J. *The Aramaic Inscriptions of Sefîre*, 1967.

Galling, K. *Studien zur Geschichte Israels im persischen Zeitalter*, 1964.

──────. *Syrien in der Politik der Achämeniden bis zum Aufstand des Megabyzos 448 v. Chr.*, 1937.

Jeremias, C. *Die Nachtgesichte des Sacharja. Untersuchungen zu ihrer Stellung im Zusammenhang der Visionsberichte im Alten Testament und zu ihrem Bildmaterial*, 1977.

Kippenberg, H. *Religion und Klassenbildung im antiken Judäa. Eine religions-soziologische Studie zum Verhältnis von Tradition und gesellschaftlicher Entwicklung*, 1978.

Kreissig, H. *Die sozialökonomische Situation in Juda zur Achämenidenzeit*, 1973.

Leuze, O. *Die Satrapieneinteilung in Syrien und im Zweistromland von 520–330*, 1935.

Olmstead, A. *History of the Persian Empire*, 1959.

Petitjean, A. *Les oracles du Proto-Zacharie. Un programme de restauration pour la communauté juive après l'exile*, 1969.

Ringnell, L. *Die Nachtgesichte des Sacharja*, 1950.

Rothstein, J. *Juden und Samaritaner. Die grundlegende Scheidung von Judentum und Heidentum. Eine kritische Studie zum Buche Haggai und zur jüdischen Geschichte im ersten nachexilischen Jahrhundert*, 1908.

──────. *Die Nachtgesichte des Sacharja. Studien zur Sacharjaprophetie und zur jüdischen Geschichte im ersten nachexilischen Jahrhundert*, 1910.

Seybold, K. *Bilder zum Tempelbau: Die Visionen des Propheten Sacharja*, 1974.

Stern, E. *The Material Culture of the Land of the Bible in the Persian Period 538–332 B.C.E.*, 1973 (ET 1982).

Wolff, H. *Haggai, Eine Auslegung*, 1951.

III. *Articles*

Ackroyd, P. "Archaeology, Politics and Religion: The Persian Period," *IR* 39, 1982, 5–24.

———. "The Books of Haggai and Zechariah I–VIII," *JJS* 3, 1952, 151–156.

———. "Studies in the Book of Haggai," *JJS* 2, 1951, 163–176.

Cross, F. "A Reconstruction of the Judean Restoration," *JBL* 94, 1975, 4–18.

Halpern, B. "The Ritual Background of Zechariah's Temple Song," *CBQ* 40, 1978, 167–190.

Koch, K. "Haggais unreines Volk," *ZAW* 79, 1967, 52–66.

Lipiński, E. "Recherches sur le livre de Zacharie," *VT* 20, 1970, 25–55.

McEvenue, S. "The Political Structure in Judah from Cyrus to Nehemiah," *CBQ* 43, 1981, 353–364.

Mason, R. "The Prophets of the Restoration," in *Israel's Prophetic Tradition: Essays in Honour of Peter R. Ackroyd*, ed. R. Coggin et al., 1982, 137–154.

———. "The Purpose of the 'Editorial Framework' of the Book of Haggai," *VT* 27, 1977, 413–421.

Petersen, D. "Zechariah's Visions: A Theological Perspective," *VT* 34, 1984, 195–206.

———. "Zerubbabel and Jerusalem Temple Reconstruction," *CBQ* 36, 1974, 366–372.

Sauer, G. "Serubbabel in der Sicht Haggais und Sacharjas," in *Das ferne und nahe Wort. Festschrift Leonhard Rost*, ed. F. Maass, 1967, 199–207.

Schottroff, W. "Zur Sozialgeschichte Israels in der Perserzeit," *Verkündigung und Forschung* 27, 1982, 46–68.

Seybold, K. "Die Königserwartung bei den Propheten Haggai und Sacharja," *Judaica* 28, 1972, 69–78.

Steck, O. "Zu Haggai 1:2–11," *ZAW* 83, 1971, 355–379.

Weinberg, J. "Die Agrarverhältnisse in der Bürger-Tempel-Gemeinde der Achämenidenzeit," in *Wirtschaft und Gesellschaft im Alten Vorderasien*, ed. J. Harmatta and G. Komoróczy, 1976, 473–486.

Weinberg, S. "Post-Exilic Palestine: An Archaeological Report," *Proceedings of the Israel Academy of Sciences and Humanities* 4, 1971, 78-97.

Whedbee, J. "A Question-Answer Schema in Haggai 1: The Form and Function of Haggai 1:9–11," in *Biblical and Near Eastern Studies: Essays in Honor of W. S. LaSor*, ed. G. Tuttle, 1978, 184–194.

HAGGAI

INTRODUCTION

As with other books that comprise the Latter Prophets, the book known as Haggai receives its title from the name of the prophet whose words and deeds the book preserves. The name Haggai *(ḥaggay)* derives from the triconsonantal Hebrew stem *ḥgg,* which means "make a pilgrimage" or "observe a pilgrimage feast." The Old Testament preserves the names of four individuals whose names derive from this primary word: *ḥaggît,* Haggith (II Sam. 3:4; I Kings 1:6, 11; 2:13; I Chron. 3:2), wife of David and the mother of Adonijah; *ḥaggiyyāh,* Haggiah (I Chron. 6:30), a Levite from the Merari clan; *ḥaggî,* Haggi (Gen. 46:16; Num. 26:15), one of Gad's sons; and the prophet *ḥaggay,* Haggai. The name of the prophet appears to hold no special secrets. It must be said, however, that when Haggai addresses the reconstruction of the major Yahwistic pilgrimage shrine—the temple in Jerusalem—as well as the ritual activity which took place at that center, his very name appears to resonate with and to provide partial warrant for focused concern on cultic matters.

Unlike some prophets who are unattested outside the books that bear their names (e.g., Amos, Hosea, Ezekiel), Haggai's name appears elsewhere in the Old Testament. In Ezra 5:1, a historian wrote, "Now the prophets Haggai and Zechariah the son of Iddo prophesied to the Judahites who were in Judah and Jerusalem in the name of the God of Israel who was over them." And in Ezra 6:14: "The elders of the Jews built and prospered through the prophesying of Haggai the prophet, and Zechariah the son of Iddo." This latter formulation is interesting since the label "the prophet" *(nᵉbiyyā'h)* following the name of Haggai seems superfluous and is not included in LXX manuscripts. And without that label, Haggai appears without either a role label or a genealogy in these two narrative accounts. This absence of specification concerning Haggai's identity is unusual when compared with introductory references to others of Israel's prophets. Of the thirteen books in the Latter Prophets which are known by the proper name of a prophet,[1] eight are identified in the opening verses by a genealogy (Isaiah, Jeremiah, Ezekiel, Hosea, Joel, Jonah, Zephaniah, and Zechariah), two by place of origin alone (Micah, Nahum). Only three remain unidentified either by genealogy or by geography: Habakkuk, Amos, and Haggai. The absence of a genealogy for Haggai is especially unusual since genealogies played a very important role in establishing continuities with the past for those who lived in the early postexilic period.[2] The absence of a genealogy for Haggai directs attention away from Haggai's origins and to the source of Haggai's authority as prophet, his communication of Yahweh's word. To this extent Haggai is viewed as having a different sort of authority from either of the officials with whom he was remembered as being directly involved, Joshua and Zerubbabel. Both of them received their authority, at least in part, by dint of genealogy. Not so with Haggai.

Some scholars have maintained that the absence of a genealogy for Haggai suggests that Haggai was not part of the group which was concerned about genealogies, i.e., he was not part of the group which returned from exile in Babylon.[3] The strongest case for viewing Haggai as one who had resided in Syria-Palestine has been made by Beuken,[4] who has been impressed by the lack of attention to Jerusalem per se in Haggai's speeches. Further, Beuken thinks Trito-Isaiah, who in all likelihood had been in Babylon, is markedly different from Haggai in his reflection on reconstruction, the "nations," and agriculture. As a result, Beuken argues that Haggai was a Judahite farmer, one who represented archaic Yahwism, a religion that did not have a significant investment in Zion election traditions. In my judgment, this assessment builds too much on the fact that Haggai mentions agricultural matters. As the commentary itself shows, much of Haggai's language about agriculture derives from futility curse language and not necessarily from Haggai's own presumed life-style or experiences as a farmer. Although there is no evidence that Haggai had been in Babylon, there is also no evidence to the contrary. In sum, Haggai's own life history remains enigmatic—and this was, I think, intended by the author. The person responsible for the book of Haggai seems intent on avoiding biographical or genealogical matters in order

[1] I exclude mention of Malachi since, in my judgment, it is not a personal name but rather a noun, "my messenger."

[2] See, for example, the description in Ezra 2 of those who had returned from Babylon.

[3] Cf. Rudolph, 21, who thinks it likely that Haggai had been in exile. Amsler, 15, maintains that there is not enough information about this matter to make a judgment.

[4] Beuken, 221–229.

to focus the reader's attention on what it was that authorized Haggai to act as prophet. It was not personal history but Yahweh's word which served that function.

Since what little information we do have about Haggai (that given in Ezra 5–6) links him to Zechariah, and since the chronologies of the two prophetic books under consideration in this volume present prophets who were active in the same year, 520 B.C.E., it is perhaps surprising that neither book provides evidence of contact between these two prophetic figures. It has been argued that the book of Haggai was written to demonstrate that Haggai, and not his contemporary Zechariah, was the primary mover behind the completion of the temple. Perhaps the references to Haggai in Ezra 5 and 6 demonstrate, more than anything else, that within one hundred years of their respective activity, Haggai and Zechariah were perceived as working for and effecting the same fundamental goal, the rebuilding of the temple. And, as we will have occasion to see, especially in the sections of this volume devoted to Zechariah's visions, this assessment by the writer of Ezra was not altogether accurate.

1. The Times

Some Old Testament prophetic literature seems to have no easily discernible specific historical context. For example, if one begins to read the book of Habakkuk, there are four obvious indicators for dating the oracles. The most one receives by way of evidence in this regard is the word "Chaldeans" in Hab. 1:6, a word that has led most commentators to argue that the general context for the book is the Neo-Babylonian period. Nevertheless, one would need much data to establish a specific historical or political setting for the book of Habakkuk. However, in other books (e.g., Isaiah) there is a more obvious relationship between historical context and prophetic utterance.[5] Many of Isaiah's oracles relate directly to the major political developments of his time. Much the same may be said for Haggai and Zechariah. It is not hyperbole to suggest that the books of Haggai and Zechariah provide the most chronologically focused literature in the Old Testament. All of the book of Haggai is dated by

---

[5] Cf. G. von Rad's comment on the book of Isaiah: "So great is the supple power of his message to adapt itself to every change in the political situation that it can show us the specific historical situation simply in the clear-cut contours of the items in the messages themselves" (*Old Testament Theology*, 1965, Vol. 2, 147).

the editor to the second year of Darius' reign, or 520 B.C.E.; more specifically, to a three-month period of that year—from the sixth (Aug.–Sept.) to the ninth (Nov.–Dec.) month. And Zechariah 1–8 dates from the eighth month of that same year, in the eighth month (Oct.–Nov.), to the ninth month (Nov.–Dec.) of Darius' fourth regnal year. The book of Haggai represents one three-month period, whereas Zechariah covers a longer period of two years. Rarely in the biblical material does such a limited time period receive such concentrated attention.

In order to understand the reason for such concentration, one needs to understand as much as possible about the overall political (international and domestic) as well as social and economic context for the activity of Haggai and Zechariah. The international situation during and several decades before the time of Haggai and Zechariah had a profound impact on what these prophets were about. The entire face of the ancient Near East—Mesopotamia, Syria-Palestine, Egypt—changed with the defeat of the Babylonian empire, an event that may be conveniently dated to the defeat of the city of Babylon in 538 B.C.E.[6] With remarkable swiftness, Cyrus was able to consolidate his military victories and to establish Persian political authority on the soil captured from Babylonia.[7] The "official" version reads, "The state of peace was imposed upon the city. Cyrus sent greetings to all Babylon. Gobryas, his governor, installed (sub-)governors in Babylon."[8] Using a system of massive provinces, a system he had developed earlier in the creation of territories such as Lydia and Taballus, Cyrus was able to incorporate Babylonian holdings as well as Babylon itself into his empire. In fact, Babylon and one province it ruled, Syria-Palestine, were joined into one huge satrapy: Babili-Ebirnari, "Babylon–Beyond the River." Gobryas was installed as governor and Cambyses, Cyrus' son, remained in Babylon as a royal representative. This heavy investment of royal and nonroyal authority figures signals the special importance this huge satrapy bore in Cyrus' mind. Interestingly, it was a satrapy that continued to link the fate of Syria-Palestine with Babylon.

What immediate effect these events had on the people and territory of Syria-Palestine is not wholly clear. It is obvious that Cyrus' activity

---

[6] On the inept rule of Nabonidus and the ease with which the Persians were able to defeat Babylon, see W. Hallo and W. Simpson, *The Ancient Near East: A History,* 1971, 147–149.

[7] On Cyrus' exploits, see M. Mallowan, "Cyrus the Great (558–529 B.C.)," *Iran* 10, 1972, 1–17.

[8] See the "Nabonidus Chronicle," *ANET,* 306.

affected those Israelites living in exile in Mesopotamia. At least one of them was able to construe Cyrus as Yahweh's anointed: "Cyrus, he is my shepherd, he shall fulfill my purposes. . . . Thus says Yahweh to his anointed, to Cyrus" (Isa. 44:28; 45:1). What Cyrus accomplished was clearly viewed with approbation by such Israelites. However, this same group must have been somewhat disappointed by the relatively gentle treatment that Babylon received from Cyrus—in contrast to the fate that Jerusalem had received at the hands of the Babylonians. Israel had anticipated that Babylon would suffer devastation, perhaps on the basis of the violence with which Cyrus attacked other Babylonian cities: "And Babylon, the glory of kingdoms, the splendor and pride of the Chaldeans, will be like Sodom and Gomorrah when God overthrew them. It will never be inhabited or dwelt in for all generations; no Arab will pitch his tent there, no shepherds will make their flocks lie down there" (Isa. 13:19–20).[9] And yet, disappointment at the lack of a violent fate for Babylon must have been in large part assuaged by the munificence that Judahites saw in the Cyrus edict, a document promulgated early in Cyrus' reign over Babylonian territories. The salient portion of the cylinder inscription reads as follows: "I returned to these sacred cities on the other side of the Tigris, the sanctuaries of which have been ruins for a long time, the images which [used] to live therein and established them for permanent sanctuaries. I [also] gathered all their [former] inhabitants and returned [to them] their habitations."[10] Israel remembered this decree as warrant for a return by some who had been in exile and also as a provision of financial support for the reconstruction of the temple (so Ezra 1:2–4; 6:2–5). For those in exile, Cyrus' defeat of Babylon may not have seemed violent enough, but the provision for the restoration of Yahwism in Israel helped make up for a sense of international injustice.

As for the territory of the Levant in contrast to Israelites in exile, it is not clear when and if Cyrus actually campaigned on Syro-Palestinian soil. Nor is it clear when those living in the Levant would have actually experienced the shift from Neo-Babylonian to Persian dominion.[11] The Cyrus cylinder, an inscription dating to 538 B.C.E., does provide some data concerning this issue: "All the kings of the entire world from

---

[9] On this point, see Galling, *Studien zur Geschichte Israels*, 1964, 54–55.

[10] *ANET*, 316. For a recent reevaluation of this document, consult A. Kuhrt, "The Cyrus Cylinder and Achaemenid Imperial Policy," *JSOT* 25, 1983, 83–97.

[11] See Ackroyd, *Exile and Restoration*, 141–142; J. Bright, *A History of Israel*, 1981³, 361 n. 42.

the Upper to the Lower sea, those who are seated in throne rooms, [those who] live in other [types of buildings as well as] all the kings of the West lands living in tents, brought their heavy tributes and kissed my feet in Babylon."[12] The tenor of this description must, of course, be tempered by its inflated royal rhetoric. However, the direct implication is that rather soon after the defeat of Babylon, those in Syria-Palestine would have known and paid homage to their new overlord. It was altogether likely that (at least to some in Syria, where Media had ruled) the conquest of Media by Cyrus in 550 would have signaled a major shift of power in the offing. As for Cyrus' own military movements, he may have campaigned in Syria on his return from Greece about 547 B.C.E.[13] Such a campaign might help to explain why Nabonidus returned to Babylon from Tema about 545. In any case, Cyrus' success in Mesopotamia, northern Syria, Anatolia, and Greece would have almost certainly been known to those in Syria-Palestine during the years 545–540.

In 537, soon after conquering Babylon, Cyrus returned to his Persian residence, Ecbatana. Little if any information is available concerning his activities during the next half decade. However, we do know that in 531/30 Cyrus felt it necessary to undertake a campaign in the far northeastern reaches of the empire. And it was there, against the Massagetae, that he fell in battle.[14] Since Cambyses had been ruling from Babylon as coregent with his father, a smooth transition of rule was possible despite the presence of a pretender to the throne, Bardiya, Cambyses' brother. Once his control of the empire was consolidated, Cambyses' first major military campaign was directed at the only territory of the ancient Near East that fell outside the control of the Persians—Egypt. And in a campaign well chronicled by Herodotus, Cambyses was able to conquer much of Egypt, a feat that may be dated with reference to the fall of Memphis in 525 B.C.E.[15] On his march into Egypt, Cambyses had crossed the Arabian desert, but on his way home he proceeded up into Syria-Palestine. It was near Mt. Carmel, in 522, that he received news of a revolt at home and died, whether by suicide or murder is difficult to determine.[16]

Darius, an officer in Cambyses' army and one who was of royal

---

[12] *ANET*, 316.

[13] See Olmstead, *Persian Empire*, 45.

[14] Ibid., 66.

[15] Ibid., 88–89; G. Posener, *La première domination perse en Egypte*, 1936.

[16] Dandamaev, *Persien*, 150–160, maintains Cambyses was murdered by the Persian tribal nobility.

blood, though not of direct descent through Cambyses, was apparently able to gain the favor of the army. He returned immediately to Media, where in that same year he was able to execute Gaumata, the rebel, and his cohort.[17]

The accession year of Darius, 522, marked the beginning of a number of insurrections across the Persian empire. In virtually every corner of its territory, rebellion took place, though interestingly no insurrection is mentioned explicitly as occurring in Syria-Palestine. In Babylon the situation was particularly severe. First, Nebuchadnezzar III, a self-proclaimed descendant of Nabonidus, declared his independence. And shortly after his defeat, another rebel, Nebuchadnezzar IV, laid claim to the Babylonian throne.[18] However difficult this period no doubt was for Darius, it seems clear that he was able, as were Cyrus and Cambyses before him, to achieve firm control of the empire in a few years, i.e., by 520, with the possible exception of the Egyptian satrapy newly acquired by Cambyses.[19]

Part of Darius' efforts to consolidate control of the empire focused on reform, especially administrative reforms of the satrapal system.[20] About 520 B.C.E., Darius began introducing Persians into regional offices that had earlier been held by natives. So Gobryas, about whom we hear nothing in Babylon after the revolts of the Nebuchadnezzars in 522–521, (perhaps he was a sympathizer?) was replaced by Ushtani (Greek, Hystanes). Persians even appeared in lower provincial administrative ranks, especially in tax and finance-related roles.

Such, briefly stated, were the vicissitudes of Persian political history immediately before and at the time of Haggai and Zechariah. How did Syria-Palestine fit into this empire? As we have seen, the satrapy in which Jerusalem and Judah sat during this period was a large one: Babylon and Beyond the River. Not only was it large, it was important as the presence of Gobryas and Cambyses in Babylon demonstrates. For Cyrus, the more important of the two subdivisions of the empire was clearly Babylon. This situation changed with the rule of Cambyses when Syria-Palestine achieved greater prominence. When he became emperor, he must have felt that Babylon was "safe"; he had, after all,

---

[17] On this issue, see E. Bickerman and H. Tadmor, "Darius I, Pseudo-Smerdis and the Magi," *Athenaeum* 56, 1978, 239–261.

[18] See Bright, *History of Israel*, 369–370, esp. nn. 65 and 66.

[19] In 519–518 B.C.E., Darius found it necessary to campaign in Egypt, thereby suggesting again the rather precarious situation in that satrapy.

[20] On the legal reform associated with Darius' name, see Olmstead, *Persian Empire*, 119–133.

ruled there for several years. Hence he was able to campaign rather
early in his reign. Syria-Palestine gained significance because it was
through this territory that major lines of communication ran from
Persia to the arena of Cambyses' military activity: Egypt. Because of
the critical importance which Syria-Palestine achieved in the period
530–520, it is altogether likely that it became necessary to have a
separate administrator for "Beyond the River,"[21] someone presumably skilled in military as well as financial matters. And it is just such a
situation that is already in place during the early years of Darius'
reign.[22] We hear of an administrator Ushtani, an individual who is
known as governor *(pḥh)* of Babili and Ebirnari. There are texts that
so designate him in the first, third, and sixth years of Darius' rule.
However, Ezra (6:6, 13) attests a certain Tattenai who is governor
(pḥh) of Beyond the River, and this at the same time during which
Ushtani would have been prefect of the entire satrapy. Although some
scholars have tried to harmonize the names of Ushtani and Tattenai
because of their identical titles, *pḥh,* it seems almost certain (so Leuze
and Galling, among others) that Ushtani was satrap or governor for
the whole of the double satrapy, whereas Tattenai was a subordinate
official, one who ruled only over "Beyond the River."[23] It may be
helpful to see the probable administrative ladder of "Judah" outlined
graphically:[24]

King of Babylon and the Lands:	Darius
Governor *(peḥāh)* of Babylon and Beyond the River:	Ushtani
Governor *(peḥāh)* of Beyond the River:	Tattenai
(Governor of Judah:	Zerubbabel)

This appointment of an official over just the territory known as
Beyond the River was a move toward the formal division of what later
became known as the fifth satrapy: the territory of Syria-Palestine and
Cyprus. According to Herodotus, this was a division that occurred
under Darius, and, if the division did occur then, it was no doubt a part

---

[21] Galling, *Syrien,* 19–24.

[22] Leuze, *Satrapieneinteilung.*

[23] On these two officials, see Leuze, *Satrapieneinteilung,* 36–42. Whether there was
another official over Babili is unclear. I doubt whether the satrap Ushtani would have
allowed a subordinate over that very important territory. On the ambiguity of the titles
in the Persian administrative structure, see Leuze, 40–42, and Galling, *Syrien,* 22.

[24] Thus Leuze, *Satrapieneinteilung,* 40.

of his overall administrative reforms.[25] The status of "Beyond the River," and accordingly of Syria-Palestine, within the context of the Persian empire was already changing very early on. Under Cyrus and his governor Gobryas, Syria-Palestine was administered jointly with Babylon. However, due to the importance of the Egyptian front for Cambyses, the territory Beyond the River, and more particularly Syria-Palestine, became a more important sector of the satrapy, its importance being manifested in increasing administrative autonomy for that area. If, as Galling has argued, the primary impetus for Syria-Palestine's administrative autonomy came with the emergence of the Egyptian satrapy, then it is likely that Tattenai, or an unnamed predecessor, was appointed about 525–522. For the same reason, we might expect him to have begun to develop a more refined administrative system within this emerging satrapy.[26]

All this is to suggest that Zerubbabel's role as "governor" should be set within the movement toward greater administrative articulation in the Persian empire and in the dual satrapy Babylon–Beyond the River. This movement, in all likelihood, received primary impetus during the latter part of the reign of Cambyses. It serves to explain Zerubbabel's presence in Syria-Palestine as early as 520. He had probably been there for a year or two, just as Tattenai would have been before him.

A separate question concerns the extent to which there were, at this time, significant subdivisions in the satrapy Beyond the River. Was "Judah" an administrative district distinct from Samaria? This is a vexing question. We do know that by the end of the fifth century, Judah was a district separate from Samaria and that Judah had its own governor.[27] In Neh. 5:14–15, Nehemiah is referred to as a governor, and there is also mention of governors before him.[28] Nehemiah 5 also allows one to infer that such district governors were responsible for, at

---

[25] See ibid., 100–117, on the territory of the fifth satrapy, and 66–76 for a discussion of the difficulty in dating these divisions. Leuze does affirm a late sixth-century date for the division. E. Stern, *Material Culture*, 238, maintains that the separation of Babili from Ebirnari occurs only at the time of Xerxes. His argument rests on the absence of "Beyond the River" in satrapal lists dating to the time of Darius.

[26] See Galling, *Syrien*, 51, map 2; M. Avi-Yonah, *The Holy Land from the Persian to the Arab Conquests*, 1966, 20–22.

[27] On Judah's borders, consult Avi-Yonah, *The Holy Land*, 15–23; G. Widengren, "The Persian Period," in J. Hayes and J. Miller (eds.), *Israelite and Judaean History*, 1977, 522; and Kreissig, *Sozialökonomische Situation*, 33–34.

[28] On attempts to reconstruct or comment on the sequence of governors in the early postexilic period, see P. Ackroyd, "Archaeology, Politics and Religion: The Persian Period," *IR* 39, 1982, 11–13; Avi-Yonah, *The Holy Land*, 13–14.

least, taxes and financial matters. How early this form of district autonomy with specific Judahite governors occurred is difficult to determine. There is little evidence that either Sheshbazzar or Zerubbabel had such prerogatives, despite the fact that they bore the ambiguous title of governor *(peḥāh)*.

Some scholars have argued that archaeological evidence may be adduced to answer this troubling question concerning the status of Judah. A number of inscriptions, primarily stamp seals, have been found that date to the postexilic period. Some of the inscriptions appear to include either the word *peḥāh*, governor, or the world *yᵉhûd*, Judah.[29] Dating these seals is difficult. However, those which include the word *yᵉhûd*, the Aramaic form for the province Judah, are generally recognized to date to the late fifth or the fourth century B.C.E. That is, they corroborate the autonomy of the district of Judah immediately after Nehemiah but they do not provide evidence for earlier provincial status. Similarly, the seals that include the word *peḥāh* appear to date to the late fifth century. Furthermore, there is some dispute about whether or not they actually read *phḥ*. Cross has argued that they should be read as *pḥr*, the potter.[30] In sum, valuable though this epigraphic evidence is for attesting to the provincial status of Judah in the middle and late Persian period, these seals do not allow one to infer that Judah had separate status during the rule of Cambyses or Darius.

The classic answer to the question, when did Judah become distinct from Samaria, is that of Alt.[31] He maintained that the territory around Jerusalem—i.e., Judah—had no real autonomy after its defeat in 587, and this despite the appointment of a local "official," Gedaliah (II Kings 25:22–26), who may never have had a successor during the exilic period. Under the Neo-Babylonian provincial system it is likely, he maintains, that the Judahite territory was administered from the nearest provincial capital, Samaria. Only with the activity associated with the name of Nehemiah does Judah achieve a measure of political and financial autonomy. Alt's view has recently been supported on

---

[29] On the seals, see Stern, *Material Culture*, 202–213; N. Avigad, *Bullae and Seals from a Post-Exilic Judean Archive*, 1976; F. Cross, "Judean Stamps," *EI* 9, 1969, 20–27.

[30] Cross, "Judean Stamps."

[31] A. Alt, "Die Rolle Samarias bei der Entstehung des Judentums," *Kleine Schriften zur Geschichte des Volkes Israels*, Vol. 2, 1964, 316–337. Cf. the responses of M. Smith, *Palestinian Parties and Politics That Shaped the Old Testament*, 1971, 193–201; Widengren, "The Persian Period," 509; and, most recently, W. Schottroff, "Zur Socialgeschichte Israels in der Perserzeit," *Verkündigung und Forschung* 27, 1982, 48.

literary grounds, on epigraphic grounds, and on the basis of general historical considerations.[32]

It is therefore licit to infer, albeit provisionally, that in 520 the territory around Judah was probably economically and politically subordinate to the regional authorities located in Samaria. The title of "governor," which Sheshbazzar and Zerubbabel received in the biblical material, does not signify for either of them a role identical to that of Tattenai, governor of Beyond the River about 520, or of Nehemiah, governor of Judah at a later time, about 440. The period of Haggai's and Zechariah's activity was one of beginnings of regional autonomy for Judah, but it was a process that took almost one hundred years to achieve.

This brief sketch of the Persian empire and the place of Syria-Palestine within it enables the reader to understand why Zerubbabel and others may have traveled to Jerusalem about 523–522 and why Haggai and Zechariah would have been active in that area several years later.[33] Cambyses was interested in consolidating control over this area, a territory that occupied a rather ambiguous position in the Persian empire. The Israelites, some of whom had been deported to Babylon, had not been particularly successful in reestablishing their community on their native soil. Israelite problems during the first foray, with Sheshbazzar, had not disturbed the Persians, since they were more interested in problems located in the northern sectors of their territory. However, when Cambyses decided to push against Egypt, a reliable, populated, and peaceful Syria-Palestine became a much more important goal for the Persians. Thus, soon after having engaged the Egyptians, the Persians authorized a delegation of Yahwists to go to Syria-Palestine from Babylon; the group included Zerubbabel and Joshua. This time the Yahwists were able to take their own funds for the reconstruction project (Ezra 2:68–69). They did not need to rely on the regional coffers administered through Samaria. This move represented a concrete impulse toward autonomy for Judah/Jerusalem, but it was an early step. Zerubbabel, as "governor," did not function as "governor" of an autonomous district— *mᵉdînāh*—of Judah. That was yet to come, in the latter part of the fifth century.

---

[32] Thus Stern, *Material Culture*, 213; Ackroyd, "Archaeology, Politics, and Religion: The Persian Period," 13–17; and more generally, S. McEvenue, "The Political Structure in Judah from Cyrus to Nehemiah," *CBQ* 43, 1981, 353–364.

[33] See similarly Beyse, *Serubbabel*, 22; Ackroyd, *Exile and Restoration*, 147; Galling, *Studien zur Geschichte Israels*, 41–42.

In any survey of the time during which Haggai and Zechariah were active, it would be a fundamental omission to limit discussion only to political and military history, since it is clear that important transformations were occurring in the social and economic conditions of those who venerated Yahweh. Archaeological data has helped us begin to understand the conditions and identify the locations of those living in Syria-Palestine during the early Persian period. W. Weinberg has presented an excellent summary of the early postexilic period as informed by archaeological data. The excavations at 'En-Gedi have been of critical importance, since it was there that local pottery of the middle and late sixth century were identified in substantial quantities. This ceramic material represents, for the most part, a direct continuation of late Iron Age forms; it is precisely that which, when found elsewhere in Judah, provides evidence of middle or late sixth century residence. And it has been found in a large cistern at Tell el-Ful and at Horvat Dorban.[34] For the most part, such pottery is being identified not at major urban sites but in smaller villages that have escaped the archaeologist's spade. Weinberg's summary is apt:

> Until very recently it has been almost impossible, either in Israel or Judah, to isolate occupation levels at any of these sites that belong to the remainder of the sixth century. A small measure of success within the last few years has begun to result in the isolation of pottery groups that can be assigned to the rest of the sixth century, after 586; some of this pottery is clearly a continuation of late Iron II wares, often degraded in both shape and fabric, but with it are pottery types that are clearly new in Palestine. A most important new factor in the archaeology of the sixth century in Palestine appears with the finding of large numbers of new sites by the recent survey; most of these are small town and village sites of the type that had not previously attracted the attention of invaders in the eighth, seventh, and sixth centuries.[35]

More recently, E. Stern has systematically collected all the archaeological evidence for the Persian period and has, in so doing, corroborated one of Weinberg's fundamental theses, that certain pottery styles point directly to those living in the early Persian period.[36]

Systematic study of the changes to which the archaeological material attests is only now beginning. It does not take sophisticated theorizing to realize that changes of some sort must have taken place among

[34] S. Weinberg, "Post-Exilic Palestine: An Archaeological Report," *Proceedings of the Israel Academy of Sciences and Humanities* 4, 1971, 83.

[35] Ibid., 88.

[36] See Stern, *Material Culture*, 39, 98, and more generally, 231–232.

Judahites and other venerators of Yahweh during this period. There was no longer a single society defined by national borders. Yahwism's days as an archaic state religion were over. By the middle of the sixth century there were groups of Yahwists in Egypt, Syria-Palestine, and Mesopotamia. And there were encounters between these groups—no doubt, not always pleasant encounters. The contact between those who had remained in Syria-Palestine after 587 and those who were returning from exile must have been particularly problematic. There are a number of hints (see Jer. 39:10 and Ezek. 11:15–16) that those who remained behind received the land of those who had left, whether it had been part of the royal holdings or the property of nonroyalty who were also taken into exile. Some who had cultivated the soil as tenant farmers prior to 586 became landowners after 587. One can imagine that the response to such new landowners by those who were returning to Judah was less than enthusiastic.[37]

Three scholars in particular have recently addressed the socioeconomic history of the postexilic period: Kreissig, Weinberg, and Kippenberg.[38] In 1973 Kreissig published a study of the social and economic history of Judah in the Achaemenid period. Though his dating of certain Old Testament literature is questionable (e.g., Job to 400–350 B.C.E.), his overall concern to address major social and economic developments is welcome. Much of Kreissig's study focuses on issues not immediately relevant to this commentary, such as the development of class conflict in a later period. Of particular value for the study of Haggai and Zechariah 1–8 is his assessment of the agricultural potential of the territory that might be described as Judah.[39] Such potential was, he argues, rather limited, both because of the labor force and because of the land itself. He also notes that this period saw a number of new landowners in Judah. Those who had earlier worked the land for the profit of others now had possession of it. The acquisition of land by this new group entailed the development of a new social reality. The extended family needed to farm plots larger than those which the tenant farmer would have worked. In Kreissig's judgment, the overall productivity of this new situation would not have been particularly high. The efficiencies of the larger estates of the monarchic period would have been lost and the major economic

---

[37] See J. Weinberg, "Demographische Notizen zur Geschichte der nachexilischen Gemeinde in Juda," *KLIO, Beiträge zur Alten Geschichte* 54, 1972, 45, on the difficulty of using the term "Judah" in this regard.

[38] See also the excellent review article by Schottroff, "Zur Sozialgeschichte Israels in der Perserzeit," 46–68.

[39] Kreissig, *Sozialökonomische Situation,* 39–54.

trading centers, especially Jerusalem but other cities as well, had been destroyed.[40]

In 1972–1973, J. Weinberg devoted two studies to the economic and social realities of the early Persian period and offered a critique of Kreissig's work as well.[41] In the first study, Weinberg argued that the postexilic Yahwistic community in Judah comprised a "Bürger-Tempel-Gemeinde," a form of society that was widespread in the Achaemenid empire.[42] Such a collectivity provided its members with an identity, a rudimentary administration, and an economic as well as administrative center, the temple. Within this community, the *bêt 'ābôt*, the "fathers' house," provided the primary unit of social organization. It was an agnatic collectivity that held land, the *'aḥuzzā/naḥᵃlā,* which it subdivided among inner segments. As such, the house, which in Iran included some 600 males, had a complex inner structure. Nehemiah 7:70–71 provides evidence of the authority structure as well as the obvious economic importance of these units. Weinberg argues for the existence of seventeen such entities in the period before 458/7. Careful genealogical justification, no doubt sometimes fictive, was critically important for these groups. The fathers' houses could trace their origins to preexilic Yahwistic clans, though Weinberg argues strenuously that the fathers' houses are fundamentally different from the earlier clan structure. By the time of the later lists (Neh. 7:61–62), those who had remained in Judah during the exile are apparently included in the Yahwistic listings.[43] This analysis suggests at least two things: (1) Although the economic basis of this new social reality developed in Syria-Palestine, those in control were, early on, those who had been in exile. (2) This system of the large "fathers' house" allowed, ultimately, for the integration of those who had been in exile with those who had remained in the land.

Finally, Kippenberg, writing after both Kreissig and Weinberg, has linked the economic concerns of Kreissig with the sociological work of Weinberg. Building on Weinberg's assessment of the father's house, he assesses the internal structure of the "house" and distinguishes it

[40] For a summary of the economic history of the early Persian period, see ibid., 101–104.

[41] J. Weinberg, "Das *bēit 'ābōt* im 6.–4. Jh. v.u. Z.," *VT* 23, 1973, 400–414; J. Vejnberg (idem), "Probleme der sozialökonomische Struktur Judäas vom 6. Jahrhundert v.u. Z. Zu einigen wirtschaftshistorischen Untersuchungen von Heinz Kreissig," *Jahrbuch für Wirtschaftsgeschichte,* 1973, 237–251.

[42] See also J. Weinberg's later study, "Die Agrarverhältnisse in der Bürger-Tempel-Gemeinde der Achämenidenzeit," in J. Harmatta and G. Komoróczy (eds.), *Wirtschaft und Gesellschaft im Alten Vorderasien,* 1976, 473–486.

[43] Weinberg, "Das *bēit 'ābōt*," 411–412.

from the earlier clan.[44] He then devotes a chapter to the economy of the Judean hill country in the period 539–332.[45] He maintains that the ability to buy formerly clan-held land, coupled with the taxes due the Persians and payable in silver, created profound changes in the society of those who venerated Yahweh. Agricultural specialization, e.g., in olives and wine, accompanied by diminished family size, was one way of handling the problem. As this economic and social process continued, class differentiation occurred within the group living in Judah, and yet at the same time a sense of religioethnic cohesiveness developed.

Such analysis of the social and economic conditions of Yahwists in Syria-Palestine living around Jerusalem during the early Persian period is only now beginning. However, the work done up to this point suggests at least three things:

1. New forms of social organization, e.g., the *bêt 'ābôt*, were evolving in the late sixth century.

2. The economy of "Judah" was not particularly productive in the early Perisan period.

3. The temple had a very important role to play for the group of Yahwists in Syria-Palestine as the name *"Bürger-Tempel-Gemeinde"* indicates.

It is, therefore, no accident that Haggai hammers repeatedly on the importance of rebuilding the temple and that the books of Haggai and Zechariah reflect inglorious economic conditions.

2. The Book

Prose or Poetry

The book of Haggai comprises speeches attributed to the prophet and various background statements which set the context for those speeches. It has been a commonplace to think that prophetic speech is poetry.[46] Thus commentators regularly feel it necessary to state what portions of a prophetic book are or are not poetry.[47] Attempts to make such judgments about the book of Haggai usually hinge on the distinction between poetry and so-called rhythmic prose, a notoriously difficult distinction to draw.

[44] Kippenberg, *Religion und Klassenbildung,* 23–41.
[45] Cf. Jer. 32:9–12.
[46] Thus, for example, D. Freedman, "Pottery, Poetry, and Prophecy: An Essay on Biblical Poetry," *JBL* 96, 1977, 21.
[47] For such judgments about the book of Haggai, see Rudolph, 23; Elliger, 86 n. 1.

The difficulty of distinguishing prose from poetry, as that is traditionally defined, in the book of Haggai is displayed fully by a comparison of *BHK* with *BHS*. Kittel's edition of the Massoretic text has the book of Haggai printed entirely as a prose work, whereas the Stuttgart edition construes much of Haggai's speech to be poetry (1:3–11; 1:15b; 2:3–9; 2:14–19; 2:20–23). My own inclination is to move in the direction of *BHS*, yet with some of the caution represented by Horst, who identified 1:9–11; 2:6–9, 10–14, 15–19 as prose and 1:3–6, 8; 2:4–5, 21–23 as having a distinct metric rhythm.[48]

Surely more important than attempts to distinguish poetry from prose is the obvious distinction between narrative and direct discourse in the book. Whether one thinks that Haggai's words are couched in poetry or prose, there can be little doubt that the book purports to present speeches of the prophet and does so by surrounding them with interpretive narrative, material that may be labeled as prose. This setting of a narrative context for all of the prophet's words serves to distinguish the book of Haggai from all other books in the prophetic canon except Jonah, which is hardly a typical example of a prophetic collection.[49]

Form of the Book

Unlike most smaller prophetic books, e.g., Amos, Nahum, Zephaniah, Haggai is not simply a collection of oracles without connective tissue. Each of the major units in the book (1:1–11; 1:12–15; 2:1–9; 2:10–19; 2:20–23) comprises words of the prophet prefaced by prose narrative discourse that introduces Haggai's words. In all units but one, 1:12–15, a date formula is included in the introduction. And in 1:12–15 the date formula is present, but at the end of the unit. Since each subdivision in the book is provided with a chronological notation, it is perhaps not an overinterpretation to state that concern for history, the recitation and interpretation of the past, was an important consideration for the author of this book. Not surprisingly, the units that are dated are also organized in chronological sequence, 6/1/520 (1:1–11); 6/24/520 (1:12–15); 7/21/520 (2:1–9); 9/24/520 (2:10–19); 9/24/520 (2:20–23). No other prophetic book evinces such a distinctive chronological ordering of a prophet's

---

[48] Horst, 203.

[49] Haggai is very much different in this regard from its chronological mate, the book of Zechariah, which has oracles either buried among the vision sequences or collected without narrative material in ch.8.

activity. Many of Isaiah's words obviously relate to one or another historical situation. However, the book of Isaiah itself is not chronologically organized as is the book of Haggai.

Is this chronological ordering an artificial editorial technique, or does the substance of the prophetic words fit the surrounding narrative so as to create a book that evinces overall unity of purpose? In my judgment, one must answer the second half of this question in the affirmative. The book of Haggai describes the effect of prophetic speech as part of an ongoing process. It is not accurate to say that Haggai's words are concerned simply with having the temple rebuilt or that the booklet itself is a memorial to the rebuilding activity. The purpose of Haggai the prophet, as well as of the book that preserves his words, is more comprehensive. The person responsible for the final form of the book was interested in process and not just in proclamation.

The person who composed the book of Haggai has provided a narrative structured on the basis of chronological sequence. As literature, therefore, Haggai stands very near to a chronicle or historical narrative and less near to a prophetic collection as we know that genre from books such as Amos or Micah. Haggai approximates history writing, and I mean history here as something more than a composition ordered on a chronological sequence. Haggai's speeches and interactions are present in a sequence. Moreover, there is something of a cause-and-effect relationship which is initiated with Haggai's first utterance and which then continues until the end of the booklet. His first words, in 1:1–11, have as their goal the construction of the temple. The second unit, 1:12–15, reports that such work was in fact successful. Haggai 2:1–9 includes a report that the populace is dissatisfied with the lack of splendor of the temple which is now emerging and then presents Haggai's words of encouragement and weal, which address this concern. Haggai 2:10–19 captures the significance of the rededication ceremony which was a relatively early component of the rebuilding process. It was a ceremony the need for which Haggai argued with the priests (2:10–14), and the ultimate results of which he commented upon in 2:15–19. Finally, with the cultus "officially" renewed, he was moved to address, in 2:20–23, the character of the emerging civil order in a rather general way with the Davidide Zerubbabel, who had been appointed a minor official by the Persians. As this sequence of prophetic words and their responses suggests, Haggai was concerned not only with physical construction but with the people's psychological response to reconstruction, with priestly responsibility, and with the civil order. Moreover, his words, especially those in 1:1–11 and 2:1–9, demonstrate a noteworthy ability to engage the people in dialogue. Such skillful interweaving of prophetic word with narrative context is unusual within the prophetic corpus. Only the prose sections of Jeremiah come close, and in those sections the prophet's words as oracular discourse are often totally in prose.

Despite the fact that both Haggai and Jeremiah use prose narration, Haggai's efforts as prophet represent a case converse to the book of Jeremiah. Whereas Jeremiah's words received a fundamentally negative response, e.g., Jer. 36, Haggai's words by contrast elicit a positive response. And even on content grounds, these two prophets seem to be saying quite different things, no doubt in part because the historical contexts in which they worked were so different. Jeremiah could say "the temple, the temple, the temple" and in so doing refer to its destruction (so Jer. 7:1–15; 26:1–6). Haggai, on the other hand, could speak of Yahweh's house and argue for the necessity of its reconstruction.

This connection between the books of Jeremiah and Haggai is not accidental. The sixth century saw a style of prose narrative develop in which speeches of a prophet were integrated into something akin to historical narratives. Two examples of this genre are to be found in the book of Jeremiah: Jer. 26 and 36, "the story of the fate of Yahweh's words under King Jehoiakim," and Jer. 37–41, "the story of the improper origins of the Egyptian *gola*." It is my contention that the book of Haggai is also an example of this genre, a booklet that might be provisionally entitled "The story of Haggai's involvement in the restoration of Judah."

In 1978, N. Lohfink published a study in which he identified the genre of the *historische Kurzgeschichte,* or the historical short account.[50] Lohfink noted that the two texts mentioned above (Jer. 26 and 36; Jer. 37–41) shared a generic similarity with II Kings 22–23, a narrative he entitled "The story of the covenant's ratification under Josiah," and to a lesser extent with the books of Ruth and Jonah. Though most of Lohfink's attention in the study was devoted to an analysis of these narratives and not to a general description of the genre, it is possible to abstract the following list of characteristics for this genre:

1. It is a relatively short prose narrative; the longest example runs some four chapters.

[50] N. Lohfink, "Die Gattung der 'Historischen Kurzgeschichte' in den letzten Jahren von Juda und in der Zeit des Babylonischen Exils," *ZAW* 90, 1978, 319–347.

2. The narrative focuses on an important person or persons.[51]
3. These accounts are narratives that purport to be history, i.e., they provide a sequence of events often with chronological or other explicit time markers.
4. The stories are made up of several different scenes.[52]
5. Dates regularly mark the boundaries between the individual scenes.[53]
6. The scenes comprising the accounts are often of unequal length.
7. Such accounts often have a virtual apologetic focus, e.g., the Egyptian *gola* is wrong or Josiah's reforms are good.

It does not require great ingenuity to recognize that the book of Haggai may be construed as approximating this genre, especially if one follows *BHK* and labels all of the book as prose. Even following *BHS*, however, there is sufficient prose to justify the contention that Haggai is fundamentally a narrative that includes a number of prophetic utterances. It is, of course, brief. It does focus on Haggai but also, in its final form, on two other important persons, Joshua and Zerubbabel. The book, with its chronological references as well as its attention to the flow of events, has a distinct historiographic purpose, namely, to explain how it was that the temple was rebuilt and what the immediate repercussions of that rebuilding were. The book of Haggai is made up of several scenes, each of which is marked by a chronological reference point. And, as with other examples of this genre, the scenes are of uneven length. Three components are rather long—1:1–11; 2:1–9; and 2:10–19—and similar in structure, whereas 1:12–15 is much shorter and, like 2:20–23, different in structure from the aforementioned blocks.

Having identified Haggai with a genre also present in Jer. 26 and 36; Jer. 37–41; and II Kings 22–23, I find it necessary to address the genre label that Lohfink applied to these texts, the *historische Kurzge-schichte*. I would prefer something such as "brief apologetic historical narrative."[54] Each of the narratives Lohfink identifies seems to be making a very specific point, that the Egyptian group in exile is in error, that the ratification of the covenant under Josiah was salutary, that Jehoiakim's response to Yahweh's word was in grievous error. So too with Haggai, one important aspect of this dossier is the positive response to the construction of the temple and to the restoration of the temple cultus in the form it actually took. The book serves to buttress

---

[51] Lohfink, ibid., 321, even speaks of a hero at one point.
[52] Thus II Kings 22–23 is made up of four basic narrative parts.
[53] Lohfink, "Gattung," 328.
[54] Cf. Rudolph, 1976, 22, and his use of the term *Apologie,* though without specific form-critical implications.

or reinforce the correctness of Haggai's words and actions as they affected the early postexilic Jerusalem situation. It must have been written by someone who viewed the temple with approbation. It was written by a person who wrote using a literary genre also present in works edited by these attributed to the deuteronomistic tradent.[55] The book is, in sum, a short apologia, comprising Haggai's words placed within a historical narrative. The book of Haggai is not a typical prophetic collection, but is rather an apologetic history that uses prophetic oracles as its essential source.

From this perspective, the book of Haggai serves at least four functions:

1. It memorializes a major cultural achievement, the rebuilding of the temple. From its perspective, Haggai's words provided the impetus whereby reconstruction was carried on.
2. The book highlights the role of Haggai as he assisted the people in dealing with the restoration of the temple compound—in initiating reconstruction, in responding to negative perceptions of the temple, in facilitating the official restoration of the sacrificial cultus.
3. The book provides for the prospect of future weal. Judah is now obeying a prophet's words. Since, according at least to the deuteronomistic history, disobedience of a prophet's words resulted in destruction, obedience to Haggai's words should yield prosperity.
4. The temple compound, now in operation, and the cultus, recently reinstituted, deserve the support of the people.

Form of Haggai's Speeches

If, as I have argued, the book of Haggai is a short historical narrative designed to focus on a brief period and on the role of Haggai (as well as Zerubbabel and Joshua) during these times, then it is not surprising that the individual prophetic speeches do not shine through in their distinctness as they do with some of Israel's earlier prophets. Further, there is every reason to think, on the basis of Hanson's assessment of the speech forms present in Deutero-Zechariah and Trito-Isaiah, that the speech forms of sixth-century prophets were moving away from the forms as we know them in earlier prophetic books, e.g., Amos.[56] Haggai's speeches had already been collected, edited, and perhaps reshaped even before the final editor, the composer of the book as we

---

[55] Cf. R. Mason's assessment of the book's editorial structure, "The Purpose of the 'Editorial Framework' of the Book of Haggai," *VT* 27, 1977, 413–421.

[56] See P., Hanson, *The Dawn of Apocalyptic,* 1975, 106–107, on the so-called salvation-judgment oracle.

now have it, did his work.[57] Hence, the form-critical task, if we mean by that the designation of separate *Gattungen* and the identification of these forms, is difficult indeed. On the basis of the studies of Beuken, Koch, and Whedbee, we are enabled to maintain that fragments of major speech types known elsewhere in the prophetic literature may be discerned. So Beuken labels Hag. 1:3–11 in the following way: 3, *Wortereignisformel* (word-occurrence formula); 4, *Scheltwort* (reproach); 5–6, *Mahnwort* (warning); 7–8, *Auftrag und Heilswort* (charge, word of redemption); 9, *Disputationswort* (disputation); 10, *Spruch* (sentence); and 11, *Eingreifen Gottes* (divine intervention). Such analysis suggests that Haggai was drawing on the rhetorical reservoir available to earlier prophets, and a good bit less innovatively than had another prophet or prophetic tradition living in a slightly earlier period, namely, Deutero-Isaiah. It also suggests, as Koch's labels for vs. 7–8, 10, and 11 demonstrate, that not all of Haggai's words may fit easily within the standard speech type used by other prophets.

Composition

As the foregoing discussion has made clear, the book of Haggai is something other than a random or even an ordered collection of prophetic oracles. Rather, Haggai's speeches have been integrated into a historical sequence. As such, the book bears stronger similarities to certain short prose historical compositions of the sixth century than it does to short preexilic prophetic collections. How are we to explain this development of the so-called prophetic book?

The definitive study of the composition of Haggai (and Zechariah 1–8) is that of W. Beuken.[58] He was impressed by the way in which the oracles of Haggai had been incorporated into a comprehensive editorial framework. His thesis about the origins of the editorial work is quite straightforward. Haggai's oracles, which had originally included chronological notices, were edited by someone from the same religious and intellectual milieu as that of the Chronicler. That person or those persons added introductory formulae, e.g., 1:1 or 2:1–2, and in so doing created episodes out of what had earlier been isolated prophetic oracles.[59] They also added comments concerning the effects

---

[57] On the notion of a preliminary collection and subsequent redaction, see Beuken, and see K. Koch, "Haggais unreines Volk," *ZAW* 79, 1967, 52–66.

[58] Cf., for a more limited discussion, O. Steck, "Zu Haggai 1:2–11," *ZAW* 83, 1971, 355–356.

[59] See Beuken, 231–232, for a summary of this argument.

of the prophet's words, e.g., 1:12–14. Vocabulary and phraseology, as well as theological perspective, betray this editor's systematic hand. Having isolated a Chronistic overlay in the book, Beuken was able to point to a preliminary collection, e.g., 1:3–11 and the "historical" Haggai, a person of the rural Judahite population who had not been deported in 586, a person who represented a conservative, agriculturally based Yahwism.

Ten years after Beuken's influential study appeared, R. Mason published a reassessment of the redaction of the book of Haggai. In Mason's judgment, there is evidence of a thoroughgoing redaction in the book, as Beuken had claimed. However, Mason maintained that such a redaction, which he observes in 1:1, 3, 12, 13a, 14, 15; 2:1, 2, may not be located specifically within a Chronistic milieu. Mason identifies those elements which characterize the redactional material, e.g., the formula *hāyāh dᵉbar yhwh bᵉyad,* and argues that the usage is not peculiarly Chronistic, as Beuken had maintained, but instead "accords more with Deuteronomistic usage."[60] He discovers the same to be true with other elements in the redactional stratum, e.g., the delivery of the prophetic word to the community's leaders as well as the notion of addressing the community as a whole.[61] Mason's analysis suggests that the editing of Haggai "does not need to be tied as closely to the 'Chronicler' as Beuken suggests."[62] Further, the editorial framework serves to effect something akin to a realized eschatology: "If not all the signs which the prophet foretold of the new age had yet appeared, nevertheless its day had dawned."[63]

The work of Beuken and Mason does, despite their attribution of the editorial task to different circles, agree in discerning one fundamental and systematic redaction of the book.[64] Furthermore, the identification of the book of Haggai with a particular genre of short historical narrative is not inconsistent with the observations of Beuken, and especially, that of Mason.

What were the sources for the person writing this narrative? It is difficult to be definitive here. Some have argued that the author of the narrative inherited a collection of Haggai's words and simply included them in his composition. Beuken has taken a different tack. He identifies 1:3–11, 12b; and 2:15–19 as pre-Chronistic compositions.

---

[60] Mason, "Framework," 415–416.

[61] Ibid., 416–418.

[62] Ibid., 421.

[63] Ibid., 420.

[64] And this process is, according to Beuken, different from the more complex process that produced the book of Zechariah 1–8.

They provide more than just words and are akin to an eyewitness account, or as he puts it in another place, an *Auftrittskizze*.[65] He affirms the existence of a pre-Chronistic collection of Haggai's words, a collection with minimal editorial material, i.e., dates, connecting the oracles. Beuken argues that some of Haggai's followers made this collection. Koch's work in identifying three similarly structured units in the book of Haggai also suggests a preliminary stage in the creation of this book.[66] More than these preliminary penetrations of the final form of the book are difficult. And it is perhaps just as well since the oracles now set within this short, apologetic historical narrative make such eminent sense that reconstructuring a different setting yields unconvincing, even artificial, results.

Text

The Massoretic text of Haggai per se presents few problems to the translator. Only three emendations are proposed below: 1:12; 2:16; and 2:19 and the textual notes concerning these verses. One of the texts discovered in the Dead Sea environs, the minor prophets scroll from Wadi Murabba'ât, includes major portions of the book of Haggai. In no place does the Murabba'ât text (Mur) offer a reading superior to that of the MT.[67] Mur clearly presents a text similar to MT, and both MT and Mur differ consistently against the more expansionistic LXX. This agreement between MT and Mur is to be expected, given the second century C.E. date of Mur.

At several points, LXX includes material that is obviously late interpolation into the text (at 2:9, 14, 21, 22). And in one instance, MT includes interpolated material (at 2:5a) that is absent in the LXX manuscripts.[68] These data would suggest the existence of two textual families both of which were expansionistic, though at different points. The LXX or Egyptian tradition is, in Haggai, clearly more expansionistic than is MT.[69]

---

[65] Beuken, 184–216.

[66] Cf. J. Whedbee, "A Question-Answer Schema in Haggai 1: The Form and Function of Haggai 1:9–11," *Biblical and Near Eastern Studies*, 1978, 184–194.

[67] See, e.g., the Mur reading of *'el* on 2:1 for the more unusual MT *b'yad*.

[68] On this issue, see P. Ackroyd, "Some Interpretive Glosses in the Book of Haggai," *Journal of Jewish Studies* 7, 1956, 163–167. In my judgment, Hag. 2:17 is not to be construed as a late interpolation.

[69] On the Messianic interpretation of Hag. 2:7 in the Vulgate, see the standard commentaries and G. Krause, "'Aller Heiden Trost,' Haggai 2:7," in *Solange es "Heute" heisst. Festgabe für Rudolf Hermann zum 70. Geburtstag*, 1957, 170–178.

COMMENTARY

Haggai 1:1–11

While this house lies in ruins

1   In the second year of the reign of Darius the king, on the first day of the sixth month, the word of Yahweh was conveyed by Haggai the prophet to Zerubbabel son of Shealtiel, governor of Judah, and to Joshua son of Jehozadak, the high priest:

2   "Thus says Yahweh of Hosts:
This people says,
    'The time has not come,
      the time to rebuild the house of Yahweh.'"[a]

3   Then the word of Yahweh was conveyed by Haggai the prophet,

4   "Is it time for you to dwell in your paneled[b] houses,
    while this house lies in ruins?"

5   Now thus says Yahweh of Hosts,
    "Consider seriously your situation.

6   You have planted much
    and harvested little.
You have eaten without becoming full.
  You have drunk without satisfaction.
    You have put on clothes without becoming warm.
Whoever works industriously for wages
    has a purse with a hole in it."

7   Thus says Yahweh of Hosts,
    "Consider seriously your situation.

8   Go up to the hill country:
    Bring back timber
    and build the house.
I will accept it and be glorified,"
    says Yahweh.

9   "You have expected much,
    but there has been little.

When you have brought it home,
I would blow it away.
Why?" says Yahweh of Hosts.
"Because of my house which lies in ruins.
But you run, each to his own house.
10   Thus, the heavens have withheld their dew from you,[c]
the earth has withheld its produce.
11   I have summoned a drought upon the land,
upon the hills and upon the grain,
upon the new wine and upon the oil,
upon all which the ground produces,
upon humanity and beast,
and upon all the toil of their hands."

a. On this translation, cf. Rudolph, 29; Ackroyd, *Exile and Restoration*, 155.
b. For a discussion of the Hebrew word *s⁽ᵉ⁾pûnîm*, see on v. 4, below, and the standard commentaries.
c. One may also read, "Therefore the heavens have withdrawn their dew." LXX lacks *ᵃlêkem;* thus *ᵃlêkem* in MT may be the result of dittography of the initial two words of the verse, *'al-kēn*.

[1] The book associated with the name of Haggai is introduced by a long prose sentence. Such introductions occur in other prophetic books, e.g., in Jer. 1:1-3. One is tempted, therefore, to read this verse as a general introduction to the entire book. However, despite the programmatic nature of this verse, providing as it does the date—the first day of the sixth month—it serves to introduce 1:2-14 and all the oracles and reports in the book. Put another way, ch. 2 is designated for a different audience and was delivered on a different date. Haggai 1:1 serves, therefore, to identify the initial time and audience for only some of Haggai's words.[1]

Of interest at the outset is the chronological reference point offered by the editor. Earlier prophetic books were dated to the reigns of Israelite or Judahite kings. Thus, for example, Amos begins, "The words of Amos, who was among the shepherds of Tekoa, which he saw concerning Israel in the days of Uzziah king of Judah and in the days of Jeroboam the son of Joash, king of Israel." Now with the absence of Yahweh-venerating territorial states headed by monarchs, such references are no longer possible. Instead, the book of Haggai is dated

[1] Cf. R. Mason, "The Purpose of the 'Editorial Framework' of the Book of Haggai," *VT* 27, 1977, 413–421.

to the monarch with power over Mesopotamia, Syria-Palestine, and now even Egypt: Darius I Hystaspis (522–486). He is, to use the succinct phraseology of v.1, "the king." One need not specify that he is (in the language of the Cyrus cylinder, a text glorifying Darius' penultimate predecessor) "king of the world, great king, legitimate king, king of Babylon, king of Sumer and Akkad, king of the four rims of the earth" (*ANET*, 316). To be part of the Persian empire, as were Judah and Jerusalem at this time, was to know only that king, the all-powerful Persian lord.

If Darius' reign is the chronological reference point for Haggai's prophetic activity, one needs to ask if there is any special significance to the specific day or year cited in this initial verse. That Haggai's oracles are dated to the early part of Darius' reign has been observed by many. And it is common knowledge that the year 522 was a difficult one for the Persian empire. One Gaumata had claimed kingship in Persia while Cambyses was returning from a campaign in Egypt. On receiving word of the revolt, Cambyses apparently committed suicide. Darius, a military officer who claimed royal lineage, was able to wrest the throne away from Gaumata, but even so, he had to quell rebellions in numerous sectors of the Persian empire.[2] Some have felt that the temporary loosening of the Persian grip may have led to patriotic outbursts in Syria-Palestine, e.g., aspirations for the restoration of monarchy in Israel, a restoration that many scholars think is depicted in 2:20–23. However, the dating of Haggai's words is not to the accession year of Darius, the year when the Persians were especially vulnerable. And clearly, since Cambyses died in Syria-Palestine, the knowledge of either Cambyses' death or Darius' accession would have been available to the Israelites. Rather, the book dates to the year when Darius was apparently able to gain firm control of the empire. In fact, during the early months of 520 Darius was consolidating the Persians' hold on the most distant district. Gobryas had been removed as regional governor and Hystanes was now the prefect over the satrapy Beyond the River, which included Syria-Palestine.[3] This situation suggests that Haggai was speaking not on the basis of an unstable condition but rather on the basis of a situation that had just become stable. And to this extent there is a distinct parallel between this first verse of Haggai and the first vision of Zechariah, which comprises a lament against the permanence of an unsatisfactory status quo.

[2] See Olmstead, *Persian Empire*, 1948, 107–108; J. Bright, *A History of Israel*, 1981[3], 369–370; Dandamaev, *Persien*, 108–214.
[3] Thus Olmstead, *Persian Empire*, 133.

Just as the year 520 B.C.E. has significance as a time of relative calm early in Darius' reign, so too the other elements of the date formula, month and day, are important. If the seventh month mentioned in Ezra 3 is to be dated to 520—and the context would suggest that it is—then, according to the sequence of the events in Ezra 3, we are situated in the month immediately prior to the reconstruction of the altar. And interestingly, Ezra 3 indicates that with the reconstruction of the altar, and not with the rebuilding of the temple, things such as "offerings of the new moon" (Ezra 3:5), i.e., the ritual performed on the first of the month, were undertaken. "From the first day of the seventh month, they began to offer burnt offerings to Yahweh" (Ezra 3:6). Put another way, Haggai is remembered as having uttered the words preserved in 1:2–11 on the first day of the month preceding the rededication of the altar. In 1:1, therefore, we are at a point just before the restoration of the sacrificial cultus.[4]

The specific day mentioned in the date formula is also significant.[5] The first day of the month was the occasion for special sacrifices (Num. 28:11–15; Ezek. 46:6-7). And apparently it was a feast especially connected with royal patronage (II Chron. 31:3; Ezek. 46:6; II Kings 4:23). Further, this day, the first of the month, was regularly linked to the Sabbath (Amos 8:5; Isa. 1:13, 14; 66:23; Hos. 2:11). Psalm 81:3 would suggest that on this first day of the month, along with the cessation of activity as on the Sabbath, there was special celebration. And yet without the altar, and without the temple, the sacrifices appropriate to this feast day were impossible to perform. Haggai was therefore addressing the Judahite community at a particularly poignant moment, a time when they should be keeping the new moon festival, a celebration which it was impossible to observe in the prescribed ways because of the lack of both altar and sanctuary. Haggai 1:1, therefore, introduces a note of contrast, even tension, into the discussion. Haggai speaks on a day that is a time for celebrative worship while arguing that there is no appropriate place for worship to take place. The first day of the month was an especially appropriate moment for such words to be spoken.

The first verse also identifies the author of these words. He is Haggai the prophet. As noted earlier, Haggai's own name provides a wordplay with the Hebrew word for festival, *ḥag,* an appropriate

---

[4] Of the altar, in contradistinction to the temple, we hear nothing explicit in Haggai 1. And Ezra 5:1, 14 has it that the impact of Haggai and Zechariah is associated with temple reconstruction and not with the rebuilding of the altar or the attendant cultic renewal.

[5] Note the wordplay implicit in the name of the prophet, *ḥaggay,* and the Hebrew word for feast, *ḥag.*

assonance, given the lack of a restored ritual center for Israel prior to Haggai's own prophetic activity. Not only do we learn who the prophet is, we learn the essence of his prophetic activity according to the editor: "The word of Yahweh was conveyed by Haggai." This is an unusual way of putting the matter. Normally the word comes to _('el)_ the prophet rather than having the prophet act as a functioning intermediary.[6] Though the language here is obviously formulaic, there is a certain wisdom in having Haggai understood as someone passing on rather than simply receiving Yahweh's word, since Haggai's rhetorical tactics are innovative and involve the prophet in a more dialogic enterprise than is found in other prophets of Israel.

Not only are we given a precise date for the first proclamation of Haggai; an audience is designated as well: Zerubbabel and Joshua. This designation of audience occurs elsewhere in the booklet, at 1:12; 1:14; 2:2. And in every instance, Zerubbabel's name occurs first. Since Hebrew syntax regularly affords pride of place to the first element in a sentence, we may infer that Zerubbabel is at least as important as (if not more important than) Joshua the high priest.[7]

Zerubbabel, an Israelite who bore an Akkadian name, Zerbabilu, was without doubt a member of the Davidic line, a nephew of Jehoiachin, the Judahite king taken into exile in Babylon (so I Chron. 3:17–19).[8] More problematic than his royal blood or actual father is the title that Zerubbabel was given, _phh_. There is little in the biblical or extrabiblical record to enable one to argue that Zerubbabel was a permanent administrator of the Persian empire.[9] Further, there are numerous seals from the postexilic period that apparently have the term _phh_ engraved upon them.[10] Hence, although the label _phh_ is used later to refer to an official governor of Judah, it is not clear that the title refers to a role of permanent administrator during the period before Darius' administrative reforms. The use of the label to designate someone early in the postexilic period may in fact represent an

---

[6] See Beuken, 28; Mason, "Purpose of the 'Editorial Framework,'" 413–421, on the background of this formula. Beuken argued that it was characteristic of the Chronistic milieu, whereas Mason contended that the formula is attested in a variety of settings, e.g., Dtr. and P.

[7] No oracle of Haggai has been preserved as direct address to Joshua. Cf. Horst, 209.

[8] Thus Rudolph, 31, and the standard commentaries.

[9] See the discussion by P. Ackroyd in "Archaeology, Politics and Religion: The Persian Period," _IR_ 39, 1982, 10–11, and Leuze, _Satrapieneinteilung_, 18–19, on the ambiguity of _phh_, since this title was used for functionaries in different levels of the bureaucracy.

[10] See Stern, _Material Culture_, 214; N. Avigad, "Bullae and Seals from a Post-Exilic Judean Archive," _QMIA_ 4, 1976.

Israelite attempt to give Zerubbabel a title consonant with his apparently temporary task of rebuilding the temple in Jerusalem. And since the label *pḥh* was used later, of Elnathan and others, it seemed appropriate, in retrospect, to use that term for Zerubbabel as well.[11]

If the title *pḥh* remains somewhat enigmatic, the description of Joshua as "the high priest" *(hakkōhēn haggādôl)* seems clear. This use of the phrase "high priest" is, in all likelihood, the first instance in which anyone bears this title in ancient Israel.[12] As was the case with Zerubbabel, we are dealing with a person who was viewed as having authority by reason of genealogy, and who also had been in exile. Jehozadak, Joshua's father, had been taken into exile (I Chron. 5:40–41 [6:14–15E]), and Jehozadak's father, Seriah, was chief priest *(kōhēn hārō'š)* when Judah was destroyed in 586 (II Kings 25:18–21).

By addressing these two individuals, Zerubbabel and Joshua, and by addressing them in this way, i.e., by emphasizing genealogy and title, the author of these verses is indirectly stating that the authorities in the community are those returning from exile. Further, he indicates that these individuals gain their authority by linkages to those who had held authority in monarchic society prior to the catastrophe in 587. One may, therefore, understand Haggai to be making a claim for continuity with the past social structure and value system and, more specifically, with one group of Yahwists, those who have experienced exile in Babylon. Put another way, authority in the community was understood as tied to the past authority structures and tied to those who had been forced into exile and not to those who had remained in the land.

---

[11] Much of the debate about the significance of the term *pḥh* rests on the judgment of whether or not Judah was a subdistrict separate from the district of Samaria. This is a much-disputed question. A. Alt maintained that Judah was a southern annex of the Samaritan province during the Persian period; it had no autonomy ("Die Rolle Samarias bei der Entstehung des Judentums," *Kleine Schriften*, Vol. 2, 1964, 316–377). This is a view which has come under severe attack. G. Widengren has recently written, "There is no doubt that Judah from the beginning of the Persian period was given the status of a province by the Persian government" ("The Persian Period," in J. Hayes and J. Miller (eds.), *Israelite and Judaean History*, 510–511). And see similarly M. Smith, *Palestinian Parties and Politics That Shaped the Old Testament*, 1971, 193–201. Ackroyd's assessment is moderated by the evidence from Neh. 2:2, a text which suggests that the Samaritan regional authorities had some sort of economic prerogatives over Judah, at least before the time of Nehemiah ("Archaeology, Politics and Religion," 13–17). Perhaps it can be argued that Judah was a separate subdistrict but was required to interact with the Persians through the established regional headquarters in Samaria. Samaria, as a regional district for the administration of Syrian-Palestinian territories by Mesopotamian powers, dates to the Neo-Assyrian period.

[12] See similarly Rudolph, 31.

[2] Verse 1 specifies two individuals as the recipients of Yahweh's words. Verse 2 indicates the basic issue about which Yahweh and his prophet are concerned—what others, the people *(hā'ām)*, have been saying and not doing. Immediately after the so-called messenger formula, "Thus says Yahweh of Hosts," the oracle begins with mention of a social unit, *hā'ām*.[13] There is little reason to think that "the people" refers to an entity different from "the remnant of the people" in any of these texts.[14] If there is a distinction drawn among Israelites in Hag. 1:12, it is between the community's leaders and those living in the Judahite territory, not between Judahites who have had different historical experiences.

Even though the people are addressed, 1:1–2 does suggest that Yahweh's words are, in the first instance, spoken directly to Zerubbabel and Joshua. Yahweh is understood to be working through these particular agents to engender action in the people. To put it another way, the prophet—from the perspective of the final form of the text—is speaking through Zerubbabel and Joshua and not directly to the people as some earlier prophets had done. Such a perspective serves to emphasize the important roles that the book of Haggai attributes to the prophet and to the community's leaders. Haggai as prophet had a role or status similar to that of the Davidide (the Davidic heir, i.e., Zerubbabel) and the high priest. Just as prophets spoke only to kings at the inception of Israel's monarchy (as Nathan and Gad spoke only to David), so now Haggai, with something akin to the reinstitution of the old order, is again speaking to the Davidide (and to the high priest) and not to the larger populace, although clearly, in 1:2ff., they are the subject of his concern.

Interestingly, Yahweh's word begins with a quotation. The people were remembered as having said,

> The time has not yet come,
> the time to rebuild the house of Yahweh.

The people are presented as making a bald assertion. No reason is given for their claim. Their statement does presume a history. It seems to imply that someone, perhaps Haggai, has said that the temple should be rebuilt. Or it may refer to certain Israelites' reactions to Sheshbazzar's attempt to have the temple rebuilt. Or, given what

[13] Cf. mention of "the remnant of the people" (Hag. 1:12, 14; 2:2) and other references to "the people" (Hag. 2:4, 14).

[14] Rudolph, 32–33, argues that this phrase refers to those who have returned from exile and to them alone. Cf. E. Janssen, *Juda in der Exilzeit*, 1956, 119 n. 13.

follows in the text, it may reflect particular conditions, difficult economic times, during which the people had little time or energy to spare from their everyday activities. Whatever the raison d'être for this quotation, it points to a demonstrable unwillingness, by at least a part of the people, to participate in the reconstruction of the temple.

[3] With the people's position articulated, we find reiterated in the text a clause also present in v. 1, a form of the verb *hāyāh* together with *d*ebar *yhwh* and *b*eyad, though this time without the designation of audience. Some have argued that the absence of such a designation is evidence that the oracle which follows (vs. 4–9) was spoken directly to the people by the prophet and not immediately to Zerubbabel and Joshua, the more so since the second masculine plural pronominal suffix (used twice in v. 4) indicates direct discourse. This is, of course, possible. However, v. 1 indicates clearly that the final editor wanted to create a picture of Haggai presenting this word to the two human functionaries, Zerubbabel and Joshua, and then to have them convey these sentiments to the entire population of Judah. Here the redactor has effected a different setting for the oracle than the probable original setting.

[4] In direct response to the people's assertion, the deity levels a rhetorical question building upon the people's own words and yet challenging their primary thesis.

> Is it time for you to dwell in your paneled houses
> while *this* house lies in ruins?

Two details require attention here. *(a) sāpûn* may refer either to a roof (cf. the noun *sippun*, I Kings 6:15) or to the interior paneling of a building (*sāpûn bā'erez*, "paneled with cedar," I Kings 7:7).[15] The strongest contrast possible is between "this house in ruins and your nicely finished houses," not between "this house in ruins and your houses with roofs." The presumption is that the people's houses would have had roofs, since they were, according to the question, living in them. *(b)* Some ancient manuscripts (LXX, S, T, V) read "houses" instead of "your houses." Nevertheless, the MT remains, in my judgment, the better reading. With the pronominal suffix, the noun is made definite and the presumption that the people's houses are in existence and inhabited is made much stronger. And this seems to be exactly the point raised by the question. The populace is now living in well-built homes while Yahweh's house is still in ruins.

---

[15] See O. Steck, "Zu Haggai 1:2–11," *ZAW* 83, 1971, 362, who translates "roof." I follow (among others) Ackroyd, *Exile and Restoration*, 155, in translating "paneled."

The use of the adjective *ḥārēb* to describe the temple in ruins is apt, the more so since that same word is used in several texts to refer to the destructions wrought in 587 (Jer. 33:10–17; Ezek. 36:35, 38; Neh. 2:3, 17). Jeremiah, in 33:10–17, describes Jerusalem ("the cities of Judah and the streets of Jerusalem") as a wasteland. The streets are now uninhabited, and yet they will become the scene of joyful activity, of marriages and thank offerings. And interestingly, this time of future bliss will require the reconstruction of the temple, so that there may be a place to which the thank offerings can be brought (cf. Jer. 33:11, "as they bring thank offerings to the house of Yahweh"). From Haggai's perspective, this process of restoration from desolation to prosperity has begun, but it remains radically incomplete without the reconstruction of the temple. Busy streets and rebuilt houses do not comprise the final restoration envisioned either by Jeremianic traditionists or by Haggai.

The adjective *ḥārēb* is appropriate in this context for another reason. It occurs in the first verse of the oracle delivered to Zerubbabel and Joshua, and ultimately to the people. And in the final verse of this same oracle (v. 11), the prophet uses a term—*ḥōreb*—composed of the same three root consonants, *ḥrb*, to describe the divine fury in the form of a drought that has afflicted the land of Judah. This root, *ḥrb*, establishes an *inclusio* around this almost essay-like collection of prophetic rhetoric and thereby emphasizes the dire situation the Judahites confront—one of devastation and drought.

[5] As with all proper rhetorical questions, the one in v. 4 receives no explicit answer but invites the addressee to reflect on the issue under discussion. Such reflection is mandated by the clause that follows, "Consider seriously your situation," an idiom used more than once in this short book (see also 1:7; 2:15, 18). This clause echoes language found in Deut. 32:45, "Consider all the words which I enjoin upon you this day." However, in Haggai the people are not commanded to focus on Yahweh's words as they were in Deuteronomy; they are, through their leaders, admonished to consider their own situation and their own inaction. This formulation borders on the ironic, since it asks people to consider not what they have done but rather what they have not done.

[6] What follows is a tightly and carefully constructed series of contrasts. In each instance, what is contrasted is human activity or initiative and its lack of consummation: planting and not having crops, eating but still being hungry, drinking and not being satisfied, putting

on clothes and remaining cold, receiving wages but having no money.[16] This series, to be effective, must have reflected serious problems in the actual conditions in and around Jerusalem. It could not have been a particularly good time. And yet the situation of those addressed must have been reasonably adequate. If they built paneled houses, life was not all that bad. Put another way, Haggai is doing more than reporting in a neutral way social and economic conditions in 520 B.C.E. He is spurring reflection on one essential topic: house/houses. And what is unsaid is probably as important as what is said. The prophet implies: "You build houses and yet you have not enjoyed security."[17]

Hillers has identified the language used in v. 6 as that found elsewhere in so-called futility curses.[18] Such formulations comprise the description of an activity in a protasis and then of the futility of that activity in an apodosis. Such curses are attested in both biblical and extrabiblical material (Deut. 28:38, "You shall carry much seed into the field and shall gather little in"; see also Hos. 4:10; *Sefîre* I). As these examples suggest, such curses regularly appear within a treaty context. Haggai is using well-known language from a well-known context. However, his use of this material is unusual.[19] The curses are written in the past tense.[20] Rather than threats encouraging obedience, they function as historiography. Things have happened in such and such a way because . . . To put it another way, reconstruction of the temple is treated as a covenant duty that, because it has not been accomplished, has brought on the futility curses of an abrogated covenant. Such a view represents a significant reformulation of the covenant norms, a focusing on the cult center per se, something that is markedly absent from other covenant stipulations preserved in the Hebrew Bible.[21] Not only are the people living an existence cursed because of the 587 disaster; their existence is also cursed because of their reaction to the result of that earlier cursing, the destruction of the temple.

[7–8] The author/editor of this section marks a break in the flow of

---

[16] The drinking referred to here is neither drunkenness nor "making merry" (Gen. 9:21; 43:34). Rather, the author refers to a routine slaking of thirst.

[17] It is impossible to identify a specific group receiving this indictment; i.e., it is difficult to follow Steck and see vs. 2–8 as referring to those who had remained in the land whereas vs. 9–11 addressed those who had returned from exile.

[18] D. Hillers, *Treaty Curses and the Old Testament Prophets*, 1964, 28.

[19] Cf. Beuken, 190–191.

[20] See Amos 4:8 for the same use of the past tense.

[21] This notion has important implications for the idea of the existence of the Sinaitic covenant after 587 B.C.E.

the argument by reiterating the messenger formula used at the beginning of v. 2 (in which the words of the people are quoted) and used again to introduce the "consider" formula in v. 5. In v. 7 the messenger formula is paired with the "consider" formula as it was in v. 5. However, immediately after this formulaic language mirroring the earlier rhetoric, we find imperative verbs—and this instead of the expected object of the imperative *śîmû* ("consider"), viz., past action of the people about which they should reflect. Rather than consider their former ways, as they were asked to do in vs. 5–6, the people are now asked, albeit implicitly, to consider future action: going up to the mountains, bringing back lumber, building the temple. The important contrast between their action—going, bringing, building—and the verbs detailed in v. 6 is clear. Now the people's action will bear fruit. Their ends will be achieved. They will successfully rebuild the deity's residence. That the outcome will be satisfactory is made explicit by verbs having Yahweh as the subject. The hoped-for success will come not as an automatic result of human action, as in the cases adduced in v. 6. Rather, success will finally derive from Yahweh's response to their human initiative.

Yahweh promises to be pleased with, or better, to accept this action. The verb *rṣh,* as many commentators have remarked, often refers to the acceptance of a sacrifice or gift in the ritual sphere (II Sam. 24:23; Jer. 14:10, 12; Ezek. 20:40, 41; 43:27; Mal. 1:10, 13; Pss. 51:18 [17E]; 119:108; Micah 6:7; Amos 5:22). And—another divine reaction—God will be glorified (for niphal uses of *kbd,* see Isa. 26:15; Ezek. 28:22; 39:13). Some commentators (e.g., Rudolph, 34) have connected this verb with the motif of the return of Yahweh's *kābôd* as outlined in Ezek. 43:1ff. However, none of the niphal uses of this verb which refer to Yahweh entail his cultic presence. Instead, they signify Yahweh's gaining prestige or revenge. Haggai is therefore speaking of glory, Yahweh's having greater prestige now that this house is finished, and not of the sanctification of his house. And with that promise by Yahweh, the divine speech apparently ends, concluded by the terminal formula *'āmar yhwh.*

[9] Surprisingly, at least from a form-critical point of view, the divine speech continues. The analytical rhetoric of v. 9 carries forward the perspectives of v. 6. Infinitives absolute and verbs in the perfect tense provide grammatical continuity with the foregoing material. The latter verse is, however, different in its tone from the former. Whereas the activities described in v. 6 are specific—planting, eating, drinking, clothing, earning—the verbs in v. 9 are unhesitatingly general: expect (infinitive absolute) and bring (perfect). The first of these two verbs

refers to no particular action but instead of a general outlook of the people. They were expecting a magnificent future. And it is not difficult to imagine what sort of future they hoped for. The promises made by Deutero-Isaiah were clear: "I will make your pinnacles of agate, your gates of carbuncles, and all your wall of precious stones" (Isa. 54:12). This expectation was, in all likelihood, held especially by those who had returned from exile—no doubt fired to return by such grandiose promises. And yet, despite such hopes, there had been little by way of satisfactory evidence for such a glorious future.

The final clause in v. 9 is both problematic and decisive: problematic because the noun *habbayit* is ambiguous; decisive because only at this point does the reader or listener learn the reason for such consistent Judahite misfortune. As for the first issue, there are two quite different translations possible for the clause *wah*ᵃ*bē'tem habbayit.* "You brought it to the temple" would emphasize the definite article preceding the word "house" and understanding the house as Yahweh's house. "You brought it home" would refer to the already completed homes of the Judahites (cf. v. 4).[22] A decision between these two options is difficult. It does, however, seem improbable that *the* house, i.e., the temple, would be referred to as a place of pilgrimage or sacrifice at this time, since the whole point of Haggai's discourse is that the temple has not yet been rebuilt. On these grounds alone, a reference to the house of each person is more likely, though the actual Hebrew phraseology is peculiar. Equally unclear is the use of the idiom *nph* + *b* to refer to destructive or disruptive activity (cf. Ezek. 37:9 and Isa. 64:6 for this use of the biblical idiom). The sense is apparently that when something was brought to one's house, it disappeared, just as wages did according to v. 6. However, the position is advanced beyond that expressed in v. 6. We now learn why wages disappear and why things brought home no longer stay put. Yahweh is behind it all. It is not simply a matter of multiple and causeless misfortune. Such negative experiences result from Yahweh's direct intervention in human affairs.

To know the source of such action is not to have a rationale provided for it. Therefore the divine agent himself raises the obvious question, "For what reason?" and immediately provides an answer. Interestingly, the answer provides no new information. It repeats what was adduced in v. 4, namely, that Yahweh's house lies in ruins. In v.4 we hear about "the house," whereas in v. 9 the language has become

---

[22] On this matter, see F. Peter, "Haggai 1:9," *TZ*, 1951, 150ff., and the standard commentaries.

personalized. There is now reference to "my house." And again, as was the case in v. 4, the contrast is between the houses of the Judahites and the house of Yahweh. In v. 9, the completed houses are the objects of intense desire—people are running toward them; and this is in contrast to the temple, which people are apparently avoiding. In sum, both the beginning and the end of this subsection (vs. 4–9), which provide an indictment of the people for not completing Yahweh's house, are unified by these formulations involving house and houses.

[10–11] One might have thought that the state of affairs described in v. 6 and its attribution to Yahweh in 9a would prove sufficient to move the people to action. Such, however, was not the case. Yet another element of prophetic rhetoric was deemed necessary. Conjoined to the earlier reflections on house/houses is a short poem introduced by "therefore" *('al-kēn)*, a formula that often introduces the concluding portion of a judgment oracle. What is peculiar about this section is that it echoes the past-tense discourse of 6–9a. The punitive action of the deity is already in effect. The word "thus," or "therefore," does not point to future punitive action so much as it introduces an explanation of the punitive action already in effect. This section further explains the specific problems that Israel has been experiencing: "The heavens have withheld their dew . . . , the earth has withheld its produce." Lack of crop yield is here explicable as action of the heavens and the earth. Though formally paired, these first two cola do reflect a cause-and-effect situation. If the heavens do not yield their water, the earth will not yield crops. The sequence is clear but the reason for the heavens not yielding dew is less so. Hence what follows in v. 11 is logically necessary, for in this verse (as was the case in 9a), such action is attributed to Yahweh. In v. 11 the prophet uses a wordplay correspondence not dissimilar to more famous instances in Amos (8:1–2) and Jeremiah (1:11–12). Yahweh has called for a drought, *hōreb*, a word that contains exactly the same three consonants as the word for ruins, *hārēb*, which occurs in vs. 4 and 9. It is not accidental that this word also appears in the list of maledictions in Deut. 28:22. What is here being described is a cosmic curse, affecting both the earth and the heavens. In v. 11, not only the ultimate source but also the particular effects of the curse are detailed. The *hōreb* is directed not only against the earth and its hills, but more particularly against plant and animal life on earth: against grain, wine, and olive oil (that which the ground produces) and against human and beast (everything they attempt to do). The description here is odd and yet precise: earth / grain, wine, oil // animals and humans / their labors. Through this formulation it becomes clear that the drought represents more than just a lack of water. It refers to a total lack of production and productivity by the heavens and the earth, by animals and humans. What God is understood to have done is to put an end to all productivity: agricultural, animal, and human. Humans may, without insight, think they are suffering through a bad year, but those with the benefit of insight from Haggai's oracles understand that Yahweh is behind such misfortune, and they understand that such misfortune has come because the temple still lies in ruins. Rarely has the temple been so clearly linked to cosmic notions, though completion of a temple and the resultant fertility is a standard motif in the ancient Near East.

In sum, 1:2–11 is an essay-like conflation of prophetic formulae, rhetorical questions, quotations, and divine speeches, a unit that addresses and then readdresses an issue of paramount concern for the prophet. The message is not only that restoration of the Judahite community without the reconstruction of the temple is impossible, but also that the lack of a temple engenders a curse.[23] Israel is living an existence that is doubly cursed. By failing to restore its cultic center, the people still suffer the effects of the curses engendered in 587 B.C.E., and they are also already suffering under a new curse because they have not acted wisely in response to the possibilities for restoration open to them through the Persian government. The Persians had explicitly allowed for the reconstruction of the temple and had provided materials for such projects.[24] Yet, even with this financial and administrative support, the Judahites had still not rebuilt the major Yahwistic shrine. What was politically and financially possible was not being done. In Haggai's eyes, the situation is something other than progressive restoration. The status quo is of continuing, even increasing, punishment, a cursed existence that would continue until the temple is rebuilt.

[23] On this section of Haggai, see esp. the following. O. Steck ("Zu Haggai 1:2–11," *ZAW* 83, 1971, 355–379) argues that these verses comprise "discussion sayings," with Hag. 2:4–8 addressing Judeans and 2:9–11 addressing those who returned from Babylon. J. Whedbee ("A Question-Answer Schema in Haggai 1: The Form and Function of Haggai 1:9–11," in G. Tuttle, ed., *Biblical and Near Eastern Studies*, 1978, 184–194), while agreeing basically with Steck's form-critical arguments, maintains that it is impossible to distinguish the audiences with such conviction and that the speech is essentially "an organic unity."

[24] See A. Kuhrt, "The Cyrus Cylinder and Achaemenid Imperial Policy," *JSOT* 25, 1983, 83–97, for a realistic assessment of the Cyrus edict.

Haggai 1:12–15a

They worked on the house of Yahweh

12 Then Zerubbabel son of Shealtiel, and Joshua son of Jehozadak, the high priest, and all the remnant of the people heeded[a] Yahweh their God, because of[b] Haggai the prophet, whom Yahweh had sent to them,[c] and as a result the people feared Yahweh.[d] **13** Thereupon Haggai, the messenger of Yahweh, spoke Yahweh's message to the people: "I am with you, says Yahweh." **14** Then Yahweh inspired Zerubbabel son of Shealtiel, governor of Judah, and Joshua son of Jehozadak, the high priest, and all the remnant of the people, so that they came and worked on the house of Yahweh of Hosts, their God. **15a** This was on the twenty-fourth day of the sixth month.

a. The idiom *šm' b⁰qôl* is properly translated "heed" or "obey" and not woodenly, "hear the voice of . . ."

b. *'al-dibrê* as a causal construction. On causal *'al*, see Williams, *Hebrew Syntax, and Outline*, §291, and the standard grammars.

c. Reading with LXX *'ᵃlêhem (pros autous)* rather than MT *'ᵉlōhêhem*, the latter a dittographic expansion on the basis of the *'ᵉlōhêhem* that occurs earlier in the sentence.

d. On the idiom *yr' min*, see art. *"yr',"* BDB, 431.

[12] Haggai 1:12–15a commences with a cast enlarged beyond the characters cited in Zech. 1:1.[1] Now "all the remnant of the people" have joined Haggai, Zerubbabel, and Joshua. Given the immediately foregoing material, vs. 2–11, the inclusion of this new group makes a good deal of sense, since it seems clear that Haggai has—in those earlier speeches—been interacting with the larger Judahite community and not just with its officials. In vs. 12–15 we hear the people's responses to Haggai's (and Yahweh's) formulations. Initially we are told that all parties involved heed Yahweh.[2] However, credit is to be

[1]On this entire section, see Beuken, 31–49. He contends that the notions of covenant and covenant renewal are the controlling issues in Haggai 1.

[2]On the idiom *šm' b⁰qôl yhwh* and its special prominence in the deuteronomistic corpus, see Beuken, 33–34, and more generally, A. Fenz, *Auf Jahwes Stimme hören. Eine biblische Begriffsuntersuchung*, 1964. Both Beuken and Fenz maintain that the proper context for understanding such obedience to Yahweh is his covenant with Israel. This would appear to be true in Hag. 1:12, especially since the covenant curses of futility are prominent earlier in that chapter.

shared. The author of this history of Haggai seems interested in highlighting the importance of Haggai the prophet. Just as Zerubbabel receives the label of governor, and just as Joshua is known as high priest, so Haggai receives an official title in order to have a similar standing with his peer functionaries. All three major characters receive role labels. Yahweh had, to be sure, sent Haggai, and Haggai was directed to speak Yahweh's words. Without this specific human agent, Yahweh's words would not have been communicated in an appropriate way. Such is, at least, the perspective of the author of these verses in the book of Haggai.

With their present lamentable condition, as interpreted in vs. 2–11, the people react in such a way as to demonstrate that they know the cause of their problems, of the lack of fertility and prosperity. They fear Yahweh as the agent responsible for their plight.[3] Haggai's speeches in vs. 2–11 had been effective. This reaction of fear is that of the overall populace—the people. It is interesting that the narrator focuses on the people and not on high officials at this point in the interchange. Perhaps this shift in audience occurs because the author recognizes who must actually do the work of temple reconstruction. It is not just the officials who must work.

[13] By way of prefacing Haggai's response to the people, the author yet again highlights the importance of Haggai in these goings-on. And he uses a wordplay to do it.[4] Haggai is a *mal'ak yhwh*, a messenger of Yahweh, who is conveying the *mal'ᵃkût yhwh*, the message of Yahweh. Again it is clear that the impetus for response lies with Yahweh, but Haggai has distinctive authority as Yahweh's agent.

The author has here gone to significant trouble to demonstrate that the prophet's words have had an effect, that this messenger from Yahweh had been given serious attention by those whom he was addressing. Given Israel's earlier experience with Yahweh's messengers, this situation is new and therefore noteworthy. In recounting the fate of Judah, the Chronicler—who wrote only a few years later than Haggai—observed:

> Yahweh, the God of their fathers, sent persistently to them by his messengers, because he had compassion on his people and on his dwelling

[3]See J. Becker, *Gottesfurcht im Alten Testament,* 1969, for a discussion of the notion of fearing Yahweh. Becker suggests that this concept had two quite different foci: ethical and ritual "fear of God," notions at home in the wisdom and deuteronomistic traditions respectively.

[4]The presence of the wordplay explains the otherwise unusual designation of Haggai as a *mal'āk.*

place; but they kept mocking the messengers of God, despising his words, and scoffing at his prophets, till the wrath of Yahweh rose against his people, till there was no remedy. (II Chron. 36:15–16).

In the premonarchic period, Yahweh's prophets were not always given the respect which they deserved and their words were not obeyed in the way in which Haggai's words were received by those in Judah about 520 B.C.E. Perhaps the historian is here suggesting that a new age has arrived, one in which Israel's prophets would become effective and one in which the community would no longer suffer the sort of fate that it had earlier experienced and was, in fact, currently experiencing.

Yahweh's message to the people is short and traditional: "I am with you."[5] Such language is most prominent in cultic usage, in the so-called priestly oracle of salvation.[6] This particular sentence is, however, only one part of the larger oracle and therefore has something of a cryptic quality here. However, two things do stand out in this use of the "I am with you" formula in 1:13.[7] First, it is associated with the notion of fear and is, therefore, similar to other usages of this word of assurance:

"Fear not, O Jacob . . . for I am with you." (Jer. 30:10–11)

"Fear not, for I am with you." (Isa. 41:10)

"Fear not, for I am with you." (Isa. 43:5)

Similarly, in Hag. 1 the people have reacted to Haggai's explication of their situation by becoming fearful. And although Haggai does not admonish them not to fear, the use of the assurance formula is altogether consistent with its use in other such texts as a solution to the people's fears.

Second, the "I am with you" statement is not a static assurance. Yahweh's current presence has significance for the future. This facet of Yahweh's activity is especially clear in those same texts which contain the "fear not" formula.

> For I am with you to save you,
> says Yahweh;
> I will make a full end of all the nations
> among whom I scattered you,
> but of you I will not make a full end.
> (Jer. 30:11a)

[5]There is little warrant for thinking v. 13 is secondary, as some commentators have suggested. Rather than being superfluous to the narrative, this verse records Haggai's direct response to the people's response to his earlier words.

[6]See Begrich's still-valuable essay "Das priesterliche Heilsorakel," *ZAW* 52, 1934, 81–92, for an assessment of the *Beistandsformel* or "word of assurance."

[7]Cf. the use of this formula in Hag. 2:4.

Fear not, for I am with you,
  be not dismayed, for I am your God;
I will strengthen you, I will help you,
I will uphold you with my victorious right hand.
                                                    (Isa. 41:10)

Fear not, for I am with you;
  I will bring your offspring from the east,
  and from the west I will gather you.
                                                    (Isa. 43:5)

When this "fear not" formula is used, the people's fear is understood to be addressed by the future action of Yahweh. Hence, Haggai's words were, though terse, no doubt as effective as his earlier words of admonition because of the connotations created by this traditional formulation. His earlier speech had engendered a sense of severe apprehension among the people, and now he had to respond to that reaction.

[14] With these brief words of assurance spoken, the narrator continues his history of temple rebuilding as it took place in 520 B.C.E. Yahweh acts, and this is a bit unusual. We might have expected the story to continue with 14b, *wayyābō'û* . . . ("and they came . . ."). Haggai had provided words of assurance to the people after they learned that they were now being punished for not rebuilding the temple. We might have thought that the people would have then proceeded to rebuild the temple. Not so. The people apparently needed assistance. However, despite the presumed effectiveness of Haggai's words, Yahweh intervened to force the people to action. There is, therefore, a resulting tension in 12–15a. On the one hand, Haggai's words were effective (v. 12); on the other hand, Yahweh had to act in order to guarantee that work on the temple would take place. And Yahweh acted vigorously. The phrase *'wr rûaḥ*, here translated "inspire," is used elsewhere to describe Yahweh inciting the Medes to make war (Jer. 51:11), the Assyrians to attack Israel (I Chron. 5:26), and the Philistines to attack Judah (II Chron. 21:16). Perhaps most important of such "stirring up" texts are the final verses of the Chronicler's history and one portion of the first chapter of Ezra.[8]

Now in the first year of Cyrus king of Persia, that the word of Yahweh by the mouth of Jeremiah might be accomplished, Yahweh stirred up the

[8]The prominence of the Chronicler's texts here does not warrant the conclusion that this verse in Haggai is attributable to the Chronicler's hand, as Beuken, 31, argues. Cf. Rudolph, 38.

spirit of Cyrus king of Persia so that he made a proclamation throughout all his kingdom and also put it in writing: Thus says Cyrus king of Persia, "Yahweh, the God of heaven, has given me all the kingdoms of the earth, and he has charged me to build him a house at Jerusalem, which is in Judah. Whoever is among you of all his people, may Yahweh his God be with him. Let him go up." (II Chron. 36:22–23).

Then rose up the heads of the fathers' houses of Judah and Benjamin, and the priests and the Levites, every one whose spirit God had stirred to go up to rebuild the house of Yahweh which is in Jerusalem . . ." (Ezra 1:5)

Just as Yahweh had acted so that Cyrus would authorize the reconstruction of the Jerusalem temple, and just as he had given impetus to those in Mesopotamia to return to Syria-Palestine, so he had to continue to act to enable the Judahites to carry out this rebuilding activity. One even senses that Haggai is fulfilling the promise proclaimed by Cyrus in II Chron. 36. Cyrus had said of the exile who would return and rebuild the temple, "May Yahweh his god be with him" (36:23), and now Haggai had indeed spoken those performative words: "I am with you, says Yahweh." Earlier, Yahweh had acted to fulfill words spoken by another prophet, Jeremiah (II Chron. 36:22–23). In Hag. 1, Yahweh acts in a similar way to further the prophetic work of Haggai.

What is it then that this brief report of Haggai's work was intended to convey? Our historian observes that the people, in concert with Zerubbabel and Joshua, worked on the temple. He does not say that they began such work; that had happened earlier, presumably under Sheshbazzar's leadership. He does not say that they finished the work; that happened in 515 B.C.E. He does not say that they worked on the altar; that is the concern in Ezra 3. He does not enter a report about the official rededication ceremony, which is the subject of Ezra 3 and 7, and of Zech. 4:6–10. Rather, the point being made in Hag. 1:12–15a seems to be that Haggai's words, in conjunction with Yahweh's direct intervention, have an effect upon the community and upon the community's leaders. Work on the temple does take place. And that fact is so important that the date for such renewed building activity is given, the twenty-fourth day of the sixth month in 520 B.C.E.

[15a] The date has complex significance. Many commentators, following Rothstein, propose placing this date before Hag. 2:15. It does, of course, emphasize the fact that work on the temple took place. It also indicates, however, that Haggai's initial speech, delivered on

the first day of the sixth month, was not immediately effective. There is a process of speech, reaction of the people, assurance by the prophet, and then direct, invigorating action by the deity. What our historian has done here is present a vignette of how prophetic words become effective. In so doing, he presents us with a picture of Haggai as a successful agent, and yet not magically so. The prophet's initial words (vs. 2–11) have an effect, but it is not immediate. Furthermore, the prophet's words require a follow-up, an assurance by the prophet and the inspiring activity of the deity.

The relation between the deity and the people of Israel is illumined significantly by this chapter in Haggai.[9] Haggai's and Yahweh's logic is such as to suggest that God's covenant with Israel is still in force. If Yahweh could punish the people for not rebuilding the temple—and if the people could still be charged with violating Yahweh's will for them—then some legal instrument must be in force that enabled Yahweh to have a claim on the people. The covenant could not have been utterly abrogated by the events of 587 B.C.E. There was still structural continuity with the past. Haggai's work on behalf of temple reconstruction was not therefore a futile attempt at establishing the older order. Part of the older order still remained, at least from the deity's perspective. It remained for the people to recognize this fact and to respond accordingly, by rebuilding the house of Yahweh. And this they did.

Haggai 1:15b–2:9

Is it not as nothing in your eyes?

1:15b In the second year of Darius the king,
2:1 in the seventh month, on the twenty-first day of the month, the word of Yahweh was conveyed by Haggai the prophet:[a]
2 Speak to Zerubbabel son of Shealtiel, governor of Judah, and to Joshua son of Jehozadak, the high priest, and to the remnant of the people:
3 "Who is there left among you who saw this house in its former glory?
How do you see it now?
Is it not as nothing in your eyes?

[9]Here I argue against the notion of Beuken that Haggai 1 represents a covenant-renewal ceremony.

4 Now, be steadfast, Zerubbabel!" says Yahweh.
"Be steadfast, Joshua son of Jehozadak, high priest!
Be steadfast, all you people of the land!
Work, for I am with you!" says Yahweh of Hosts.
5 (The matter which I covenanted with you when you came out of
Egypt)[b]
"My spirit resides among you.
Do not fear!"
6 For thus says Yahweh of Hosts,
"In just a little while,[c]
I will shake the heavens and the earth,
the sea and the dry land.
7 I will shake all the nations,
the precious things of all the nations will arrive,[d]
I will fill this house with glory,"
says Yahweh of Hosts.
8 "The silver is mine,
the gold is mine," says Yahweh of Hosts.
9 "The glory of this latter house shall be greater
than that of the former one," says Yahweh of Hosts.
"In this place I shall establish prosperity," says Yahweh of Hosts.[e]
(and peace of soul as a possession for all who build,
to erect this temple)[f]

a. Mur reads *'el* instead of *b^eyad*. The principle of *lectio difficilior* as well as
the reiteration of the formula used in 1:1 makes MT the preferable reading.

b. Haggai 2:5 presents a serious textual problem. Verse 5a, "The matter
which I covenanted with you when you came out of Egypt," appears to be a
prosaic intrusion into the poetic discourse of the prophet. Furthermore, LXX
does not include these words. Regrettably, the Murabba'ât manuscript is
fragmentary at this point, but the space missing would appear long enough to
include these 29 letters. Further, the penultimate word *bs'tkm* is, in all
likelihood, present in the MS. Since the Murabba'ât MS. is closely allied to the
MT textual tradition, agreement between Mur and MT against LXX should
not be surprising. An appeal to the Sinaitic tradition seems rather beside the
point here, in a section devoted to the other major Israelite election
tradition—that of Zion, the place of Yahweh's residence. In sum, 2:5a can be
construed as intrusive. On the reason for its inclusion, see the commentary
below.

c. The first four words of the divine oracle are difficult. As Ackroyd
observes, they would read literally, "yet one, and it is only a little one" (*Exile
and Restoration*, 153–154). LXX is of little help, since it apparently translates
only the first two words: *eti hapax*, "yet once." The key issue is whether the

anticipated action of the deity is a repetition of something done earlier, as the RSV suggests with its "once again," or whether it is a way of making indefinite the moment at which the cosmic shaking will occur (so JPS): "in just a little while longer." Since this language of Yahweh shaking treasure out of the nations is not used earlier in Israelite traditions, the notion of repetition is not likely to be in the text. Hence, something like the JPS translation is preferable.

d. On a plural meaning for the singular noun *ḥemdat*, see the commentary below.

e. The ambiguity inherent in the Hebrew preposition *b* makes possible two quite different translations: "in this place" or "from this place." See the commentary below for a discussion of the options.

f. Immediately after the concluding formula in MT, LXX includes the following clause: "and peace of soul as a possession for all who build, to erect this temple," *kai eirēnēn psychēs eis peripoiēsin panti tō ktizonti, tou anastēsai ton naon touton.* Especially since these words occur after the final formula *nĕ'um yhwh ṣĕbā'ôt* they appear to be a scribal reflection on the notion of *šālôm* promised by the prophet. See the commentary below.

[**1:15b**] Dates are used to introduce all the major sections of this compendium of prophetic words and the results they achieved or hoped to achieve. And as we are beginning to see, dates serve as major markers in the architecture of this small prophetic collection; thus in 1:1 and 1:15a they mark the initial reception of Yahweh's word and the major response to Yahweh's word. And now in 1:15b, the date formula points to the growing impact of the people's response to Yahweh's word. The year is the same as it was when Haggai first began his public discourse, and almost one month has passed since Yahweh invigorated the community and its leaders to continue with work on the temple.

[**2:1–2**] Just as the day of the month had special significance in 1:1, so here the twenty-first day of the month places Judah in the final part of the feast of booths (on which see Lev. 23:33–36) at a time when a major congregational gathering took place for "an offering by fire to Yahweh." This feast was, at least from the perspective of Ezek. 45:25, *the* feast.[1] With people gathering in Jerusalem and with attention focused, as it no doubt was, on the temple under reconstruction, it was very important for Haggai to respond to concerns about the temple and its status. Further, there can be little doubt that Joshua, and especially Zerubbabel, would have attended the great assembly associated with this feast, since the royal leader was apparently of

---

[1] See Wolff, *Haggai, Eine Auslegung*, 1951, 27–28, on the resonance with the dedication of the first temple and the overall significance of this date.

some significance in this particular celebration (I Kings 8:2, 65). Even though it is possible to label Hag. 2:1–2 as editorial or redactional in origin, these verses remain in all likelihood accurate indicators of the time, audience, and overall context in which the words of Haggai were spoken.

The same cast active in the previous unit—Joshua, Zerubbabel, and the people—continue in 1:15b–2:9. Further, these parties had responded favorably to Yahweh's admonitions by working on the temple. And yet, despite their efforts and despite the earlier energizing action of Yahweh, things were obviously not progressing in a wholly satisfactory way. Haggai is speaking to a situation in which some Judahites think the new temple under construction is a pale copy of the old one. We do not, however, have their exact words. Rather, we have Haggai's response to this dissatisfaction. Put another way, we must infer this response of the people from what we are told in 1:15b–2:9 and from other reports of this basic period. In a narrative written at a slightly later date (Ezra 3:10–14), the people's reaction to the foundation stone ceremony is, in fact, preserved. Despite the festivities that surrounded such an occasion, the writer of this text informs us about a distinct ambivalence in the community's response to this event. On the one hand, "all the people shouted with a great shout, when they praised Yahweh, because the foundation of the house of Yahweh was laid" (Ezra 3:11). On the other hand, "many of the priests and Levites and heads of fathers' houses, old men who had seen the first house, wept with a loud voice when they saw the foundation of this house being laid" (Ezra 3:12). Surely it is this kind of situation which set the context for Haggai's speech—people were present who remembered the earlier temple and could express dissatisfaction with the new one.

As Haggai has desired, work on the temple had gone forward. And yet such work created its own problems, just as some of Haggai's earlier words had created a disabling fear that required a response by the prophet. Now with their work apparently well under way on the temple, some of the older generation sensed that this new building did not compare well with the one built by Solomon. And their reaction had an impact on the perceptions and the activity of those who had not seen that earlier temple. It is no accident that Haggai—in dealing with this problem—addresses Zerubbabel, Joshua, and all the people. The impact of the dissenters' criticism would have been contagious, affecting the entire community.

[3] Haggai does (and properly so) begin with direct address to the source of such concerns. One senses an adroit politician at work here.

Going immediately to the root of the problem, he asks a question of those who had most reason to be dissatisfied, those who could remember that earlier Solomonic temple (3b). In a tactically brilliant maneuver, Haggai expresses agreement with the perspectives of those expressing dissatisfaction: "Is it not as nothing in your eyes?" Such a formulation elicits their response and in so doing establishes rapport with that sector of the community which is dissatisfied.

In engaging those who were unhappy about the temple, Haggai was able to supply a vocabulary that would suit both his hearers' perceptions and his own ability to respond to their situation. He defined the issue as a difference in *kābôd*. This Hebrew noun is ambiguous, especially when it is used with reference to a temple. The temple may house Yahweh's holiness, his *kābôd* comprising an indwelling holy presence. However, Yahweh's *kābôd* does not seem to be at issue here. Rather, *kābôd* in vs. 3 and 9 refers to the obvious ornamentation that holds a prominent place in the description of Solomon's temple in I Kings 6–7. That temple was remembered as impressive not only in its structural outline but in its ornamentation of wood and precious metals. And despite the return of at least some of the temple vessels from Babylon (Ezra 1:8–11), the overall perception was that the splendor of this second temple would not match that of the Solomonic structure. Interestingly, the issue, as Haggai articulates it, is not of the temple's size or style. Indeed, there is little reason to think that the second temple was markedly different from the Solomonic structure in either respect.[2] It was apparently easier for Haggai to propose a remedy in regard to the splendor of the temple than in regard to the essential size or style of the structure itself.

[4] After broaching dissatisfaction about the temple directly with the older generation, who felt such dissatisfaction, Haggai addresses those who have been influenced by the older generation. Zerubbabel, Joshua, and the entire community receive imperatives from Haggai. Each party is told to stand firm, to be strong. And collectively, they are told to work—almost certainly meaning to work on the temple. They are to work because of a divine guarantee. Haggai utters again the so-called formula of assurance, "I am with you," which is linked to the imperatives with a causative *kî*. This formula is, as we saw in the discussion of 1:13, taken from time-honored language, especially as it was uttered in the ritual context of the priestly oracle of salvation. In this particular context, the formula may have special significance

---

[2] We know embarrassingly little about the second temple. See, e.g., the discussion in *IDB* IV, 547–550.

because of the assonance between the independent personal pronoun *'ᵃnî* in 2:4 and the negative particle *'ayin* in 2:3. The correspondence in sound is matched by a dissonance in meaning.[3]

[5] The traditional connection of "fear" to the priestly oracle of salvation is present in 2:5 as it was in 1:13. Here we read *'al-tîrā'û*, "Do not fear," the standard accompaniment to the word of assurance in the priestly oracle of salvation.

Standing in synonymous parallelism with the word of assurance is 5b, "My spirit resides among you." This is one way to restate the notion of Yahweh's presence with Israel. It is a restatement based upon language used earlier in the book. Just as Yahweh had awakened the spirit or inspired certain parties to work in 1:14, so now Yahweh's spirit is in the midst of the people.[4]

Beuken has subjected 1:15b–2:9 to intense scrutiny and has argued that 2:4–5 represent quite a different form from that of 2:3 and 2:6–9.[5] He notes that vs. 3 and 6–9 focus on the temple, whereas vs. 4–5 represent what Lohfink[6] has designated as an investiture, a form normally comprising three parts:

    I. *Ermutigungsformel* (formula of encouragement)
   II. *Nennung einer Aufgabe* (assignment of a task)
  III. *Beistandsformel* (formula of assurance)

For Beuken's purposes it was important to recognize that this same form is used six times in the Chronicler's history, instances in which the verb *'śh* occurs as a description of the task to be performed, as it is in Haggai.

Unusual in this speech, according to Beuken, is the phrase *kol-'am hā'āreṣ*, which he thinks may reflect a pre-Chronistic stage in the text; i.e., Haggai spoke to the people and the editors later construed him as having been active with Joshua and Zerubbabel.

Beuken also attributes the formulations "I am with you" and "Do not fear" to the hand of the editor since they are, he argues, superfluous to the prophetic task. This is, in my judgment, an inadequate approach to this language, given the rhetorical task that

---

[3] Cf. Wolff, *Haggai, Eine Auslegung*, 30.
[4] Cf. Wolff's reflection on *rûaḥ* within the context of late prophetic texts (e.g., Isa. 63:11), in *Haggai, Eine Auslegung*, 31.
[5] Beuken, 49–64.
[6] N. Lohfink, "Die deuteronomistische Darstellung des Übergangs der Führung Israels von Moses auf Josue," *Scholastik* 37, 1962, 32–44.

Haggai confronted. Such language would have been appropriate to the difficult task of convincing people to continue in the work of rebuilding a less than fully glamorous temple. And as for the expression "My spirit resides in your midst," Beuken sees it, not surprisingly, as a function of the Chronicler's historiography, referring to the activity of the prophetic *rûaḥ* as exemplified by Haggai himself.

As I have noted earlier, Beuken's work represents an intense search for Chronistic elements in Haggai and Zechariah 1–8. On occasion, the Chronicler uses language from older Israelite traditions, e.g., the "I am with you" formula present in Hag. 1:13 and 2:5. Such language is not inherently Chronistic. I have argued that the dynamics of Haggai's situation required him to use traditional language in order to address successfully the distresses created by the reconstruction of the second temple. One may maintain that the Chronicler, as well as Haggai, is drawing on the stock of acceptable phraseology, and not that the Chronicler has inserted such language into the book of Haggai.

This divine oracle conveyed by Haggai is complex, entailing both words of admonition and words of comfort. It is also remarkably general: Be steadfast. I am with you. My spirit is in your midst. Do not fear. This is—all of it—highly stereotypic language. In order to give this oracle a distinctive character, a prophetic traditionist has introduced language focusing on a concrete event, the exodus, and a specific relationship, the covenant at Sinai, as a basis for Yahweh's admonitory language here. Yahweh is with Israel now, this traditionist claims, because of the specific relationship made possible by Yahweh's covenant with Israel. Such commentary is hardly surprising, given the traditional linkage between the feast of booths, the time at which this speech is dated, and the exodus. "You shall dwell in booths for seven days . . . that your generations may know that I made the people of Israel dwell in booths when I brought them out of the land of Egypt" (Lev. 23:43).

The use of consistently traditional language here by the prophet is interesting. He is attempting to deal with a difficult issue inside the community—one inspired by those who remembered the glories of the good old days. To respond effectively to this situation, Haggai has chosen "good, old" language, not only to define the situation but also to attain the goal of having people continue to work on the temple with the feeling that their concerns about the lack of glory have, in fact, been dealt with in a serious manner.

[6] After words of encouragement directed to Zerubbabel, Joshua, and the people in 2:4–5, Haggai presents an oracle that, because of the causative *kî* introducing v. 6, is understood to provide warrant for the foregoing admonitions and the brief formulae of assurance in vs. 4–5.[7] Translations of the first four words of this oracle vary a good bit. As suggested in the textual note, the thrust of the phraseology is to plead for time: "In just a little while," the hoped-for time of weal will occur. The prophet is not expecting the repetition of some earlier event but rather a new sort of glorious activity in the very near future.[8]

Future weal will depend upon Yahweh's direct intervention. Haggai conveys Yahweh's intentions to all concerned: "I will shake the heavens and the earth, the sea and the dry land," a statement the first part of which occurs again in 2:21. We are obviously dealing here with more than earthquakes or tremors. As J. Jeremias has shown, the language of the mountains shaking derives from Israel's theophanic traditions. Yahweh appears and the world reacts violently.[9] However, as Jeremias points out, Haggai has used this traditional language in a distinctive way. In Haggai, the shaking of the earth is not a reaction to Yahweh's appearance per se but rather is linked to new activity of Yahweh on behalf of his people. Further distinguishing this language from typical theophanic descriptions is the scope of such violent agitation. It is no longer just the mountains which quake. The entire cosmos vibrates, as indicated by the two polar sets: earth–heavens, sea–dry land. These elements define the entire cosmos, not simply four parts of it. The shaking of these elements serves as a nonverbal proclamation that Yahweh is acting decisively on behalf of his people, a community gathered around the rebuilt temple.

[7] Moreover, Yahweh's activity will have something other than a cosmic or geographic focus. "He will shake the nations," whose wealth or precious things will become available for the temple. The particular word used to indicate precious things, *ḥemdāh*, is problematic.[10] This

---

[7] Beuken thinks 2:6–9a may be attributed to Haggai, whereas 9b is Chronistic—with its shared emphasis on *šālôm* and the phrase *māqôm hazzeh;* cf. I Chron. 22:9–10a.

[8] Mason, "The Prophets of the Restoration," in R. Coggin et al. (eds.), *Israel's Prophetic Tradition*, 1982, 144, insists that the prophet is thinking eschatologically. Cf. Rudolph, 43.

[9] J. Jeremias, *Theophanie*, 1965, 66–69.

[10] The Vulgate takes very seriously the fact of a singular noun and gives the word a distinct Messianic connotation: *et veniet Desideratus cunctis gentibus*, "and the desire of all the nations shall come." Attention to the Hebrew syntax, viz., the plural verb, makes such a translation and interpretation impossible. See Amsler, 34–35; G. Krause, "'Aller Heiden Trost,' Haggai 2:7," in *Solange es "Heute" heisst*, 1957, 170–178.

word, when used to describe wealth, often occurs as part of the phrase
k°lî ḥemdāh, meaning precious objects or vessels (Hos. 13:15; Nahum
2:10 [2:9E]; II Chron. 32:27; 36:10; cf. Ezra 8:27). This very fact
suggests that Haggai does not expect ingots of gold but, rather,
precious vessels and other metallic accoutrements for the temple
cultus. Such vessels were, after all, taken away at the time of the defeat
in 587 (II Kings 25:13–17). According to the Ezra report of
Sheshbazzar's delegation, these vessels were returned (Ezra 1:5–11).
To what extent this actually happened, and what fate these objects
might have suffered in the period between Sheshbazzar and
Zerubbabel is unclear. In any case, precious objects belonging to the
temple had been lost to the nations. And their return was a necessary
part of a proper restoration.[11] Haggai's ideas here are probably not
dissimilar from those being expressed in Zechariah's first two visions,
that the nations are prospering improperly when compared with the
dismal fate of Judah. This cosmic and international imbalance must be
redressed. Haggai manages the matter by having the nations
plundered. Both in Zechariah 1–8 and in Haggai, Yahweh had to act in
order to right the lamentable status quo.

A comparison of Haggai's expectation of riches from the nations
with Isa. 60:5–11 is instructive. Here too there is talk of treasure
flowing to Jerusalem. However, a different traditio-historical background is clearly at work in this deuteroprophetic text. The motif in
Isa. 60:1–11 is that of the pilgrimage of the nations to Jerusalem: "and
nations shall come to your light." In Haggai, the language derives from
theophanic traditions and carries a punitive undertone toward the
nations, an element missing from Isa. 60. In Haggai the nations are
being shaken in order to jar loose their wealth.

The purpose of such action is not simply to plunder the nations, nor
is it to provide wealth for the Judahites, wealth that, according to Hag.
1:6, they did not have.[12] Instead, Yahweh will use the precious objects
to fill the temple with glory. The possessions, rather than God, will
provide kābôd. Hereby the concerns expressed in Hag. 2:3 are
addressed. There was "former glory" and there will be future glory.
And since there is no tradition of Yahweh shaking the world to provide
treasure for the Solomonic temple, Haggai seems to be suggesting that
the future glory will be even more marvelous than that known by those
who had experienced Solomon's temple. This is made explicit in 2:9.

[11] For the notion of riches in the nations which are available for plunder, see Nahum
2:10.
[12] Cf. the view of the nations in Zech. 8:22.

[8] The first part of 2:8 is intriguingly ambiguous: "The silver is mine, the gold is mine." What is the point of such a claim? Two different implications are possible. First, Yahweh might be claiming that all silver and gold are ultimately his in order to justify taking them away from the nations. Second, Yahweh might be making this claim in order to keep the Judahites from thinking that the silver or gold was by right or would become theirs when it appeared (or better, reappeared) in Judah. Both options are possible at the same time: Yahweh has the right to remove gold and silver from the nations and also the right to claim such material for this temple.

The emphatic claim in v. 9 that the glory of this house shall be great emphasizes the second of these two options, that the gold and silver are designated for the temple and not for the deficient purses in which the Judahites had stored their wealth.

It is difficult to read this section in Haggai and not to reflect on the "silver and gold" text in Zech. 6:9–15. There too, silver and gold were coming from the nations, from Babylon. Yahwists were bringing this accumulated wealth in order to provide the objects appropriate for the worship and rule of Yahweh in Jerusalem. The mood in this Zechariah text is mundane, one of fund-raising by a group of persons who venerate Yahweh. In order to achieve the goal of accumulating such objects, Haggai does not think of the community contributing out of their own pockets, but rather of the necessity of Yahweh intervening decisively to provide such wealth for his people. The contrasts between these two perspectives are considerable: Where does one look first for financial assistance? Who is the real provider?

[9] As the motifs of silver and gold resonate with a section in Zechariah 1–8, similarly the penultimate colon in Hag. 2:9 emphasizes a quality mentioned in Zech. 8:12 and 19: *šālôm*, peace or well-being. The temple, according to Haggai, will become the source of *šālôm*, whether he establishes it in or from this place.[13] This contention seems a move beyond the insistence on glory and highlights a different function of temple completion, that of guaranteeing overall prosperity for the community in a way similar to the claims presented in Hag. 1.

Some scholars have argued that a wordplay is involved in this use of *šālôm*, a wordplay either on the name of the first temple's builder,

---

[13] *māqôm* often has the technical meaning of holy place or temple; see Jer. 33:1–13; 14:13; Hos. 9:19; Gen. 22:3ff.

Solomon, or on the city in which the temple was built, Jerusalem. Both
words include the consonants *šlm*.[14] Both options are possible,
although neither is, in my judgment, likely.

A final comment seems appropriate about the afterlife of 2:9. The
final promise in the pericope, "In this place, I shall establish
prosperity," is ambiguous because it is difficult to know precisely what
Yahweh is promising: Peace for those who come to the temple? Peace
for all, as such peace proceeds out from the temple? And of these two
options, is it lack of war, lack of material prosperity, or lack of
dissension concerning ritual matters which *šālôm* means here? The
ambiguities inherent in the Hebrew formulation elicited reflection
apparently in response to the following question: For whom will
Yahweh provide this *šālôm?* Some exegete/scribe wrote an answer into
the margin of the book which found its way into Septuagint
manuscripts, an answer that linked these glorious promises to the
pragmatic admonitions articulated in Hag. 1. This author believed that
the *šālôm* would not be something of material sort, but a spiritual
condition resulting from a specific activity, actual participation in the
construction of the temple. What was for the original speaker a
material form of prosperity has, in LXX, become a highly spiritualized
concept: "and peace of soul as a possession for all who build, to erect
this temple."

Haggai 2:10–14

That which they bring near is unclean

10 On the twenty-fourth day of the ninth month in Darius' second
 year, the word of Yahweh came to Haggai the prophet:
11 "Thus says Yahweh of Hosts,
 Ask the priests for a ruling.[a]
12 'If a person lifts consecrated flesh with the skirt of his garment,
 and then, if that person's skirt touches bread, stew,[b]
 wine, oil, or any other kind of food, does it become holy?'"
 The priests responded, "No."
13 Then Haggai said,
 "If a person unclean from contact with a corpse
 touches any of these, does it become unclean?"
 The priests responded, "It becomes unclean."

---

[14] See Amsler, 35; Baldwin, 49.

14 Thereupon Haggai responded,
"So it is with this people,
and so it is with this nation
before me," says Yahweh.
"So it is with all the work of their hands:
That which they bring near is unclean."[c]

a. The clause may be translated literally, "Ask the priests for a torah."
b. The word translated here as "stew" occurs only two other times in the Hebrew Bible, Gen. 25:29 and II Kings 4:38. These contexts suggest something akin to what we know as vegetable stew.
c. Not only does the Septuagint include material not found in MT at this point, it also provides a quite different notion of the final clause "and whosoever shall approach them shall be defiled." People, rather than things, is the subject of reflection in LXX. The material that is in LXX and not included in MT is, for lack of a better term, best described as heterogeneous: "Because of their early profits, they shall be pained because of their toil, and you have hated those who reprove in the gates" *(heneken tōn lēmmatōn autōn tōn orthrinōn odynēthēsontai apo prosōpou ponōn autōn kai emiseite en pylais elegchontas)*. Clearly the final clause in the LXX represents an insertion into the text based on Amos 5:10, though in the second and not the third person as in MT and LXX of Amos 5:10: "They hate him who reproves in the gate" (LXX, *emisēsan en pylais elegchonta*). This dependence on the LXX of Amos for a gloss in the book of Haggai is suggestive of the scribal work present in the deuteroprophetic material, i.e., the insertion of one part of the canonical text as commentary into yet another part of the canon. As for the other material in LXX, at least one commentator has argued that *heneken . . . autōn* represents a translation from a Hebrew *Vorlage* and that *tōn orthrinōn* represents a mistaking of *śḥr*, "bribe," for *šḥr*, "dawn" (see Mitchell, 73; Rudolph, 45). Mur is fragmentary at this point. Since the dialogue with the priest and Haggai's use of that dialogue both have to do with holiness and uncleanness, the moralism present in LXX appears to be a secondary expansion. Ackroyd (*Exile and Restoration*, 169–170) rightly sees the LXX material as an early interpretation, pushing the notion that becoming *ṭāmē'* was due to moral failure, a view lacking in MT.

[10] It is difficult to know the precise significance of the date in 2:10, at least on the basis of its occurrence here for the first time in the book of Haggai.[1] As far as we know, the twenty-fourth day of the month—in and of itself—has no special meaning, either as historical commemoration or as ritual moment in the calendrical festivals. The number

[1] Cf. Hag. 2:15, "now," which points to this particular day, and Hag. 2:18, which reiterates this same date.

twenty-four does resonate with the date in 1:15, the twenty-fourth day of the sixth month. Put another way, it had been—at least according to the editor's perspective—three months to the day that substantive work on the temple had been going on. Further, it had been a little more than two months since Zechariah had admonished the people to continue with their work on the temple. In both these earlier situations, Haggai was remembered as having addressed the community and its leaders, specifically Zerubbabel and Joshua. Haggai 2:10 presents the reader with something new. The date formula, at least formally, remains the same. But once the matter of the way in which Haggai receives Yahweh's work is broached, things change. The shift is subtle, but it is nonetheless there; and it is a change that occurs again in 2:20. Haggai now receives rather than conveys Yahweh's word. The overall picture is of having the word come *to (ʾel)* Haggai rather than having Yahweh's word conveyed by *(bᵉyad)* Haggai to someone. The change appears to be slight,[2] but it is significant since it reflects a change in the process of communication within which Haggai was involved. And interestingly, the two texts that record Yahweh's word coming to Haggai have Haggai speaking to a discrete audience rather than to the entire community. In 2:10–14, Haggai is in dialogue with the priests, and in 2:20–23, the prophet speaks directly to Zerubbabel. Yahweh, through Haggai, is directing words to more discrete sectors of the Judahite community now that a basic impetus for the reconstruction of the temple has begun. (The reasons for this shift in audience will become clear as we proceed with the commentary.)

[11] The words Haggai received are introduced by the standard "messenger formula," words that had occurred earlier in the book (1:2, 7; 2:6). The oracle so introduced comprises, in the first instance, imperative directions to the prophet: "Ask the priests for a ruling!" With these words we are introduced to a special realm of discourse, the priestly decision-making procedures, a basic knowledge of which is necessary to understand the ensuing verses in Hag. 2.

A good deal has been written about the so-called priestly torah or priestly decision-making process and the topics covered by such deliberation. Begrich's essay remains a classic and yet has received numerous corrections over the years, especially in the form of enlarging the realm of questions about which the priests might be

---

[2] P. Ackroyd had earlier recognized this same shift ("Studies in Haggai I," *Journal of Jewish Studies* 2, 1951, 169) but had argued that it was not important. Cf. Beuken, 65–66.

consulted.[3] Nevertheless, in 2:11–14 the priests are clearly exercising judgment about ritual matters: holiness and impurity.

For the purposes of this volume, it is important to establish several points about the priestly torah:

1. One of the major duties of the priests was to provide *tôrāh* instruction to the people. This is indicated clearly by the ancient poem in Deut. 33:10: "They shall teach Jacob your judgment, and Israel your *tôrāh*." This general expectation is reiterated in other texts, especially in Micah 3:11; Jer. 18:8; and Ezek. 7:26.

It seems to be the case that certain types of priests were responsible for particular kinds of judgment. In Lev. 10:10–11 the Aaronite priests are given an overall charge:

> You are to distinguish
> between the holy *(qōdeš)* and the common *(ḥōl)*,
> and between the unclean *(ṭāmē')* and the clean *(ṭāhôr)*;
> and you are to teach *(yrh)* the people of Israel
> all the statutes which Yahweh has spoken to them by Moses.

The Aaronites appear to have their realm of inquiry focused on matters involving the sacrificial cultus and ritual purity.

The situation with the Levitical priests seems to be a bit different. In Deut. 17:8–13, those situations which should be sent for resolution by the Levitical priests are described as follows:

> If any case arises requiring decisions between one kind of homicide and another, one kind of lawsuit and another, or one kind of assault and another, any case within your gates which is too difficult for you . . . then you shall do according to what they declare to you . . . according to the *tôrāh* with which they instruct you.

Here the entire appellate judiciary seems to fall within the purview of the Levitical priests, since they are given responsibility for all difficult cases. Equally apparent is the much broader range of topics which this system of providing *tôrāh* entails. Anything subject to legal process could receive a *tôrāh* and this in contrast to the prescriptions which direct the Aaronites to focus on issues of holiness and purity.

2. Israel's priests were subject to indictment when they did not do their duty in providing *tôrāh*. Thus Ezek. 22:26, "Her priests have

[3] J. Begrich, "Die priesterliche Tora," *ZAW* 66, 1936, 63–88. Begrich had maintained that only matters of holiness were involved in *tôrāh* decisions. Lescow, Deissler, Jensen, and Renker, among others, have challenged this view. For bibliography, see A. Renker, *Die Tora bei Maleachi*, 1979, 164.

done violence to my law *(tôrāh)* . . . ; they have made no distinction between the holy *(qōdeš)* and the common *(ḥōl)*, neither have they taught *(yrh)* the difference between the unclean *(ṭāmē')* and the clean *(ṭāhôr).*"[4] Most such indictments seem to focus on the Aaronite responsibility for distinguishing clean from unclean, holy from profane, and, in so doing, to charge the priests with having allowed radical desecration.

3. If one considers specifically the type of decision-making referred to in 2:11–14, it seems to be of the variety given into the hands of the Aaronite priests, i.e., dealing primarily with distinctions appropriate to the cultus, *qōdeš-ḥōl, ṭāhôr-ṭāmē'.* In Haggai, the terms used are *qōdeš* (holy) and *ṭāmē'* (unclean). These two words seem a peculiar combination, since one normally thinks (on the basis of texts such as Lev. 10:10–11) in terms of two binary opposites: holy versus profane, clean versus unclean. Yahweh's question, which Haggai asks of the priests, apparently disturbs these two lexical and conceptual sets. One does, therefore, wonder if the question makes sense, given the normal usage of these particular terms for holiness and uncleanness.[5]

One may infer from a survey of the salient texts that these two sets—holy and profane, clean and unclean—do overlap. In Deut. 14:2, 3, 21, we are informed that the people of Israel are holy *(qādôš)* to Yahweh and that they should not eat any abominable thing *(kol-tô'ēbāh).* Such abomination is then described in terms of clean *(ṭ'hôrāh,* v. 11), and unclean *(ṭāmē',* v. 10).[6] To eat an unclean animal is to risk defilement, the opposite of the state of holiness. Such texts demonstrate that the sets of holy-profane, and clean-unclean, are related, since something that is unclean may clearly affect a person's state of holiness.

It is probably best to think of these terms, which are normally placed in two binary sets, as standing in something of a continuum: *qōdeš, ṭāhôr, ḥōl, ṭāmē'.* Of these notions, *qōdeš* (holiness) and *ṭāmē'* (impurity) are the truly powerful forces. The middle terms do not entail such power and represent something akin to neutral states. Neither cleanness nor profaneness per se are typically capable of passing on their qualities. Cleanliness *(ṭāhôr)* is close to, and may be used to approach, something holy, and ordinariness *(ḥōl)* is akin to

---

[4] Cf. Ps. 79:1; Zeph. 3:4.

[5] On the vocabulary of cleanliness, see W. Paschen, *Rein und Unrein. Untersuchungen zur biblischen Wortgeschichte,* 1970. For a valuable overview of biblical notions of purity and impurity, see J. Neusner, *The Idea of Purity in Ancient Judaism,* 1973, 11–31.

[6] Cf. the similar distinction in Lev. 11.

uncleanness but clearly does not have the contagious power of something that is actually unclean.[7]

The contagion of uncleanness, *tāmē'*, is responsible for much of the material in Israelite religious structures (see, e.g., Lev. 11 on clean and unclean animals).[8] Impurity may be passed on by direct contact or even close proximity. The situation with holiness is a good bit more complex. Some have suggested that holiness is contagious in the same way as *tāmē'* is contagious. Haran writes:

> Any person or object coming into contact with the altar (Exod 29:37) or any of the articles of the tabernacle furniture (30:29) becomes "holy," that is, contacts holiness and, like the tabernacled appurtenances themselves, becomes consecrated. At the opposite extreme there is a tangible, contagious defilement. But contagious holiness has one advantage over the latter: it cannot be removed from a person or object. It is possible to purify one who has contracted uncleanness since this substance may be thrust out of the community into the desert. Contagious holiness, by contrast, actually exists at the very centre of the camp, in the tabernacle, and we are told of no activity or rite which can deprive a person or object of it.[9]

Haran's observations are apt and yet do not provide the whole story. The system he describes is designed for an unravaged community, for a situation in equilibrium or stasis. When forces external to the society impinge, the system is thrown totally out of kilter. The center of the society, tabernacle/temple/Jerusalem, could be, and in fact was, defiled. Texts describing the fall of Jerusalem and the destruction of the temple make this evident (Lam. 1:8–9a; 4:14–15; Ezek. 8). However, the basic thrust of these texts is not what we might expect. Most of these texts assume that the defilement actually occurred earlier than the destruction, that the blood was already flowing (thus Lam. 4) before Jerusalem was actually sacked. And according to Ezek. 8–9, Yahweh's glory had been offended by the impurity of idolatrous worship in the temple and was therefore constrained to leave the temple precinct.[10] Spilling of blood at the ritual center, the temple,

---

[7] On the relation of *tāmē'* to *hōl*, see Lev. 21:4, "He shall not defile (*tāmē'*) himself as a husband among his people and so profance (*hōl*) himself."

[8] Cf. the enlightening discussion of M. Douglas, *Purity and Danger: An Analysis of Concepts of Pollution and Taboo*, 1966.

[9] M. Haran, *Temples and Temple-Service in Ancient Israel*, 1978, 176. Haran suggests that non-P material shares this same sentiment (e.g., I Sam. 6:19–20 and II Sam. 6:6–9). These texts, however, do not attest a contagious holiness but rather the danger of the sacral power bound up in a holy object.

[10] See Ezek. 9:7, *tamme'û 'et habbayit.*

had—according to Israel's perceptions of the events—begun prior to the attack of the Neo-Babylonians, an attack that surely entailed even more radical desecration of the temple compound than had occurred earlier.[11]

The fact that the temple did become unclean in 587 raises the more general question relevant to this text: How does a person become unclean? In certain specialized cases it could come about as a result of genealogy and improper aspiration, if one aspired to the priesthood without having appropriate genealogical credentials (Ezra 2:62). Normally, however, it was a function of contact, of coming close enough for the contagion of uncleanness to move to a person from the unclean object or person (see Lev. 5:3). Toombs has argued, following Num. 5:2–4, that three forms of uncleanness are especially virulent: leprosy, bodily discharges, and corpse defilement.[12] "In these instances of uncleanness, there were prescribed ways for cleansing the radical impurity" (see, e.g., Lev. 13–14, concerning bodily discharges).

[12] As should be clear at this point, much may be said about holiness and profaneness, cleanness and uncleanness. It is now appropriate to focus the foregoing statements by means of the particularities in Hag. 2:11–14. The first case that the priests are asked to adjudicate involves carrying meat that has been consecrated. Presumably this is an instance similar to the one described in Lev. 6:26–27, the law of the sin offering, in which the priest eats the flesh of the animal in a holy place, and "whoever touches its flesh shall be holy"; also note the sacrificial variety in Lev. 7:11–21, and especially v. 19b, "All who are clean may eat flesh." At some point in the ritual procedure, flesh that had been roasted was taken to an appropriate place and consumed—in the sin offering, by a priest; in the peace, votive, or freewill offerings, by the supplicant. The prescriptions for the guilt offering make explicit that at least this offering had to be eaten within the temple precinct: "It shall be eaten in a holy place." But the flesh of the votive or freewill offering could still be eaten on the day after the sacrifice had been made. The clear implication of this time frame is that the flesh could be carried to one's domicile and consumed there, the more so since the prescription "It shall be eaten in a holy

---

[11] It is, of course, the case that the temple had been defiled earlier than the events surrounding the destruction of 587. Because of Ahaz' cultic improvisations, Hezekiah was constrained to cleanse the temple (II Chron. 29:12–19; cf. Neh. 13:9 in a similar regard). Especially important in this connection are the prescriptions for cleansing the temple found in Ezek. 40–48: in particular 43:20–22 on the ordinances for the altar and 45:18–20 for the cleansing of the sanctuary proper.

[12] *IDB* I, 644.

place" is lacking in the laws concerning thanksgiving, freewill, or votive offerings.[13]

What becomes apparent from a brief look at these sacrificial regulations is that either priests or nonpriests could carry roasted and sanctified flesh and that such flesh could be carried either within the temple precinct or beyond, to someone's house. In sum, there were several situations in which Haggai's question was relevant. The query was neither strange nor inappropriate.

A further observation is in order. The sacrifices just mentioned were to be made on the so-called great altar (so Lev. 1:6; Ex. 40:6). The fate of this altar in the destruction of Jerusalem in 587 is unclear. II Kings 25 suggests the total destruction of the temple compound.[14] The temple was burned, and all valuable metallic objects, whether gold, silver, or bronze, were removed. Nothing, however, is said about the altar. Whether or not it was actually torn down, it was perceived, at least by one tradition, as defiled, no doubt by the presence of non-Yahwists in the temple area at the time of destruction and by the altogether likely presence of Israelite corpses in that same area. Ezekiel 43:13–26 provides specific instructions for the reconstruction of the altar as well as for its rededication. Although the function of the material in Ezek. 40–48 is open to much debate, it does seem proper to infer from this text that the altar was in need of rededication, if not, in fact, reconstruction.[15]

If the activity described in Hag. 2:10–14 presumes the existence of the altar and its function within the sacrificial cultus, and if we may infer from Ezek. 43 that the altar was at some point defiled, if not torn down, then during the time before the altar was rededicated (and rebuilt) Haggai's question would have been especially pointed. His query would have referred to activity that could not or should not have been undertaken because of the current state of impurity in which the altar existed, if it did exist. Put another way, Haggai's question makes sense as a question about the actual operation of the cultus only if the altar had actually been rebuilt. With the altar in existence, the question would function as a pointer and prod con-

---

[13] It seems wholly inappropriate to treat the details of this or the following question as allegorical elements to be decoded. Cf. Rothstein, *Juden und Samaritaner,* 34ff., who treats the flesh as God's presence and the garment as those returning from exile; or cf. André (as summarized in Mitchell, 69), who understands the flesh to mean Israel and the garment to mean the land of Palestine.

[14] Ps. 79:1 is equally explicit: "O God, nations entered your inheritance. They polluted your holy temple. They have turned Jerusalem to ruins."

[15] See Ezra 3:1–7 for an account of the altar in the postexilic period.

cerning the as yet impure character of the Yahwistic cultus.

Haggai's question goes on, i.e., it deals with more than the character of the flesh which had been consecrated within the sacral context. Haggai asks: If the garment in which the consecrated flesh is being carried touches another food—bread, stew, wine, oil, or anything else—do any of these foodstuffs become holy?

One important observation must be made before the priest's answer is examined. This list of food does not allow one to infer that the contact so described has occurred within the temple precinct. The word for stew, *nāzîd,* is never used explicitly within a ritual context.[16] One may therefore infer that the situation presumed by Haggai's question is that of a layperson returning home with meat consecrated from a sacrifice and carrying the roasted meat in his or her garment and, in so doing, touching the garment to other foodstuffs.

The answer to this typically binary question is given simply: "No." None of these foodstuffs will become holy.[17]

This simple answer raises a profound religio-historical question: To what extent was the holy *(qādôš)* contagious? As noted above, Haran does argue that the holy is contagious—on the basis of texts such as Ex. 29:37 (someone who touches the altar becomes holy) and Ex. 30:29 (someone who touches the altar and its utensils becomes holy). But these are special cases; they refer only to a priest touching things which only priests are supposed to touch. Those of priestly lineage are, potentially, holy, and by contact with holy objects they could become (more?) holy. Put another way, nonpriest was not to touch either the altar or the tabernacle appurtenances. Those individuals would not be holy, they would be dead—defiled—as was Uzzah in II Sam. 6:7. From this perspective, the contagious character of the holy would appear to be radically limited. Unless something bears the explicit potential in itself of being holy, then it is impossible for that thing, person, or place to be holy. And when a person not having this potential contacts the holy, he or she is made the opposite of holy, i.e., dead and thereby unclean. It is therefore difficult indeed for the holy to be contagious beyond certain rather obvious, well-defined categories such as holy people, priests, or holy objects, such as altar paraphernalia. In sum, the priests' answer is fully consistent with other Israelite prescriptions and is therefore not open to serious challenge.

[16] See Gen. 25:29, 34; II Kings 4:38ff.

[17] An interesting question is whether the garment itself would have been construed as holy. On the basis of the way in which Haggai's question is put, one might presume that the garment was at least neutral, i.e., clean. It did not, at least, sully the flesh.

[13] The second case that Haggai raises is not just the converse insofar as it involves uncleanness instead of holiness. If it were simply the converse, we would expect *ḥōl* (profaneness) rather than *ṭāmē'* (impurity) as the binary mate for *qādôš*. This second situation involves someone who has become impure as a result of direct contact with a corpse. The ancient Israelite strictures concerning this form of impurity were very clear. Anyone who touched a corpse became unclean for a minimum of seven days. Such uncleanness could be overcome by cleansing rituals, using the "water for impurity" on the third and seventh days of a person's impurity. Without such purification, a person "defiles the tabernacle of Yahweh and that person shall be cut off from Israel" (Num. 19:13). This is strong language indeed and reflects the severity and virulence of such contamination, obviously frequent though this form of impurity must have been in ancient Israelite culture.[18]

It is about such *ṭāmē'* that Haggai inquires. If someone who is unclean from contact with a corpse touches any of the above-mentioned foodstuffs, will these items become unclean? The priests answer in the affirmative. The *ṭāmē'* is contagious. Just as it can defile the *miškān* (dwelling place) of Yahweh, so too it would cause impurity in those foodstuffs.

Even with no explicit commentary on these two questions, an obvious point has been made by this series of inquiries, although it might not be the final point Haggai is himself making. Uncleanness and holiness function as something of polar opposites, though not as lexical binary opposites, as we have just seen. And yet despite their apparent complementary polarity, these two qualities function in quite different ways. *Qādôš* is not contagious in the same way in which *ṭāmē'* is contagious. Only a very few things may become *qādôš*, whereas virtually everything is open to defilement by something which is unclean, e.g., by leprosy or a corpse.

[14] Such is the way holiness and uncleanness function in one cultural system. And yet these general issues are apparently of no interest to Haggai. He is not a historian of religion. Rather, Haggai is interested in suggesting that what the people are now doing is, somehow, *ṭāmē'*. If Haggai's argument reflects the ritual rules of his time, what the people are doing is *ṭāmē'* not because of some morally repugnant action they have performed but because of their having come in contact with something that is *ṭāmē'*. An Israelite was not innately *ṭāmē'*. One became *ṭāmē'* either through the contagion of

[18] On this ritual, see J. Milgrom, "The Paradox of the Red Cow (Num 19)," *VT* 31, 1981, 62–72.

an impure object or by having one's body exist in a *ṭāmē'* condition such as menstrual uncleanness (v. 14). Haggai's own interpretation—or better, Yahweh's interpretation—of the realities of holiness vs. impurity is presented in v. 14. And it is around this verse that most debate concerning the significance of this passage has swirled. Four straightforward questions are raised by it: (1) Who are "these people//this nation"? (2) What is impure? (3) Where does the impurity manifest itself? and (4) What is the source of the impurity? The answers to these four questions will provide the basis for a proper interpretation of the entire passage.

1. What is the identity of "this people//nation"? Since the time of Rothstein, one answer has dominated the critical literature.[19] Rothstein and others following his lead have contended that these terms refer not to Judahites who have returned from exile or to those who remained around Jerusalem during the period 587–520.[20] Instead, the two parallel terms refer to those who settled in Israelite territory after the defeat of the Northern Kingdom in 721, a group which had become heterodox Yahwists.

Rothstein's approach to Hag. 2:10–14 is to juxtapose it with the narrative in Ezra 4:1–5. In that text, a historian narrates opposition to the rebuilding of the temple on the part of those who had been brought into the land during the time of Esarhaddon. These are known in Ezra as "the people of the land *('am hā'āreṣ)*, in opposition to the people of Judah." These early "Samaritans," i.e., those living in and around Samaria, were those whom Haggai terms "this people//this nation" and they were, because of their foreign origins and heretical beliefs, unclean. To this extent, Rothstein understands Hag. 2:10–14 to be a word directed to the Judahite community admonishing them to remain unsullied by heterodox Yahwists who have not undergone the experience of defeat and exile. This interpretation remains influential in many recent studies.[21]

[19] Rothstein, *Juden und Samaritaner*, 5–41.

[20] Rothstein, among others, has argued that the audience of 2:10–14 must be different from those addressed in 2:1–9 since in the latter passage, blessings are promised, whereas in the former, charges of impurity are leveled. The problem with Rothstein's appeal to necessity is his judgment that Haggai is asserting that the people are impure. This the text itself never states. See below for a discussion of "the work of their hands" as impure and not "they" themselves.

[21] See, e.g., Rudolph and Beuken. See Amsler, 38–39, for a discussion of the basic interpretive options. Beuken, 67–68, adduces a separate argument in defense of Rothstein's position. Since the people are addressed in the third person, it is likely that a foreign entity is being addressed (as in the "Oracles against the nations"). However, it must be noted that since only the priests are capable of providing for the requisite purification, it is fully appropriate that they, the priests, be addressed directly and that the people be referred to impersonally.

In my judgment, Rothstein's interpretation of this phrase founders for several important reasons. First, there is no evidence in sources dating to the sixth century, e.g., Isa. 56–66, for a proto-Samaritan–Judahite split. It is therefore improper to introduce the perspectives of Ezra 4 into this earlier period.[22] Second, referring to people with the demonstrative pronoun *hazzeh* does not engender a negative connotation, as some have contended. As Koch rightly points out, Haggai refers to "this house" (1:4; 2:3, 9) and "this day" (2:15, 18) without any pejorative sense; cf. also Isa. 6:9, "this people," which demonstrates the applicability of this phrase to the Judahite community.[23] Third, the term *haggôy*, which occurs in synonymous parallelism with *hā'ām*, has no special negative meaning in the biblical material. Cody has argued convincingly that the noun *gôy* is used importantly as a description of Yahweh's own people.[24] He also observes that when the noun *gôy* is used of Israel, it has certain special implications; e.g., it points to political power and possession of land, whereas *'am* refers more often to internal social or covenantal relations of the Judahite community. One may expand upon Cody's argument and maintain that Haggai's use of the term *gôy*, referring here to the Judahites, is especially apt. By using this particular noun, Haggai is able to suggest that Judah, properly understood, will again possess land and be a political structure.[25]

One does well to compare Haggai's use of this collective terminology to that of others in the sixth century. The linguistic usage of priestly circles reflects clearly the impact which the loss of statehood had on Israel's self-consciousness. No longer is Yahweh's promise to Abraham construed as a promise of statehood as it was by the Yahwists: "I will make of you a great nation" (Gen. 12:2). Rather, that promise is now construed by the priests as "I will make nations of you" (Gen. 17:6); "You shall be the father of a multitude of nations" (Gen. 17:4); "A nation and a company of nations shall come forth from you" (Gen. 35:11). This gives a strong impression of a plurality, as opposed to a singular entity. The priests are here "realistic" in a way that, perhaps, Ezek. 37:22 was not ("I will make them one nation in the land . . . and they shall be no longer two nations and no longer divided

---

[22] See also K. Koch, "Haggais unreines Volk," *ZAW* 79, 1967, 65, who accepts Rudolph's argument that Ezra 4 represents a historian trying to explain why it took twenty years to rebuild the temple after Cyrus' decree had been promulgated, and this on the basis of political conditions in the author's own time.

[23] Ibid., 61.

[24] A. Cody, "When Is the Chosen People Called a *gôy*?", *VT* 14, 1964, 1–6.

[25] Cf. Ezek. 37:22.

into two kingdoms") and—even more—Haggai was not. For Ezekiel, if Israel was once a single nation, then Israel could be that again sometime in the future. For Haggai, the language of *gôy* and '*am* could be used in the present. What Israel had been, Israel still was. No far-distant moment was necessary to use this language. Haggai's vocabulary reflects his perception that Israel has not undergone fundamental change through the vicissitudes of the sixth century.

The term *gôy* has a certain proleptic, even prescriptive, quality in this text. Its use represents a very real hope by Haggai that Israel will be something more than a nondescript outpost of the Persian empire. In sum, the word *gôy* need not be presumed to refer to a foreign nation as the plural form of this same noun does in 2:22. It is best, therefore, to follow the judgment expressed by H. May, "It seems most reasonable to identify 'this people' and 'this nation' with Yahweh's own people."[26]

2. What is impure? The answer has regularly been: This people//nation are impure. However, a careful reading of 2:14 demonstrates that it is not specifically the '*am/gôy* but "the work of their hands" which Yahweh and Haggai label as unclean. The text points in particular to their work and not to the people themselves as being unclean.[27]

Further, all too often there has been a presumption that the phrase "the work of their hands" refers to work of the '*am/gôy* on the temple.[28] Two arguments militate against such a notion. First, even if Ezra 4:1ff. were an accurate description of the period around 520 B.C.E., this account suggests that the Judahites did not, in fact, allow other Yahwists to become involved in the activity of rebuilding the temple; i.e., it is unlikely that the rebuilding activity would have been impure as a result of "Samaritan" help. Second, and more telling, this same phrase, "the work of their hands," is used elsewhere in Haggai (1:11 and 2:17) to refer to the work of Judahites.[29] Further, this phrase refers

[26] H. G. May, " 'This People' and 'This Nation' in Haggai, " *VT* 18, 1968, 190–197. See similarly Ackroyd, *Exile and Restoration,* 167 n. 71; Koch, "Haggais unreines Volk," 52–66. Cf. S. Talmon, "Synonymous Readings in the Textual Traditions of the Old Testament," *Scripta Hierosolymitana* 8, 1961, 343; T. Townsend, "Additional Comments on Haggai 2:10–19," *VT* 18, 1968, 359–360.

[27] For a similar interpretation, see Ackroyd, *Exile and Restoration,* 168: "The emphasis in Haggai's own message to the people concentrates on the uncleanness of the people's offerings in the shrine."

[28] Thus many standard commentaries; also Beuken, 73; and, most recently, R. Mason, "The Prophets of the Restoration," 144.

[29] Cf. Mitchell, 68, who points to the use of this phrase in Deut. 24:19; 28:12, 30:9.

to the Judahites' activity in one specific sphere: agriculture. That which the Judahites produce—wine, oil, grain, cattle—comprises "the work of their hands" according to Haggai. Put another way, the work of their hands is some concrete thing, agricultural produce, not simply activity on a building project. And it is that concrete material, their agricultural produce, which is viewed as impure. The strong implication of this formulation is that the people become impure because of the impurity of their hands. They, the people, are not innately *ṭāmē'*, or impure.

3. If the work of their hands is agricultural produce, where is such produce becoming impure? Israel clearly has a high view of its land and the agricultural bounty that the land produces. Neither the land nor its yield is inherently impure. Rather, agricultural commodities provide the wherewithal for approaching Yahweh. The "work of their hands" bears innate potential for acceptability by the deity. Hence the question we have raised here is especially pointed: Where (and how) does such produce become impure?

Of particular importance in addressing this question is the specific vocabulary used to describe what the people are doing and where they are doing it. They "bring near" *(yaqrîbû)*. The hiphil use of *qrb* is classical, even technical, language for bringing an offering or presenting a sacrifice. The term can (rarely) be used absolutely to refer to making an offering (Num. 7:2, 18). More frequently, especially in the priestly source and in Ezekiel, it refers to making various discrete offerings, e.g., *zebaḥ* (Lev. 7:16); *'ōlāh* (Num. 29:13); *minḥāh* (Lev. 2:8). With such a technical meaning virtually implicit in *qrb*, the picture—when coupled with *šām* referring in all likelihood to the temple in Jerusalem—is of Judahites bringing sacrificial offerings from their crops and flocks.[30] They would bring such offerings to the altar in the temple complex and the priests would pronounce the offerings as either clean (acceptable) or unclean (unacceptable). This conclusion seems especially warranted since the people are described as *l'pānay* Yahweh. One is "before Yahweh" in the temple setting (e.g., Ex. 16:9, 33, 34; Lev. 1:5, 11).

The priestly pronouncement is provided as the terminal section of this oracle: "It is unclean." It—in Hebrew the third masculine singular independent personal pronoun—could refer to one of two words in the foregoing sentence, *šām* ("there") or *kol-ma'ăśēh* ("all the work"). The latter option is surely the more likely. That which they bring *there* is unclean. Or put in explicit answer to the question, the uncleanness is

[30] Beuken, 72, asserts that *šām* refers to a Samaritan cultic site.

manifest explicitly at the temple complex where sacrifices are being brought. Impurity is, ironically, occurring at the temple or altar.

4. What is the source of the impurity? Rothstein had an obvious answer. If this "nation//this people" referred to heterodox Yahwists, then they themselves were the source of the defilement. Such an explanation would not, however, fit the analogy Haggai is drawing, i.e., contact defilement as opposed to innate defilement. What is more important—if, as we have argued, "this people//this nation" refers to orthodox Yahwists, i.e., Judahites, then the impurity must come from something external to the people themselves.

The assonance provided by *šām—ṭāmē'* provides a clue for the best answer to this question. What is being brought is unclean, or rather, becomes unclean because it is presented at a place that is unclean. Everything, all that they bring, is unclean. Surely such a claim could not be made about the normal fare of sacrificial offerings. At least some would pass muster. But this is obviously not the case in Hag. 2:14. Nothing that the people present for sacrifice is acceptable. If the people are not inherently tainted (and there is no reason to think that they are), and if it cannot be said that all produce presented for sacrifice is inherently tainted, then the impurity can only derive from the place to which the sacrifices are being brought: the altar and the temple compound.

One must therefore ask what there was about the place to which sacrifices were being brought which would impute uncleanness to them, all of them? Could the temple or the altar be impure, i.e., a potential contaminate? According to Ezek. 40–48, the temple did need to be purified from earlier uncleanness. Especially germane to this particular issue is the altar. It is likely the altar was rebuilt well before the completion of the temple, presuming that it had, in fact, been torn down.[31] And yet it was probably not purified in the appropriate manner, since reconstruction of the temple would have been thought to be a requisite for altar rededication. In Ezek. 43:18–25, the writer provides explicit instructions for the altar's rededication. Had this seven-day process not been undertaken, and had individuals brought sacrifices to this altar, it would have been fully appropriate for the priests to reject the material for sacrifice—"the work of their hands"—as unclean, and this because of the uncleanness of the cultic site itself, whether temple or altar. The temple, and more

[31] See the report of altar reconstruction in Ezra 3:1–6. This narrative clearly points to a restored if not purified cultus prior to the official rededication of the temple (Ezra 3:6b, "But the foundation of Yahweh's temple was not yet laid").

particularly the altar, may well have become a source of defilement for Israel as they brought their sacrifices to present to Yahweh.

If these four questions have been answered properly, the meaning of v. 14 becomes clear. Haggai is arguing that when Judahites appear at the temple to present sacrifices, what they offer becomes unclean because it comes in contact with an altar and temple that have not yet been purified. This judgment is particularly powerful since it has been created out of priestly *tôrôt* that are themselves not moot, either in purely rhetorical terms or on the basis of general notions concerning holiness and impurity. The clarity of the priests' answers provides evidence to support Haggai's judgment in v. 14.[32] Further, in these verses Haggai seems to be calling for the official rededication of these cultic foci—altar and temple—especially now that work on the rebuilding of the temple is proceeding apace. The reason that the temple area and the altar are unclean is not that they are not yet fully rebuilt. They are unclean because the appropriate rituals of cleansing and rededication have not yet been performed. What the people bring—"the work of their hands"—becomes *ṭāmē'* because their grain and animal offerings come in contact with a temple compound and an altar that are unclean. Such a situation creates radical dissonance with normative Yahwistic traditions in which Israel is construed as "a nation of priests, a holy people." It is a situation that stands in need of correction. And what follows—in Haggai 2:15–19—reflects the solution to the problem which Haggai has clearly articulated by means of dialogue with the priests. And, after all, it was appropriate to raise this issue with the priests since the priests were the only group that could cleanse the temple and the altar.[33] They and only they could effect the removal of *ṭāmē'* from "the work of their (the people's) hands."[34]

Haggai 2:15–19

From this day on, I will send blessings

15 "But now, consider this day and its future significance![a]
Before stone was set upon stone
in the temple of Yahweh,

[32] Elliger, 95, maintains, and I agree, that most laypersons would have known the answer to these two questions.
[33] For a similar argument, see Amsler, 39.
[34] Contra Beuken, 65.

16   how did you fare?[b]
If one went[c] to a heap of twenty measures,
there were but ten.
If one went to the wine vat to skim off fifty units,
the press[d] would yield only twenty.
17 I attacked you with blight and mildew,
all the work of your hands with hail.
But you did not side with me,"[e] says Yahweh.
18 "Consider this day and its future significance!
The twenty-fourth day of the ninth month,
the day on which the foundation
of Yahweh's temple was laid.
Consider!
19 Will the seed in the granary still be diminished?[f]
Will[g] the fig tree, the pomegranate, the olive tree,
continue not to bear fruit?[h]
From this day on, I will send blessings."

a. Literally, "from this day and forward." For a similar expression indicating a time period beginning at a specific moment and continuing into the indefinite future, See I Sam. 16:13; 30:25: *mēhayyôm hahû' wāmā'‹lāh*. There is no warrant for translating *wāmā'‹lāh* as "backward." See Beuken, 209–210. See JPS for this past-tense option; and see Mitchell, 73–74, for the history of this particular interpretation.

b. Reading *mah-h‹yîtem* instead of MT *mih‹yôtām*. Cf. LXX *tines ēte*, "What sort of people were you?" See Beuken, 211ff.

c. Some have proposed repointing MT *bā'* (here understood as a 3 masc. sg. perfect) to read *bō'*, an infinitive absolute used as a finite verb (here with the 2 masc. pl. subject as specified by the reconstructed *h‹yîtem*). The suggestion is not without warrant, since 1:6 and 9 utilize infinitives absolute as finite verbs.

d. On *pûrāh*, see the discussions of Mitchell, 75, and Rudolph, 45–46. On the basis of Isa. 63:3, it seems clear that *pûrāh* (like *yeqeb*) refers to a part of a winepress; *pûrāh* means the pressing chamber, and *yeqeb*, the collecting unit. See similarly JPS.

e. The Hebrew is, as Ehrlich (*Randglossen*, V, 323) has aptly observed, "barbaric." A literalistic translation would yield, "You were not with me." LXX reads *kai ouk epestrepsate* (or Heb. *w‹lō' šabtem*). Haggai twice uses the formula "I am with you" (*'anî 'itt‹kem*, 1:13; 2:4), which would suggest the possibility of creating the converse of such a formula: "You are not with me." However, there are more felicitous ways to phrase this negative notion—e.g., *lō' 'attem 'ittî*.

One expects a verb here (i.e., Yahweh has acted), but the hoped-for action, siding with or turning to, has not occurred. The translation here favored includes the verbal notion, but in a neutral way in keeping with the nonverbal clause in MT.

It is interesting that both Hag. 2:14 LXX and 2:17 MT seem to reflect material in Amos. Much actually depends on whether one construes the Haggai text to be based upon Amos 4:9. Both texts share similar words and syntax: hiphil of *nkh*, *'etkem*, *b* of instrumentality followed by a series of natural disasters (in Haggai—blight, mildew, and hail; in Amos—blight, mildew, [and locusts]). The disjunctive negative clauses are also similar (Haggai—*wᵉ'ên 'etkem 'ēlay;* Amos—*wᵉlō' šabtem 'āday*).

f. The first colon seems to require a verb, which has apparently been lost by haplography. *BHS* proposes two forms of *grʿ*, either the participle *migrāʿ*, or the perfect *nigrāʿ*, a proposal followed in this translation. LXX seems to have read a form of *ydʿ: ei epignōsthēsetai epi tēs halō*, "whether this shall be known on the threshing floor." Cf. Beuken, 212–213.

g. Reading with LXX, V, *wᵉʿōd* instead of MT *wᵉʿad*.

h. On *nśʾ* meaning "to bear fruit," see esp. Ezek. 17:23; 36:8; Joel 2:22.

[15] The word with which Hag. 2:15 commences, *wᵉʿattāh* ("but now"), has been understood by some as a rhetorical marker of considerable force such as to allow the argument that vs. 15–19 mark a new speech by the prophet.[1] However, attention to the use of this word in 1:5 suggests a much different situation, since the word serves there to introduce the "consider" formula within the context of a larger speech or literary construct rather than to initiate a totally new unit. In 1:5, *wᵉʿattāh* is placed before *śîmû lᵉbabkem* just as these two phrases are conjoined in 2:15.[2]

Also important as an argument for the unity of Hag. 2:10–19 is Koch's form-critical observation that 1:2–8; 2:3–7; and 2:11–19 share a similar threefold structure: reference to the situation—1:2, 4; 2:3; 2:11–13; the present moment as a turning point—1:5–6; 2:4–5; 2:14; announcement of salvation—1:7–8; 2:6–7; 2:15–19.[3] If Koch's basic judgments about these texts are correct, then the particle *wᵉʿattāh* serves to introduce minor subdivisions in two of the larger units. And yet, interestingly, in one instance (1:5–6) it introduces the second element of the form, and in another (the text under consideration here, 2:15–19), it introduces the third element in the form. What is important for our purposes is that in neither case does the word

---

[1] Consequently, many commentators recommend taking the putatively out-of-place date in Hag. 1:15a and placing it before 2:15–19. Thus Weiser, Horst, Rothstein, Chary, Wolff, and Amsler, among others.

[2] In Hag. 1:5 the two units are divided by the presence of the stereotypic messenger formula: *kōh 'āmar yhwh ṣᵉbā'ôt*.

[3] K. Koch, "Haggais unreines Volk," *ZAW* 79, 1967, 52–66.

introduce the first element in the unit; $w^{e\prime}att\bar{a}h$ would appear to be used to initiate a subunit rather than to begin a new one. For these reasons, therefore, it is licit to view 2:15–19 as a continuation of the foregoing verses (2:10–14), a continuation introduced by $w^{e\prime}att\bar{a}h$.

If, in Hag. 1:5 and 7, Judahites are asked to consider their ways in response to an admonitory discourse by Haggai, in 1:15 and 18 they are asked to consider a quite different object, "this day" and its future significance. According to the final form of the text, the day was not only definite ("this day") but it was, and is now, datable within the context of Darius' reign, being the twenty-fourth day of the ninth month in the second year of that reign.

What was this day that it had such special meaning? Fortunately, these verses provide enough evidence for a specific answer. It was a day when "stone was set upon stone" (15b); "the day on which the foundation of Yahweh's temple was laid" (18), "a day upon which Yahweh will begin to send blessings" (19b). There can be little doubt that what Hag. 2:15–19 here describes is an event mentioned in two other places, though there without a specific date: the laying of the foundation stone of the second temple.[4]

The hands of Zerubbabel have laid the foundation of this house. (Zech. 4:9)

And when the builders laid the foundation of the temple of Yahweh . . . (Ezra 3:10)

And all the people shouted with a great shout when they praised Yahweh, because the foundation of the house of Yahweh was laid. (Ezra 3:11)

All these texts focus on one important ceremonial event, the foundation stone ceremony. In this regard it is important to differentiate between labor on the foundations of the footings of the temple and the ceremonial deposition of the temple's foundation stone. There is, of course, evidence that Sheshbazzar had undertaken some preliminary work on the clearing of rubble and early work on the foundations of the temple. According to Ezra 5:16, Sheshbazzar came and laid "the foundations of the house of God ('uššayyā' dî bêt 'ĕlāhā') which is in Jerusalem." The vocabulary there is different from that of Hag. 2:18, or Ezra 3:6, 10, 11, or Zech. 4:9, where the root ysd is used to refer to the foundation.[5] In order to explain the peculiar formulation

---

[4] Cf. Baldwin, 19, 52–53, on the supposed conflict between Ezra 3:8 and the activity described in Haggai. Worry about temporal inconsistency could be avoided if the significance of the foundation-stone ceremony were appreciated as an act distinct from mundane rebuilding activity.

[5] On this rather ambiguous term, see Baldwin, 52–53.

in Ezra 5:16, Tuland has argued, in my judgment convincingly, that *'uššayyā'* is a Sumerian loanword (*uš*) which has been transmitted through Akkadian into Aramaic and which means foundations of a specific sort, footings on bedrock. Following Tuland's analysis, what we find described in Ezra 5 is work on the temple footings undertaken by Sheshbazzar. There is little reason to think, on the basis of Ezra 5:16, that Sheshbazzar was involved in the actual laying of the foundation stone or the attendant ceremonies.

It is equally important to note that work on the reconstruction of the temple could have been taking place, under the leadership either of Sheshbazzar or Zerubbabel, prior to the ceremonial rededication of the temple and the laying of the foundation stone. In both texts which purport to recount the process by means of which the temple was rebuilt, Hag. 1–2 and Ezra 3:1–13, it seems clear that work on the rebuilding of the temple began under Zerubbabel's leadership and then, at a later time, the foundation stone of the temple was laid.[6] Rather than presenting a chronological inconcinnity, this order of events is exactly that which we should expect. Work on the footings and some basic construction would have been necessary before the formal ceremony of rededication could have been undertaken. In sum, the sources that report the rebuilding of the temple, though hardly identical, do affirm that some reconstruction took place prior to the "laying of the foundations."

What then was the foundation stone ceremony? I have already suggested that certain phrases in Hag. 2:15–19 reflect such a ceremony and I have, in another place, argued that Zech. 4:6–10 provides evidence of a rededication ceremony for the second temple, a ceremony necessary for the formal rededication of a temple that had been destroyed and defiled.[7] More recently, B. Halpern has expostulated on the entirety of Zechariah 1–8 as a reverie on this ceremonial rededication of the temple. In this context, Halpern attempts to reconstruct the salient features of the so-called *kalû* ceremony on the basis of Babylonian and Seleucid sources (Halpern, pp. 171–172). There were, as might be expected, prescribed readings and sacrifices, as well as the obligatory laying of the actual foundation deposit.[8] On

---

[6] On the relation of these accounts, see P. Ackroyd, *Exile and Restoration*, 1968, 147–148; and more recently, "Faith and Its Reformulation in the Postexilic Period Sources, Prophetic Material," *TD* 27, 1979, 323–346.

[7] See D. Petersen, "Zerubbabel and Jerusalem Temple Reconstruction," *CBQ* 36, 1974, 366–372; R. Ellis, *Foundation Deposits in Ancient Mesopotamia*, 1968.

[8] B. Halpern, "The Ritual Background of Zechariah's Temple Song," *CBQ* 40, 1978, 171–172.

the basis of my earlier work and on Halpern's more recent essay, there can be no doubt that an Israelite version of the *kalû* ritual was performed as an early part of the rebuilding process for the second temple. Language of the foundation, *ysd* (Ezra 3), "the former stone" (Zech. 4:7), the tin tablet as foundation deposit (Zech. 4:10a), and "this day" (Hag. 2:15) all point to such a ceremony designed to achieve ritual purification and cultic continuity.

The pressing question raised by Hag. 2:15–19 is, how do these verses relate to this important day? According to Koch, on form-critical grounds these verses should provide words of weal. Do they, and if so, in what fashion? After addressing certain Judahites, in all probability the priests, Haggai places "this day" in a temporal sequence, a time with a before and an after. Verses 15b–17 comprise the "before" and culminate with an indictment of the people. The first component of the "before" section serves to emphasize the concrete activity of rebuilding: "before stone was set upon stone in the temple of Yahweh." It is altogether licit to presume that such language reflects actual placement of stone upon stone; indeed, perhaps it refers to the ritual manipulation of the "former" stone mentioned specifically in Zech. 4:7, a stone designed to guarantee ritual continuity with the earlier holy building. Or perhaps the phrase refers simply to masonry construction appropriate to the rebuilding of the temple walls. Whatever the case, "this day" was remembered as a time before "stone was set upon stone," whether a ritual or a nonritual laying of stone upon stone.

[16] After this temporal clause, the prophet asks the people to reflect on their condition in this prior period: "How did you fare?" (i.e., how did you fare before the temple was ritually purified and before rebuilding began?). As with other questions that Haggai was remembered as asking (e.g., 1:4; 2:3), no answer is provided by the people. Rather, the answer—or, perhaps better, the response—is given by Haggai, and this with the kind of rhetoric we would expect in a judgment oracle. Not surprisingly, Haggai continues to describe the people's fortunes within the context of agricultural activity (as in 1:6). And here, just as earlier, Haggai focused on the harvest and its final yield. The imagery, at least in 2:16b, is different from that in 1:6. In 1:6 the problem was that there had been only a low yield after aggressive planting. However, the imagery provided in 2:16 is of the crops already harvested, whether grain or grapes. The amount in storage is mysteriously disappearing; if one went to a pile of grain containing twenty measures, one would find only ten.[9] Or if one pressed grapes in

---

[9] See Neh. 13:15 and Ruth 3:7 for the notion of a deposit of agricultural goods.

the upper chamber of a wine press, the yield in the lower chamber, which one expected to contain a vast amount of wine, would be only a limited amount.[10]

[17] What follows in v. 17 is difficult to relate, both syntactically and conceptually, to the foregoing verse. Had there been a *w* or *kî* prefixing *hikkêtî*, it would be possible to construe v. 17 as having a causal relationship to v. 16; Yahweh's "I smote" would serve to explain the mysterious diminution of agricultural commodities that Israel had experienced. Without such syntactic connective tissue of the sort just described, it is not clear whether v. 17 provides the cause for what happened in v. 16 or whether it is designed to offer yet another instance of difficult times prior to the time "stone was set upon stone."

To achieve leverage on the situation, one must ask: (1) Are blight or mildew ever understood to affect crops after harvest? and (2) What is the relation of this verse to Amos 4:9, as well as to other traditions in the Bible to which it appears to be directly related? That Haggai is utilizing specialized discourse in this verse becomes obvious when one surveys the usage of the nouns *šiddāpôn* (blight), *yērāqôn* (mildew), and *bārād* (hail) elsewhere in the Hebrew Bible. For example, the noun *yērāqôn* is used only in conjunction with the noun *šiddāpôn* (Amos 4:9; Deut. 28:22; I Kings 8:37; II Chron. 6:28; and Hag. 2:17). These two nouns comprise something of a formulaic pair. Hence it is difficult to gain a sense of precise nuance for either noun separately. However, in the texts in which these two nouns do occur, it is clear that such agricultural maladies are under the control of the deity: as an enacted curse warranted by a covenant with the deity (Deut. 28:22); as a problem that the deity can alleviate (I Kings 8:37); or as a direct action of the deity (Amos 4:9; Hag. 2:17). To this extent, Haggai's use of these nouns is typical. Blight and mildew are simply examples of agricultural disease that may exemplify the power and control of the deity. The situation with *bārād,* hail, is slightly different. The noun—though it does occur in theophanic descriptions (Ps. 18:13) and in a few other texts—is strongly linked to the plague traditions (Ex. 9 and Pss. 78:47, 48; 105:32). And it is the usage there (Ex. 9:25, "The hail struck down every plant of the field and shattered every tree of the field") which fits with the usage in Hag. 2:17. Hail, like blight and mildew, is an agent that Yahweh may use in attacking a nation's agricultural goods.

[10] On winepresses, see *IDB* IV, 850. For the importance of agricultural activity at the temple, see L. Stager and S. Wolff, "Production and Commerce in Temple Courtyards: An Olive Press in the Sacred Precinct at Tel Dan," *BASOR* 243, 1981, 95–102.

Of particular interest in this regard is the form of the agricultural goods under attack. Reference to hail as a destructive agent (as in Ex. 9:25) directly implies that the attack is on crops in the field, before they have been harvested. The same may be said for references to blight and mildew. They are diseases that apparently affect grain and grapes before harvest. And to this extent, the imagery of v. 17 is different from that of v. 16, where the focus is on agricultural commodities after they have been harvested. There is therefore reason to think that v. 17 provides yet another instance of difficulties but one that is now already attributable to the action of Yahweh.

Haggai 2:17 is also illumined by attention to its similarities to Amos 4:9. Amos reads: I attacked you with blight and mildew *(hikkêtî 'etkem baššiddāpôn ûbayyērāqōn);* Haggai 2:17 begins with exactly the same wording. Amos continues by listing other means by which Yahweh assaults the people and then concludes, "yet you did not return to me *(wᵉlō' šabtem 'āday)."* Haggai too lists another (though only one other) means of divine attack, hail, and follows with the statement "but you did not side with me" *(wᵉ'ên 'etkem 'ēlay).*

There can be no doubt about the chronological priority of the formulation in Amos 4:9 over that in Hag. 2:17.[11] And since there appear to be influences from Amos elsewhere in the book of Haggai, in both MT and LXX (e.g., Hag. 2:14), it is altogether likely that in this verse the prophet Haggai (or a redactor) utilized the formulations of his prophetic predecessor for his own purposes. In so doing, the author/editor struck a blow for the importance of Haggai as a prophet standing in a line that extended back to the earlier figure, Amos.

Amos 4:6–11 comprises a series of indictments that lead up to a sentence in v. 12. The formal structure in which this language is used in Haggai is unusual. Haggai 2:16–17 provides a retrospective judgment that then pivots toward a more hopeful future in vs. 18–19.

Further, Haggai (or a redactor) has worked a significant variation on the traditional material. In establishing a parallelism in the first two cola, he formulated two objects of the deity's action: you//all the work of your hands. This formulation brings the Amos text in line with the rhetoric Haggai had employed earlier. Haggai wanted to focus on what the people were doing. Thus "all the works of their hands" is placed in parallelism with "this people//this nation" in v.

[11] See Beuken, 210 n. 4; P. Ackroyd, "Some Interpretive Glosses in the Book of Haggai," *JJS* 7, 1956, 166.

14. So too in Hag. 2:17 the people ("you") are defined in terms of the work of their hands. And, as in v. 14, this "work" refers to agricultural commodities, which in vs. 16–17 are understood to be subject to ravaging disease and storm.[12] Past agricultural problems, as punitive measures, had not served to move the people to appropriate action (as they had not in Amos 4:6–11). Put in a slightly different way, the technique of communication used in the past did not work. It did not work in the time of Amos and it did not work immediately prior to the time of Haggai's activity; that is, it did not effect a change in people's actions. However, Haggai's discourse with the people, his questions and his responses, had moved especially the leaders to action in a way that Yahweh's earlier measures had not moved them. Haggai, as his booklet reports, had been able to effect the rededication ceremony and, in so doing, had (to use the phraseology from the end of 2:17) enabled the people to side with Yahweh.

[18] With v. 18, Haggai presents the chronological axis on which his activity turns. Actual work on the temple had already begun (1:12–15). People needed encouragement (2:1–9). Now the cultus needed to be restored ritually, and this could only happen as a result of the Israelite version of the *kalû*, or rededication ritual. Verse 18 provides the date for this ritual and states in no uncertain terms that it was on this day that the temple's foundation was laid. As we have seen earlier, this language refers to a foundation deposit ceremony, not simply to beginning work on the foundations or footings of the temple. It was a day on which the site was ritually purified and thus became once again functional holy space.

The day was to be of special moment. On it, the people were understood implicitly to have sided with Yahweh. And presumably, after it the punitive action of the deity (blight, mildew, and hail) would cease. The fact that the day, the twenty-fourth day of the ninth month, constitutes a boundary between a before and an after is demonstrated by means of the two *sîmû l*ᵉ*babkem* formulae, one in v. 15, which introduces the earlier lamentable situation, and one in v. 18, which introduces the future time of weal.

[19] To advance the parallelism established by the two *sîmû* formulae, Haggai uses interrogative discourse in v. 19 just as he did in

---

[12] For this reason, namely, the careful reformulation of the Amos material to fit Haggai's rhetoric, it is improper to construe v. 17 as a late addition even though the imagery of v. 17 represents crops before harvest and that of v. 16 represents crops after harvest.

16a.[13] Consistent with vs. 16–17 which depict the "before," v. 19 discusses the future in terms of agricultural commodities. What is especially significant is Haggai's effort to relate what he is now discussing with the commodities to which he referred in vs. 16–17. Earlier he had described produce in storage, whereas in v. 17 he referred to crops still in the field. Verse 19 picks up both these forms of agricultural yield: "Will the seed in the granary still be diminished?" (as it was according to v. 16); and "Will the fig tree, the pomegranate, the olive tree, continue not to bear fruit?" (as a result of infection or hail, as was the case in v. 17). The picture created by this question is one of comprehensiveness. Haggai offers different situations in which crops may be destroyed, either in storage or in the field. And then he provides a picture of different sorts of crops (in vs. 16 and 19): grapes, grain, fruit trees, and olive trees. It is therefore no accident that he speaks of *all* the work of their hands in v. 17 (and v. 14). Haggai's notion of agricultural activity is all-inclusive, in terms of both woe and weal.

The particular trees mentioned in v. 19 are significant. The economic importance of the olive tree has been fully recognized.[14] The importance of the fig tree and the pomegranate is less well known, yet both are attested as having economic value. As well as being an edible fruit, the pomegranate could be used to produce wine, and the juice of the rind was used in dyeing and tanning.[15] Figs too were apparently important for foreign trade: "Judah and Israel traded with you; they exchanged for your merchandise wheat, olives, and early figs (reading *ûpaggag* instead of MT *ûpannag*), honey, oil, and balm" (Ezek. 27:17). Interestingly, pomegranates and figs also function to symbolize the fertility of the Promised Land, so Num. 13:23 and especially Deut. 8:7–8, "For Yahweh your God is bringing you into a good land, . . . a land of wheat and barley, of vines and fig trees and pomegranates . . ." It is no accident that Haggai uses these same products to promise weal, which will spring forth from the land that has been promised to those rebuilding Judahite society.

---

[13] The syntax of the questions is difficult because of the absence of finite verbs. As indicated in the textual note, I propose emending the text to include a verb lost by haplography. If one follows strictly the MT, the text would likely be translated, "Is the seed still in the granary [present tense]: do the vine, the fig tree, and the pomegranate still not bear fruit?" Ackroyd, *Exile and Restoration,* 159, points to the ambiguity in such a formulation. It is not at all clear that this translation would allow Haggai to speak words of promise.

[14] See, e.g., M. Silver, *Prophets and Markets,* 1983, 16–17, 24–29.

[15] So *IDB* II, 288; III, 840.

Prior to "this day," these particular trees had not borne fruit. Now they would be fertile as a result of Yahweh's direct intervention. And it is on this note that the oracle ends: "From this day on I will send blessings," presumably upon the land and the people, and upon the work of their hands. This use of *brk* as a transitive verb without an explicit object is unusual. Of the seventeen occurrences of *brk* in the first-person common singular piel, this is the only one in which there is no object. More typical is the sort of formulation found in Gen. 12:2: "I will bless you." The prominence of such language in the promises of the patriarchs is noteworthy. Especially significant is the version of the promise presented in Gen. 26:3–5, which is affirmed on behalf of Isaac: "Sojourn in this land and I will be with you, and will bless you; for to you and to your descendants I will give all these lands." In Gen. 26, blessing and the giving of the land are directly linked, as are blessing and the productivity of the land in Haggai.[16] Thus, we have in Hag. 2:19 a move from indirect to direct blessing and, concomitantly, a stylistic shift from question to direct assertion.

Such are the detailed problems raised by Hag. 2:10–19. These verses are divided into two distinct subunits, one focusing on the present impurity of what is being offered at the center, which has not yet been officially rededicated, and another pointing both to the inglorious past and to the bountiful future that will result from the ceremony providing for purity and formal restoration of the cult center. Both sections, vs. 10–14 and 15–19, provide powerful rhetoric to instigate the enactment of this specific ceremony. Haggai 2:10–14 is designed to galvanize priestly sentiment against impurity. Only the priests could perform the appropriate purification rituals. Haggai 2:15–19 presents the case to the general population, though this group is only indirectly mentioned in vs. 16 ("How did *you* fare?") and 17 ("I attacked *you*").

These two examples of Haggai's rhetoric are more than just quotations of his words. Haggai's own words have been integrated into a section of the book that serves not only to record what he said but also to demonstrate that these speeches had a concrete effect: On the twenty-fourth day of the ninth month in 520 B.C.E. a ceremony of rededication did take place, a ceremony that would make pure "all the work of their hands" and that would provide for seed in the granary as well as fruit on the fig, pomegranate, and olive trees.

Haggai 2:10–19 provides the reader with yet another success story for one of Israel's prophets, not an altogether common occurrence. In

---

[16] Cf. the similar motif in the covenant context (Lev. 26:3ff.; Deut. 28:2ff.).

their present configuration, these verses attest to Haggai's ability to engage various sectors of Judahite society: the high priest, the governor, the priests, and the people (*'am*). By use of skillfully constructed dialogue, often initiated by questions rather than with the more typical prophetic diatribe, Haggai was able to add success to success, to initiate work on the temple, and to have the appropriate rites of purification performed. If II Chron. 36:15–16 has as its essential point that Israel fell because she rejected Yahweh's messengers, then Hag. 2:10–19 attests that Judah may yet succeed because the people and its leaders responded favorably to the efforts of one of Yahweh's messengers—Haggai.

Haggai 2:20–23

I will take you, O Zerubbabel

20 The word of Yahweh came a second time to Haggai on the twenty-fourth day of the month.
21 "Speak to Zerubbabel, governor of Judah:
    I am going to shake the heavens and the earth.[a]
22 I will overturn the throne of kingdoms,[b]
    I will destroy the strength of the kingdoms of the nations.[c]
    I will overturn the chariot and its riders.[d]
Horses and riders shall go down,
    each by the sword of his compatriot.
23 On that day," says Yahweh of Hosts,
    "I will take you, O Zerubbabel
    son of Shealtiel, my servant," says Yahweh.
    "I will set you as a seal,
    for I have chosen you," says Yahweh of Hosts.

a. LXX includes *kai tēn thalassan kai tēn xēran*, "and the sea and the dry land." This fuller reading is in all likelihood based on the phraseology of 2:6. Mur is fragmentary at this point.

b. Mitchell, 77, comments aptly on this construction, pointing out that the singular *ks'* may mean "rule" (I Kings 1:37), or it may be "an example of a common Hebrew idiom, the use of the singular for the plural in the construct before the plural, and translated 'thrones,' cf. GK §124, 2c." Cf. Beyse, *Serubbabel*, 55.

c. One might suggest, *metri causa*, simply "the strength of the nations." However, consistent with MT, both LXX and Mur include the more prolix "the strength of the kingdoms of the nations." The *maml*ᵉ*kôt* following *ḥōzeq* is almost certainly a dittographic expansion based on the *mamlᵉkôt* present in the first colon.

d. LXX^A adds *kai katastrepsō pasan tēn dynamin autōn kai katabalō ta horia autōn kai enischysō tous eklektous mou,* "and I will overthrow all of their power, bring down their borders, and strengthen my chosen ones."

[20] The final oracle in the book of Haggai includes the same basic formula, *hāyāh + dᵉbar yhwh + 'el ḥaggay,* as that used in the penultimate section of the book, 2:10. This so-called word-occurrence formula does, however, occur first in 2:20 (i.e., before a comment about the date of the oracle), whereas the date formula occurs first in 2:10. As I noted earlier, the word-occurrence formula with the preposition *'el* is used to introduce only the last two oracles in the book of Haggai. The reason for this situation is that different audiences were addressed in these final two speeches. Whereas earlier in the book Haggai was remembered as addressing the entire community as well as its civil and religious leaders, the audience for the last two oracles is more specialized—in 2:10–19 the priests; in 2:15–19 presumably the people; and then finally, in 2:20–23, Zerubbabel alone. And consistent with the change in audience, the formulaic introductions for those oracles are distinct from the formulae used earlier in the book.

Just as the word-occurrence formula with *'el* is shared by the final two oracles, 2:10–19 and 2:20–23, so also the date for both these oracles is identical: the twenty-fourth day of the month. The editor makes receipt of two oracles on the same day explicit by including the word *šēnît,* "a second time," within the introduction. Haggai was remembered as having ended his prophetic activity with considerable effort on one day, by directing Yahweh's words to quite different audiences, to the priests as well as the titular and hereditary political leader, Zerubbabel.

[21] Haggai 2:20–23 is the only oracle addressed to a lone individual. The oracle, Yahweh's communication to Haggai, designates not only the recipient of the words, but his official role as well, "Zerubbabel, governor of Judah."[1] The oracle directed to this individual comprises two basic parts, vs. 22 and 23. In v. 22, Yahweh, in a first-person speech, announces what he is about to do to foreign nations, and in 23 (which is separated from 22 by the stereotypic phrase "on that day") he speaks directly to Zerubbabel. One senses that v. 23 might be the most appropriate sequence to the introduction provided

---

[1] On the title *pehāh,* see the Introduction.

in 20–21, since in v. 23 Yahweh addresses Zerubbabel. However, that direct address to Zerubbabel does not occur first, and it is the more general announcement of divine activity with which we must deal first.

The divine speech commences with language used earlier in this brief book.[2] Such repetition can hardly be accidental. The identical phraseology makes a rhetorical point. By using such language the author not only emphasizes the priority of divine activity but focuses attention on that material which had not been used earlier. As we have seen in our analysis of 2:6, Haggai is borrowing language of standard theophanic descriptions and yet is expanding this discourse to include Yahweh's actions as they affect the entire cosmos. However, the theophanic language in 2:21 is briefer than it was in 2:6.[3] The reason for such brevity is not wholly clear. Perhaps the omitted words are to be understood as implicitly present in the text. Or perhaps an emphasis on the cosmic totality providing its treasure, as in 2:6–7, is not so critical for the purposes of this particular speech. We cannot be sure. We may, however, say with conviction that this oracle presents a revised and briefer form of theophanic expectation.[4]

[22] What may also be said about the connection between 2:6ff. and 2:20ff. is that there is a similar syntactic structure: *'ănî* with the masculine singular active participle followed by converted perfect verbs.[5] Further, the action narrated by the converted verbs in the perfect "tense" affects the same basic entities: foreign nations.[6] There is, however, a significant difference between 2:6ff. and 2:22–23. Yahweh is described as dealing in a different way with the nations in these two oracles. In 2:6–7, the same verb is used to describe Yahweh's action; he shakes the cosmos and he shakes the nations. In 2:21, the verbs describing what he will do to the nations are different. The imagery is uniformly martial: overturn *(hpk)*, destroy *(šmd)*. And as a

---

[2] Cf. Beyse, *Serubbabel,* 54–55, who argues that such similarity means that these two oracles were spoken for the same reason.

[3] LXX includes the longer phraseology in Hag. 2:22.

[4] G. Sauer, "Serubbabel in der Sicht Haggais und Sacharjas," in F. Maas (ed.), *Das ferne und nahe Wort,* 1967, 200 n. 10, argues that Ezek. 31:16 is the only other text in which *r'š* is linked to the object *gôyîm.* He also maintains that Haggai preserves notions about the nations found in Deutero-Isaiah: Isa. 40:4ff.; 43:14ff.; 45:1ff.; 50:2ff.

[5] See Beuken, 226, for a different form of this argument.

[6] On the regularity and importance of the oracles against the nations in the prophetic literature, see G. Wright, "The Nations in Hebrew Prophecy," *Encounter* 26, 1965, 225–237; J. Hayes, "The Usage of Oracles Against Foreign Nations in Ancient Israel," *JBL* 87, 1968, 81–92; D. Christensen, *Transformation of the War Oracle in Old Testament Prophecy,* 1975.

result, horse and rider will "go down." All this vocabulary is appropriate to military activity.

Many commentators have noted that much of the language in Hag. 2:22 is associated with important traditions or narrative contexts in the Hebrew Bible. So, for example, the verb *hpk,* "overturn," is regularly used to describe the defeat of Sodom and Gomorrah (Gen. 19:25, 29; Isa. 13:19; Amos 4:11; Deut. 29:23).[7] Interestingly, Jer. 20:16 uses this same verb and does not mention those cities by name: "Let that man be like the cities which Yahweh overthrew without pity." This development in Jer. 20:16 suggests something of a generalizing trend; it is not unlike the way in which this same verb is used in Hag. 2:22. This formulation in Haggai appears to function even more strongly as an oracle against a foreign nation or city than it does as a reference to the Sodom and Gomorrah tradition.

Though the verbs echo that tradition, the objects of the verbs do not. Rather than specific cities, in Hag. 2:22 we hear only of vague entities, literally a "throne of kingdoms, the strength of the kingdoms of the nations." The language in this verse is very general, especially in the first two cola.

> I will overturn the throne of kingdoms,
> I will destroy the strength of the kingdoms of the nations.

We do not know which nations are to be affected. Nevertheless the use of such formulations in 22a serves to place Haggai squarely within the standard discourse of Israel's classical prophets. When Jeremiah defined the normal activity of prophets, he included warnings of judgment against kingdoms, as in Jer. 28:8, "The prophets who preceded you and me from ancient times prophesied war, famine, and pestilence against many countries and great kingdoms *(mamlākôt).* When in Isa. 23:11 a prophetic writer wanted to describe Yahweh's punitive action against nations, he wrote about Yahweh shaking kingdoms *(mamlākôt).* It is therefore no accident that shaking was the manner in which Haggai described Yahweh acting toward nations in 2:21.

Further, the linkage of nations and peoples *(mamlākôt* and *gôyîm)* found in 2:22 is attested elsewhere in the prophetic corpus. Isaiah 13:4 includes the phrase *maml‛kôt gôyîm* (cf. II Chron. 20:6 for the phrase *maml‛kôt haggôyîm*) to describe the nations which are to be defeated by Yahweh. And in the same chapter (Isa. 13:19) there is an explicit linkage between the destruction of a nation—Babylon, "the glory of

[7] See similarly Beuken, 80; cf. Beyse, *Serubbabel,* 55.

kingdoms" (*mamlākôt*)—and the Sodom and Gomorrah tradition, with its typical verb *hpk* (a linkage also present in Hag. 2:22a):

> And Babylon, the glory of kingdoms,
> the splendor and pride of the Chaldeans,
> will be like Sodom and Gomorrah
> when God overthrew them.
>
> (Isa. 13:19)

A final example of the way in which Haggai's rhetoric in 2:21–22 is of a piece with the language of earlier Israelite classical prophets may be discerned in Jer. 51:20–21. In both texts there is a move from general to specific objects of destruction, more particularly a move from description of attack against nations to description of attack by means of specific elements such as horse and rider.

> You are my hammer and weapon of war:
> with you I break nations in pieces;
> with you I destroy kingdoms;
> with you I break in pieces the horse and his rider;
> with you I break in pieces the chariot and the charioteer.
>
> (Jer. 51:20–21)

The similarities between the language in Hag. 2:22a and that found in Isaiah and Jeremiah is striking. Such similarity serves to confirm Haggai's role here as a typical prophet, e.g., his inveighing against foreign nations in a manner consistent with prophets before him. Thus, general though it is, the language serves to authenticate Haggai in his role as a prophet.

Moreover, there are links between this verse and language found in Israel's psalms. Sauer has argued that Hag. 2:22 resonates with at least two of Israel's royal psalms, Pss. 2 and 110.[8] In these poems, as in v. 22, there is language about the overthrow of thrones and the ruin of nations. This connection enables one to maintain that Haggai was drawing on traditions and literature associated with the coronation of Israel's kings, and in so doing, to place the role of Zerubbabel as Davidide within a strong political context. And as I have argued elsewhere, the role of the prophet in Israel is often related to the monarchic institution. Here, too, the rhetoric of v. 22 portrays Haggai as a typical prophet.

---

[8] Sauer, "Serubbabel in der Sicht Haggais und Sacharjas," 202–203. Cf. Ps. 110:5b–6: "He will shatter kings on the day of his wrath; / he will execute judgment among the nations, / filling them with corpses; / he will shatter chiefs over the wide earth."

In 22b, Haggai continues with a verb used earlier in the oracle, *hpk,* "overturn." However, instead of mentioning general entities, nations and kingdoms, the writer specifies what it is that will be destroyed: chariots and their riders, horses and their riders. This language, too, resonates with other and earlier language of the Hebrew Bible. Reference to chariots, horses, and riders inheres in the Reed Sea tradition, in both prose and poetic versions, in both early and late texts. Hence the description by the priestly writer: "The Egyptians pursued and went in after them into the midst of the sea, all Pharaoh's horses, his chariots, and his horsemen" (Ex. 14:23). And, as Jer. 51:21 suggests, the use of this vocabulary became a convenient way to describe the military power of a nation (cf. Deut. 20:1).[9]

Two other elements in 22b provide contact points elsewhere in the Hebrew Bible. The second verb in this verse, *yrd,* is also associated with the Reed Sea traditions (e.g., Ex. 15:5, "They have gone down into the depths like a stone"). And, as Beuken and others have observed, the verb has a more general (though equally negative) meaning, "to go down into the underworld" (Isa. 32:19; Jer. 13:18; 48:15; Lam. 1:9; Ezek. 26:16; 30:6).[10] And then, the final colon of the verse reverberates with language drawn from Israel's holy-war traditions (cf. Judg. 7:22, "Yahweh set every man's sword against his fellow."[11] There is an even greater similarity to the phraseology in Ezek. 38:21. "I will summon every kind of terror against Gog, says Yahweh God; every man's sword will be against his brother" (cf. Zech. 14:13).[12]

Given all its resonances with the language and imagery of other biblical texts, Hag. 2:22 seems to have the character of a mosaic. It appears to draw on language from various Israelite traditions: holy war, exodus, oracles against the nations.[13] In using such language, Haggai is able to foster the image of a prophet espousing the religion of an earlier period. The picture created is a highly conservative one. What has appeared to most commentators as hopelessly general language is, in fact, highly affective and effective discourse, serving to

---

[9] The obvious importance of horses during the Persian period is no doubt reflected here as well as in Zechariah 1–8.

[10] Beuken, 80 n. 1.

[11] See Rudolph, 52; G. von Rad, *Der heilige Krieg im alten Israel,* 1969, 65ff.

[12] Debate has swirled around Hag. 2:21 and esp. 2:22, over the extent to which the language reflects particular political and military problems in the Persian period or is simply traditional, reflecting holy-war idioms. Beyse, *Serubbabel,* 55–56, properly rejects an either-or interpretation.

[13] See similarly Rudolph, 53–54.

link Haggai to normative Israelite traditions and to define him as an authentic prophet in his own time.[14]

[23] Such rhetoric was apparently necessary to prepare the way for the proclamation that Yahweh, through Haggai, made in the final verse of this short booklet. Verse 22 was, it must be remembered, directed to Zerubbabel. And in that verse Zerubbabel was reminded of the success and scope of Yahweh's earlier cosmic and, especially, military success. Once these rhetorical points had been made, Haggai could speak directly to Zerubbabel about his own specific situation.[15] Much has been written about the stylistic and redaction-critical significance of the phrase *bayyôm hahû'*.[16] As the use of the phrase in Deutero-Zechariah demonstrates (see Zech. 12:3, 4, 6, 8, 9, 11), the phrase was often used by prophetic traditionists to link originally distinct material together. However, as Beuken and others have correctly maintained, it is difficult to imagine that v. 23 comprises a secondary addition to an original oracle of v. 22 by itself, since v. 22 is so general in its overall import. In v. 23, *bayyôm hahû'* seems to mark a transition point; it represents the move from a general statement of weal to the more concrete promise addressed to Zerubbabel. Furthermore, the phrase "on that day" itself reinforces the theme of specific future events contained in this verse. Whereas vs. 21–22 point to Yahweh's action in the future, it remains rather vague military activity that will be undertaken in a general future. When the phrase "on that day" is used to describe such futurity, the connotations of a specific time, a day, are introduced. Moreover, when a definite day on which Yahweh will act is broached, Israel's notions of the day of Yahweh, the *yôm yhwh*, become inextricably involved.[17] Succinctly stated, the day of Yahweh was a time at which Yahweh would destroy his enemies. It had, as does v. 22, fundamental military connotations. The use of the phrase *bayyôm hahû'* does much more than provide a simple connective between vs. 22 and 23. It provides a conceptual transition from the general future to a specific moment at which Yahweh will act decisively.

Just as the language of v. 22 was chosen with great care to resonate

[14]K. Seybold, "Die Königserwartungen bei den Propheten Haggai und Sacharja," *Judaica* 28, 1972, 70–71, recognizes the presence of this traditional language and yet does not comment on its special function within the book.

[15] Thus Hag. 2:23.

[16] See P. Munch, *The Expression bajjôm hāhū': Is It an Eschatological terminus technicus?* 1936; and Beuken, 79 n. 3.

[17] See, e.g., G. von Rad, "The Origin of the Concept of the Day of Yahweh," *JSS* 4, 1959, 97–108.

with earlier Israelite traditions, and thereby to authenticate Haggai's prophetic rhetoric, so too in v. 23 the writer has selected vocabulary drawn from specialized Israelite language. But here the focus is on one and not several traditions. Although the first verb *(lqḥ)* used in this direct address to Zerubbabel is a common one in the Hebrew language, its use achieves a special effect when it has as its object a member of the Davidic line. The root *lqḥ* often occurs as a general first element in a parallel statement of election. The verb *lqḥ* is hardly a terminus technicus for Davidic election as is the case with *bḥr*, which occurs later in this verse. But *lqḥ* is used by Israel's prophets elsewhere to indicate Yahweh's choice of a place or person,[18] and it is followed by the more specific *bḥr* in 23b. However, even before the more technical *bḥr* occurs, the pronominal suffix on *lqḥ* indicates that Yahweh has selected one person, "you."

Immediately thereafter, Yahweh designated the addressee as "Zerubbabel son of Shealtiel, my servant." "Zerubbabel son of Shealtiel" occurred earlier in the book.[19] And the title "my servant" is new. This term "servant" (or worker) has a wide range of connotations in the biblical material. It is used as a royal title (e.g., II Sam. 7:5; Ps. 132:10; I Kings 11:32, 36; I Chron. 17:4; Isa. 37:35).[20] Despite the end of monarchy in Israel, such usage of *'ebed* as referring to a Davidide did not end in 587. Ezekiel (34:23; 37:24, 25) continued to look for a Davidic heir as king, one who would be known as a servant.

There is, however, a countertradition, one that in the sixth century called non-Israelite monarchs "Yahweh's servants." Jeremiah (25:9; 27:6) refers to Nebuchadnezzar as "my servant." And even more prominent in this regard is the impulse—represented in Deutero-Isaiah—to view Cyrus as Yahweh's servant (Isa. 45:1). From the perspective of this countertradition, Haggai's oracle represents something of a refocusing of civil and military authority on a Judahite, rather than foreign, monarch.[21] And to this extent, Haggai seems closely aligned with the Ezekiel material.

By the end of 23a (the fact that it is the end of an internal subdivision is marked by the phrase *ne'um yhwh*) we are clearly in the realm of discourse appropriate for a Davidide. The second part of the verse begins with the verb *weśamtîkā*, "I will set you," and stands in direct

---

[18] Thus Amsler, 41; cf. Beuken, 80.

[19] But it seems to have new significance here, since it points to the authorizing genealogy of David.

[20] See Amsler, 41; Ackroyd, *Exile and Restoration*, 164 n. 53; Beuken, 80 n. 2.

[21] Cf. Chary, 54, who argues that Haggai's use of *'ebed* is antithetic to that of Deutero-Isaiah.

syntactic consecution with *'eqqāḥ°kā*, "I will take you." And such action is immediately defined with a simile: "as a seal or signet." This particular simile appears to pick up and reformulate language used by Jeremiah in an oracle concerning another Davidide, Jeconiah:

> As I live, says Yahweh, even though Coniah the son of Jehoiakim, king of Judah, is a signet upon my right hand, I will tear you off . . . (Jer. 22:24)

This text, perhaps more than any other, serves to demonstrate the precise significance of Haggai's perspective. On the basis of Jer. 22:24 we know that the king could be conceived metaphorically as a seal upon the right hand of the deity.[22] We might paraphrase Haggai in the following manner: I set you as a signet on my right hand and, in so doing, designate you as my earthly representative, equivalent to a king in significance.

Such an interpretation, that the signet on Yahweh's hand indicates an elevated, perhaps even royal, status for Zerubbabel, is corroborated by the use of the term *ḥôtām* in Ezek. 28:12. This text describes the royal house of Tyre as corrupt, and within this indictment the following description occurs: "You were a perfect signet, fully of wisdom and perfect in beauty."[23] And in I Macc. 6:15 we hear explicitly that the signet was a symbol of royal authority: "the crown, his robe, and the signet."

The final colon of v. 23 corroborates fully this assessment of Haggai's oracle as a speech in which Haggai addressed the Davidic Zerubbabel as if he were to have royal status at some future time. The tense of the verb in this final colon is especially interesting, a perfect: "because I chose (or have chosen) you." Zerubbabel may someday be invested as king. But such investiture will not depend on Yahweh's choosing him in the future. Yahweh has already chosen, or elected, Zerubbabel by Yahweh's having designated the Davidic dynasty as the appropriate means by which civil rule would be exercised in Judah. This same verb, *bḥr*, was used by a psalmist to designate the election of David, "He chose David his servant, and took him from the sheepfolds" (Ps. 78:70). And interestingly, in this poem the psalmist uses the noun *'ebed* (servant), which also occurs in Hag. 2:23. Further, it is important to know that the verb *bḥr* is also used to describe the election of the Davidic city as well (see Isa. 14:1; 41:8; 43:10; 49:7). In

---

[22] On the relation of Jer. 22:24 to Hag. 2:23, see Seybold, "Königserwartungen," 71–72; Rudolph, 54; Ackroyd, *Exile and Restoration,* 165; K. Baltzer, "Das Ende des Staates Juda und die Messias-Frage," in R. Rendtorff and K. Koch, *Studien zur Theologie der alttestamentlichen Überlieferungen,* 1961, 33–43.

[23] I read *ḥôtam tāknît.*

sum, this colon, and indeed the entire final verse, highlights the royal prerogatives of Zerubbabel, the Davidic scion.[24]

What, then, may be said about this final oracle in the book of Haggai? This is a real question, since there has been considerable debate about whether to interpret these verses as a call to rebellion or as an eschatological (often meaning, in this case, unrealistic) expectation.[25] I would propose the following perspectives. Since there are so many allusions to discrete Israelite traditions in this verse, one of the oracle's meanings is that there is continuity between what Yahweh has done in the past and what he will do in the future. Second, this oracle establishes two stages for such action: martial activity and human political effort. This sentiment, too, affirms, the overall theme of continuity, since Israel had held for centuries that Yahweh was involved in its fate as a warrior and worked through and with human political instrumentalities. Third, Haggai was clearly interested in reestablishing something akin to the old social and religious order. Through his efforts—in the perspective of this book—the temple was well on the way to reconstruction. Now it was time to focus on other issues, including the civil polity of Israel. Fourth, Haggai would appear to be an astute politician, willing to work slowly and to muster support for his efforts. Efforts to revive the role of the Davidide, whether as ruling monarch or in some other governmental role, would require the cultivation of support within and outside Israel. Persian authorities— both regional and those actually in the homeland—as well as loyal Yahwists would need to be involved in this process. Haggai's words concerning this matter are general and open-ended. They focus attention on the Davidide, and they invite reflection.

What should be the role of the admittedly special Davidide in the new order? Haggai is less specific here than he was about the reconstruction of the temple. He hints that Zerubbabel be viewed in royal terms, but nothing explicit is said. Earlier he had said, "Rebuild the temple." He does not here say, "Crown Zerubbabel king." Why?

[24] Beuken, 81, has argued that 23b is secondary since *bḥr* is a favorite verb of the Chronistic redactor as well as of the Deuteronomist. Beuken, however, does not recognize that *bḥr*, when applied to Davidic election, is not limited to deuteronomistic or Chronistic sources but is part of the standard royal election traditions.

[25] Beuken, 78ff. (cf. Rothstein), understands the oracle in a fundamentally political way. Ackroyd, *Exile and Restoration,* 164–165, also argues against a "non-political interpretation." Cf. Chary, 34, who tends toward an eschatological interpretation. Mason, 25, takes a middle-of-the-road position: "The language of the oracle shows that Haggai saw Zerubbabel as a messianic figure and therefore envisaged political independence for the community in the new age." Presumably, such independence would occur in the near future.

An answer to this question takes us full circle to the beginning of the book. In the introduction we are told that there was already a king on the throne, one who was ultimately in charge of matters in Syria-Palestine. Darius was king. And openly to claim similar royal status for Zerubbabel would create immediate and unnecessary conflict. Haggai appears to be enough of a conservative to want to preserve a special role for the Davidide, and yet politically astute enough to realize that monarchy might not be a realistic form of government for Israel during this period. For this reason, rather than employing the more political terms *melek* (king) or *nāśî'* (prince), he used the noun *'ebed*. This term for servant or worker could, after all, refer to a king and had been subject to special reflection by several exilic writers. The ambiguity entailed in the use of this term enabled Haggai to reflect about the role of the Davidide, even to promise glory to the Davidide, without actually causing a political crisis. In contrast to those responsible for the editorial framework of the book—and, apparently, to Zechariah—Haggai had not settled on the diarchic form of government. By calling for the Davidide to be construed as servant or signet ring, Haggai used symbolic language that established linkages with the past and yet that did not specify future political developments.

The booklet ends, therefore, on an ambiguous note. The language encompasses important earlier traditions. And it is hopeful. It could serve as the stuff around which many Yahwists could rally and reflect. It is, above all, open-ended. Haggai's final oracle builds on his earlier success and provides Israel and the Davidic heir, Zerubbabel, with the opportunity to define an uncharted course, one appropriate to a new situation that was, from hindsight, not hospitable for the renaissance of Davidic monarchy. But governors, or at least some figures with civil authority, were important and would remain so for the next several centuries. And perhaps, at least for the forseeable future, the stability provided by genealogical continuity would make possible the restoration of a Judahite community that could understand itself as a continuation of monarchic Israel and yet would evolve into a fundamentally different phenomenon.

ZECHARIAH 1–8

INTRODUCTION

In this commentary I follow the critical judgment of scholars over the years who have discerned a fundamental division between Zechariah 1–8 and 9–14.[1] Such a division makes possible the creation of this volume in which two prophets are examined—Haggai and Zechariah—who were active at approximately the same time, ca. 520 B.C.E., and a second and subsequent work that focuses on anonymous, deuteroprophetic literature, namely, Zechariah 9–14 and Malachi, literature that does not stand rooted in one specific historical context.[2]

The general, historical, and social background for the books of Haggai and Zechariah have already been presented. Hence, we may address ourselves in this section to the particularity of an individual prophet, Zechariah, and the literature attributed to him.

1. The Person

Concerning the person Zechariah, little can be said. Presuming that Zechariah son of Berechiah son of Iddo (Zech. 1:1) is the same person as Zechariah son of Iddo (Neh. 12:16), we know that Zechariah was a member of a priestly house, i.e., that of Iddo. What this says about Zechariah's behavior is difficult to infer. He was known to be familiar with ritual matters (Zech. 7:2–3). Some scholars have argued that Zechariah had been in exile, and that he had direct knowledge of the plight of those in captivity, and, moreover, that he had assimilated imagery from his Mesopotamian environs.[3] Though it is difficult to argue with great conviction that Zechariah had been in exile, his

[1] For a review of the basic arguments sustaining the division of Zechariah 1–8 from 9–14, see O. Eissfeldt, *The Old Testament: An Introduction*, 1965, 435–440; B. Otzen, *Studien über Deutero-Sacharja*, 1964, 11–34. Cf. Baldwin, 62–70.

[2] See B. Childs, *Introduction to the Old Testament as Scripture*, 1979, 476–486, for an assessment of the relationship between Proto- and Deutero-Zechariah from the perspective of canonical criticism.

[3] For a discussion of this issue, see, e.g., Amsler, 49–50.

genealogy at least points to a connection between him and the group of Israelites who had lived in the diaspora.

As was the case with Haggai, the name of the prophet Zechariah resonates with his task. The name means "Yahweh has remembered." It is a conservative name, evoking a sense of continuity with earlier Israelite tradition. Such a name suggests that Yahweh remembers what he did for and with Israel at an earlier period. And it presumes that he will act again in a similar manner.

According to the chronological data provided by the book's editor, Zechariah's activity continued for a period longer than that of Haggai. The earliest date, preserved in Zech. 1:1, places the beginning of his prophetic activity in Darius' second year, the eighth month; the final date, in Zech. 7:1, places further activity in Darius' fourth year, the fourth day of the ninth month. On the basis of these dates alone, we learn that the editors of this book thought Zechariah functioned as a prophet for a period of at least two years. Whether ch. 8, or any other material in the book, suggests a later date, is moot. In any case, nothing in the book implies that Zechariah experienced, at least in his role as prophet, the completion of the temple in 515 B.C.E.

2. The Book

If little may be said about Zechariah, we are on firmer ground when we treat the book itself. It is made up of two types of literature; visions and oracles. Moreover, the book has been given a structure by the presence of date formulae in 1:1; 1:7; and 7:1. Using these formulae as organizational markers, one may argue that the book is made up of three basic sections, an introduction (1:1–6), a block of reports of visions, replete with oracular responses (1:7–6:15), and a concluding block of prophetic speeches organized around Zechariah in the role of oracle giver.

Prologue

In the first section, the person responsible for the final form of the book has provided an introduction that, among other things, establishes the credentials of Zechariah. Then, in a pastiche of prophetic discourse, the audience is reminded of the inappropriate way in which Israel had responded to earlier prophets. Israel rejected the prophets' words and expired. This earlier generation had, however, recognized the justice in the way in which they had been treated. They returned. This word, *šûb*, "return," has geographic as well as religious and ethical implications for Zechariah's hearers, and it is a word originally at home in oracles of salvation. This prologue to the book conveys hope. Just as the fathers turned, so now the current generation may (re)turn.

The Visions

Once this stage is set, the visions, the core of the book, ensue. Visions are, of course, nothing new in the prophetic corpus.[4] Vision reports are preserved in the literature of earlier classical prophets (e.g., Amos 7:1–9; 8:1–3; Isa. 6; Jer. 1:11–19; Ezek. 1:1; 8:2), and in narratives about so-called preclassical prophets (e.g., I Kings 22). The notion of a prophet receiving all his information through the visionary experience is even attested in the introductions to Amos (1:1), Isaiah (1:1), and Obadiah (1:1). Hence Zechariah stands in a venerable tradition when reporting visions as one element in the performance of his prophetic role.[5]

One basic issue must be addressed before we may consider the overall significance of these vision reports, that of the visions' coherence. The basic purport of the date formula and vision introduction in Zech. 1:7–8 and the absence of other such markers until Zech. 7:1 is that all the visions were received within a single night. Were this the case, we might well expect that all the visions would cohere.

Scholars studying dream behavior have, in fact, determined that a series of dreams—usually four to six in number—in one night is normal. Such dreams may focus on one theme or on related matters. Moreover, 70 to 80 percent of dreams reported are in color, as are Zechariah's visions. Presuming a fundamental similarity between dreams and visions, a relation recognized by ancient Greeks (waking [*hypar*] and dream [*onar*] visions) as well as modern investigators, there would appear to be prima facie evidence to support the notion of a basic coherence within Zechariah's visions.[6]

However, that these dreams or visions did occur in one experiential

---

[4] Recent valuable work on visions in the prophetic literature includes S. Amsler, "La parole visionnaire des prophètes," *VT* 31, 1981, 359–363; K. Freer, *A Study of Vision Reports in Biblical Literature* (Ph.D. Dissertation, Yale University, 1975); F. Horst, "Die Visionsschilderungen der alttestamentlichen Propheten," *EvTh* 20, 1960, 193–205; B. Long, "Reports of Visions Among the Prophets," *JBL* 95, 1976, 353–365.

[5] For a discussion of the place of Zechariah in the visionary tradition, see C. Jeremias, *Nachtgesichte*.

[6] Basic literature on dream behavior as it relates to the issues raised by Zechariah's visions includes A. Rechtschaffen, P. Verdone, J. Wheaton, "Reports of Mental Activity

context or that they all cohere has not regularly been admitted by biblical scholars. For example, K. Galling has argued that it is possible to identify a distinct historical setting for each of the visions, and that these settings are not identical. Some visions reflect conditions in Babylon before Judahites returned to Syria-Palestine (Zech. 1:8–15; 2:1–4 [1:18–21E]; 2:5–9 [1–5E]; 6:1–8); others reflect conditions in Syria-Palestine after the return and just before the rebuilding of the temple (Zech. 4:1–6a, 10b–14; 5:1–4; 5:5–11).[7]

Such a mode of interpretation presumes that the significance of the visions lies primarily outside the visions themselves, i.e., in the historical impulse that produced them. This mode of interpretation entails problems similar to that of interpreting individual psalms from their putative moments of historical origin. That style of psalm exegesis has been firmly rejected and should, on similar grounds, be subject to question for the visions of Zechariah.

In a different vein, but still involving the question of the coherence of all the visions, some scholars have argued for the basic unity of the visions but have maintained that one vision, usually Zech. 3, the fourth vision, stands apart from the other vision reports. This judgment is often rendered because that vision differs in form from the other visions and because it seems to be more highly pragmatic than the other visions.[8] In my judgment, Zech. 3 is an integral and original part of the visionary sequence, dealing as it does with a critical issue in the meta-restoration that Zechariah envisions, namely, the issue of how ritual purity may be engendered in a situation of radical defilement.

Galling and others are correct in perceiving that these visions of

---

During Sleep," *Canadian Psychiatric Association Journal* 8, 1963, 409–414; E. Kahn, William Fisher, J. Barmack, "Incidence of Color in Immediately Recalled Dreams," *Science* 137, 1962, 1054–1055; C. Padgham, "Colours Experienced in Dreams," *British Journal of Psychology* 66, 1975, 25–28; A. Rechtschaffen, W. Offenkrantz, "Clinical Studies of Sequential Dreams," *Archives of General Psychiatry* 8, 1963, 497–509; H. Roffwarg et al., "The Effects of Long-Standing Perceptual Alterations on the Hallucinatory Content of Dreams," *Psychophysiology* 5, 1968, 219–225.

[7] Galling, "Die Exilswende in der Sicht des Propheten Sacharja," *Studien*, 123ff. Some scholars prefer to speak of a literary unity within the visions, e.g., Seybold, *Bilder zum Tempelbau*, 39. Rignell, *Nachtgesichte*, 243, also speaks of literary unity and yet argues that visions reflect different historical contexts. Cf. other studies that postulate a single ritual moment which serves to explain the visions: H. May, "A Key to the Interpretation of Zechariah's Visions," *JBL* 57, 1938, 173–184; G. Wallis, "Die Nachtgesichte des Propheten Sacharja. Zur Idee einer Form," *VT Supp* 29, 1978, 377–391.

[8] For a thorough discussion of this issue, see C. Jeremias, *Nachtgesichte*, 201–225.

Zechariah entail not only a literary unity but also a progression.[9] However, the unity and progression do not reflect historical reality per se.[10] Rather the visions precede, and even enable, historical reality to take place. My own perspective is that the visions represent highly symbolic theological reflection on the process by means of which Judahite society might be (re)ordered and restored.

Zechariah's visions stand somewhere between purely mundane concerns and a utopian vision of renewal. The visions are not concrete in the way in which Haggai concentrates on agricultural yield (Hag. 2:14–19) and on the preservation of capital (Hag. 1:6), and they are not concrete in the way in which Ezek. 40–48 provides detailed measurements for the restored temple compound. Nor are Zechariah's visions utopian as are the expectations for wealth in Hag. 2:6–7 or as is Ezekiel's vision of a society without religious error (Ezek. 43:7). Zechariah's visions stand somewhere between utopian social vision and concrete physical and social detail.

The notion of "somewhere in between" is apt not only as a description of where these visions stand vis-à-vis other early postexilic literatures. This notion of "inbetweenness" also serves as an accurate indicator for the content of Zechariah's visions. In the first vision, we are conveyed to a geography which is not really of this world and is not directly that of the divine dwelling. We are near the cosmic deep, overseeing the divine corral. But we see neither the deity nor any obvious location in this world. We are between worlds. In the second vision, Zechariah looks up and sees four horns, and then four artisans approaching them. These objects are this-worldly and yet somehow removed from this world—hovering above Zechariah in the night. On moving to the fourth vision, we are presented with a scene in which Joshua is cleansed in the divine council. And yet the council lacks the one element that is regularly present, the deity himself. It is not the divine council that we have come to expect on the basis of I Kings 22 or Isa. 6.[11] In the fifth vision, the most static vision of the cycle, Zechariah sees an object that we normally associate with the temple compound. And yet the temple lampstand has no obvious cultic context, and it is surrounded by strange olive-tree people. Finally, in the sixth and

---

[9] Galling, "Exilswende," *Studien*, 123; K. Seybold, "Die Bildmotive in den Visionen des Propheten Sacharja," *VT Supp* 26, 1974, 108.

[10] Cf. B. Halpern, "The Ritual Background of Zechariah's Temple Song," *CBQ* 40, 1978, 167–190, who argues for the unity of Zechariah as a visionary experience elicited by the ceremonial deposition of the second temple's foundation stone.

[11] See the similar assessment of E. Mullen, *The Divine Council in Canaanite and Early Hebrew Literature*, 1980, 275.

seventh visions, the prophet perceives objects, a flying scroll and an approaching ephah. Both are in midair. The soaring *'êphāh* is, as the writer succinctly puts it, "between the earth and the heavens."

A second feature present in the visions is motion.[12] Things are on the move. To be sure, not all the visions are filled with movement. But even the so-called static visions function to make movement possible in the visions that follow. The first vision, which provokes a lament by the *mal'āk,* receives a divine response to move beyond the lamentable status quo. Movement must and does follow. Artisans are on their way to destroy the nations responsible for Judah's demise. An individual, probably angelic, moves out to do survey work on Jerusalem, only to be intercepted and corrected. The high priest is reclothed and thereby cleansed. Action follows hard on the heels of the inceptive, static vision.

And then, in the second, also static vision, Zechariah sees a symbol of divine presence, one flanked by two anointed figures, figures probably representing the diarchic polity of the newly restored Judahite community. This vision suggests, among other things, that a new cultic and social order is in place. As a function of this newly constituted order, further action could take place. Flying scroll, soaring *'êphāh,* and surging steeds—each with its own function— complete the visionary sequence. These complex symbols represent the working out of this new order as it affects Judah as well as the entire world. Though these visions are strange in their imagery, much is happening in them; things are up in the air; and things are on the move.

A third feature shared by these visions is the leitmotiv represented by the phrase *kol-hā'āres* In six of the eight visions, the notion of activity encompassing all the earth is stated explicitly. In both beginning and concluding visions, horses have gone out or are going out to patrol "all the earth." In the second vision, one hears of horns of the nations that have destroyed Judah, a description that surely refers to more than the Neo-Assyrians and Neo-Babylonians. The number four here, as elsewhere, symbolizes the totality of world powers. The next two visions focus on the restored Judahite community and do not, therefore, include explicit mention of worldwide scope. But in the fifth, sixth, and seventh visions, the phrase "all the earth" appears again. In the fifth, Yahweh is *'ādôn* of the whole earth. In the sixth, the flying curse is understood as proceeding out "over the face of the entire earth." And in the seventh, we hear of an *'êphāh* which represents "their sin" in all the earth. In these visions, then, Zechariah

---

[12] See similarly Seybold, "Bildmotive," 106–107.

experiences visions that focus neither on the territory of Judah nor on a localized version of Yahweh's activity. The scope of the activity is cosmic, international, as befits a deity who is sovereign over the world.

These visions, therefore, share three essential elements: things occur in an intermediate realm, things are on the move, and the notion of "all the earth" is a leitmotiv of the deity's action. How are these features to be explained? Are these elements simply a function of the dream or trance experience that Zechariah reports? Or are they a function of a presumed rededication ceremony for the Jerusalem temple? In both cases, the answer is no. Rather, another explanation is more likely—or better, two related explanations are likely.

First, Zechariah's visions comprise the doing of theology. In them, he is explaining why and how Yahweh will undo the results of iniquity; how Yahweh will be present in Jerusalem; how the community's leadership will be organized; how the problem of human error will be addressed; and how the contamination of earlier sin and unclean existence will be expunged. Second, the visions comprise Zechariah's experientially based responses to these problems of a community attempting to reorganize itself.

By way of answering the question of how Yahweh will be present in Jerusalem, Zechariah reports that Yahweh will no longer be localized in his temple. Instead, Yahweh will be a wall of fire around the city. And as for the city itself, Jerusalem will be a different urban entity from what it had been earlier. It will exist without walls. Here Zechariah may be reflecting on the Persian ritual capital Pasargadae, another city without walls and with fire altars on its perimeter. In any case, Zechariah was also being hardheadedly realistic. The city walls of Jerusalem were not rebuilt for another century.

Or—another case—purity and holiness were constitutive categories for monarchic Yahwism. In 520 B.C.E., how could the high priest and, in turn, the people be purified? The temple lay in disarray. The older cleansing practices were, therefore, impossible to carry out. Zechariah does, however, provide a solution. Joshua was to be cleansed in the ritual setting of the divine council, though not by the deity himself. Once this agent of communal purification had himself been cleansed the polity of the new community could begin to function.

These are important conceptual problems. Rather than rushing in where angels fear to tread, rather than proposing, as had Haggai, that the temple needed to be rebuilt, or that Zerubbabel was to be anointed as king, Zechariah experienced Yahweh's angelic agents and discerned how the new religious and social order was to be initiated.

What Zechariah reports in these visions is initial restoration within the cosmic order. Once Yahweh had decided to act beneficently toward what was now Judah, there were certain processes that must begin, certain issues that must be resolved, certain decisions about community organization that must be made; and all this before humans could do the mundane work of restoration. What we see in the visions is the beginning of restoration on a cosmic plane. Things are being carried out over "all the earth," not just in Judah, as Ezek. 40–48 would have it. Yahweh's steeds and angelic host are busy with the work of creating a new social and religious structure that will affect the entire world, not just Judah.

My first answer to explain the peculiar elements of these visions—that things are up in the air, on the move, and cosmic in scale—is that Zechariah is experiencing and reporting restoration within the cosmic order. In so doing, he is providing the theological rationale that will make concrete forms of restoration possible. He is not, in these visions, directly proposing or engaging in the actual work of restoration.

Why was it necessary for Zechariah to bother with such an effort when the immediate conditions of the community made mundane work so necessary? The answer to this question provides the second, and perhaps more important, reason for the peculiar configuration these visions have. Zechariah seems to be presenting an alternative vision of restoration. It revises significantly a vision included in another prophetic book, a vision that details the manner in which Judah, and more particularly the temple, is to be restored. I refer, of course, to the so-called *Verfassungsentwurf* of Ezekiel.[13] In order to make this point as clearly as possible, we must consider eight major points of contrast between the visions of Zechariah and "the visions of God" preserved in Ezek. 40–48.[14]

1. What is the scope of Yahweh's restorative activity? Ezekiel's answer is clear. "The hand of Yahweh was upon me, and brought me in the visions of God into the land of Israel" (Ezek. 40:1b–2). Everything happens in the land of Israel. Even the paradisal river, which was worldwide in the primeval history of Genesis, is in Ezekiel limited to

[13] On this block of material, see esp. H. Gese, *Der Verfassungsentwurf des Ezechiel (Kap. 40–48) traditionsgeschichtlich untersucht,* 1957; W. Zimmerli, *Ezechiel,* 1969, 977–1249; and J. Levenson, *Theology of the Program of Restoration of Ezekiel 40–48,* 1976.

[14] For an assessment of the relation between Zechariah and Ezekiel 40–48, though without benefit of higher-critical perspectives, see C. MacKay, "Zechariah in Relation to Ezekiel 40–48" *Evangelical Quarterly* 40, 1968, 497–210. MacKay's basic argument is that "Zechariah is our first expositor of Ezek. 40–48."

the land of Israel (Ezek. 47). For Zechariah, however, Yahweh's activity is cosmic in scope, as the leitmotiv *kol-hā'āreṣ* clearly indicates.

2. What will initiate the new order? Ezekiel is not explicit here, but we may infer that a newly completed temple is a requisite. Only with the temple rebuilt do the visions of Ezekiel make sense. The actual building of the temple was a necessary condition for the new order. Not so for Zechariah. A decision by the deity and activity on the part of his agents were necessary in order to set up the basic cosmic and social structure for the new order. Human beings must wait for the deity and his agents to act.

3. What will the new Jerusalem be like? Ezekiel is definite and clear. In Ezek. 48:30–35 we hear of a square city, four thousand five hundred cubits on a side. Each side will have three gates. And since we hear of gates, we may presume that the sides were those of a walled city.[15]

Zechariah's notion is quite different. For him, to talk about measurements of breadth and width is wholly inappropriate. Further, to speak of a walled city is also improper. The new Jerusalem will not have walls because it will be a different and more heavily populated urban entity. Zechariah could not differ more from Ezekiel's notion of the restored Jerusalem.

4. How will Yahweh be present in the restored city? Ezekiel is at this point characteristically straightforward. In ch. 43, we hear of the return of Yahweh's *kābôd*. The deity addresses Ezekiel, "Son of man, this is the place of my throne and the place of the soles of my feet, where I will dwell in the midst of the people of Israel for ever" (43:7). This place is, of course, none other than the temple. The glory of Yahweh entered the temple. That was to be the locus of Yahweh's presence.

Zechariah's perspective is quite different. There is no reason to think that Yahweh will be limited to the temple compound. In the third vision, a divine oracle emphasizes Yahweh's presence in a way quite distinct from the temple: "For I will be to her a wall of fire round about, says Yahweh, and I will be the glory within her" (Zech. 2:5 [1E]). Nothing in Zechariah's visions leads one to suppose that Yahweh is thought of as bound by the temple precinct in quite the same way as that notion is expressed in Ezekiel's vision.

5. How is the priesthood to be restored and renewed? Ezekiel, or a disciple of Ezekiel, contends that the Zadokites are to provide the core of priestly leadership (Ezek. 44:9ff.). They are to undertake special

[15] See Levenson, *Theology of the Program of Restoration*, 119–125.

offerings to cleanse and to rededicate the newly constructed temple (45:18–20). To put it another way, there are priests who survived the destruction and exilic experience without becoming ritually suspect.

Zechariah, however, argues that the restoration of the priesthood is to begin with a specific high priest, Joshua. He is to be cleansed, not in some standard purification ceremony but in a rite performed in the divine council. There is, in Zechariah, no mention of Zadokite versus non-Zadokite, Levite versus non-Levite. Further, there is no warrant in the visions of Zechariah to think that any priestly groups were degraded, as is clearly the case in Ezek. 40–48.

6. How is the priesthood to be ordered? The picture in Ezekiel is one of collegial activity. No particular hierarchy is present. And rather surprisingly, the role label "chief" or "high priest" is wanting. Zechariah, on the other hand, makes it clear that, despite the fact that there is a group of priests (Zech. 3:8), there is a high priest who has significant prerogatives, one whose ritual purity enables the priestly system as a whole to function properly.[16]

7. How will the new community be ruled? With Ezekiel, we are forced to consider the enigmatic *nāśîʾ*. Levenson's comments are apt: "The School of Ezekiel hoped not for a diarchy of Davidide and Zadokite such as was to emerge just after the return from Exile (Zech. 3), but for a community so fundamentally liturgical and sacral in nature that the Davidide, politics having vanished, could only be a liturgical figurehead. . . . Ezek. 40–48 hoped not for a restoration of the monarchy, but for a restoration of the monarch, who is now redefined according to his deepest and truest function as the servant of God, one devoted to the divine service, to liturgy."[17] Clearly, leadership in the restored community focuses on this utopian priest-monarch amalgam, the *nāśîʾ*.

Zechariah operates with a different ideal. In his fifth vision, he sees two olive trees, trees interpreted as being "the two anointed who stand by Yahweh of the whole earth." Commentators uniformly view these anointed figures as signifying the diarchic polity recoverable in the oracular material, e.g., Zech. 6:9–15.[18] Zechariah apparently thinks in terms of joint civil-religious leadership, though the character of the civil side of the equation remains notably unclear in the visions themselves. The visions do, however, make clear that the high priest is to have an important leadership role, and this in contrast to Ezek. 40–48.

[16] Admittedly, this material is from the oracles.
[17] Levenson, *Theology of the Program of Restoration,* 143.
[18] See the standard commentaries and C. Jeremias, *Nachtgesichte,* 176–188.

8. How will the postexilic community deal with disorder? For Ezekiel, one has the suspicion that the new community is to be without disorder. He writes: "The house of Israel shall no more defile my holy name" (Ezek. 43:7). Similar is his statement about the priests in the new order: "They shall not defile themselves by going near to a dead person" (Ezek. 44:25). One senses that this is a utopian setting, one in which Jeremiah's expectations of a new covenant are to be realized.

Zechariah, by way of contrast, appears more pragmatic. His vision of the new order includes mention of those who have violated covenant norms and yet go unpunished. This situation is addressed in the sixth vision (Zech. 5:1–4), a vision that is designed to solve that problem by having a flying curse punish those for whom punishment is appropriate. The admonitory material elsewhere in Zechariah 1–8, though outside the bounds of the visionary texts, buttresses this notion of a not-so-perfect society.

These eight questions and the presumed answers of Ezekiel and Zechariah surely suggest that Zechariah has presented an alternative to or a revision of the notions of restoration present in Ezek. 40–48.

In summary, one may contend that Zechariah was, in and through the vision reports, speaking from within the context of normative Israelite religious traditions and explaining how Yahweh was again to interact with his chosen people. That was, for Zechariah, no easy task. The covenant curses had been called down; the people and the land were now unclean. Yahweh had left his holy place; the community had been disbanded. Further, there was an alternative proposal available, that of Ezek. 40–48. Moreover, the visions of Zechariah are not, as some have contended, either general expressions of salvation to the newly agglomerated postexilic community, nor are they, as others have maintained, directly linked to a cleansing or rebuilding ritual. Haggai may have been fired to propose immediate action in response to the poetry of Deutero-Isaiah or to the program of Ezekiel. Not so Zechariah.[19] He provided the theological prolegomenon to restoration, a theological warrant for the more mundane work of restoration to follow. Zechariah provided a theological perspective relevant to a new situation, that of a Yahwism without an independent territorial state. Although Zechariah's visions are grounded in the political, economic, and social reality of the early postexilic period, and although they address fundamental issues such as the appropriate

---

[19] Cf. W. Harrelson, "The Trial of Joshua the High Priest—Zechariah 3," *EI* 16, 1982, 116*–124*.

polity of the evolving Yahwistic community, the visions remain highly symbolic, open to a variety of responses.

The Oracles

Interspersed among the visions are oracles, some of which may stem from the hand of Zechariah, some of which may not.[20] The oracular material in Zechariah 1–8 occurs in two blocks. A number of oracles are scattered throughout the vision sequence, whereas others are collected at the end in chs. 7–8. These two bodies of prophetic-style speeches each appear to be accomplishing separate purposes. On the one hand, the oracles in and around the visions respond to the visions, drawing out various implications and even correcting them. On the other hand, the oracles at the end of the book depict Zechariah in the nonvisionary mode and serve to enhance his status as a prophet, as an Amos, capable of a variety of prophetic styles. Moreover, this second block of oracles has a particular focus, the transition from a time of lamentation to a time of celebration, especially as this will occur in Jerusalem. Also, this latter collection includes more admonitory rhetoric than do the oracles included among the visions.

Oracles in Zechariah 1:7–6:15. I would make five basic observations about the oracles included within the visionary material.

1. Not all visions are followed or interpreted by oracles. The second, sixth, and seventh visions start without benefit of oracular utterance. It is perhaps no accident that these are the shortest and, in some ways, the most straightforward visions. The implications of these three visions do not raise difficult theological problems, nor do they represent unusual solutions as does, e.g., the third vision. The second, sixth, and seventh visions, despite the bizarre imagery of the latter two, reflect standard, often covenant, ideology and do not, therefore, call for elucidation or correction.

2. When oracles do occur in Zech. 1:7–6:15, they function as responses to, elucidiations of, or corrections to the visions. The oracles are not inserted willy-nilly among the visions but comprise reactions to issues raised by the visions. For example, 1:14–17 is an oracular response to the first vision. That first vision concludes in v. 13 with a very general statement of good news, "Yahweh then answered the messenger who spoke to me with kind and consoling words." And yet, what precisely was the purport of those kind and consoling words? It is

---

[20] Beyond the commentaries, two monographs are of special significance for the study of the oracular material: Beuken, op. cit., and Petitjean, *Oracles.*

the answer to this question which the oracular additions address. Zechariah 1:14–16 define that good news as a promise to Jerusalem and as an assurance that the temple will be rebuilt. Zechariah 1:17 is less concrete and tempers the emphasis on Jerusalem by advocating good news for other cities as well. Zechariah 1:14–17 is a natural explication of the general message of the first vision.

Another example. The fourth vision treats the ritual purification of the priest. Following that vision, there is a block of prophetic speech, 3:6–10. Within that section, there are two competing interpretations of the vision. In 3:6–7, 9, the prerogatives of the high priest are presented in conditional language. But in 3:8, the status of the Branch, no doubt the royal figure, is presented in an unconditional way. The vision was open-ended about the significance of the high priest's purification and about the relation of the priest to the Davidide. The oracles explore these issues by commenting on the status of the high priest and that of the royal figure. Needless to say, it is unlikely that both oracles stem from one hand or authorial tradition, since they advocate competing positions.

A final example, ch. 4, the so-called *mᵉnôrāh* vision, presents an idealized view of the postexilic polity, high priest and Davidide functioning with equal status. Inserted into this vision are two oracles, 4:6–7 and 4:8–10. The first enhances the status of Zerubbabel at the expense of Joshua, and the other focuses on the role of Zerubbabel as temple builder. Both oracles work in complementary fashion to correct or revise the notion of egalitarian rule articulated in the vision.

In sum, it appears that the visions were so general—at least from the perspective of those involved in the programmatic work of restoration—that they allowed for, perhaps even required, those preserving them to comment on, expand, or even correct their implications.

3. Whenever an oracular response is made to a vision in Zech. 1:7–6:15, it always entails more than one saying. It is appropriate, therefore, to speak in every instance of oracular additions to the visions. After the first vision, there are two oracles, 1:14–15 and 1:16–17; after the third vision, a collection comprising 2:10–17 [6–13]; after the fourth vision, 3:6–7, 9; and 3:8; inside the fifth vision, 4:6–7; 4:8–10; and 4:12; and after the eighth vision, 6:10–11, 14; and 6:12–13. Since the oracles following the fourth vision push in different directions, and since the second of the oracles following the first vision appears to depend on the first oracular response to that vision, it is almost certainly the case that the variety represented in these multiple sayings may be attributed to more than one redactional hand.

4. There are certain issues, one hesitates to say themes, common to

many of these oracles. For example, whereas the visions provide a prominent place for the high priest, the oracles present the royal figure as having special importance (Zech. 4:6–10; 6:12–13). The oracles also emphasize the important role of the prophet (Zech. 2:13, 15 [9, 11E]; 4:9; 6:15). To this extent the oracles are conservative, buttressing two traditional and complementary roles, Davidide and prophet—which stem from the polity of the monarchic period. Moreover, the place of Jerusalem, the city of Yahweh, as site of his blessing, is emphasized in the oracles (1:14–16; 2:12 [8E], 14). This too is evidence of a traditional stratum, the conviction that Yahweh will reside where he did in an earlier period.

5. Despite the fact that the oracles support or correct the visions, there are elements of continuity between the visions and oracles. There is, for example, continuity between the cosmic imagery of the four winds in the final vision and the notion of four winds in Zech. 2:10, although one should note that this oracle is conjoined to the third and not the final vision. Moreover, both visions and oracles share certain images with those present in the book of Isaiah: the personified Zion (Isa. 40:9); the cities of Judah (Isa. 40:9) the nations coming to Zion (Isa. 56:6–7); foreign nations going beyond Yahweh's limits (Isa. 47:5–7); myrtle and water (Isa. 41:18–19); the notion of brief punishment (Isa. 54:7); Zion shouting for joy (Isa. 12:6). The list could go on. Such continuities between oracle, vision, and Isaiah suggest that despite certain differences in perspective, there is shared discourse between the prophetic traditionists of the Isaianic circle, the prophet Zechariah, and those preserving Zechariah's visions and oracles.

In sum, the oracles preserved in Zech. 1:7–6:15 may be construed as responses to Zechariah's visions. They are heterogeneous, presenting one and then another perspective, drawing out the implications, even correcting these highly symbolic and reflective reports in which Zechariah envisions the meta-restoration of Judah.

Oracles in Zechariah 7–8. The situation in Zech. 7–8 is markedly different from that of the prior oracles. Here we see Zechariah in a nonvisionary mode at the outset, responding to a question with standard prophetic rhetoric and presenting additional oracles as well. This section may strike the casual reader as highly disparate, and indeed it is made up of diverse oracles. However, there is a structure and logic to the complex. There are three basic parts: Zech. 7:1–14; 8:1–17; and 8:18–23. Zechariah 7 begins with a question from individuals sent from Bethel concerning appropriate fasting requirements. To this query, Zechariah responds with counter-questions that broach fundamental issues concerning fasting. Then in a historical essay, 7:8–14, the author adduces typical preexilic prophetic oracles, which are followed by the response of the people to such prophetic admonitions, and then, the ensuing judgment by Yahweh. What was an apparently innocent question becomes the occasion for two speech units that become increasingly negative in tone.

That negative tone changes in Zech. 8:1–17. Here, in highly allusive language and in a series of short oracles, we learn that Yahweh has become jealous for Zion, that Yahweh will dwell in Jerusalem, that Zion will also be repopulated by humans, that the restoration will be glorious, and that Yahweh will accomplish the return of his people. In this subcollection of oracles, 8:1–8, there is singular focus on weal for Jerusalem. Then occur two longer blocks: 8:9–13 and 8:14–17, both of which entail historical reprise; things were bad, now they will be better. Both of these units contain admonitory language as a condition for future well-being in Jerusalem. These two compositions appear to present the pragmatic implications of the salvific news expressed in 8:1–8.

In the third and final component of this oracular collection, 8:18–23, Zechariah provides the long-awaited answer to the question broached in 7:3. Fasts shall become feasts. But, consistent with the tone of 8:9–17, this good news is conditioned by the admonition to "love truth." Then in the final two oracles, 8:20–22 and 8:23, the urban theme struck in 8:1–8 is reasserted. This time, though, it is foreign people coming from foreign cities to Jerusalem, rather than Israelites returning to Jerusalem from diaspora settings. Also, the foreigner/Israelite dichotomy is enhanced by reference to the ability of the individual Israelite to interact with ten foreigners. These two oracles represent the most utopian elements in the collection.

The oracles in Zech. 7–8 rehearse in a less symbolic way issues broached in the visions and their oracular responses, e.g., the presence of Yahweh in Jerusalem (8:3/2:9 [5E]); concern for justice (7:9–10; 8:16–17/5:1–4); concern for proper ritual (7:4–7; 8:18–19/3:1–5). However, in this later and more prosaic section, other issues not addressed in the visions are discussed, e.g., the way it will be for those living in the new Jerusalem (8:3–8, 12–13, 20–23). This particular theme appears to be a continuation of the Isaianic and Deutero-Isaianic focus on the urban entity of Zion. What Yahweh will do for his venerators will be done in Jerusalem. Beneficent life will occur there. The only blessing not centering on Jerusalem is that of agricultural prosperity, which will redound to the glory of Judah.

It is tempting to think that the visions represent the seminal experience of Zechariah and that the oracles in chs. 1–8 comprise material of secondary importance, a more mundane expression of visionary depth. And to a certain extent this may be true for chs. 1–6. However, chs. 7–8 are more than an oracular appendage to the visions of chs. 1–6. Chapters 7–8 present a picture of the prophet which enlarges that given in the visions. In the earlier section, Zechariah was a visionary, whereas in the latter block, he is oracle, responding to queries and presenting admonitions, historical assessments, and good news, topics frequently addressed by others of Israel's prophets. Together, chs. 1–6 and 7–8 constitute a picture of the well-rounded prophet, to use an admitted anachronism. Zechariah is depicted as prophet comfortable in two modes: vision and audition. And to this extent he stands in a line of other Israelite prophets who presented both oracles and vision reports, e.g., Amos. Equally to the point, Zechariah may be distinguished from Haggai, whose book contains no visions. Some scholars have maintained that the book of Haggai is written to buttress his role as prime instigator of temple reconstruction. If such is the case, the booklet of Zechariah presents a response, a picture of Zechariah as one who used the full repertoire of oracle and vision to exercise his role. In this regard, it is surely no accident that in chs. 7–8, Zechariah is presented in a way similar to Haggai, becoming involved in dialogue on ritual matters. Zechariah is able to do what Haggai can do, but he is able to do more.

Formation of the Book

I have already argued that Zechariah 1–8 comprises three basic sections: 1:1–6; 1:7–6:15; and 7:1–8:23. The vision cycle and inquiry-response concerning fasting practices provide the core visionary and auditory prophetic activity of Zechariah. Out of this bipartite prophetic discourse, an editor created a book of three parts. The core prophetic material has been prefaced by a hope-engendering introduction wrought out in typical prophetic language. This was, however, not the only supplement to the prophetic material. There were additions in the latter two parts as well. In the second and longest section, all but three of the visions were interpreted or even corrected. And the final two chapters fill out the picture of Zechariah as oracle giver, standing in the tradition of prophets who speak admonitions as well as words of promise.

Some scholars have recently argued for the existence of one

fundamental redaction in the book of Zechariah.[21] In my judgment, the variety within the oracular responses to the visions, as well as the difficulty of denying certain oracles in chs. 7–8 to Zechariah the prophet, makes difficult the identification of such a single redaction. Nonetheless, someone ordered the book, including as it does the discourse of Zechariah as well as oracular additions to that original material. I have argued that the organization of the book seems designed to enhance the picture of Zechariah as prophet with comprehensive abilities rather than to argue for a distinctive theological position; that was done in the visions themselves. Moreover, the material, especially the oracles in chs. 1–6, seems designed to soften the proposals for high-priestly authority that are expressed in the visions. Hence one may say that the redactor and the book in its final form are not only interested in portraying Zechariah in a favorable light. They are also concerned to articulate a particular, pragmatic view of the visions, a view that preserves a special place not only for the city of David but for the Davidide himself. Such views are not foreign to the book of Haggai.

Text

As was the case with Haggai, the text of Zechariah 1–8 is relatively free of textual problems. That is, of course, not to say that the MT is always easy to translate. I have found it necessary to offer readings different from MT in the following instances: 1:4; 2:11–12 [7–8E]; 3:2, 5; 4:2, 7, 9; 5:6; 6:3, 6–7; 7:13; 8:6, 16.[22]

---

[21] For the notion of one primary redaction, see Beuken, op. cit., and, to a certain degree, P. Hanson, "Zechariah, Book of," *IDB Supp,* 1976, 982–983. For a more stratified approach, see Seybold, *Bilder zum Tempelbau,* 22–23. See also Amsler, 45–48, for a more organic view of the growth of the book.

[22] Studies with a strong text-critical interest include: E. Lipiński, "Recherches sur le livre de Zacharie," *VT* 20, 1970, 25–55; Petitjean, *Oracles;* Ringnell, *Nachtgesichte.*

COMMENTARY

Zechariah 1:1–6

As for your fathers, where are they?

1 In the eighth month, in the second year of Darius, the word of
Yahweh came to Zechariah son of Berechiah son of Iddo, the prophet:
2 "Yahweh was angry because of your fathers."
3 Now you should say to them:
"Thus says Yahweh of Hosts,
Return to me,
says Yahweh of Hosts,[a]
so that I may return to you,
says Yahweh of Hosts.[a]
4 Do not be like your fathers, to whom the earlier prophets said:
'Thus says Yahweh of Hosts,
Turn from your evil ways and evil actions.'[b]
They did not obey or pay attention to me.
5 As for your fathers,
where are they?
And the prophets,
did they live forever?
6 However, my words and my statutes,
concerning which I charged my servants the prophets,
did they not overtake your fathers?
Then they turned and said,
'Yahweh of Hosts has done to us
according to our ways and deeds,
just as he had intended to act with us.' "[c]

a. The word $ṣᵉbā'ôt$ is missing in many LXX manuscripts.

b. Both Ketib, $ûma'ᵃlylêkem$, apparently a form of $'ᵃlîlāh$, and Qere,
$ûma'ᵃlalêkem$, apparently a form of $ma'ᵃlāl$, reflect an haplographic omission
of the second *mem* in the probable original word, $ûmimma'ᵃlālêkem$, "from
your (evil) deeds."

c. The sense is difficult here. What group is the subject of the verbs *wayyāšûbû* and *wayyō'm⁽ᵉ⁾rû?* Is it "the fathers" who turned and admitted that they had received just recompense for their deeds or is it the audience of Zechariah which has already been referred to by the 2 masc. pl. pronominal suffix in this same sentence: *'ᵃbōtêkem.* A strict construction of the Hebrew syntax would suggest the latter option, the interpretation which I accept. Cf. Ackroyd, *Exile and Restoration,* 202, 203 n. 107; Rudolph, 70; Petitjean, *Oracles,* 49.

[1] The book of Zechariah commences with a date formula and a formula for the reception of the prophetic word very similar to the language found in Hag. 1:1. In both instances, the reader is informed that the prophetic word was received during the second year of Darius. However, the Zechariah formula provides the dates in a different order—month before year instead of year before month as it appears in Haggai. Also, the Zechariah formula provides less detail than does the Haggai introduction. Haggai reads "Darius the king," whereas Zechariah has the more succinct "Darius." Haggai includes the day of the month on which the oracle was conveyed; Zechariah includes only the year and the month.

Just as Haggai's name resonates with the issue of the restoration of the cult, so too Zechariah's name is significant vis-à-vis the relationship of Yahweh to his people in the late sixth century. The name means, literally, "Yahweh has remembered." For a people decimated by defeat and exile, a prophet who is promising cosmic restoration and who has a name that signifies Yahweh's continuing relationship with his people will be remembered as especially important.

The introductory verse of Zechariah is, when compared with Haggai, expansive at one point—in its identification of Zechariah. Haggai was identified simply as *hannābî',* "the prophet." Zechariah, on the other hand, is introduced as "son of Berechiah son of Iddo, the prophet." This designation of Zechariah differs from the two texts in Ezra that mention him (Ezra 5:1; 6:14), texts that define Zechariah simply as the son of Iddo. As Rudolph rightly points out, we need not assume this difference to comprise a contradiction since the Hebrew word *bēn* can mean grandson as well as son.[1] More to the point is the question of what such a genealogy is meant to signify. That Neh. 12:16, in a listing of priestly houses, includes a "Zechariah" as "of Iddo" suggests strongly that the genealogy in Ezra 5:1 and 6:14, which lists Zechariah just as the son of Iddo, and the genealogy in Zech. 1:1,

---

[1] Rudolph, 67.

which traces Zechariah back another generation to an Iddo, are both emphasizing Zechariah's connections to a priestly house and also to the group of Yahwists that had been in exile. Both claims are achieved by linking Zechariah to Iddo.[2]

When the nuances of Hag. 1:1 and Zech. 1:1 are compared, it becomes clear that Zechariah's authority is defined in terms of his priestly genealogy and his solidarity with the group which had been in Babylon as well as his reception of the prophetic word. The book of Haggai, on the other hand, makes a more limited claim for the authority of Haggai, as a prophet who achieves prominence by conveying the prophetic word.

[2] One might expect an integrated oracular unit to follow the introductory verse. Not so. Verse 2 sits loosely in its present context. There is no indicator of audience for this retrospective statement: "Yahweh was angry with your fathers." The addressee (as the second-person masculine plural pronominal suffix in the phrase "your fathers" implies) is a group and not the prophet himself. And yet, the identity of this group is not provided in a clear fashion. The verse appears to have been drawn from another, and more original, context and used here for a different purpose. The syntax of the phrase in v. 3, *wᵉʾāmartā ʾᵃlēhem*, "you say to them," is just as problematic as to audience identification. The verb, a converted perfect, requires a preceding verb, something other than the *qṣp* in v. 2. And the *ʾᵃlēhem* stands without an appropriate referent. Again, as with v. 2, one senses something drawn out of its original context and placed in a new setting, one appropriate to introduce a book.

Only with the formula "Thus says Yahweh of Hosts" in 3ab do we have something that might be construed as an oracular unit. Here the author sets the tone for this prophetic collection by commenting on the past, and this in a highly unusual way. For the purposes of this author, the past was made up of a particular kind of relationship between two parties. The parties are Yahweh and "your fathers" and the character of the relationship is "anger." The author could have said, as did Deutero-Isaiah, "I am angry with my people." The author of Zech. 1:2 avoids such a statement, for good reason. His formulation serves, on the one hand, to tie those addresses to an earlier generation, their fathers, and, on the other hand, it functions to distinguish between the current generation and that of the fathers.[3] This use of the term "your

[2] Perhaps the Iddo mentioned in Zech. 1:1 is the one mentioned in Neh. 12:4, 16.
[3] In the prophetic corpus, the use of the verb *qṣp* in the qal conjugation with Yahweh as the subject is limited to exilic and postexilic texts.

fathers" to refer to an early and culpable generation is most prominent in Jeremiah and Ezekiel. So Ezek. 20, and especially Jer. 7:25–26, "From the day that your fathers came out of the land of Egypt to this day, I have persistently sent all my servants the prophets to them, day after day, yet they did not listen to me, or incline their ear, but stiffened their neck. They did worse than their fathers." There is, therefore, a history to what Zechariah says in v. 2: "Yahweh was angry because of your fathers." Furthermore, Yahweh is angry because of the way Israel had and has responded to his prophetic agents, of which Zechariah is now one.

The terse formulation in v. 2 has an implication that is warranted by v. 5, the rhetorical question: Your fathers, where are they? The answer to this question is, on the basis of the parallel question (Did they live forever?) is: No, they are dead. And if the fathers are dead, then one might hope that Yahweh's anger had been satiated, since it was the fathers who provoked Yahweh's attack on Judah. The implication of Zechariah's terse retrospective assessment is that Yahweh has been angry—and yet that this anger need not continue.[4]

In sum, this introductory historical comment in v. 2 does at least three things: (1) it summarizes past relationships between Yahweh and Israel; (2) it establishes a link between generations; (3) it allows for a distinction between various generations and their relationships to Yahweh.[5]

[3] Interestingly, the retrospective statement in v. 2 is, in the final form of the text, a "word" to the prophet and not to the larger audience. That which the author or editor wants us to perceive as the oracle to be communicated (vs. 3ff.) is introduced by the problematic phraseology "Now you should say to them." Verse 3 is peculiar in its own right. There are more formulaic words than there are words in the oracle itself. The oracle comprises only four words in Hebrew, *šûbû 'ēlay wᵉ'āšûb 'ᵃlêkem*, "Return to me so that I may return to you," whereas the formula surrounding and even penetrating these words includes ten Hebrew words. The few words of the message seem to be overwhelmed by the more stereotypic phraseology. To be sure, some texts (e.g., LXX) omit the introductory and closing formulae. However, the picture of few words surrounded by "proper" prophetic language is such as to convince one that the formulae belong at the primary level of the book. These formulaic expressions serve to authenticate Zechariah's words in the eyes and ears of the intended audience.

---

[4] See also Isa. 57:16: "for I will not contend forever, nor will I always be angry."
[5] Cf. Ezek. 20 on the same problem.

The oracle itself is framed in the imperative mood. "Return to me!" Again, this is language also shared by the Deutero-Isaianic collection. Cf. Isa. 44:22: "Return to me *(šûbāh 'ēlay)*, because I have redeemed you." The primary verb, *šûb*, is, in both Zechariah and Deutero-Isaiah, an ambiguous word. In Isa. 44:22, we discern language used elsewhere, in Israel's lament rituals, i.e., Yahweh should return to Israel and correct a lamentable situation. Just as Israel could call on Yahweh to return, so too Yahweh could call on Israel to return to him. Joel 2:12 represents a similar sentiment: "Return to Yahweh, your God, for he is gracious and merciful, slow to anger, and abounding in steadfast love, and repents of evil."

In order to return or turn to Yahweh, one must turn from something, i.e., a fundamental reorientation is required for one to turn to Yahweh. Further, such reorientation to Yahweh, whether geographic or metaphoric, and it is probably both in Zechariah with his insistence that people return to Judah from Babylon, is to be done for a concrete reason, so that Yahweh will return to Israel. Language requesting Yahweh to return to Israel was no doubt part of the liturgical language of the exilic and postexilic communities. The oracle "Return to me so that I might return to you" should therefore be read from the perspective of communal laments such as Ps. 126:4, "Restore *(šûbāh)* our fortunes, O Yahweh," and Ps. 85:5 [4E], "Restore us *(šûbēnû)* again."

The response of Zech. 1:3 to such language of collective lament is that Yahweh's return to Judah depends upon a return of the people to Yahweh.

Since there is considerable ambiguity in the language of "return,"[6] return from what or where, the prologue to Zechariah's cycle continues beyond the discrete boundaries of this tersely formulated admonition.

The tone of admonition continues in v. 4 with the command "Do not be like your fathers." What was formulated in vs. 2–3 as two separate issues: "Yahweh was angry with your fathers" and "Return to me," is here integrated into a single thought. The fathers with whom Yahweh was angry were earlier admonished to "return."

[4] From this point in the text, the author or redactor functions as a historian in order to clarify the situation of "your fathers," as it is relevant to those living ca. 520 B.C.E. Of primary importance for this author is the claim that prophets had earlier spoken words similar to

---

[6] The same "return" formula occurs in Mal. 3:7, an apparent borrowing from Zech. 1:3.

those which Zechariah was then proclaiming. Interestingly, the phrase "the former prophets" occurs only in Zechariah 1–8 (see 7:7, 12), and it clearly implies prophetic status for Zechariah. Zechariah stands in a line of prophetic succession, a notion very much in line with the hereditary designation of authority in 1:1. The time of prophecy was not yet past, from the perspective of this writer, though, to be sure, there had been some fundamental changes because of the events surrounding 597–587, changes such that prior to 587, prophets could be grouped together and labeled as "the former prophets."

The first "historical" claim is, therefore, that prophets in an earlier time spoke to the fathers of the Judahites to whom Zechariah was now speaking. The second claim is that of quotation, i.e., v. 4b represents the sort of things that earlier prophets had said. The oracle is introduced with exactly the same formula as that which is used in v. 3 to introduce the admonition directed to the audience of this oracle. This identity of formula is important because it functions to imply, initially, that despite the differences in prophets, former versus contemporary, their authority is identical—they speak Yahweh's words directly, within the context of a particular historical situation. Moreover, the oracles—those of Zechariah and his prophetic predecessors—begin with the same word, *šûbû.* Here, however, the similarity between their discourses ends. Whereas Zechariah's admonition advised the hearer to return to Yahweh, the second *šûbû* continues by advocating the turning *from* evil ways and evil deeds. This putative quotation resembles other prophetic texts, especially those in the books of Jeremiah and Ezekiel.[7]

> Return, every one from his evil way, and amend your ways[8] and your doings. (Jer. 18:11)

> Turn now, every one of you, from his evil way and wrong doings. (Jer. 25:5)

> Turn now every one of you from his evil way, and amend your doings. (Jer. 35:15)

Present in all these texts is the masculine plural imperative *šûbû,* the nouns *derek* (way) and *ma‘ᵃlāl* (deed), and the context of so-called Jeremianic prose. Not dissimilar are certain texts in the book of Ezekiel that admonish Israel to "return" (cf. Ezek. 14:6; 18:30; and, more particularly, Ezek. 33:11, which advocates "return from your evil ways"[9]). One may infer that the author of Zech. 1:4 has viewed

---

[7] Thus also Beuken, 98.

[8] *darkêkem* is missing in Syro-hexaplaric and Lucianic manuscripts.

[9] *hārā‘îm* is missing in LXX.

such texts as Jer. 11:18; 25:5; 35:15; Ezek. 33:11 as typical of pre-586 prophetic language and has appropriated it as the sort of things such prophets said. This activity on the part of the author of Zech. 1:4 presupposes that he had access to some form of the nascent prophetic collections, one that in the case of Jeremiah included the recently written deuteronomistic prose. Zechariah 1:4b comprises not so much a single quotation but the sort of thing people in 520 would have expected such prophets to say.

After the citation from prophets of the past, the historian reported that the fathers did not obey the oracles of the earlier prophets. This is not an innovative judgment. It is, in fact, shared by another postexilic biblical text, II Chron. 24:19. Interestingly though, that text ("Yet he sent prophets among them to bring them back to Yahweh; these testified against them, but they would not give heed") is not a judgment on the downfall of the Judahite state but is, instead, a commentary about Judah's reaction to the prophets.[10] Again, this section of Zechariah, 1:1–6, appears to be a conflation of various statements concerning Israel's interactions with its prophets, especially generalizations in this regard.

[5–6] With vs. 5–6, the historical reprise terminates and the author again explicitly addresses several rhetorical questions to his audience. The first two questions reintroduce two of the parties just discussed, the fathers and the prophets: "As for your fathers, where are they? And the prophets, did they live forever?"

Rhetorical questions they may be, but they do not have obvious answers. The first question, Where are your fathers? inspires at least two different possible answers—they are in exile or they are dead.[11] The second question, which stands in formal parallelism with the first question, is most likely similar in meaning. The second question, Do the prophets live forever? is to be answered in the negative: No, they are mortal. Inspired and powerful though these messengers of God might be, they do not achieve immortality as a result of their services to the deity.[12] In fact, the prophets—who presumably obeyed the

---

[10] Cf. also II Chron. 36:15–16.

[11] Cf. the text in Lamentations, "Our fathers sinned, and are no more; and we bear their iniquities" (Lam. 5:7). This notion suggests strongly the negative connotations that Zechariah's first question might engender.

[12] Some have maintained that the death of the (no doubt) sinful fathers must be that of punishment, and by implication so must the death of the prophets. Hence some have maintained that Zechariah is here referring only to the so-called false prophets. The contrast between both fathers and prophets versus the words of the deity make such a contention inappropriate. Cf. Rudolph, 69; Beuken, 100.

deity—suffered the same fate as those who did not heed the deity's words. Both obedient and disobedient humans belong together in one set when distinguished from the set of realia mentioned in v. 6—"my words and my statutes."

In v. 6, the author does argue that although the prophets (and the fathers) have expired, the power of their words lives on.[13] The word "overtook" *(hiśśîgû)* your fathers. Used this way, this verb bears the distinct military and punitive connotations of the root *nśg*.[14] Yahweh's anger itself may be construed as overtaking his enemies (cf. Ps. 69:25). Clearly, here the words and statutes are understood to be the overpowering curses of Yahweh's covenant with Israel.

Interestingly, this comment on the past is put in the form of a question—did this not happen? Those alive in 520 could affirm an easily remembered history, the events of 597–587. Those acts could clearly be understood as the covenant curses foretold by the prophets. The interpretive structure provided by the prophets assisted those who could perceive that what had happened to Israel was consistent with a fulfillment of Yahweh's words proclaimed by his prophets. Their words lived on, even though they themselves had died.

As a result, they ("your fathers") turned. The word "turned" is the key thematic word in this introductory section of the book.[15] And in a quotation from this group, the language of words and deeds present in v. 4 is reiterated. The events of the defeat and exile are understood as Yahweh's response to errant ways. In sum, the prophet's words, though they had forced the people to return before 587, did in fact allow the people to return after 587. They were effective as punishing, interpreting, and enlivening words.

As a prologue or introduction, these first six verses recount a lamentable history and yet one with a hopeful final note for Zechariah's audience. Although punishment had not been averted, the deity's actions had been properly understood by those who had suffered through the enactment of the covenant's curses. Moreover, they—the people—had finally returned to Yahweh. The stage had been set for restoration and, in this literary setting, for the articulation of Zechariah's visions to that end. The fathers had returned, thereby

[13] On this verse, see Beuken, 101–102, and Lohfink, who views it as a *Promulgationssatz*.

[14] See esp. Hos. 10:9 and Jer. 42:16 and notice the use of *nśg* within the context of covenantal curses overtaking those who have violated the covenant's strictures (as in Deut. 28:15, 45).

[15] For a study of this root, see esp. W. Holladay, *The Root šûbh in the Old Testament,* 1958, 262–263.

reinforcing the imperative to return that Zechariah directed to his audience.[16]

This introduction comprises a pastiche of typical prophetic materials as those were known to the author of this part of the book of Zechariah: typical prophetic formulae, typical prophetic rhetoric, typical prophetic vocabulary.[17] The use of such materials demonstrates Zechariah's place within this prophetic tradition. He stands in a line of prophets, since he is using the same language as they did and since he is admonishing the people to act, to turn, just as did the prophets of old. However, he also seems to be saying that the current generation ("you") may learn from the past. What it took disaster to teach their fathers, they may learn without such punitive measures. But they do need to turn, just as their fathers finally did.

The fathers had repented. The stage was set for a glorious future. Yahweh is enabled to return, if the current generation returns as well. The positive tone of this section is markedly reinforced by the origins of such language of return. Such discourse is at home not in oracles of admonition but in words of salvation.[18] The issue now becomes: How does Zechariah's first vision corroborate or stand in tension with the positive expectation articulated in these first verses of the book?[19]

[16] One senses that the verb "to return" must, in Zechariah, also entail the sense of geographic movement, i.e., from Babylon to Syria-Palestine. For the nonmetaphoric use of *šûb*, see Zech. 1:16; 8:3.

[17] A similar comment on the stereotypic character of the material is made by Beuken, 111, though I do not share his assessment of the disparate origins of these verses.

[18] Thus H. Wolff, "Das Thema, 'Umkehr' in der alttestamentlichen Prophetie," *Gesammelte Studien zum Alten Testament*, 1965, 133–145.

[19] Much has been made, by Beuken among others, about the similarity between the redactional material in Haggai and Zechariah 1–8 and the Chronicler's tradition. It is not surprising, therefore, that Beuken has noticed the striking congruence between II Chron. 30 and Zechariah 1. The text in Chronicles comprises a report of Hezekiah's Passover and, more particularly, a report of the letter that Hezekiah sent throughout the nation exhorting the people to celebrate the Passover in Jerusalem. The exhortation in II Chron. 30—to have the Passover in Jerusalem—is quite a different matter than the admonition in Zech. 1:1–6, which is to "turn" to Yahweh. Nevertheless, the language, especially the use of the verb *šûb* and the reference to the fathers, holds both words together. Despite this similarity in vocabulary, the respective authors appear to be using it in quite different ways. The verb *šûb*, "return," in II Chron. 30 has primary geographic connotations: Return to Yahweh, who resides in Jerusalem. Moreover, the return of Israelites to Jerusalem is linked to the return of people who might return to this land, a reference which in the literary context of Chronicles can only refer to those taken from the land by the Neo-Assyrians, but which, in the historical context of the Chronicler, could mean as well those taken into exile in the sixth century. In sum, although the

Zechariah 1:7-17

All the earth is dwelling peacefully

7   On the twenty-fourth day of the eleventh month, that is the month of Shebat, in the second year of Darius, the word of Yahweh came to Zechariah the prophet, son of Berechiah son of Iddo:

8   I had a vision last night.[a] A man was riding[b] upon a dark chestnut horse. He was positioned among the myrtle bushes[c] which were near[d] the cosmic deep.[e] And behind him were dark chestnut, light bay, and white horses.[f]

9   I said, "What are these, my lord?"
And the messenger who spoke with me said,
   "I will let you see what they are."

10 Then the man[g] who was standing among the myrtle bushes responded,
   "These are they whom Yahweh has dispatched
   to range back and forth over the earth."

11 They[h] then reported to the messenger of Yahweh as he stood among the myrtles:
   "We[h] have ranged back and forth over the earth.
   All the earth is dwelling peacefully."

12 The messenger of Yahweh then responded:
   "How long, O Yahweh of Hosts,
   before you have compassion
      upon Jerusalem and upon the cities of Judah,
      which you have cursed for these past seventy years?"

---

vocabulary of these two texts is remarkably similar, the points being made by their respective authors are quite different.

Beuken, however, adds a form-critical argument to the discussion, stating that both texts include the form of the Levitical sermon (Beuken, 91–92). Here too, in my judgment, there are problems. To be sure, both texts, i.e., Hezekiah's letter and the oracle commencing in Zech. 1:3, begin with imperative discourse. And both texts include reflection on the past. However, especially in this latter section, there is a considerable difference between them. Zechariah is able to point to a past that ends on a positive note, whereas II Chron. 30 ends with an essentially negative judgment. Further, there are no parallels in II Chron. 30 to the issues broached in Zech. 1:5–6, the contrast between the death of humans and the vitality of Yahweh's words. Finally, whereas II Chron. 30:6–9 gives the impression of being a carefully written and rhetorically consistent text, Zech. 1:3–6 appears as a pastiche of prophetic discourse: v. 3—admonition; v. 4—retrospective judgment; vs. 5–6—reflection on the prophetic word and its power.

13 Yahweh then answered the messenger who spoke to me with kind and consoling[i] words.
14 The messenger who spoke to me then said:
Proclaim!
"Thus says Yahweh of Hosts:
I have become very zealous
on Jerusalem's and on Zion's behalf.
15 And I am very angry about the nations which are untroubled.
Though I was only angry for a little while,
they helped turn it into evil.
16 Therefore," thus says Yahweh,
"I am returning with compassion to Jerusalem.
My house shall be rebuilt in her,"
    says Yahweh of Hosts.
"A measuring line shall be stretched out over Jerusalem."
17 Proclaim further:
"Thus says Yahweh of Hosts:
My cities shall again overflow with plenty.
Yahweh will once again comfort Zion.
He will once again choose Jerusalem."

a. Literally, "I saw this night." Cf. NAB, JPS.

b. Or "mounted upon."

c. For MT *bên hahadassîm*, LXX reads "between overshadowing mountains," (i.e., Heb. *hehārîm*). This LXX reading almost certainly represents an attempt to harmonize the imagery of the first with the last vision.

d. Cf. similarly C. Jeremias, *Nachtgesichte*, 115.

e. MT *bammᵉṣulāh*, apparently read as *bammᵉṣillāh* by LXX. MT should be understood as deriving from the root *ṣwl*, *mᵉṣulāh*, "the deep; ocean depth," e.g., Jonah 2:4; Ps. 69:3, 15; Job 41:23; Ex. 15:5. (Thus JPS and Horst, 218. Cf. Rudolph, 72, who translates "place of prayer.")

f. On the horse colors, see commentary. LXX adds a color, apparently by way of harmonizing with the vision in Zech. 6:3, 6 (*psaroi*, dappled). Some commentators propose amending MT *sᵉruqqîm* to *šeḥōrîm* (black), again for the sake of consistency with the vision in Zech. 6.

g. I assume that this individual is the one mentioned in v. 8.

h. The referent of these plural verbs is not specified. We are probably correct in thinking that the riders of the horses are presumed, and not the horses themselves.

i. *niḥumîm* is unusual as an adjective. It is attested as a noun in Isa. 57:18. In Hos. 11:8, *niḥûmāy* is regularly emended to *raḥᵃmāy*.

The First Vision

[7] As was the beginning of the book, so also the cycle of night visions is introduced by a chronological formula. In contrast to the first formula, however, the one introducing the visions is more precise. It specifies not only the day—the twenty-fourth of the eleventh month—but the name of the month as well. The name of the month, šᵉbāṭ, is taken from the Babylonian calendar, as is Chislev in Zech. 7:1.[1] Not only does the royal referent create a different perspective from that which was created by earlier Israelite dating formulae, e.g., "In the fourth year of Jehoiakim the son of Josiah, the king of Judah (Jer. 36:1). The month name, and the calendar with the spring new year which that calendar entails, also witness to the new context for understanding Yahweh's activity. It is an imperial context in which Israel is no longer even a vassal state, much less an independent nation. Reference to the Persian kingdom precludes mention of Israel or Judah or mention of a monarch by means of which to date Zechariah's work. Yahweh's activity must be dated to a Persian king and to the Babylonian calendar which the Persians also used. This introductory formula is therefore of great significance. It does more than simply provide a chronological setting in which Yahweh and Israel find themselves. It emphasizes the "foreign" context in which Yahweh and Israel find themselves—one controlled by a foreign ruler and by foreign vocabulary. And this by way of setting the context for a lament and for visions which display Yahweh vigorously reasserting his cosmic dominion.

[8] With the eighth verse, and the inception of the visionary material, Zechariah 1–8 shifts gears radically from what had occurred in the first verses. Instead of having to do with the previous generation or with Israelites as a group, the concerns enlarge to worldwide scale.

The translation proposed here is one way of handling an awkward formulation in the Hebrew text, the verb "I saw," followed by the noun "night" prefixed by the definite article. Normally one could translate "I saw this night," since the definite article prefixed to units of time indicates the present-tense value, as, for example, haššānāh, "this year." Since there is no preposition, the translation "I saw in the night" could not be easily justified. Surely the referent is to this night just passed, i.e. last night. And as for the use of the verb rā'āh, "to see" as meaning, more specifically, to have a vision, see Isa. 30:10; I Kings

---

[1] These are the earliest attestations of Babylonian month names in the Hebrew Bible. Heretofore, the so-called Canaanite names were used, though the Canaanite name for the eleventh month has not been preserved in the biblical text.

22:17, 19. I take this statement to function as an introduction to all the visions, since there is no ipso facto reason that would have prevented these visions/dreams from being received in one night.[2]

What, then, did Zechariah include in his vision report? He reports, first, an individual riding on horseback. The use of the term *'îš* precludes thinking of this individual as necessarily a mortal. There is a hint of motion—the phrse *rkb 'al* means "riding on" more often than it means simply "mounted upon" (so Num. 22:22 and II Sam. 18:9)—but the emphasis is clearly not on the motion that this mounted rider conveys.[3] Further, at least at first glance, the vision is not populated with mounted cavalry, an image known from martial descriptions elsewhere in the Hebrew Bible (II Sam. 1:6; I Kings 20:20; Jer. 50:42). Rather, we receive the impression of an overall scene with minimal action. The prophet spends more time describing the place at which the horses are located and the horses themselves.

As for the first issue, the place itself, the explicit mention of water and the existence of flora is of signal importance. The term *mᵉṣulāh* is regularly used in the Hebrew Bible to refer to the ocean depth. There is no reason to think, however, that Zechariah envisions the horses hovering above the oceanic deep. Rather, this use of the term "deep" in all likelihood refers to one of the singular places at which the deep bubbles up at the surface of the earth. This notion is attested not only in the biblical imagery, but elsewhere in the northwest Semitic ambit.[4] So, for example, El, the cosmic God of the Canaanite pantheon, is remembered as living on a mountain, at the foot of which water was present. So

> Then they set face
> Toward El at the sources of the Two Rivers
> In the midst of the pools of the Double-Deep.[5]

Clifford has studied this language within the context of the notion of the divine abode and has argued that it reflects old Mesopotamian poetry which places the god in paradise, the source of life-giving waters. Rather than some threatening sinkhole, then, the reference of *mᵉṣulāh* is to the waters that fructify, that allow beneficent life.

This Edenic imagery is further enhanced by reference to flora, *hahᵃdassîm*, which is commonly construed as myrtle shrubs. Myrtle,

---

[2] See the introduction for a discussion of dream sequences in one night.
[3] Thus Rudolph, 74–80, speaks not of a movie but of a moment (*Aufnahme*).
[4] For the biblical examples, see Gen. 2; Ezek. 47; Zech. 13:8; Joel 4:18.
[5] R. Clifford, *The Cosmic Mountain in Canaan and the Old Testament*, 1972, 48.

which is not poisonous (as is its look-alike, oleander), is a rather hardy shrub with dense growth and bright green leaves. It is a striking ornamental plant, giving the impression of well-watered, luxuriant growth.[6] For this reason, a poet living only a few decades before Zechariah could write:

> I will open rivers on the bare heights,
> and fountains in the midst of the valleys;
> I will make the wilderness a pool of water,
> and the dry land springs of water.
> I will put in the wilderness the cedar,
> the acacia, the myrtle, and the olive.
>
>   (Isa. 41:18–19a)

And similarly,

> Instead of the thorn shall come up the cypress;
> instead of the brier shall come up the myrtle.
>
>   (Isa. 55:12)

The first of these texts from Deutero-Isaiah is particularly informative, since, like Zechariah's first vision, it links the presence of water with the presence of myrtle. The two together mark a scene of fertility in Isa. 41:18–19a and in Zech. 1 as well. It is, however, best not to be too precise about assigning a location to this place. It is not the divine dwelling per se, nor is it the official entry into the divine abode. But it is clearly near the divine abode and is inhabited with supernatural beings with a divine mission.[7]

If the place of the scene is a fertile garden near the residence of the deity, what may be said about the creatures that inhabit the garden? A great deal. However, several subsidiary questions must be addressed by way of answering this larger central question.

1. Are the colors themselves, two versions of red and one white significant or symbolic in and of themselves?

---

[6] Contra Bič, *Nachtgesichte*, 11, who perceives this to be related to the cult. Cf. K. Seybold, "Die Bildmotive in den Visionen des Propheten Sacharja," *VT Supp* 26, 1974, 100.

[7] C. Jeremias, *Nachtgesichte*, 1977, 114; Beuken, 239. On this general issue, Jeremias and Horst have noted the combination of motifs in the first and last visions of Zechariah—the myrtle, the two mountains, the watery deep, the marks of the heavenly assembly—and maintained that together they signify the divine dwelling. To be sure, horses and divine council imagery are present in both visions, but the bucolic, pleasant, even peaceful imagery of the first vision is to be contrasted significantly with the metallic straining of the second vision. They picture a different atmosphere, and, if not altogether, a different place.

2. Are the numbers, three colors, or number of horses important to the meaning of the vision?

First, regarding the colors of the horses. Two of the three words present in v. 8 present obvious color characteristics for a horse, red (here rendered "dark chestnut") and white. The third word, *śeruqqîm*, appears much less frequently in Hebrew and probably refers to a light reddish tone, here translated "light bay."[8] Put another way, the colors describe two states of red, dark and light, as well as white.

Perhaps the most obvious question that one needs to ask is whether these colors might reasonably be used to describe horses. Fortunately, descriptions of horse colors occur elsewhere in the ancient Near East and have, as such, been the subject of academic study. Salonen, in particular, has classified descriptions of horse colors according to the historical period in which they were written.[9] Black, white, brown-red, fox red, and dappled are labels that occur from the Old Babylonian through the Neo-Assyrian periods. And if one pursues this issue into modern discussion of animal science, one discovers that there are five basic horse body colors: bay, black, brown, chestnut, and white. One may, therefore, with no difficulty, conclude that Zechariah reports seeing normal horse colors in his vision.[10]

The colors that Zechariah reports here comprise three of the five—and in Zech. 6, four of the five—basic body colors of horses. Further, these body colors are all attested in antiquity. These three colors yield a distinct flavor of verisimilitude to the vision. Zechariah is reporting typical horses with typical horse colors. Had he just seen white horses, one might have greater reason for thinking the horse colors entailed symbolic meaning.[11] According to Xenophon, Persians used white horses to pull cultic wagons. Moreover, Herodotus reports that the Persian magi sacrificed white horses to the river god. In Assyria, white horses were considered holy and played a not insignificant role in the cult of Ashur.[12]

If such a "commonsense" interpretation for the horse colors is available, need one seek further meaning in the specific colors mentioned in Zech. 1:8? Such interpretations have been pursued. (1) Rignell, for example, has argued that in the first vision, two basic

---

[8] See R. Gradwohl, *Die Farben im Alten Testament*, 1963, 21–22; A. Brenner, *Colour Terms in the Old Testament*, 1982, 114–115.

[9] A. Salonen, *Die Landfahrzeuge des alten Mesopotamien nach sumerisch-akkadischen Quellen*, 1951.

[10] Cf., similarly, Seybold, "Bildmotive," 100.

[11] E. Weidner, "Weisse Pferde im Alten Orient," *Bib Or* 9, 1952, 157.

[12] Cf. II Kings 23:11 as a political-religious example of the horse cult in Israel.

colors have been used: red and white.[13] And these two colors symbolize, respectively, war—the spilling of blood, and then victory—weal. (2) Rothstein argues that the three colors are the colors of the sunrise, just before daybreak.[14] Zechariah as priest (Neh. 12:4) could have been at work in the early morning in order to oversee the earliest sacrifices. And he might have seen clouds, in the shape of horses, which were colored by the early rays of the sun. Moreover, myrtle bushes could have been growing on the eastern edge of the temple site. The sunrise could have symbolized a new day, that victory and salvation were dawning for Israel, and the permanent green of the myrtle would have symbolized God's constant capacity for fostering growth, especially as the season of fertility approached. (3) Bič proposes that the three colors symbolize the three world regions: heaven, earth, and sea.[15]

It seems clear that all such virtually allegorical interpretations move far beyond the significance of the colors as they actually occur in the text.

Interestingly, Ensminger[16] attests an Arabian proverb of indeterminate date that deals with four horse colors, all four of which are present in the sixth vision and three of which are present in the first vision:

> The fleetest of horses is the chestnut,
> the most enduring the bay,
> the most spirited the black,
> and the most blessed the white.

This adage is direct testimony for allowing the significance of the colors to reside in the horses themselves and not in allegorical sunrises or in cosmic geography.

In sum, the significance of the vision is not to be plumbed by symbolic exegesis of the horse colors. What the colors do attest is the cogency of the vision as including real horses and not otherworldly creatures, which we see in later visions.

A second major question revolves around the actual number of colors, and by implication, horses themselves. Gese takes the number three, for three colors, seriously and argues that the three colors refer to the three known continents of the ancient world.[17] And yet one

---

[13] Rignell, *Nachtgesichte*, 34, 206.

[14] Rothstein, *Nachtgesichte*.

[15] Bič, *Nachtgesichte*. For another geographic interpretation, see H. Gese, "Anfang und Ende der Apokalyptik, dargestellt am Sacharjabuch," *ZThK* 70, 1973, 20–49.

[16] M. Ensminger, *Horses and Horsemanship*, 1977, 100.

[17] Gese, "Anfang und Ende der Apokalyptik," 34–35.

wonders, how do these specific colors refer to these three continents? There is no direct linkage between brown and Asia, red and Europe, or white and Africa.

One could as well argue that the text does not indicate the critical issue in the contrast between the first and last visions—three colors mentioned in the first vision and four in the final vision. The number four was regularly understood as a symbol of completeness in the ancient world. By inference, therefore, three was a sign of incompleteness. The first vision, with its three colors, communicates that, though things are at rest, they are improperly so. Things are not in balance and will need future resolution before proper stability can be achieved.

Further, it is important to note that the text does not indicate the actual number of horses, just the number of colors. There may be six horses, or twenty-six. All we know is that a dark chestnut horse is in the foreground, and that a herd of unknown proportions is behind it.

For those who insist on emending the number of colors in the initial vision on the basis of the colors in the final vision, there is another series of options: e.g., Duhm—four directions, McHardy—four abbreviated horse colors, and Horst—four planets. However, since these visions are markedly different in imagery and in meaning, an emendation to make them similar is unwarranted.[18]

We may recompose, provisionally, Zechariah's vision report. He has a dream or vision in color, as is typical for most dreams. In that dream, he sees horses which, not surprisingly, have typical horse colors. The vision is of a well-watered, flora-filled place near the divine dwelling. The garden functions rather like a pasture or corral. It is that part of the divine realm in which the horses are quartered. The scene is peaceful and pleasant with minimal movement and disturbance. The scene is Edenic, unlikely to create dissatisfaction. What distinguishes this scene from the normally apprehended world is not the color or number of horses but rather the place itself and its bucolic qualities, a peaceful place beyond the access of normal mortals.

[9] This picture, almost a color slide, is puzzling, so much so that Zechariah immediately asks a question,[19] "What are these, my lord?" "My lord" has not hitherto been introduced either as part of the vision

---

[18] Ibid., 34; C. Jeremias, *Nachtgesichte*, 127; Rudolph, 75.

[19] This simple fact should serve as a damper on speculation about the meaning of various elements in the vision. Zechariah himself offers nothing by way of immediate explanation, a fact that might well lead us to think there is no obvious explanation for the single elements which comprise the total picture.

or as part of the larger literary context. However, since this messenger who functions as interpreter appears not only here but elsewhere in the Hebrew Bible (cf. Dan. 8:10), we may presume his presence to be a given of the genre vision in this particular cultural setting. The text immediately informs us that this individual is a "messenger," one whom Zechariah understands as an individual who will speak regularly with him.

Then, somewhat surprisingly, the messenger offers to show or let Zechariah see (and this by way of continuing the visionary imagery)—rather than offering to explain verbally the significance of that which Zechariah has already seen. This particular vocabulary is important since it serves to project Zechariah back into the visionary world. And we are told, not too subtly, that the vision is not at this point self-interpreting.

[10] The individual whom Zechariah saw riding on a horse, and not the messenger himself, responds to Zechariah's question. Zechariah, apparently while "seeing," is told that "they (the horses) are the ones whom Yahweh has dispatched to range back and forth over the earth." This language of a charge by the deity for someone to range back and forth over the earth is informed significantly by the use of similar language and notions elsewhere in the biblical text.[20] The semidivine beings who make up Yahweh's council range over the face of the earth and report to the deity about human affairs. The vision of Zechariah is therefore linked to the notions of the divine assembly and the ways in which the deity is informed about earth. However, Zech. 1:7 is not a vision of the divine council in session, nor is it of the deity himself. (Cf. the picture of the council itself in I Kings 22 or Isa. 6—contra Jeremias, 117.) Rather, the picture is of the divine garden and corral to which the horses and presumably their riders (though this latter group is not expressly identified) have just returned after an earthly patrol. Zechariah's vision is of a sort of paradise, but a rather unglamorous one; it is a garden in which Yahweh's steeds are quartered, not in which Yahweh himself is readily accessible.

[11] The use of horses to cover the vast distances of the Persian empire is well attested. Herodotus writes:

Nothing mortal travels so fast as these Persian messengers. The entire plan is a Persian invention; and this is the method of it. Along the whole line of road there are men (they say) stationed with horses, in number equal to the number of days which the journey takes, allowing a man and horse to each day; and these men will not be hindered from accomplishing

[20] Cf. Job 1:6; 2:1–2.

at their best speed the distances which they have to go, either by snow, or rain, or heat, or by the darkness of night. (*History,* VII, 98)

This Persian pony express was renowned in its ability to cover vast territory in a variety of directions. And if the Herodotus commentary is apt, we learn that all horses had riders, a fact that allows us to make sense of what follows in Zech. 1:11: "they," the riders, responded to the messenger.

Presumably the fact that they respond to the messenger clarifies the high status of the *mal'āk* as a messenger of the deity. Earlier he was referred to simply as a messenger—now he is the messenger of Yahweh. The ability of the *mal'āk* to move into the scene further emphasizes his preternatural abilities. He is able to communicate with these riders who sit mounted among the myrtle bushes. The visionary process is, at this point, fully consistent with what the *mal'āk* had said earlier to Zerubbabel, "I will let you see what all this means." In order to do this, the messenger himself was constrained to enter the scene, and in so doing he elicited an "internal" interpretation. The riders' report to the *mal'āk*, "We have ranged back and forth over the earth. All the earth is dwelling peacefully." We discover that these riders had a mission to carry out and that it has been completed. They can therefore report about the entire earth that it is—like the garden itself, whose imagery reinforces their message—at rest, peaceful.

There are at least two critical terms in the patrol's report. First, the patrol does not report about one city, one province, or even one empire. The scope of its activity is cosmic. Hence it reports about "all the earth." Equally important is the judgment which the patrol has reached. It reports that the earth is dwelling peacefully. This term "peacefully," *šōqāṭet,* is regularly used to describe geographic areas: cities (II Chron. 23:21), nations (Josh. 11:23; Jer. 48:11), and even "all the earth" (Isa. 14:7), regions not involved in military activity or civil strife. The participial construction, living in peace, may be used to describe a group of people living at peace, so Judg. 18:7. And interestingly, this term is used as something of an antonym for Yahweh's military activity, and this especially in exilic and postexilic prophet texts: cf. Ezek. 16:42; 38:11; Isa. 62:1; Jer. 47:6–7. If Yahweh acts as divine warrior, he is not *šqṭ* (see esp. Isa. 62:1). Especially informative is Jer. 47:6–7, a text in which lament language is used in connection with the notion of rest, the converse of the situation in Zech. 1: "Woe, sword of Yahweh, how long until you rest? Put yourself into your scabbard, rest and be still!" (Jer. 47:6).

The report of the messengers is, therefore, of cosmic peace, both of the deity and of the world. It is a report reinforced by the bucolic garden. All the world, including the divine dwelling and its surroundings, is restful. The specific elements in the vision serve to authenticate this theme in the text. There is no disturbance, whether by earthly or divine agents. For most Israelites at most times in their history, this message would have been utterly welcome. Not so this time.

[12] In v. 12, the peaceful scene is shattered. Just as in Jer. 47:6–7 a lament is uttered by way of responding to the absence of Yahweh's peace, so here, the *mal'āk* utters a lament about the presence of cosmic peace. The *mal'āk* responds to the status quo and in so doing makes a sudden shift in the workings of the vision, just as he did by engaging the members of the divine patrol in conversation (v. 11). As a result of the special surroundings in which this vision takes place, the divine garden and pasture-stable, the *mal'āk* is apparently spurred to address the deity himself, "Yahweh of Hosts." And it is no accident that he uses this particular title for Yahweh, since the term "hosts" has explicit military connotations.[21] The *mal'āk* seeks an end to the peaceful state of the cosmos precisely through the instrumentality of this Yahweh, who had an army, who could act as divine warrior.

The form of speech which the *mal'āk* uses is significant, if for no other reason than that it virtually requires a divine response. The *mal'āk* introduces his speech with a phrase that has distinct associations in the Hebrew poetic corpus: *'ad-mātay,* "How long?" This term regularly occurs near the beginning of an individual or a communal lament, so for example in individual laments, Pss. 6:4; 13:3, and in communal laments, Pss. 79:5; 80:5; 90:13. Research on the function of the lament within the ritual context of ancient Israel has demonstrated that the lament was regularly spoken in the temple context. Either at some point during the recitation of the lament, or after the lament had been completed, an officiant priest would speak words of weal, a priestly oracle of salvation, words that would be construed as having answered the lament of the worshiper. Only such a procedure can explain the expressions of thanksgiving that regularly recur near the end of many laments. Though the normal context for laments was the temple and its services, the time at which this vision was thought to have been received precluded the normal temple function; there was no temple. However, since the temple was the prototype of the divine dwelling, the heavenly dwelling, and since this first vision of Zechariah apparently envisioned an area near to the

---

[21] See, e.g., P. Miller, *The Divine Warrior in Ancient Israel,* 1973, 152–153.

divine dwelling, it was natural indeed for the *mal'āk* to utter a lament in this place.

Zechariah has used a rhetorical form that is designed to elicit a response from the deity and to call attention to the plight of the now incomplete cultic center, the temple complex.

The stereotypic quality of the phrase *'ad-mātay* in most laments present in the Psalms is pronounced. One does not expect a direct answer to the question, and such temporal responses do not often occur in oracles of salvation. In vs. 12ff., one senses that the phrase *'ad-mātay* does, in fact, have a more specific temporal connotation than it normally bears in liturgical texts,[22] and this because the question concludes with a comment about a specific period of time, seventy years.

What, precisely, has the *mal'āk* done in this specific lament? One may answer this question by pointing to three specific issues, each of which requires brief discussion.

1. The language that Zechariah uses to describe Yahweh's attitude toward Jerusalem and Judah is especially appropriate to the formulation of a lament. So, for example, Ps. 79:8, a communal lament, includes the following formulation:

> Do not remember against us the iniquities of our forefathers;
> Let your mercy come speedily to meet us.

The Hebrew word for mercy in this psalm is *rḥm*, the same word used in Zech. 1:12, "How long will you have no mercy?" Similarly, in Ps. 7, an individual lament, the following sentence occurs (v. 11):

> God is a righteous judge
> and he never curses.[23]

Here too, the notion of cursing, present in the psalm lament, is also integral to the lament spoken by the *mal'āk*. Yahweh has cursed Jerusalem and the cities of Judah for decades. The two verbs that the author has used to describe Yahweh's attitude toward Israel are therefore appropriate to the language of lament. They belong to the language of lament as that is attested elsewhere in the Israelite psalm corpus. When Yahweh is said "not to have mercy," and indeed "to curse," there is necessarily a lamentable situation.

2. The attitudes and actions of Yahweh are understood as taken in relation to particular entities: Jerusalem and the cities of Judah. This

---

[22] Cf. the usage in Isa. 6:11a.
[23] Reading *'al* for *'el* with LXX.

particular description is interesting because it suggests that the lament has a focus larger than the destroyed temple, one place in the city of Jerusalem. This notion of lament for something more than the destruction of the temple is attested elsewhere, as in Ps. 69:36 [35E], another lament:

> For God will save Zion
> and rebuild the cities of Judah.[24]

However, the extent of the area, the cities of Judah mentioned in this psalm, is difficult indeed to specify. It might be claimed that the poetic parallel "Jerusalem/cities of Judah" is simply a case of synonymous parallelism, that "cities of Judah" really means nothing more than Jerusalem and the immediately surrounding environs. And in some texts, the pair does appear to constitute no more than synonymous parallelism.[25] However, as evidence of a certain regional expectation for future weal, some texts refer to the cities of Judah alone as destroyed (Jer. 5:17, "your fortified cities"; and Jer. 10:22, "cities of Judah"). Similarly there is a distinct regionalism in the promises of restoration: "Say to the cities of Judah, Behold your God" (Isa. 40:9; cf. 61:4).

Further emphasizing the regionalism of this lament and expected restoration are two other texts, one from Zechariah 1–8. Zechariah 7:7 speaks of a former time "when Jerusalem was inhabited and in prosperity, with her cities round about her, and the South and the lowland were inhabited." Jerusalem is and shall be in the future no island. Similarly, in Neh. 11:1–3, we learn that residents of Judah could be divided on the basis of where they lived—whether in Jerusalem or in "the towns of Judah." Thus Neh. 11:3 states: "These are the chiefs of the province who lived in Jerusalem, but in the towns of Judah every one lived on his property in their towns." Jerusalem, even as a cult center, was not a city in isolation.[26]

The importance of cities qua cities for postexilic Judah is evident from the names given to the districts that made up the governate of Judah.[27] These districts were named for the regional centers located in

---

[24] Cf. Isa. 64:10.

[25] Lam. 5:1; Jer. 7:17, 34; Isa. 44:26.

[26] The extent to which these expectations of the restored cities of Judah reflects a hope for the reappearance of the "fortified cities of Judah" is unclear; cf. Jer. 34:7; 26:2; II Chron. 17:9; 31:1.

[27] M. Avi-Yonah, *The Holy Land from the Persian to the Arab Conquests,* 1966. Interestingly, Jer. 40:5 states that Gedaliah, whom the king of Babylon appointed as governor of Judah, was appointed over the cities of Judah.

them, and so, similarly, were the subdistricts (see Neh. 3). In sum, the lament on behalf of Jerusalem and the cities of Judah points to a regional notion of community, not simply an exclusive urban focus on Jerusalem.[28]

3. In the lament, the *mal'āk* has specified the length of the period during which Yahweh has not had mercy upon Jerusalem and the cities of Judah. This feature is highly unusual since laments do not regularly include a description of the length of the lamentable state.[29]

Of course, one of the problems raised by this phrase is, which seventy-year period is meant if a specific seventy-year period is actually presumed? If one takes literally the date introducing this vision, the second year of Darius, which is 520 B.C.E., and if one takes the seventy-year period literally, the presumed period extends from 590/89 to 520/19. As Rudolph notes, Neo-Babylonian preparations for the siege against Jerusalem were taking place as early as 589/88 and Jerusalem was defeated in 588/87. Hence an obvious seventy-year period, ca. 590–520, would make sense as the lamentable time referred to in Zech. 1:12. Such was the extent of Judahite diaspora, a time when the temple was in ruins.[30] This particular seventy-year period also would fit the use of that phrase in Zech. 7:4.[31]

The issue is however, complicated because this phrase, "seventy years," is present elsewhere in ancient Near Eastern texts, both biblical and extrabiblical. Lipiński[32] notes that this same time period is used to describe the length of time during which a god, Marduk, would show displeasure toward Babylon. And in an Isaianic oracle against Tyre, we learn that Tyre would "be forgotten for seventy years" (Isa. 23:15). Such evidence strongly suggests the existence of a literary convention by which seventy years was the standard length for a period in which a nation suffers degradation because of divine displeasure. And one may infer that when the number is used, it should not be taken in a rigidly literal way.

[28] On regional interaction, see Jer. 36:9.

[29] There is little warrant to follow C. Whitley, "The Term Seventy Years Captivity," *VT* 4, 1954, 63, in excising *'ªšer zā'amtāh zeh sib'îm šānāh* at the end of 1:12.

[30] Thus also, among others, C. Jeremias, *Nachtgesichte,* 131, 135.

[31] On the notion of a seventy-year period, see Whitley, "The Term Seventy Years Captivity," 60–73; A. Orr, "The Seventy Years of Babylon, *VT* 6, 1956, 304–306; P. Ackroyd, "Two Old Testament Historical Problems of the Early Persian Period," *Journal of Near Eastern Studies* 17, 1958, 23–27; C. Jeremias, *Nachtgesichte,* 131–138; Petitjean, *Oracles,* 311–312; and the standard commentaries.

[32] E. Lipiński, "Recherches sur le livre de Zacharie," *VT* 20, 1970.

The use of the phrase "seventy years" in the book of Jeremiah is another example of this convention:[33]

These nations shall serve the king of Babylon seventy years. (Jer. 25:11)

When seventy years are completed for Babylon, I will visit you. (Jer. 29:10)

Here, quite clearly, the seventy-year period refers to a period of Babylonian rule in the ancient Near East, and not necessarily to a period of Judahite suffering. If one calculates the fall of Babylon at 539, at a time when the Neo-Babylonian empire ceased to exercise a significant role, then a literal calculation of the seventy-year rule of Babylon would extend back to about 610, which is only two years after the fall of Nineveh to the Neo-Babylonians. The year 612, in a very real way, represented the symbolic beginning of Babylonian rule in the ancient Near East.[34]

The use of the seventy-year convention in Jeremiah has quite a different referent than does its use in Zechariah. Whereas in Zechariah the seventy years refers to a lengthy period of Judahite devastation, a time in which Babylonian rule gives way to Persian dominion, the seventy years in Jeremiah refers to the period during which Babylon would exercise hegemony in the Near East. In both the Jeremianic and the Zechariah usages of this seventy-year motif, what is surprising is the extent to which this convention comes very close to the actual period which it purports to describe: in Jeremiah, the period of Babylonian rule, and in Zechariah, the period of Judahite degradation.

In retrospect, what strikes one is the "creative conventionality" of this lament. It is an assemblage of time-worn elements appropriate to laments of all sorts (e.g. *'ad-mātay,* "How long?" also "Have compassion"; "You have cursed"). What is unique in this particular lament is the use of the seventy-year convention. The conventional character of this temporal span allows us to understand more fully what the *mal'āk* was doing in this utterance. This is no *vaticinium ex eventu.* Rather, the *mal'āk* appears to be saying, the time for divine displeasure as that is known throughout the ancient Near East, a period of "seventy years," is now about over. And yet the cosmos still appears to be at rest. The lament is therefore not over the situation of Judah but rather about the expected end to the divine displeasure which all Judahites knew would eventually come. Deutero-Isaiah had been saying this several decades earlier. Therefore, the cry *'ad-mātay*

---

[33] On the relation of the Jeremianic to the Zecharian use of this tradition, see C. Jeremias, *Nachtgesichte,* 1977, 133–138.

[34] Cf. the later use of this seventy-year tradition in II Chron. 36:21 and Dan. 9:2.

achieves a certain penetrating quality. If not "seventy years," how long indeed? The rest which the riders report violates the expected end to Yahweh's seventy-year displeasure with Judah. How much longer, the messenger asks on behalf not only of Zechariah but all Judahites, will Yahweh, who, as his title "Yahweh of military troops" ("of hosts") suggests, has cosmic power and military might, wait before again taking pleasure in and comforting his people?

[13] In v. 13, the first answer to this individually expressed but nonetheless communal lament comes in a most prosaic way. Rather than recording a priestly oracle of salvation[35] (words of the deity conveyed directly to the person who makes a lament), v. 13 presents only a narrative description of the divine response. The *mal'āk* apparently hears words of comfort, "good words, consoling words." The lack of visual language and the repetition of *dᵉbārîm*, "words," emphasizes the verbal character of this communication. The communication between the *mal'āk* and Yahweh is not visual, though it is recounted within the context of Zechariah's vision. Zechariah sees nothing; and we are not sure that he has heard anything. How these words, good as they are, address the lamentable state of Jerusalem and the cities of Judah, we do not know. Presumably, they are somehow like those presented in the two oracles preserved in vs. 14–17, words that the *mal'āk* presents to Zechariah. However, all the text tells us explicitly is that Yahweh, in a veiled way consistent with his action and presence up to this point in the vision, responds positively to the lament of the *mal'āk*.

[14] Once the interaction between the deity and the *mal'āk* terminated, the *mal'āk* again turned to Zechariah, in v. 14, this time with a command: "Proclaim." Such an imperative to speak out is not without a certain history both in the book of Zechariah and elsewhere in sixth-century B.C.E. literature. Though not used in the imperative in v. 4, the same verb *qr'* is used there to describe the activity of earlier prophets: "They proclaimed to your fathers." To be a prophet was to *qr'*. Similarly, *qr'* in the imperative mode is used in the command to the personified Zion in the context of the commissioning narrative in Isa. 40:1–11. There, within the context of a divine council setting,[36] someone said, "Proclaim," whereupon the prophetess Zion responded, "What shall I proclaim?" After the stereotypic objection, "All flesh is grass," we hear that which Zion is supposed to proclaim:

---

[35] On the priestly oracle of salvation, see the classicial study of J. Begrich, "Das priesterliche Heilsorakel," *ZAW* 52, 1934, 81–92.

[36] Cf. the commissioning narrative in Isa. 6.

Say to the cities of Judah,
"Behold your God."
(Isa. 40:9c)

She is to tell the cities of Judah that Yahweh is coming as divine warrior and that he will treat those in exile as a shepherd treats his flock. Noteworthy here is a certain commonality of texts in Deutero-Isaiah and Zechariah. In both, the prophet is understood as a "proclaimer." In both, the object of the prophet's discourse is identified explicitly as the cities of Judah. And, in both texts, the notion of Yahweh coming (Isa. 40:10 and Zech. 1:16) is prominent. The command to proclaim is, therefore, a command to engage in prophetic activity as such activity was understood in the middle of the sixth century B.C.E. It is not, however, a commissioning narrative in the full form-critical sense of that term.[37] The command of the *mal'āk* to Zechariah does not introduce him into his prophetic role or provide a general warrant for that role. Rather, the command introduces a particular message—two oracles that the prophet, as prophet, is supposed to proclaim.

What is Zechariah commanded to proclaim and how is it similar to and yet different from that which the prophetess Zion, in Isa. 40, is required to do? One is immediately impressed by the structural complexity of the oracle material that is preserved in Zech. 1:14–17. The material is so complex that critical opinion in the last century has favored identifying only a core of genuine Zechariah speech in these verses. In order to make such judgments, however, the form-critical issues must be surveyed. If we follow the standard formal markers, similar to those which occur elsewhere in the prophetic corpus, we may delineate the following structure in the text:

v. 14   "Proclaim"
Messenger formula: "Thus says Yahweh of Hosts"

vs. 14b–15   Reason

v. 16   "Therefore, thus says Yahweh"

v. 16b   Action

v. 17   "Proclaim" again
Messenger formula: "Thus says Yahweh of Hosts"
Oracle of promise

---

[37] N. Habel, "The Form and Significance of the Call Narratives," *ZAW* 77, 1965, 297–323.

On purely structural grounds, it would appear that Zechariah is presented with two different oracles, both of which represent formal types well attested in the prophetic literature. On formal grounds, there is little reason to question the intelligiblity of this material.[38]

The first of these oracles is bipartite. It comprises a reason for and then a statement of Yahweh's beneficent action. The reason, vs. 14b–15, is itself made up of two quite different elements. On the one hand, Yahweh is zealous for Jerusalem and Zion. This particular expression of Yahweh's intense relation to this place is relatively infrequent in the Hebrew Bible. It is attested in Joel 2:18; Zech. 8:2; and Ezek. 39:25. All these texts appear to date to the post–587 context in Israel.[39] The oracle in Zech. 8:2 is difficult. One may, however, observe that Yahweh's jealousy is related to his wrath *(ḥmh)*. It is interesting to observe precisely that which such zeal entails in the non-Zechariah texts. In Ezek. 39:25, we learn that such zeal is associated with Yahweh's promise ("I will be jealous for my holy name") to restore Israel: to have mercy, to bring the people back to the land. And in Joel 2:18, "Then Yahweh became jealous for his land, and had pity on his people" is part of Yahweh's response to a communal lament which almost surely reflects the devastation of the sixth century. The divine response to the lament in Joel is instructive because it is remarkably similar to Hag. 2:19. Both texts express well-being for the returned and newly established community, and there is a promise of "grain, wine, and oil." Such is an appropriate response to the lament expressed in Joel, and such is an appropriate response to the apparent agricultural failures as those are attested in the book of Haggai. Yahweh's zeal for Israel, whether in Ezekiel as an expression for return or in Joel as an expression of viable and productive existence, is not simply a deeply felt emotion, as the typical translation of "jealousy" would suggest. In these two cases, Yahweh acts in a particular way because of his jealousy.[40] Hence we should expect the expression of zeal in Zech. 1:14b to imply, as well, beneficent action on behalf of Jerusalem/Zion.

[15] On the other hand, Yahweh is related to another entity, and this in quite a different way.[41] If Yahweh is zealous for Jerusalem/Zion, he is also angry with the nations which are untroubled. And

---

[38] See Beuken's position on this point, op. cit., 243.

[39] On this basic point see Petitjean, *Oracles*, 79ff.; Rudolph, 79.

[40] On the notion of Yahweh's jealousy, see Baldwin, 101–103; Petitjean, *Oracles*, 79–81.

[41] Note the continued use of "emotional" language, first jealousy, then anger.

here we return to the interpretation of the earlier vision. Surely the "untroubled nations" represent the same notion as "all the earth dwelling peacefully." Since these nations have provoked Yahweh's anger, there is a reason for this emotion, and this in contrast to the absence of a specific reason for his zeal. The nations have turned Yahweh's action to evil. The nations as instruments of Yahweh's purpose have overstepped their bounds. What Yahweh intended to happen for a short time period, they have improperly extended. One senses here the linkage between the lament of the *mal'āk* (these past seventy years) and the divine response (a little while). Both the *mal'āk* and the deity are using time language. And interestingly, the *mal'āk* and Yahweh appear to agree that things have gone on too long. They have continued beyond the time that Yahweh had originally intended. What was originally conceived as proper chastisement has been turned into evil.

This notion of nations which have gone beyond what they were supposed to do is present elsewhere in sixth-century literature. Compare Deutero-Isaiah:

> Sit in silence, and go into darkness,
>   O daughter of the Chaldeans;
> for you shall no more be called
>   the mistress of kingdoms.
> I was angry with my people,
>   I profaned my heritage;
> I gave them into your hand,
>   you showed them no mercy;
> on the aged you made your yoke exceedingly heavy.
> You said, "I shall be mistress for ever,"
>   so that you did not lay these things to heart
>   or remember their end."
>
> (Isa. 47:5–7)

This oracle against a nation, Babylon, is made because of Babylon's improper exercise of power toward the object of Yahweh's anger, Israel. More particularly, Babylon is indicated because she showed no mercy (*rḥm;* so also Zech. 1:12, "How long will you have no mercy?"), and because she thought she would be a "mistress forever." Both the kind of the action (the lack of mercy) and the length of the presumed action (forever) serves to indict Babylon. However, there is a difference between the viewpoint of Deutero-Isaiah and that of Zechariah. For Deutero-Isaiah, the length of Babylon's hegemony is at issue, but for Zechariah, Babylon is no longer the issue at all. Babylonian hegemony had ended almost two decades prior to the time of Zechariah's visions. Instead, the issue is the continued degradation of the Judahite community. Despite the destruction of the neo-Babylonian empire, and despite the installation of a beneficent Cyrus and later Darius on the Persian throne, the temple in Jerusalem had not yet been rebuilt. Judah was still a nonentity on the international scene. And there was no reason to expect a radical change, because all the earth was dwelling peacefully under the now-secure rule of Darius. For Zechariah, therefore, anger at specific foreign nations is no longer appropriate in quite the same way that it was for Deutero-Isaiah. The scene had changed radically with the "punishment of the Babylonians" and with the beneficent rule of the Persians. There is no easy target, i.e., a particular foreign nation, against which Yahweh can be angry.

Displeasure with the one in control, Yahweh, seemed more appropriate, hence the existence of a lament to the deity by the *mal'āk*. In Deutero-Isaiah we also read:

> For a brief moment, I forsook you,
>> but with great compassion I will gather you.
> In overflowing wrath for a moment
>> I hid my face from you,
> but with everlasting love I will have compassion on you,
>> says Yahweh, your Redeemer.
>
> (Isa. 54:7–8)

Again, time language and the character of the action are the two critical categories. However, here the time language is that of brevity; Yahweh had intended the anger, his anger, to be brief; and yet, by reference back to Isa. 47:5–7, the nations had subverted that purpose and made it last longer than Yahweh intended. However, common to Isa. 47:5–7 and 54:7–8, and to Zech. 1:12, is a notion of Yahweh's anger and curse against Israel. The issue is not foreign nations but the contrast between Yahweh's expected graceful action and the perceived continuation, improperly so, of Yahweh's anger. The *mal'āk,* in fact, laments precisely about the absence of the compassion *(rḥm)* which is promised by Deutero-Isaiah; there the same verb is used to describe Yahweh's anger as is used in Zech. 1:15 *(qṣp)*. The issue now, as the *mal'āk* presents it, is Yahweh's attitude toward Israel. He has seen to it that Babylon has been punished. Nations are at ease, and yet no one nation is to be indicted.

The "reason" part of the oracle establishes the grounds for Yahweh's action by referring to two different parties and two different motivations: zeal for a city, Jerusalem, and anger at certain undefined nations.

[16] In v. 16, introduced by the messenger formula, is a statement by Yahweh of what will happen to redress the situation. We are told three basic things. First, the verb šûb is used to depict what Yahweh is about to do or what he has just done.[42] In the introductory oracle of the book, vs. 1–6, the verb šûb is used to define action appropriate to the people: they should return or turn. Now it is Yahweh who is turning or returning. Does this assertion mean he will be present again in Jerusalem, i.e., in his house? Or does it indicate a quality of attention that Yahweh will now direct toward Jerusalem? The text is ambiguous, and probably intentionally so. On the one hand, with the reconstruction of the temple, Yahweh can properly be spoken of as residing in Jerusalem—he can (meta)physically return to his house. On the other hand, since Zechariah emphasizes the existence of the deity's cosmic abode as evidenced by the presence of the divine garden in the first vision, the notion of Yahweh turning toward Jerusalem with favor is equally apt. Whether turning toward or returning, Yahweh will act with rḥm, and this in response to the complaint of the mal'āk, in 1:12, that Yahweh has no mercy on Jerusalem.[43]

If the first colon is somewhat vague, the next two cola indicate the sort of effects that Yahweh's presence will create.

> My house shall be rebuilt in her . . .
> A measuring line shall be stretched out over Jerusalem.

What precisely do these apparent words of weal signify? First, they entail the reconstruction of the temple, pure and simple. What is not said here is as important as what is said. The use of the passive voice allows the agent of this reconstruction to remain veiled. We do not know who will build the temple or how it will be built. Those issues are not of interest—and this in direct contrast to Haggai. Second, and more interesting, is the statement that a measuring line, qāwh, will be stretched out over Jerusalem. (It is important to observe that this is a different word from the measuring cord mentioned in Zech. 2:5 [1E], ḥebel.) This notion of stretching out a measuring line is ambiguous. It is used in both a constructive and a destructive sense in the Hebrew Bible. And in both these senses it may be used literally as well as metaphorically. As for the destructive sense, examples of literal uses include:

---

[42] There is an apparent problem with the tense of the verb (see Rudolph, 79).
[43] Cf. Ezek. 10:18–22; 11:22–23; 43:1–5 on Yahweh's return to Jerusalem.

> Yahweh determined to lay in ruins
> 　the wall of the daughter of Zion;
> He marked it off by the line;
> 　he restrained not his hand from destroying.
> 　　　　　　　　　　　　　　　(Lam. 2:8)

and of more metaphoric senses:

> He shall stretch the line of confusion over it,
> 　and the plummet of chaos over its nobles.
> 　　　　　　　　　　　　　　　(Isa. 34:11)

Even more important for this text are the so-called constructive uses of this image. Literally: "The carpenter stretches a line, he marks it out with a pencil; he fashions it with planes, and marks it with a compass" (Isa. 44:13). And a constructive metaphoric instance would be:

> Who determined its measurements—surely you know!
> 　Or who stretched the line upon it?　(Job 38:5)

Most important of all are those texts in which the image of measuring by means of a line is used in the language of the restoration of Judah:

> Going on eastward with a line in his hand, the man measured a thousand cubits, and then led me through the water; and it was ankle-deep. (Ezek. 47:3)

> Behold, the days are coming, says Yahweh, when the city shall be rebuilt for Yahweh from the tower of Hananel to the Corner Gate. And the measuring line shall go out farther, straight to the hill Gareb, and shall then turn to Goah.　(Jer. 31:38–39)

To stretch the line, in the last two contexts, is to measure the extent of Yahweh's restorative blessing. The marvelous cosmic water attested in Ezekiel and the expanded city in Jeremiah both reflect a new reality, not simply a reconstruction of Jerusalem. Hence, we may well infer that the urban renewal implied in v. 16 will be preternatural.

The first oracle, then, an oracle of promise, gives reasons for Yahweh's actions and sets forth several different ways in which Yahweh's beneficent action will develop toward his holy city, Jerusalem.

[17] There is every reason to think that v. 17 introduces yet another oracular response to the lament of the *mal'āk,* another of the "gracious and comforting words" from Yahweh. Unfortunately, commentators have been so impressed by the disjunction between vs. 16 and 17 that they have said little about the latter, other than that it is a secondary addition to the text, or an expansion of v. 16. That v. 17 is structurally

distinct from the preceding oracle is clear. It commences with the messenger formula "Thus says Yahweh of Hosts," which is introduced here by the same command that is present in v. 14, *qᵉrā' lē'mōr*, "Cry aloud," here joined with the particle *'ôd*, "again." This structural integrity is, however, in itself no argument for the secondary character of v. 17. Rather, this second oracle is simply of a different basic type. Unlike the prior oracle, v. 17 offers no reason for the good news, because no such reason is structurally necessary in an oracle of this type. Just as the priestly oracle of salvation provides immediate words of weal to the petitioner and no reasons need be given to the supplicant, so v. 17, constructed in the mold of the priestly oracle of salvation, is an immediate response to the lament of the *mal'āk*. On purely structural grounds, therefore, v. 17 is every bit as cogent a response to the *mal'āk*'s lament as is the oracle of promise in vs. 14–16. It is an answer directly tied to the specific language of the lament. Whereas the *mal'āk* speaks about "Jerusalem and the cities of Judah," the oracle of salvation speaks of "my cities, Zion/Jerusalem." "The cities of Judah" in v. 12 have become "my cities" in v. 17. In sum, there is significant reason to think that the latter verse is an appropriate response to the lament of the *mal'āk* and not simply a secondary accretion to the text.

When one compares the first with this second oracular response to the lament of the *mal'āk*, one is impressed by the pragmatically prosaic language of the first oracle and, by contrast, the richer, more allusive language in the final oracle. Whereas in vs. 14–16 we hear about a house being rebuilt and a measuring device being employed, in v. 17 we read, "My cities will again overflow with plenty."[44] One might expect the more typical imagery of mountains dripping with sweet wine or hills flowing with milk, as in Joel 4:18 [3:18E]. But here it is urban—or perhaps better, suburban—centers that are overflowing with prosperity. The image is unusual, this metaphor of urban prosperity flowing over the brim (of the city wall?). Secondly, Yahweh will comfort Zion. Again, we normally expect this verb, *nḥm*, to be used to define the actions of a people or god toward other people. But here Zion, a place, is personified. Zion, a rocky ridge, is conceived as a person who can be comforted. Here, Zechariah uses the language of another poet, Deutero-Isaiah. The very first words in Isa. 40, the famous imperatives, provide the background for Zechariah's rhetoric: "Comfort, comfort my people . . . Speak tenderly to Jerusalem." The verb *nḥm* is used in Isa. 40 and in the Zechariah text. However, in the

---

[44] A not well attested sense of *pwṣ*; cf. Prov. 5:16.

Deutero-Isaiah formulation, the ambiguity of people and place is expressed concretely (my people/Jerusalem), whereas in Zechariah all explicit language is that of place (cities, Zion, Jerusalem). Only by using the technique of personification is Zechariah able to express sentiments similar to those of Deutero-Isaiah. Thirdly, Yahweh will choose Jerusalem. This is a rather remarkable assertion. As Petitjean aptly observes,[45] Zechariah is the only prophet who speaks of an election, a choosing of Jerusalem (1:17; 2:16 [12E]; 3:2). This notion of Yahweh "choosing" is more regularly associated with the choosing of the Davidic house.[46] Nevertheless, the verb *bḥr* is used to describe Yahweh's designation of Jerusalem outside the prophetic corpus (see, e.g., I Kings 8:44, 48, "the city which you have chosen"). In this context, the choosing of Jerusalem is contingent with the placement of "the house," the temple, which is in that city. And in I Kings 11, while the temple is not explicitly mentioned along with the "Jerusalem which I have chosen" (vs. 13, 32), the presence of the temple is implied in v. 36, where Yahweh speaks of "the city where I have chosen to put my name." By way of contrast, Zechariah's use of this language of election in 1:17 includes no specific mention of the temple. The emphasis appears to be exclusively on the city, not on the building of the temple.

Verse 17 is therefore replete with rich language. Expressions such as cities overflowing; Yahweh comforting Zion; and Yahweh choosing Jerusalem tap fundamental ideas of blessings and election, and even basic notions about the character of Yahweh in Israel's religious heritage.

On purely formal grounds, the richness of this oracular response to the lament is colored by the tension between first- and third-person discourse in this terse utterance: "my cities" versus "Yahweh." This tension is real and can probably be explained if we infer that v. 17 is constructed from originally independent phrases from Zechariah's utterances. This lack of agreement in person is, however, consistent with the hazy presence of the deity for Zechariah—immediate and yet intermediate. And the consistency between lament and oracle of salvation—the explicit focus on place and not on people—makes v. 17 an utterly appropriate response to the *mal'āk*'s lament.

On purely formal grounds, then, the conclusion of the first vision block, vs. 7–17, presents two separate oracles that Zechariah is commanded to proclaim, examples of Yahweh's gracious words to the *mal'āk*. The first, an oracle of promise, has a bipartite structure

[45] Petitjean, *Oracles,* 71.
[46] See, e.g., I Sam. 10:24; 16:8, 9, 10; Ps. 78:70.

(reason-action) and focuses on the reconstruction of Jerusalem and the temple. The second is an oracle of salvation, the genre expected following a lament. In this oracle (v. 17) the issue of reconstruction per se, that very pragmatic issue, is not broached. Rather, the rich language of election and weal is used to describe Yahweh's response to the lament. In neither oracle, is the question of the *mal'āk,* "How long?" answered in any specific way. However, the stereotypic position of the question in laments should prevent one from presuming that some specific response in temporal terms was expected. It was enough to know that Yahweh would act on behalf of the petitioner, in this case, on behalf of the concerns of the *mal'āk* as they affect the cities of Judah.

If one may identify an odd element in this divine response to the *mal'āk,* it is that Yahweh's action in the future is directed—explicitly, at least—only toward Israel. He will act beneficently toward Jerusalem; it will be "chosen" and rebuilt. Further, the cities of Judah will be viewed as Yahweh's cities, and as such they will grow prosperous. There is, however, in the first vision block no explicit indication that Yahweh will act cosmically with or against the nations, and this despite the fact that it is "the world at rest" which elicits the lament from the *mal'āk.* In a way, this silence about foreign nations is understandable, since the foreign nation that destroyed Judah had itself been destroyed by the time of Zechariah. Babylon had fallen in 539 B.C.E. And the Persian empire with Cyrus, and now Darius, at its head is not perceived as an enemy of Israel during this period. Cyrus is, after all, according to Deutero-Isaiah, Yahweh's anointed. Hence, despite the fact that the cosmic—or at least the international—situation is lamentable from Israel's perspective, there is no nation that could be singled out to receive Yahweh's displeasure in this context. It is proper, therefore, to construe the vision and its response as one of weal for Jerusalem and its immediate surroundings and not necessarily one of woe to the nations against whom, according to the oracle of promise, Yahweh is angry.

Zechariah 2:1–4 [1:18–21E]

I looked and saw four horns

1[18]   I raised my eyes and looked and saw four horns.
2[19]   I said to the angel who had conversed with me,
          "What are these?"

He said to me, "These are the horns
which scattered/winnowed Judah, Israel, and Jerusalem."[a]
3[20] Then Yahweh showed me four artisans.
4[21] Whereupon I said, "What are they going to do?"
He said, "These horns are the ones which scattered Judah
so that no one could raise his head.[b]
Now these [artisans] have come to terrify them,
to throw down the horns of the nations
which raised a horn against the land of Judah
in order to scatter it."

a. Some have proposed deleting *'et-yiśrā'ēl wîrûšālām* because only Judah is mentioned in 2:4 [1:21E]. *'et-yiśrā'ēl* is missing in LXX. However, the correspondence between the totality of Israelite and Judahite destruction argues against such an excision.
b. On *k*pî*, see BDB, 805.

The Second Vision

If the first vision is difficult to understand because of its complexity and because of the lament and oracular response which it elicited, the second vision is difficult to comprehend because of its conciseness and the lack of a response or of oracular material.[1] Further, the lack of a date formula introducing this vision, i.e., something paralleling what is present in 1:1 and 1:7 and the ensuing visions, suggests that for the writer/editor this second vision is to be construed as part of a larger visionary sequence. In addition, the significant structural similarities between this and the earlier example, and the recurrence of the question "What are these?" suggest construing the visions as a unit. Finally, since on the basis of recent studies of dreams we know that sequential dream experiences are not uncommon, such a complex visionary experience was, empirically speaking, plausible. All this speaks for understanding, at least partially, the second vision within the terms set up by the first. Nevertheless, this second vision, like each of the other visions, must be treated in its own right as an integral unit before linkages between the preceding and following visions may be explored.

[2:1–2 (1:18–19E)] The vision begins with language that in later visions becomes formulaic for the introduction of a vision: "and I looked up and saw," "behold" (see 5:1; 6:1).

[1] For an incisive analysis of this text, see R. Good, "Zechariah's Second Night Vision (Zech 2, 1–4)," *Bib* 63, 1982, 56–59.

Whereas the first vision involves a geographic setting, apparent movement, and a scene populated by animals and human-like beings, the second vision apparently comprises a single object—or at least objects that can be described by a two-word phrase. And the immediate question posed for the reader by these horns is the same question that Zechariah asks the messenger, "What are these?" This question was apparently as difficult for the messenger as it has been for contemporary interpreters.[2] The angelic interpreter does offer an interpretation, a geopolitical interpretation, in 2:2, 4 [1:19, 21E]. These horns obviously symbolize nations or ethnic units of some sort: "the horns of the nations." However, few modern critics would suggest that this interpretation allows us to know precisely what sorts of horns Zechariah saw. And for the purposes of this vision in its final form, the specific identification of these horns is relatively unimportant. Nevertheless, suggestions about the identity of these four horns abound. Prominent among the suggestions are (1) two pairs of animal horns[3]; (2) the four horns of the altar[4]; (3) horns in the ground[5]; and (4) horned helmets. In my judgment, any assertions concerning the nature of the horns are premature until all the explicit evidence which the vision report provides has been assessed.

Whatever Zechariah saw and termed "four horns," the messenger interprets metaphorically. These horns are understood to have "scattered" Judah, Israel, and Jerusalem. The horns are clearly identified as political-military entities that have wrought destruction on Judah and Israel. That *qeren,* "horn," can be used to symbolize a nation is attested elsewhere in the Hebrew Bible (e.g., Jer. 48:25, "The horn of Moab is cut off and his army is broken, says Yahweh"). Similarly in Deut. 33:17 the fate of "Joseph" is described in the following way:

> His firstling bull has majesty,
>   and his horns are the horns of a wild ox;
> with them he shall push the peoples,
>   all of them to the ends of the earth.

---

[2] And this in contrast to some interpreters who find an obvious meaning here. Baldwin, 103, writes: "The meaning of this vision is straightforward"; for a similar view, see Rignell, *Nachtgesichte,* 72.

[3] Thus, e.g., Good, "Zechariah's Night Vision," 56–59; Horst, 222; C. Jeremias *Nachgesichte,* 131.

[4] B. Halpern, "The Ritual Background of Zechariah's Temple Song," *CBQ* 40, 1978, 177–178.

[5] Rudolph, 82.

Both these texts indicate that the symbolism of a horn may be used to describe a nation, especially a nation's military activity.[6] And the verse from the Blessing of Moses in Deuteronomy suggests a concrete source for the symbol there, the horn of a bull. The interpretation of the *mal'āk* is, therefore, consistent with the symbol of the horn as used elsewhere in the Hebrew Bible. Despite this interpretation, however, we have not yet learned the uninterpreted identity of the horns that Zechariah saw.

Another interesting feature of the *mal'āk's* interpretation is the list of what has been "scattered" by the horns: Judah, Israel, and Jerusalem. This list allows one to conclude that the scattering includes not only the activity during 597–587 but the demise of Israel in 721 as well. The scattering meant the destruction of all "Israel," both the northern and southern countries. Further corroborating this notion of the total destruction of "Israel" is the numerical symbolism present in the four horns. The number four in the Hebrew Bible is regularly used to symbolize totality, as in the four directions of the compass, for example.[7] For this reason, it is difficult to think literally, or in this case allegorically, about the identity of four specific nations which destroyed Israel and Judah.[8] There is no early tradition to the effect that four specific nations brought down Israel. Hence an obvious option is to think about the total destruction of Israel and Judah (including Jerusalem, which may be a secondary addition because of the emphasis on the city itself in Zechariah) as having resulted from all the world's powers. From the perspective of the *mal'āk's* interpretation, then, Zechariah has seen something which means or calls to mind the totality of Israel's defeat and the multiple international agents which had a hand in that destruction. That is what, according to the *mal'āk*, the vision means; though again the *mal'āk* has not explained for us what it is that Zechariah has "actually" seen.

[2:3–4 (1:20–21E)] Immediately after the horns have been given their political-military interpretation, Zechariah is shown more objects, and these are perhaps in motion, since they are described by an active participle—"coming." Not only do the *ḥārāšîm* appear to be moving, they are also specially "shown" to Zechariah by Yahweh. They stand in contrast to the horns which Zechariah apparently just "saw."[9]

---

[6] On horns as symbols of power, see Horst, 39, 222; Rignell, *Nachtgesichte*, 61; Bič, *Nachtgesichte*, 61.

[7] C. Jeremias, *Nachtgesichte*, 161; Horst, 222.

[8] For attempts to do this, see Baldwin, 104; Ringnell, *Nachtgesichte*, 61–62.

[9] This same pattern of Zechariah seeing something and then being shown something also appears in the first vision: "seeing" in 1:8 when compared with "being shown" in

The significance of these four objects is at least as difficult to determine as is that of the four horns. *Ḥārāšîm* can signify, and has often been translated, "smiths," i.e., metalworkers. However, someone described as a *ḥārāš* could work with wood as well (Isa. 40:20; 44:13; Jer. 10:3; Ezra 3:7; II Sam. 5:11; II Kings 24:16), or could work stone (so Ex. 28:11). II Kings 24:16 suggests, in fact, that a metalworker, *masgēr,* can be distinguished from a *ḥārāš.* It is more proper, therefore, to translate *ḥārāš* in the Zechariah text as "artisan," the more so since, in Ezek. 21:36 [31E], the phrase *ḥārāšê mašḥît* is used metaphorically to mean "artisans (or creators) of destruction."

As with the horns, the term "artisan" itself allows for no easy identification. Hence, just as with the first symbol, the seer asks: *māh-'ēlleh,* "What are these," and then adds, "coming to do?" Zechariah's question clearly focuses on the significance of the *ḥārāšîm.* The answer that follows is therefore strange, or at least begins in an odd manner, given the clear focus of the question. It is as if the *mal'āk* is commenting further on the significance of the horns and ignores the artisans. Interestingly, it is only in this putative explanation of the artisans that the action of the "horns" is given a clearly negative assessment. The action of the horns is more clearly focused on the southern society; they are now horns that have scattered "Judah." The extent of the scattering is described: "so that no one could raise his head." This metaphoric language derives, of course, from military experience. Those "who raise their heads" are engaged in military or similar action (Ps. 83:3 [2E]). And when one is subjugated, one cannot lift up one's head (Judg. 8:28). This metaphor is exemplified on numerous ancient Near Eastern reliefs in which a king is pictured with his foot on the head of a supine, defeated enemy. By using this metaphor, the author is able to create a picture of the total defeat, just as he was able, by using the number four, to symbolize the totality of foreign powers responsible for Israel's destruction, and just as he was able, by using the key words Judah, Jerusalem, Israel, to signify the totality of what Israel had once been. The destruction of everything by all the enemies of God's people had been total.

This total destruction is apparently the raison d'être for what the *ḥārāšîm* were coming to do.

1:9. However, in the first vision, Zechariah is shown again the same objects, the horses in the garden. In the second vision, he is shown new objects. In both cases, the meaning of what he has initially seen is interpreted by what the seer is shown in the second instance. In a real sense, then, what Zechariah is shown—the *ḥārāšîm*—serves to interpret what he saw first, the *qᵉrānôt.*

Only after we learn that the horns signify military agents that created total destruction for Judah do we learn what it is that the *ḥārāšîm* will do. They are to terrify and to cast down the horns. And only with this action are the horns themselves given a more definite meaning—they are the horns of the nations that raised a horn against the land of Judah. For raising their horns, the nations will have their horns destroyed. Their punishment is therefore ironic. What served as a symbol of attack will now be that which is punished.

As a closing addendum, the author indicates in a purpose clause what it was that the nations intended to do by raising a horn, namely, to disperse the nation Judah. Here the referent is clearly the exile of 587 (and perhaps that of 721). This statement provides a fitting enclosure with an earlier part of the oracle, because it uses the term *zērû*, which was used in 2:2 [1:19E] to describe this scattering effect of the horns.

Only at this point, after a study of the entire vision, is it appropriate to designate what it is that Zechariah actually might have seen, and to argue for a certain visionary coherence. One may proffer such an interpretation, one that takes into account the horns, the artisans, the scattering and the casting down. I would argue, along with Halpern, that the four horns are those of an altar. The altar was a well-known cult object. Since the reestablishment of Jerusalem as a cultic center is one of the major themes in the Zechariah visions, an altar is utterly appropriate as a primary object in the visions. The purpose or significance of the horns of an altar, however, is not immediately self-evident. The only clear function which the horns of the altars had in Israel was that of providing refuge. However, the notion of refuge is turned on its head in this vision. And, on these grounds, the *mal'āk* has license to interpret these enigmatic horns. The way the *mal'āk* treats the horns is not unlike the way Yahweh treats the *qāyiṣ* that Amos sees (8:1–2) and the almond branch that Jeremiah sees (1:11–12). What the prophet or visionary sees and might infer about an object, a basket of summer fruit, an almond rod, or, here, the horns of an altar, is unimportant. Rather the envisioned object provides an occasion for the deity to make a point which is, at best, tangentially related to that which was actually seen. Summer fruit signifies the end, the almond branch signifies an observant Yahweh. Similarly, the horns of the altar allow the *mal'āk* to comment upon the fate of Israel and its attackers. Immediately after the prophet reports seeing four horns, Yahweh shows him four artisans, apparently approaching the altar. The number of artisans obviously corresponds to the number of the horns. Since artisans, *ḥārāšîm*, can work in stone, we are shown here the sort of craftsman who could be responsible for creating a stone altar.

Further, they are artisans fully capable of destroying that which they had created. And since the horns now deserve to be destroyed, it is presumably in this latter capacity that they appear here. Artisans could lop off the horns of the altar and could, in so doing, throw down the horns, which symbolize foreign nations. This way of viewing the horns and artisans has the advantage of explaining the literal significance of the various elements in the vision, as well as making possible the symbolic interpretation of the *mal'āk*. The vision, therefore, works at several levels, and these levels are connected in an ironic way. The most literal level is that of a horned altar, with the horns suggesting the notion of refuge and safety. The introduction of artisans, however, introduces the possibility of destruction, countering the initial impulse of the vision. The interpreted level translates the horns into foreign nations and yet leaves the artisans untranslated. Are they, too, foreign nations, or are they semidivine beings of the sort that populated the first vision? We are not told.

It is important to note that Zech. 2:1–4 [1:18–21E] is necessary, given the content of the first vision. In that vision, Zech. 1:15, the issue of international justice and responsibility is raised. The nations that furthered disaster are at ease. But this issue was not resolved. Yahweh is dealing only with Jerusalem and the cities of Judah. To them, words of weal are spoken, but no words of woe are uttered to the nations that remain at ease. In the second vision, this problem is addressed. Foreign nations, though they remain unnamed, will be cast down. Moreover, by addressing the problem of theodicy, a note of discord is introduced into this visionary cosmos which has been at peace. With the actions of the artisans against the horns, the earth no longer dwells in tranquillity. The state of balance that had existed is now disturbed by Yahweh, with results that will work themselves out in the ensuing visions. What is important to note is that the action which destroys equilibrium is itself an action of destruction.

Zechariah 2:5–9 [1–5E]

I will be to her as a wall of fire

5[1] Then I raised my eyes and looked:
        There was a man in whose hand was a measuring line.
6[2] I said,
          "Where are you going?"
        He said to me,

"To measure Jerusalem,
to discover its breadth and length."[a]

7[3]   Then, as the angel who had spoken with me was going away,
another angel was coming to meet him.

8[4]   The latter said to the former,
"Run, speak to that young man:
'Jerusalem will exist without walls,
since men and animals will be so numerous in her midst.

9[5]   I will be to her,' says Yahweh,
'as a wall of fire around her.
I will be glorious in her midst.'"

a. The tense value is difficult to capture. Cf. JPS: "To measure Jerusalem, to
see how long and wide it is to be."

The Third Vision

[2:5 (1E)] The third vision constitutes a significant departure from
the first two visions, despite the fact that the formulaic beginning of
this vision and that of its predecessor in 2:1 [1:18E] prevents those
distinctions from being perceived immediately. Nevertheless, despite
certain formal similarities between this and the foregoing visions,
remarkable new elements appear. The scope of the vision begins to
narrow and the visionary prophet is able to enter into the visionary
world.

As with the preceding visions, there is a vision inception formula and
a brief description of that which has been seen. In this instance,
Zechariah has seen an individual holding some sort of measuring
implement. The two-word phrase describing the measuring tool—
hebel middāh—occurs only here in the biblical material. Elsewhere (in
Zech. 1:16 and in relevant texts such as Ezek. 40:3) where measuring
lines or rods are mentioned, other words or phrases are used. The
phrase present in the Zechariah text, *hebel middāh,* is therefore not
easy to interpret. The use of *hebel* in other contexts, i.e., when it is not
modified by *middāh,* is, nevertheless, informative. Though *hebel* can
mean "rope" or "region," among other things, it can also refer to a
method by means of which a line or rope is used to divide tracts of land.
In Micah, we find the following case:

In that day they shall take up a taunt song against you,
and wail with bitter lamentation,
and say, "We are utterly ruined;
he changes the portion of my people;

how he removes it from me!
Among our captors he divides our fields."
Therefore you will have none to cast the line by lot
in the assembly of the Lord.

(Micah 2:4–5)

And similarly in Amos (7:17): "Your land shall be parceled out by line." Both texts suggests that the *hebel* was used to divide or measure out land. In particular, the passage in Amos 7 implies that the measure was relative, e.g., that a given field could be divided in half. More important, to use a *hebel* is to presume that there is a particular entity to be measured, i.e., a particular field. To use a *hebel* is not, therefore, to create a new entity. To use it is, rather, to determine relative measurements within an already given context. One would not be able to measure a field five by five hectares. One would instead be able to speak of sections of equal size within a given area.

[6 (2E)] At this point the seer enters the action. Previously, in 1:9 and 2:2 [1:19E], the visionary asked a question of the angelic intermediary, "What are these, my lord?" "What are these?" In the third vision, what the prophet sees is apparently clearer. So, rather than ask about the identity of the envisioned person and object, Zechariah enters the visionary world. He is now, by the third vision, apparently accustomed enough to its workings that he is able to participate in this strange world. He does so by again asking a question of the person: "Where are you going?" To that question, the person responds in a straightforward manner, "To measure Jerusalem, to discover its breadth and length."

Despite the seeming clarity of this answer, contemporary translators have had difficulty in assessing its significance. City size in the Hebrew Bible is not usually described by using these categories. For example, Nineveh, in Jonah 3:3, is remembered as requiring three days to walk across. However, neither of the two terms found here, *rōḥab* and *'ōrek,* is used in Jonah. Often simply the phrase "a large city" is used when referring to a major urban site. The phrase used in Zechariah regularly appears when buildings are described, especially the temple. The two terms are especially frequent in the book of Ezekiel. The use of the phrase "length and breadth" in Zech. 5:2, describing a scroll, is much more typical than is the usage in 2:6 [2E], describing a city.

Much has been made of the impulse to measure Jerusalem as it might have related to the reconstruction of Jerusalem's walls.[1]

---

[1] Thus, e.g., Rothstein, *Nachtgesichte.*

However, the use of these particular terms, length and breadth, does little to substantiate this suggestion. The most prominent use of these terms in connection with the city of Jerusalem occurs in texts that date to the early postexilic period—to be found in another block of visionary material, the picture of the restored temple community in Ezek. 40–48. In that literature, the geography and configuration of the holy city are spelled out in clear terms.[2] It is to be 5,000 cubits in breadth and 25,000 cubits in length. This description of Jerusalem in terms of breadth and length is unique to Ezek. 40–48 and to Zech. 2:6 [2E]. One may infer, therefore, that the person with measuring line in hand is going out to take measurements of the sort described in Ezekiel's perceptions of the restored Jerusalem. For Ezekiel, Jerusalem was to be a fixed entity, part of a holy subdivision with clearly defined boundaries on all four sides. It is no accident that Zechariah, like Ezekiel, saw a person with measuring implements in hand.[3]

[7–9 (3–5E)] Just after beginning their dialogue, Zechariah and the person he has seen are interrupted. The angelic intermediary with whom Zechariah had spoken earlier commands another of the semidivine beings to run and speak a divine oracle to the young man. What the young man had said elicited an immediate response from the divine realm.[4] The command from one creature to another is, in itself, significant. The fact that the messenger is told to run indicates the urgency with which the task must be performed. Second, the individual with the measuring tool is here described as a *na'ar*, a term often used to indicate youth or minor status. Some have wanted to see the use of this term as connoting derogation.[5] Since, however, the term *na'ar* has other meanings, i.e., that of steward, such a negative tone is probably not present in the text.

The oracle itself, which the heavenly interlocutor apparently had already received, presents the divine response to the activity proposed by the person with measuring line in hand. Moreover, this response appears to challenge notions of restoration in Ezek. 40–48.

---

[2] See esp. Ezek. 48:15ff.; 45:1–8, and the standard commentaries.

[3] On the contrast between Ezekiel and Zechariah on this general issue, see D. Petersen, "Zechariah's Visions: A Theological Perspective," *VT* 34, 1984, 195-206.

[4] The first hint in the Hebrew text that the purpose of this oracle is corrective comes with the syntax in Zech. 2:7 [3E]. Immediately after we learn what the *'iš* intends, a disjunctive narrative sequence is used: "but the *mal'āk* who had spoken with . . ." This construction indicates discontinuity with the preceding encounter between the individual and Zechariah.

[5] Baldwin, 106.

There are a number of important claims made in this oracle:

1. Jerusalem will exist without walls.
2. Humans and animals will populate the city.
3. There will be many humans and animals.
4. Yahweh will be a wall of fire around the city.
5. Yahweh will be inside Jerusalem.

Each of these points requires some discussion.

1. Jerusalem will exist without walls. The syntax in 2:8b [4bE] is awkward, since one expects a preposition before *pᵉrāzôt,* and there is none.[6] Nevertheless, the claim is clear. Jerusalem will be something other than a straightforward walled city. It is better described using a plural noun, *pᵉrāzôt,* apparently because of the great number of its inhabitants. The actual noun is difficult to understand since it is used only four times in the Hebrew Bible. As such it apparently refers to small villages, towns without walls.[7] Another noun from the same triconsonantal root corroborates this sense. In I Sam. 6:18, a contrast between the fortified city and *happᵉrāzî,* the unwalled village, is maintained.

2. There will be many humans and animals there. The notion of a greatly repopulated Jerusalem inheres in restoration expectations. Jeremias correctly maintains that the phrase "humans and animals" is a stereotypic phrase used to describe all living things (so Zeph.1:3).[8] This phrase is used to foretell the destruction of Jerusalem: "Human and beast shall perish from that place" (Jer. 21:6; Ezek. 14:21). And the phrase is used to describe the repopulation of the land after its conquest (Ezek. 36:11 and Jer. 31:27). However, it remains for Zechariah to focus the promise not on "the house of Israel and the house of Judah" but on Jerusalem alone. What was an expectation for the entire nation in the eyes of other Israelites now centers, in Zechariah's vision, on one city.

3. There will be many people and animals, so many that the notion of *pᵉrāzôt* is more appropriate than that of *'îr.* This idea, too, resonates with earlier post–587 aspirations for restoration. So compare Isa. 49:19, "Surely now you will be too narrow for your inhabitants"; and 54:3 "for you will spread abroad to the right and to the left, and your descendants will possess the nations and will people the desolate cities." However, here again the notion of significant repopulation

---

[6] Cf. Rudolph, 83.

[7] See esp. Ezek. 38:11; see also Esth. 9:19; Judg. 5:7.

[8] C. Jeremias, *Nachtgesichte,* 171.

entails a repopulated land and cities and not just a repopulated Jerusalem as is the case with Zechariah. Zechariah alone concentrates exclusively on the city as the place of this preternatural repopulation.

4. Yahweh will be a wall of fire around Jerusalem. The notion of Jerusalem as a city without walls naturally creates the picture of a defenseless urban entity. Major cities of this period had walls. How could Jerusalem attain significant status without city walls? Yahweh responds by claiming to function as a wall of fire. Whence did this notion derive? Some have claimed that it represents the motif of the divine guardian to Eden (Gen. 3:24).[9] But how could what was a symbol of punishment become so easily transformed into a motif of protection? Such a question is, in my judgment, impossible to answer. Fortunately, however, we may understand the significance of an unwalled city that is inhabited by the deity and that is surrounded by fire in quite another way. The royal city of the Achaemenid kings, Pasargadae, was built without benefit of walls.[10] In and around it were a number of fire altars that symbolized the cosmic god Ahura Mazda. Such a city, impregnable, symbolizing dynastic strength and the presence of the god, would have been well-known to the inhabitants of Syria-Palestine, especially those in direct contact with the Persian authorities, as were, no doubt, the leaders of the renascent Judahite community. Yahweh as fire in an unwalled city probably reflects Persian notions of a mighty, ritually proper urban complex.

5. Finally, Yahweh proclaims that he will be or become holy or glorious inside Jerusalem. This statement is ambiguous. It is possible that there is a direct reference to the holiness of the temple itself,[11] especially since Ezekiel understands Yahweh's return to Jerusalem as the return of his *kābôd* to the temple. However, because this third vision of Zechariah seems designed to refute certain expectations propounded by Ezekiel, appeal to Ezekielian traditions to argue that this colon refers directly to expectations of rebuilding the temple seems unwise. As Jeremias points out, for Zechariah the city is the crucial entity; for Ezekiel, the temple alone is what matters.[12]

One suspects, therefore, that the crucial idea expressed in this oracle is that Yahweh's holiness will be accessible throughout this city of weal—it is described as on the perimeter, the walls, and inside the city. One might infer that the vision presents a view of Yahweh's presence which is in contrast to standard temple ideology. It does not support a

---

[9] Ibid., 174.
[10] D. Stronach, *Pasargadae*, 1976, figs. 3 and 4.
[11] C. Jeremias, *Nachtgesichte*, 175.
[12] Ibid., 176.

view such as that of P or Ezek. 40–48, namely, that Yahweh's holiness is limited to the temple. What is most important for Zechariah is not the reconstruction of the temple but rather the reestablishment of Jerusalem, and that in a new form. To this extent, continuities exist between Zechariah and Deutero-Isaiah.[13]

In sum, the oracle in 2:8b–9 [4b–5E] comprises Yahweh's word to Zechariah, to the *'îš/na'ar,* and to the people. Yahweh's word means that the measuring which was about to take place was erroneous in its intent. What Israel took to be a given, a measurable Jerusalem with walls, is not what Yahweh had in mind. Rather than exist in its pre-587 form, Jerusalem was to be a city without discrete boundaries and without Yahweh's being localized in the temple. The issue was not that of rebuilding Jerusalem's walls but rather of a proper conception of the new Jerusalem.

This third vision comprises a focusing of issues. From the first vision, which treats of the cosmos, and from the second, which focuses on the foreign nations, Zechariah moves to the third, which treats of one delimited area, Jerusalem. By the third vision, the transition has been made from the cosmic arena to the particular dwelling of the Judahites and their god. Just as the survivors of defeat and exile needed to be informed about the true character of the cosmic scene, so too they needed to be corrected in their presumptions about the character of the restored Jerusalem. Such was the task of the third vision and the oracle it contained.

Zechariah 2:10–17 [6–13E]

Flee from the northland

10[6] "Listen! Listen![a]
        Flee from the northland," says Yahweh,
        "for it was I who scattered you[b]
        like the four winds of heaven," says Yahweh.
11[7] "Listen, O Zion! Escape!
        O dweller in Fair Babylon!"[c]
12[8] For thus says Yahweh of Hosts,
        After (the) glory sent me[d]
            to the nations who despoiled you.

---

[13] On this vision, cf. B. Halpern, "The Ritual Background of Zechariah's Temple Song," *CBQ* 40, 1978, 178; Galling, *Studien zur Geschichte Israels,* 115–116; Beuken, 247.

"Indeed, whoever strikes you
touches the pupil of my eye.[e]

13[9] Indeed, I am wielding my hand against them
so that they shall become spoil
for those who served them."
Then you shall know that Yahweh of Hosts
has sent me.

14[10] "Sing and rejoice,
Fair Zion!
For I am coming,
I will dwell in your midst," says Yahweh.

15[11] Many nations will join themselves
to Yahweh on that day.
They shall become a people for him.[f]
And he will make his dwelling in your midst.[g]
You will know that Yahweh of Hosts has sent me to you.

16[12] Yahweh will take possession of Judah as his portion
upon the holy ground,
and he will again choose Jerusalem.

17[13] Be silent, all flesh, before Yahweh.
He has indeed roused himself
from his holy abode.

a. For *hôy* meaning "Listen," see Isa. 18:1; 55:1; Jer. 47:6.

b. On MT *pērastî*, meaning "spread out," see G. R. Driver, "Studies in the Vocabulary of the Old Testament, II," *JTS* 32, 1931, 251–253, and Petitjean, *Oracles*, 97–100.

c. Reading *bᵉbat* instead of MT *bat;* see similarly Rudolph, 87. On the translation of *bat*, literally "daughter of" (2:11, 14 [7, 10E]), see *JPS*. Clearly, we are dealing with the technique of personification. However, "daughter" has diminutive connotations which the translation "Fair Babylon" or "Fair Zion" avoids.

d. *'aḥar kābôd šᵉlāḥanî* is extremely difficult. See the myriad proposals, e.g., Rudolph, 87; T. Vriezen, "Two Old Cruces," *OTS* 5, 1948, 88–91; Rignell, *Nachtgesichte*, 84–88; Beuken, 322 n. 3; Ackroyd, *Exile and Restoration,* 180 n. 31. LXX reads "after the glory sent me," which is a literal rendering of the Hebrew and which is included, for lack of a more convincing alternative, in the translation here.

e. Reading *'ênî* instead of MT *'ênô.* Cf. E. Robertson, "The Apple of the Eye in the Massoretic Texts," *JTS* 138, 1937, 57–59.

f. Reading *lô,* following LXX and S, instead of MT *lî.*

g. Reading *šākan* instead of MT *šākantî.* The MT form is probably the result of assimilation to the phrase in v. 14.

[10 (6E)] The first words after the third vision report signal the beginning of a new unit. The particle *hôy*—regularly translated "woe"—most often occurs to introduce a woe oracle, as at Amos 6:1. However, it may also function in a more general way to call attention to what will follow.[1] In both cases, the word *hôy* regularly occurs at the beginning of a rhetorical unit containing direct discourse.

Direct discourse continues the urgent mood of *hôy*: "Flee from the northland." Some have seen here, in the presence of the verb "to flee," an echo of holy-war language.[2] Bach identified a particular rhetorical form, the call to flight, which is especially prominent in the book of Jeremiah, e.g., 6:1ff.[3] And to be sure, there are a number of texts in which the verb *nws* is used to describe people in flight before an enemy, e.g., Judg. 4:15. However, the sense in Zech. 2 is not of escaping from before the enemy but of fleeing from a land of captivity. Perhaps the best context in which to observe this notion elsewhere in the biblical material is that of Jer. 46:6:

> The swift cannot flee away *(yānûs)*,
>   nor the warrior escape.
> In the north by the Euphrates
>   they have stumbled and fallen.

Such language could well describe the fate of the Israelites in Babylonian captivity. They have not been able to flee from their captivity in Babylon, i.e., in the northland. Now, however, things have changed. The deity has been provoked to action. Past wrongs are about to be righted. A new and different Jerusalem is being envisioned. All this serves, for the writer-editor of this short collection of sayings, as a reason for imperative discourse directed to those in exile. Whereas earlier the people could not escape, now they are commanded to flee from "the land of the north, the arena of their captivity."[4]

A comment is perhaps necessary on the notion of Babylon as the land of the north. As a glance at any atlas will show, Babylon is to the east and not to the north of Judah. This fact has caused some to suggest that the use of "north" here is figurative.[5] Perhaps it is enough to point

---

[1] See esp. Isa. 1:24; 17:12; 18:1; 55:1; Jer. 47:6. In this sense it is an imperative particle and may be continued by an imperative verb. Interestingly, Petitjean maintains that Isa. 55:1–5 has an analogous structure to Zech. 2:10–17 [6–13E], *Oracles*, 95–96.

[2] R. Bach as cited by Ackroyd, 179; Beuken, 317–320.

[3] See R. Bach, *Die Aufforderungen zur Flucht und zum Kampf im alttestamentlichen Prophetenspruch*, 1962, 15–50.

[4] On the phrase "land of the north," *'ereṣ ṣāpôn*, cf. Zech. 2:10 [6E]; 6:6, 8.

[5] Thus, e.g., Baldwin, 108.

to the tradition articulated in the book of Jeremiah, that Israel's enemies would come from the north (Jer. 6:22; 10:22) and that it was from the north that the exiles would return (Jer. 3:18; 16:15; 23:8; 31:8).[6] In sum, the "north" functions here as, at least, a geographic convention for the Babylonian enemy and place of exile.

What is truly peculiar about the formulation here is the singular emphasis on "the north" and then the ensuing reference to geographic diversity, to people scattered as the four winds of the heavens. How is it possible to speak about people returning from the north when they must, by implication, return from north and south, east and west? Again, linguistic usage in the book of Jeremiah helps us to understand this problem, if not to answer it in a fully satisfactory way. The following texts in Jeremiah not only point to the north specifically but also have a more general geographic reference:

A people is coming from the north country;
   a great nation is stirring from the farthest
   points of the earth."
                                        (Jer. 6:22)

As Yahweh lives who brought up the people of Israel
   out of the north country
and out of all the countries where he had driven them.
                                        (Jer. 16:15)

As Yahweh lives who brought up and led the
   descendants of the house of Israel out of the north country
   and out of all the countries where he had driven them.
                                        (Jer. 23:8)

Behold, I will bring them from the north country
   and gather them from the farthest parts of the earth.
                                        (Jer. 31:8)

Clearly, Israel could be thought of as both in the north, and scattered to the far points of the world as well. The "north" serves as both a literal statement (one needed to travel north through Syria to reach Mesopotamia) and as a more symbolic statement about the far reaches of the earth (i.e., it reflects as Israel's perception about its existence vis-à-vis its geographic center, Jerusalem). The mention of winds coming from four directions also serves to link this description of diaspora with the view of total divine action promulgated in the final vision, i.e., that of the horses heading out in the four major directions.

[6] See B. Childs, "The Enemy from the North and the Chaos Tradition," *JBL* 78, 1959, 187–198.

The second imperative does emphasize the current location of those being addressed. The first command states, implicitly, that the people are in the north. The second command states explicitly that they are in Babylon. And consistent with the technique of personifying Zion is the literal reference to "the daughter of Zion," best translated "Fair Zion."

The imagery created by this personification of the female Zion living within the female Babylon is one of tension. How does one person, Zion, live in or reside in another, and foreign, individual? The rhetoric of personification here serves to help make the case for change. In the context of these particular and peculiar personal terms, Fair Zion and Fair Babylon, the status quo is problematic.[7]

The phrase *bat-bābel*, "Fair Babylon," is itself interesting. It does occur elsewhere (Jer. 50:42; 51:33; Ps. 137:8; cf. Isa. 47:1). The use of the word *bat*, literally "daughter," to refer to the population of a city or region is well known.[8] As these texts clearly show, such usage serves to call to consciousness all the negative sentiments that Babylon held for Israel. Babylon, which had been the mightiest of empires, will be brought low, whereupon Zion will be able to leave her position in captivity. Zion will replace Babylon as the significant city.

Syntactically, 2:10b [6bE] serves as the reason for the imperative expressed in the first part of the verse; it warrants the command to return, since this clause points out that it was Yahweh who drove the people into exile, not Babylon by her own devices. Hence, it is only Yahweh who is able to command and assist the return of those people to Syria-Palestine. Two primary images, the wind as the seat of the deity, and the total dispersion created by all four winds working together at the order of the deity, serve to buttress the deity's ability to command return.[9] Only the deity can command the winds. Moreover, all four winds are necessary to gather up those who have been dispersed throughout the world.

[11 (7E)] If the first imperative was directed toward all Israelites, the second imperative phrase achieves a certain focusing: "Escape, O Zion."[10] If the usage is the same as that of Deutero-Isaiah (see especially 51:16), the figure of Zion in all likelihood refers to Israel, or

---

[7] Thus Isa. 52:2; Lam. 4:22; and the writer of Zech. 2:14 [10E]. Cf. Isa. 52:1–2 for the use of "Zion" and "Fair Zion" in the same rhetorical unit.

[8] There has been no thorough study of the image of the daughter. For a brief statement, see H. Haag, *"bat," TWAT* I, 867–872.

[9] On this issue, see Petitjean, *Oracles,* 102–103.

[10] Cf. Rudolph, 86–87, who does not adopt a vocative reading. See also Petitjean, *Oracles,* 104–105.

a special part of Israel. In any case, Israel, now viewed as a person, is commanded to flee, a sentiment similar to the initial command in v. 10.

[12 (8E)] Here another section in this agglomeration of sayings commences. The messenger formula is prefixed by an emphatic *kî.* Unfortunately, the message itself is difficult to translate, or at least the first three words of it are. They may be rendered literally "after glory sent me." However, this makes little sense if, as a commonsense reading suggests, this commentary would refer to the prophet being sent to foreign nations. There is no warrant for thinking that Zechariah is, in this or any other section of the book, being sent directly to the nations. For this notion one needs to see Jeremiah (e.g., Jer. 1:10) or the various blocks of oracles against the nations preserved in many prophetic books.

The second colon, is, however, clear. Something or someone is being directed to the nations who despoiled Israel. This notion of Judah being despoiled is attested elsewhere in the prophetic corpus (cf. Isa. 10:6; Hab. 2:8). What the writer does here is to provide the rationale for the despoliation of the nations predicted in 2:13 [9E]. Until the textual problem is resolved, more than this cannot be said about this half verse, i.e., about who or what is interacting with the nations.

If the first half of the verse is a conundrum, 12b [8bE] presents a couplet including one of the most famous phrases of the Hebrew language as it is popularly understood, "the apple of his eye." This bicolon is introduced by another emphatic *kî.* The action is defined, again using the technique of personification. That which is described is—seemingly—neutral action, "touching." However, the phrase *ng' b* (cf. Gen. 26:11; Josh. 9:19; II Sam. 14:10; Jer. 12:14) denotes harmful touching, hitting, even killing. Malevolent action is under discussion here. But toward what? Study of the second colon allows a material advance over earlier notions of the apple of someone's eye. The author is here referring to the eyeball and its pupil. Once it is clear that the eyeball is intended, the force of this almost proverbial expression becomes clear. Anyone who acts injuriously toward Israel is, at the same time, acting injuriously toward Yahweh, toward one of the most sensitive and important parts of Yahweh's being. It is no accident that the eye is referred to here. It is a supremely sensitive part of the human (or divine) organism, and it is used as a symbol in the book of Zechariah, albeit in the plural—"the eyes of Yahweh" (Zech. 4:10b). This poetic piece, therefore, attests to the unbreakable and protective relationship that Yahweh has with Israel.

[13 (9E)] A bodily metaphor entailing touch, the eye, continues with another bodily reference, the hand of Yahweh. Again this occurs in a clause introduced by an emphatic *kî* and one identifying the actor with an active participle. Used with the preposition *'al*, this word, Heb. *nwp* (wield), refers to violent, military-like action with Yahweh as the subject (cf. Isa. 11:15; 19:16). Yahweh will wield his arm against them, presumably referring to those who will or would touch his eye. While the effect of such military action is surely punitive and destructive, total devastation of the enemy is not the ultimate goal. To the contrary, those who injure Yahweh or, at least, damage his eye shall become spoil for those who have worked in servitude. Just as the nations despoiled Israel, so (see the preceding verse), the nations will now become spoil for Israel. Reversal of fortune is clearly the highlight of this punitive action from Yahweh's mighty hand.

All this has a purpose, and it is not—at least from the perspective of the author of these verses—to make Israel feel good. Rather, such action is designed to provide legitimation for the writer, to enable the people to know that Yahweh has authorized and sent the writer. Such visions of future weal—the despoliation of the enslavers—may have sounded like so much pie in the sky. Hence, it was important for the author of such statements to be recognized as someone reliable, as someone speaking the message of the deity.

A strict construction of these words, however, makes it clear that Israel would know that the speaker was sent by Yahweh only when such miraculous despoliation occurred. Only then would it be possible for his authority to be verified. To this extent, Zechariah's authority was similar to that of the classical prophets, who often depended upon future verification of their words.[11]

In vs. 12–13 [8–9E], what began and still functions as an oracle of promise—that the enemies of Israel will be despoiled for the benefit of Israel—ends on a modulated note having to do with the relationship of the speaker to those whom he is addressing. It is one thing to speak glorious promises to a defeated and disoriented people; it is another to have those assertions taken seriously by the people themselves. This problem is reflected here. And the speaker apparently recognizes that he is unlikely to achieve acceptance until the glorious future which he envisions comes to pass. Such is the human side of the prophetic equation.

[14 (10E)] Yet another unit in this series of imperatives associated with personifications occurs in the next three verses. As with the

---

[11] See the Deuteronomic legislation concerning this matter, Deut. 18:15–22.

language in Zech. 2:11 [7E], a personified (daughter of) Zion is the subject of the imperative.[12] However, the character of the imperatives has changed radically. Whereas earlier Zion was commanded to escape, now she is commanded to respond vocally and, perhaps, liturgically to what is now and what will happen. The people are to "shout for joy." Such language, surprisingly, is not very common in the Hebrew Bible. Interestingly, the strongest parallels to such discourse, i.e., feminine singular imperatives of *rnn,* involve the presence of Yahweh in Jerusalem.

The shorter of these similar texts occurs in Isaiah:

> Shout, and sing for joy,
> O inhabitant of Zion,
> for great in your midst
> is the Holy One of Israel.
> (Isa. 12:6)

A longer example of similar rhetoric occurs in Zephaniah:

> Sing aloud, O daughter of Zion;
> shout, O Israel!
> Rejoice and exult with all your heart,
> O daughter of Jerusalem!
> Yahweh has taken away the judgments against you,
> he has cast out your enemies.
> The King of Israel, Yahweh, is in your midst;
> you shall fear evil no more.
> (Zeph. 3:14–15)

This is language very much like that of the so-called enthronement psalms celebrating Yahweh's royal presence in the Jerusalem temple. Only here and in Zeph. 3:14 do we have the terms *rnn* and *śmḥ* juxtaposed as feminine singular imperatives. And since the emphasis here is on Yahweh's arriving in Israel's midst, as it is in Zeph. 3, there is good warrant for thinking that we have here traditional language designed to celebrate, or, more accurately, command celebration of Yahweh's arrival in Jerusalem.

Just as Babylon was personified in the expression *bat-bābel* in 2:11 [7E], so now Israel is construed as the daughter of Zion. Such daughter language is not infrequent, and is used with special frequency both in songs of joy and in lament.[13] Beuken thinks that the phrase also refers

---

[12] Petitjean argues for a structural parallel between 2:10–13 [6–9E] and 2:14–16 [10–12E]; see *Oracles,* 128.

[13] Petitjean, ibid., 129–130, sees this as an instance of metonymy.

specifically to the women of the city since a subgroup of women would normally have undertaken lament language.[14] Be that as it may, the author has achieved symmetry, a critical concern in the surrounding visions, by using daughter language to refer both to an Israelite and to a non-Israelite city.

The next clause, after the imperatives directed to the daughter of Zion, states that the reason for such exultation is Yahweh's arrival in Jerusalem. As the text in Zeph. 3 suggests, such a reason is not unusual in this sort of discourse. However, the enthronement or theophanic notion in the context of Zech. 2 is charged with new meaning. Whereas in preexilic enthronement texts Yahweh was in Jerusalem prior to the ritual celebration of his enthronement, now, in 520 B.C.E., Yahweh was not understood as present in Jerusalem. His "house" was under construction. His presence had not recently been celebrated in Jerusalem according to the standard rituals outlined in the priestly regulations of the first temple. Hence, to say that Yahweh was coming to dwell in Israel's midst had special significance at this moment, more so than if such a statement had been made by a prophet prior to the defeat of 587.[15]

Not only was Yahweh coming to Judah. He promises to dwell *(škn)* in the people's midst. The verb *škn* with the preposition *bᵉtôk* is used to describe Yahweh's remaining presence. It especially picks up pentateuchal references to the residence of the deity in Israel's midst.[16] Given this particular linguistic background, it is difficult to gainsay the ritual implications of this formulation, that Yahweh's presence will dwell in the temple. If, earlier in these sayings, Jerusalem was a person, a *bat,* a daughter, now it again functions as a place for the temple, a *bêt.* The word play *bêt-bat* reinforces the particularity of the prophet's message.

[15 (11E)] Yahweh's ritual presence in Jerusalem will have a miraculous effect: "Many nations will join themselves to Yahweh on that day." Presumably the day of Yahweh's ritual entry and the celebration of his presence in the temple is meant. An opposite notion is expressed in Ps. 83:3–9 [2–8E], namely, that a coalition of nations is forming against Yahweh. Judah had actually experienced such a coalition arrayed against itself. Hence, it is not surprising that when expecting the peaceful age to be ushered in by Yahweh, they would

---

[14] Beuken, 324.

[15] Just such a return of Yahweh to Israel was part of the expectations of the exilic poet Deutero-Isaiah. Isaiah 52 speaks explicitly of singing when Yahweh returns to Zion.

[16] See Ex. 25:8–19; 29:44–46; Lev. 16:16; 26:11–12; Num. 6:3; 35:34. Cf. I Kings 6:9–13; Ezek. 37:24b–28; 43:1–9. See also Petitjean, *Oracles,* 123–124.

expect a markedly different sort of experience with other nations. Isaiah 60:1–14 expresses one belief in this regard, that former oppressors will "come to your light" and "build up your walls." In other texts (e.g., Esth. 9:27; Isa. 14:1) one finds the expectation that foreigners will join more equally with Israel. However, the strongest parallel expression to this text, apart from inner Zechariah resonances (e.g., Zech. 8:20–23), occurs in the tightly constructed speech in Isa. 56:3–8:

> And the foreigners who join themselves to Yahweh
> to minister to him, to love the name of Yahweh,
> and to be his servants,
> every one who keeps the sabbath,
> and does not profane it,
> and holds fast my covenant—
> these I will bring to my holy mountain,
> and make them joyful in my house of prayer;
> their burnt offerings and their sacrifices
> will be accepted on my altar;
> for my house will be called a house of prayer
> for all peoples.
>
> (Isa. 56:6–7)

Clearly, in the early postexilic period there was the expectation, at least by some, that those from non-Israelite territories and those who had earlier not venerated Yahweh were eligible for inclusion in the temple ritual. To be sure, this perspective was not shared by all who worshiped Yahweh, as can be seen in the fate of "mixed marriages" recorded in Ezra-Nehemiah.

Precisely, how "foreigners" (Isa. 56:6) or those from foreign lands (Zech. 2:15 [11E]) might join with Israel or with Yahweh is not entirely clear. However, it is the case that when the verb *lwh* is used to describe some sort of linkage between parties, the word "treaty" or "covenant" also occurs. Jeremiah 50:5 is clear in this regard, "Come, let us join ourselves to Yahweh in an everlasting covenant which will never be forgotten." So too the important passage Isa. 56:3–5 speaks clearly of those "who hold fast my covenant." To stand in covenant relationship is to have joined with Yahweh. Israel and Judah could stand in such a relationship (Jer. 50:5). And now in the early postexilic period it becomes possible to think of "foreigners" having this same relationship with Yahweh. It is not popular to speak of universalism in the Hebrew Bible, and yet both the text in Isa. 56 just cited and the short verse we are considering clearly suggest that the Israelite/non-Israelite distinction is losing ground to a distinction between those who venerate Yahweh and those who do not. Territorially defined religion of the Iron Age, the religion of monarchy, religion in the service of the state, is in the process of evolving into a quite different form. Jerusalem, the former capital, remains important, but now it is important for more than just those who could claim kinship with Israel's ancestors.

The result of this joining of foreigners to Yahweh will be, according to this author, the creation of an *'am*, a single people. Here the writer is moving beyond the notions expressed in Isa. 56. In Isa. 56:7 we read that "my house shall be called a house of prayer for/by all peoples (*'ammîm*)." The multiplicity of ethnic and political communities will remain. However, the vision of Zechariah moves to that of a utopian state, as indicated by the presence of the technical eschatological phrase "on that day." He looks for the creation of a single *'am*, one comprising the disparate elements known as *gôyîm*. The distinctions that will be maintained according to Isa. 56:7 (and for that matter Isa. 2:1–4) will, according to Zech. 2:15 [11E], be abrogated.

From the perspective of our own period, such an expectation for the breaking down of national and ethnic boundaries might appear attractive. However, one must wonder if the Judahites who were presumably addressed by this author would have viewed this promise of a new type of Yahwism with approbation. Not surprisingly, the very next verse allocates a special place to Judah, just as previous verses had reflected on the importance of Zion as a group of people. Nevertheless, this utopian promise must have impressed some as a wholly inappropriate way of viewing the reconstituted community centering around the newly rebuilt temple. What could the careful attention to genealogies provided in Ezra-Nehemiah mean if all foreigners and many nations could achieve unity with Yahweh and could achieve important status as functionaries within that religious community?[17]

For this reason—the integrity of the traditional religious community—it is not at all surprising that the focus shifts from an inclusive view back to the traditional Israel. At 2:15b [11bE] the editor has reintroduced material used in the immediately preceding verses, i.e., at the position in which such material belonged in the first instance. The clause "I will dwell in your midst" first appeared as part of the announcement of Yahweh's return to Jerusalem in the preceding verse. Now the clause functions as iteration, to assure Judah that Yahweh will function as he did earlier, as an indwelling temple presence. Although something startling and new will come about—the

---

[17] Cf. Ezek. 40–48 for an opposing view.

presence of nations within the Yahwistic community—there are continuities with other promises that reflect the older (covenantal and statist) order. Also reappearing is the clause "and you shall know that Yahweh of Hosts sent me to you." This sentence serves to unite the "universal promise" with more particularistic expressions of future weal such as the promise that plunder will flow into Jerusalem. These repetitions are not errors of copyists or scribes. They serve to affirm that Judah and Zion do have a special place in Yahweh's plan, which has now become a plan for unity among all nations, a covenant relationship of a new type.

[16 (12E)] As a part of this renewed emphasis on the special place that Judah has in the divine economy, the author concludes by mentioning explicitly Judah ("the holy ground") and Jerusalem in the strongest possible way. Yahweh is presented as an active agent vis-à-vis Israel. He will "take possession" of Judah and "choose" Jerusalem.

The first verb, *nḥl* ("take possession") is employed in an unusual way. We often hear that Israel will inherit or take possession of the land.[18] Or we hear about Yahweh's servants taking possession of the land or holy mountain (Isa. 57:13; Ps. 69:37 [36E]). We even hear about all the nations as Yahweh's possession (Ps. 82:8), or about Israel as Yahweh's inheritance (Ex. 34:9). However, nowhere else is the verb *nḥl* used with Yahweh as the subject and the land as a reference. Such usage is clearly innovative with Zechariah, an attempt to reintroduce the specific relation of Yahweh to the land, and this in face of the more universal pronouncement at the beginning of v. 15 [11E]. Similarly, the expression *'admat haqqōdeš* is singular, without precedent in the Hebrew Bible. (The expression *'admat qōdeš* does occur in Ex. 3:5.) To be sure, Mt. Zion is called holy, even at Zech. 8:3. However, that designation is never given to the *'ᵃdāmāh* of Israel. Again, by using this new formulation, the author is emphasizing the special character, the sacrality, of Israel within the context of weal to all nations.

The notion of *ḥelqô*, "his portion," also emphasizes the particularity of Judah's status. This community is Yahweh's portion among the nations. Interestingly, the notion of Israel receiving her appropriate portion after having suffered in exile is included in Isa. 61:7. Further, the *nāśî'* in Ezek. 45:7, Yahweh's specially chosen official within the postexilic polity, has his role. So also the tribes are important in Ezek. 48:8, 21. However, the notion of a special territory portion for Yahweh

---

[18] See, e.g., Ex. 23:30; 32:13; Josh. 14:1; 17:6; 19:49; Ezek. 47:13–14; Deut. 19:3.

is not usually included in such hopes. Zechariah is, again, stressing the special place of Judah vis-à-vis its deity.

The final way in which the unique character of Israel is indicated occurs in the last part of this verse. The idiom *bḥr b* serves to conclude a unit just as it does in Hag. 2:23b, though there the reference is to the choosing (or, better, "election") of a person. Here it is not a Davidic heir but Jerusalem, the holy city, that is the subject of Yahweh's special attention. The particular way in which this action is formulated emphasizes that such action is a repetition of Yahweh's earlier action toward Jerusalem. Once before he chose it, and he will choose it once again. This perspective serves to emphasize the special place Judah and her capital have in Yahweh's eyes. The imagery in this final verse of promise is markedly tangible: take possession, earth, Jerusalem. The author seems to be attempting to ground the promises in the land and capital of Judah. Yahweh's restoration is not ethereal reality but is, instead, based on the very soil of his special possession. To that extent, the author creates an effective *inclusio,* linking this promise of land to the imperative to flee from the land of the north in v. 10 [6E].

[17 (13E)] We now find what seems to be a change in perspective from the foregoing material. To be sure, the imperative mood picks up on the imperative *nws* in v. 10 [6E]. However, the total phrase "Silence, all flesh, before Yahweh," has a formulaic ring.[19]

Two uses of the imperative bear striking similarity to its situation in this verse:

> But Yahweh is in his holy temple;
>   let all the earth keep silence before him.
>   (Hab. 2:20)

> Be silent before the Lord Yahweh
>   For the day of Yahweh is at hand;
> Yahweh has prepared a sacrifice
>   and consecrated his guests.
>   (Zeph. 1:7)

The text in Zephaniah uses this idiom to introduce an oracle concerning the day of Yahweh, his theophany. Zechariah also includes the notion of theophany here in v. 17b [13bE]. And the similarities between Hab. 2:20 and this verse are even stronger. Both refer to an entirety of response, all flesh/all the earth. Both require such silence before him *(mippᵉnê / mippānāyw).* And both texts refer to the divine dwelling. Perhaps most important is the relative position of these two

---

[19] Thus also Elliger, 111; cf. Beuken, 327–328; Petitjean, *Oracles,* 151ff.

verses. Zechariah 2:17 [13E] caps off a series of promises concerning restoration. Habakkuk 2:20 also appears at the end of a series of sayings—in this instance, woe oracles. Such usage strongly suggests that the author-editor of the three preceding verses in Zechariah had available fairly stereotypic language that could be used to mark the end of a collection of this sort.

What unites this verse with the immediately preceding unit is the use of *haqqōdeš* in v. 16 [12E] and *qodšô* here. In the earlier verse, the deity inherits his holy ground. And in v. 17 [13E] we hear about the deity moving out from his holy habitation. Put another way, there is something of a sequential relation between these two verses. Yahweh first had to take the land as his possession, had to choose, again, Jerusalem as his capital. Only then could he or did he have a holy habitation from which he could come forth. And such procession or "coming forth" is clearly envisioned in the second half of this verse.

The precise significance of the term *mā'ôn*, habitation, is not entirely clear. Does it mean earthly temple—or supernal dwelling?[20] Petitjean maintains, on the basis of Deut. 26:15; II Chron. 30:27; Jer. 25:30, that the reference is to the heavenly abode of the deity. However, in Ps. 26:8 and II Chron. 36:15 the reference of *mā'ôn* would appear to be the earthly temple. Further, the parallel expression to this phrase in Hab. 2:20 would suggest that the Jerusalem temple is intended. And if the temple is meant by the term "abode," then just as Israel is "grounded" in v. 16, so too Yahweh is fixed by reference to his habitation, something made possible by the previous verse, in which he again chose Jerusalem.

A final comment. In this verse, we discern something of a resonance with v. 15 [11E]. There a theme of universalism was struck. Many nations will join Yahweh. Then in the next verse a movement back toward the specific was achieved with emphasis on Judah, the land, and Jerusalem. Both elements, the particular and the universal, are brought into the final verse. "All flesh" establishes linkage with many nations, and Yahweh's "abode" calls to mind the place of Yahweh's home, Jerusalem. This final verse, therefore, encompasses both the new and the old vision of restoration.

Zechariah 2:10–17 [6–13E] comprises, therefore, a disparate series of utterances—some are divine oracles—2:10–11, 12–13, 14 [6–7, 8–9, 10E]; others derive from the prophet's hand—2:11, 15–16 [7, 11–12E]. They clearly breathe a spirit different from that of the visionary cycle. The deity's sayings are filled with imperative discourse: listen, flee,

---

[20] Thus is, of course, not a natural disjunction.

sing, escape; and they announce a new act of the deity—his liberation
of those in exile. The prophet, on the one hand, comments on the
outcome of this action—2:15–16 [11–12E]—and, on the other hand, on
his own prophetic role—2:13b, 15b [9b, 11bE]. It is difficult to be sure
that Zechariah, to whom we attribute the visions, wrote any or all of
these sayings. Nevertheless, their purport is clear: someone was
encouraging those who were residing in exile to return to Jerusalem.
Yahweh was about to act decisively to enable the restoration of his
holy city, Jerusalem, and his holy territory, Judah.

Zechariah 3:1–10

I have removed your guilt from you

1   Then he showed me Joshua, the high priest, standing before the
    messenger of Yahweh, and the prosecutor[a] standing at his right
    hand to prosecute him.
2   Then (the messenger of)[b] Yahweh said to the prosecutor,
    "May Yahweh rebuke you, O prosecutor!
    May Yahweh who has chosen Jerusalem rebuke you!
    Is not this individual a burning stick[c]
        pulled out of the fire?"
3   Now Joshua was standing before the messenger
    and dressed in filthy garments.[d]
4   And he[e] said to those standing before him,
    "Take off his filthy garments!"
    And he said to him,
        "See, I have removed your guilt from you,
        and I will clothe you with stately robes."[f]
5   Then he[g] said,
    "Let them set a ritually pure crown on his head."
    Then they set the ritually pure crown on his head
        and they put clothes on him
        while the messenger of Yahweh stood there.
6   Then the messenger of Yahweh admonished Joshua:
7   Thus says Yahweh of Hosts,
    "If you walk according to my ways,
        and if you keep my charge,
        if you administer my house,
        and if you oversee my courts,
    then I will let you move around among these standing here.

8   Now, listen, Joshua, O High Priest,
        you and your colleagues who sit before you,
        for these are indeed men of portent!
        I am indeed bringing my servant, the Branch.
9   For, behold, this stone which I set before Joshua,
        on a single stone with seven eyes
        I will engrave its inscription," says Yahweh of Hosts,
        "and I will remove the evil of that land in one day."
10   "On that day," says Yahweh of Hosts,
        "each of you will call to his friend
        to sit under his vine, under his fig tree."

a. On *haśśāṭān* (literally "the satan") as "the prosecutor," see the commentary.

b. Syriac has "angel of Yahweh," instead of simply "Yahweh," the MT reading. For reasons of consistency within the vision scene, I adopt the Syriac reading.

c. On *'ûd*, see Amos 4:11; Isa. 7:4.

d. For *ṣô'îm*, see Deut. 23:14; Ezek. 4:12; Isa. 4:4; 28:8; 36:12; Prov. 30:12.

e. The subject is, presumably, the messenger.

f. The term *maḥᵃlāṣôt* is attested only in one other place, Isa. 3:22.

g. I follow V, S, T, and LXX in reading a third-person verb, *wayyō'mer*, "he said," instead of MT *wā'ōmar*, "I said."

The Fourth Vision (3:1–5)

[1] It has become a commonplace for modern commentators on Zech. 3 to observe that the fourth vision differs in certain formal ways from the other visions. (1) The typical introduction, "I saw" or "I lifted up my eyes and saw," is missing. (2) The usual questions, either from Zechariah or from the messenger, play no role in the vision. (3) There is no puzzling symbol or person which requires elucidation. What Zechariah sees is, at least to him, self-evident. (4) And because of the apparent clarity of the scene, the interpreting angel has no role vis-à-vis Zechariah apart from "showing" him the scene. These and other differences have led many to question the place of this vision in the cycle—whether or not it may be attributed to Zechariah; and if it may be attributed to Zechariah, whether or not it dates to the same period in which the other visions were composed.[1] Important though these critical judgments may be, a consideration of them is most

[1] See C. Jeremias, *Nachtgesichte*, 201–203.

appropriate after a detailed study of the vision in question has been made.

Despite the apparent clarity of the vision for Zechariah, the significance of this unit is as murky as are those visions with more recondite imagery. The very beginning of the pericope is ambiguous. The text states, without identifying a referent, "He showed me . . ." Who is the "he"? There are at least two possibilities. Agents have shown something to Zechariah two times earlier in the book. In 1:9, the interpreting angel responds to Zechariah, "I will show you what they are," by way of responding to Zechariah's query concerning the identity of the horses. And in 2:3 [1:20E] we read, "Then Yahweh showed me four smiths." Clearly either Yahweh or the interpreting angel could show Zechariah something. However, in these other visions, neither Yahweh nor the angel initiate the envisioned scene by showing Zechariah an object. Such action occurs only after the scene has begun to unfold. Here the phrase "He showed me" occurs at the inception of the vision in Zech. 3. Since the deity elsewhere never initiates communication with Zechariah, it is probable that here the "he" is a member of the divine assembly, perhaps the angel who "spoke with Zechariah."

What Zechariah does see is three individuals: Joshua, an angel of Yahweh, and the satan. Two of these characters are new to Zechariah's visionary world and they, therefore, require some comment, as does the role of the *mal'āk yhwh* in this vision.

1. Joshua, the high priest. On the most literal level, we are given a name and a role label. Since they are conjoined at this place in the narrative, it does not make a great deal of sense to argue that this vision is one in which Joshua becomes high priest, as will become clear later.[2]

Who is this Joshua, the first "historical" character, apart from Zechariah, to appear in the night visions? We are told regularly, in Haggai, in Zechariah, and in Ezra-Nehemiah, that Joshua was the son of Jehozadak. And Jehozadak was, in turn, son of Seraiah, the chief priest *(kōhēn hārō'š)* during the time that Jerusalem was defeated in 587.[3] Seraiah was executed at Riblah, and his son, Jehozadak, was taken into exile. Jehozadak apparently sired Joshua in Babylon, from where he returned to Jerusalem along with another hereditarily designated agent, Zerubbabel, scion of the Davidic line. Prominent though Joshua's name is in the literature that surrounds the reconstruction of the second temple, no specific action is attributed to him.

---

[2] Contra Beuken, 284; cf. also C. Jeremias, *Nachtgesichte,* 211.
[3] Thus I Chron. 6:40–41; II Kings 25:18//Jer. 52:24.

The consistency with which Joshua is labeled high priest is striking. That label is used only infrequently to describe priests prior to the exile. Cody goes so far as to maintain that the title "the high priest" *(hakkōhēn haggādôl)* is absent in authentic preexilic usage.[4] Whatever the case, it seems clear that the role of the high priest achieved certain prominence in the early postexilic period.

2. A second personage is *haśśāṭān,* "the satan." It is important to observe that this individual is not the more familiar Satan of the New Testament nor is it the even more familiar Miltonian devil. "The (a) *śāṭān*" as such is attested rather infrequently in the Hebrew Bible. A satan can be, simply, a human adversary, so I Sam. 29:4, a text in which the Philistines use the term to refer to David. To be sure, there are several instances in which the human adversary is understood to be divinely inspired (e.g., I Kings 11:14, 23). Also, an angel of the Lord, a *mal'āk yhwh*—a personage of great importance in the Zechariah visions—can act as a *śāṭān* (Num. 22:22). Perhaps the closest analogues to the notion of *śāṭān* present in Zech. 3 occur in the following three texts:

a. Psalm 109:6. In this psalm we read:

> Appoint a wicked man against him;
> let an accuser [a satan] bring him
> to trial [lit., stand at his right hand].

This same idiom, that of the satan standing at the right hand, is also used in Zech. 3:1, a fact which strongly suggests that the Zechariah scene is one of legal proceedings. Further, the psalm text indicates as well that the satan functions as prosecuting attorney. The parallelism of the psalm (wicked man//accuser) also suggests that this prosecuting attorney is more than just neutral. He is, to use a contemporary idiom, "out to get someone." There is therefore a certain negative connotation to a satan and his duties.

b. I Chronicles 21:1. This text is particularly informative when compared with its historical parallel, II Sam. 24:1. The II Samuel text reads as follows:

> Again the anger of Yahweh was kindled against Israel, and he incited David against them, saying, "Go, number Israel and Judah."

---

[4] A. Cody, *A History of Old Testament Priesthood,* 1969, 103 n. 53; cf. R. de Vaux, *Ancient Israel,* Vol. 2, *Religious Institutions,* 1965, 397–398; J. Bailey, "The Usage of the Post Restoration Period Terms Descriptive of the Priest and High Priest," *JBL* 70, 1951, 217–225.

I Chronicles 21:1 recounts this same episode in the following manner:

Satan stood up against Israel, and incited David to number Israel.

At least two important changes have taken place in this latter version preserved in Chronicles. First, Yahweh's anger has been personified as a satan. Second, this personification has been understood to function within a legal nexus. The satan appears against, *'md 'al*. This phrase, used in Ps. 109:6, describes an appearance in litigation. What remains the same, however, is the basic negative connotation associated with the figure of the satan. He leads David astray, incites him to act against Yahweh's will. This sort of legal action probably is best understood as occurring not in a human legal assembly but rather in the divine council, the place where lying spirits are understood as receiving their authorization (I Kings 22).[5]

c. *Job 1–2*. The well-known picture of the satan in the prologue of the book of Job is consistent with the usages listed above. A basic negativity is readily apparent in his actions. He challenges Yahweh's perceptions of Job's situation and appears in the cosmic legal assembly, the place in which the sons of the god assemble with the high deity. As one who can appear in the divine assembly, we may infer that the satan is, in Zechariah as in I Chron. 21:1 and in Job 1–2, a divine creature.

In Zech. 3, then, the satan appears to be an individual consistent with the other appearances of a creature by that name: one who acts in a legal context, one whose action inspires a negative connotation, one of the divinities functioning in the divine council.

3. The *mal'āk yhwh*. It should perhaps be surprising to have to comment upon the presence of the *mal'āk yhwh* in this vision. After all, the *mal'āk yhwh* has appeared in each of the previous three visions. However, in the fourth vision the *mal'āk* exercises a quite different function from that in the preceding visions. He does not have the role of interlocutor or interpreter for Zechariah. He is not there to act as a bridge between the visionary and the "real" world. Rather, in the fourth vision the *mal'āk* works exclusively within the visionary world. He is part of the scene that Zechariah "sees." More pointedly, he appears to convene, to act as ultimate authority in the council. Joshua and the satan stand before the *mal'āk*. The *mal'āk* (see the text-critical comments; here we are following the versions) responds to the satan's indictment. Moreover, the *mal'āk* gives directions for Joshua's change

---

[5] For a recent study of the divine council, see E. T. Mullen, *The Divine Council in Canaanite and Early Hebrew Literature*, 1980.

of apparel. The *mal'āk* removes the *'āwôn* that Joshua has borne. The *mal'āk* is, quite simply, the supreme authority in the council. He acts in place of the normal supreme authority, Yahweh. Such a role for the *mal'āk* is consistent with the remarkable absence of Yahweh in the other visions. Whereas the visions appear to depict the working out of Yahweh's will, they do not function to display immediately the divine presence. The visions are at a distance of one removed from the deity himself.[6] (Similarly, when the divine dwelling is envisioned in ch. 1, Zechariah is not shown the deity.) Hence, it would have been inappropriate for the deity himself to appear, even in his normal role in the divine assembly.

After considering these three individuals, we may conclude that the setting of the vision is the divine council. The procedure is a legal one, as the phrases *'md 'al* and *'al-y'mînô* indicate. The satan is prosecuting attorney, the *mal'āk* is judge, and Joshua is defendant.

[2] Once the scene is set, action proceeds. In fact, it is more accurate to say that action continues, since something has already happened. The satan has already leveled some sort of charge against Joshua, though we are not privy to his particular claim. After the satan has made an assertion, Zechariah experiences the goings-on and hears the next speech, that of the *mal'āk*, which is addressed to the satan. The speech begins with strong language: "May Yahweh rebuke you, O satan." The verb *g'r,* when Yahweh is the subject, is regularly used of action directed against the national enemies of Israel and against those who act against Yahweh's will (Isa. 17:13; Ps. 9:6; 119:21). In this case, the reason for the rebuke is hidden; it was expressed in the speed of the satan that has been made prior to the reception of the vision by Zechariah. The rebuke is, however, reasonably clear. The rebuke of Yahweh is reiterated in such a way as to reveal an arena of Yahweh's positive action. Yahweh is the god who has chosen Jerusalem. This may not appear to be an innovative claim, and yet it is. The idiom *bḥr b* is classic language of Davidic and Israelite—but never Jerusalemite—election. Further, the idiom is obviously current in the early postexilic period; Haggai uses it in 2:23, though of the Davidic line and not the Davidic city. Use of this election idiom serves to establish contact with the normative traditions of the monarchic period, traditions having to do with the monarchic place and person: Jerusalem and David.[7] Similarly, explicit reference to Jerusalem is important, since the notion

---

[6] See also C. Jeremias, *Nachtgesichte,* 205; however, I do not follow him in seeing such strong links with Isa. 6.

[7] Cf. Zech. 1:17; 2:16.

of Jerusalem is that of a city in which Yahweh takes residence.[8] And since Yahweh takes residence in a temple, human agents—priests, and more particularly here, a high priest—become necessary. The indictment of Joshua is, at least indirectly, viewed as something of a challenge to Jerusalem and the God who chose it. He—the satan—is apparently viewed as challenging the wisdom of a human agent necessitated by Yahweh's residence in Jerusalem.

This, however, is not the only reason for the rebuke issued by Yahweh. A rhetorical question is used to broach the manner of Joshua's appearance and status: "Is not this individual a burned piece of wood pulled from the fire?" The imagery used in this question is intriguing and complex. Further, the phrase "burned piece of wood snatched from the fire" was used by the prophet Amos in his retrospective curses which depict Yahweh's relationship with Israel.[9] In Amos 4:11 there are two similes used to describe Israel's fate:

as when God overturned Sodom and Gomorrah

as a burned piece of wood snatched out of the fire[10]

Yahweh was understood to have overthrown *some* of Israel in a manner similar to the destruction of Sodom and Gomorrah. In this action, Israel became like a partially burned piece of wood. And yet, despite Yahweh's action, Israel did not return to him. The similes used by Amos function to describe destruction which was not total, which was designed to make it possible to "return" to Yahweh.

What was simile in Amos appears in Zechariah as metaphor, a stronger literary convention. Further, the image that Amos used to describe a community is now used in Zechariah to refer to a sole individual, though he may be representative of the community in certain ritual contexts.

This metaphor of the burned and partially consumed piece of wood is a complex literary image, one that affords various perspectives on the individual so visualized. (1) A piece of wood plucked out of the fire is something that has survived a conflagration. Though the conflagration may have destroyed some materials, the piece of wood was not destroyed. The Amos usage would suggest that the survival may be construed as intentional. Fire can be a modest punishment, a

---

[8] Cf. the previous vision for an expression of the importance of Jerusalem.

[9] Though in Amos 4:11 the word used is *śᵉrēpāh* instead of *'ēš*, which occurs in Zech. 3:2.

[10] On this section, see Wolff, *Joel und Amos*, 1977, 221–222; J. Mays, *Amos*, OTL, 1969, 80–81.

punishment that does not entail total destruction. (2) When something survives severe burning, the survivor may be understood as having passed a test, of enduring an ordeal. The survivor is, by dint of survival, viewed as innocent.[11] Given the legal language and setting of the vision in Zech. 3, this nuance is appropriate to the surviving Joshua. He is, in some meaningful way, innocent. (3) Someone or something pulled out of a fire is dirty. Soot and smoke discolor; fire creates a powerful odor and char. Such an object yanked from a fire will appear much different from the way it did before it was put into the fire.

Which of these three nuances—or others—controls the metaphor is not clear. But at least one may assert that the metaphor is powerful and complex. It serves to explain the nature of the fire; it was intended by Yahweh. It also serves to suggest Joshua's innocence; and it serves to explain his disheveled appearance.

[3] Not surprisingly, given the visual implications of this metaphor, Joshua's appearance is commented upon directly in a grammatical aside. The second part of the comment is redundant; it reiterates what is to be found in 3:1, that Joshua was standing before the *mal'āk*. The crucial element in 3:3 is, then, the appearance of Joshua, especially his clothes. His garments are filthy. This is strong language. The word translated into English as "filthy" may refer to human fecal contamination and to the lack of holiness and the contamination it entails.[12] More generally, the word may also indicate radical contamination of an indefinite sort, so Prov. 30:12. Perhaps most interesting is a deuteroprophetic text, Isa. 4:2–4, in which the notions of the restored Jerusalem, the filth of the inhabitants, and fire—three salient elements also present in the Zech. 3 vision—are conjoined:

> And he who is left in Zion and remains in Jerusalem
>   will be called holy,
> every one who has been recorded for life in Jerusalem,
> when Yahweh shall have washed away the filth of the daughters of
>   Zion
>   and cleansed the bloodstains of Jerusalem from its midst
>   by a spirit of judgment
>   and by a spirit of burning.
>
> (Isa. 4:3–4)

There is, however, an important difference between the Isaianic and the Zecharian texts. In Isaiah, *ṣ'h* ("filth") is put in parallelism with "blood of Jerusalem." Blood has here the connotation, as it has in Isa.

---

[11] See also Isa. 43:2; Ps. 66:12.
[12] See esp. Deut. 23:12–14; Ezek. 4:12.

1:15, of bloodguilt, not simply bloodstains, i.e., blood from being injured. Similarly, the cleansing of which the Isaianic traditionist speaks is to be accomplished by a spirit of judgment//burning. Fire is designed to rid Jerusalem of its moral impurity. The situation is quite different in the Zechariah material. Here filthy garments result from the punishing//purifying fire. Further, the filth is not located in Joshua as is the case with the "daughters of Zion." Rather, Joshua's clothes are filthy, and this as a function of the fire, not his own impurity. The filth in Zechariah is, therefore, of a qualitatively different sort. And since it rests in the clothes and not in the person, its removal will, presumably, be easier—at least if done by a deity. That such is the case is attested later in the vision when the expected lustration rites do not occur.

[4] After the circumstantial clause completing v. 3, action resumes with v. 4. The *mal'āk,* who is clearly in control of the divine council, responds to the foregoing situation by using the standard language of "response"—'*nh*—as that occurs in the other visions (1:10, 11; 4:4). He issues a command to those standing before him—the third time this particular phrase "before him" has been used, a usage no doubt designed to buttress the authority of the *mal'āk* in the council. Those standing before him, minor deities of the divine council, are charged to remove the filthy garments that Joshua is wearing. After issuing the command, the *mal'āk* addresses directly the object of this action, Joshua:

> See, I have removed your guilt from you,
> and I will clothe you with stately robes.

A proper understanding of this command and the attendant direct address are crucial to a proper understanding of this vision. The identical prepositions are used: "the clothes from upon him" *(mēʿālāyw)* and "your guilt from upon you" *(mēʿāleykā).* This strongly suggests that the removal of the '*āwôn* is effected by the removal of the filthy garments.[13] The removal of the '*āwôn* is not just performative utterance, a pure word-event. The *mal'āk* effects the removal of guilt by commanding and eliciting action.

Further, the term for guilt/iniquity used here is complex. Its presence here has to do with Joshua's role as high priest, and his ability to function properly in that role. The standard lexicons define '*āwôn* as a general word for ethical transgression. The word may also signify the state of guilt that exists after a particular deed has been committed.

---

[13] There is every reason to think that the command is performed immediately by the divine attendants.

And it can refer to the punishment of a particular deed (Gen. 4:13). Interestingly, the effects of *'āwôn* can be transferred. So we read in Lam. 5:7, "Our fathers sinned and are no more, and we bear their iniquities" (their *'āwôn*); see also I Sam. 25:24; Isa. 53:6, 11.

Clearly, someone other than the transgressor can bear the guilt or punishment of the errant party. For the priest, Joshua, therefore, to have or bear *'āwôn* does not necessarily mean that he has erred. In the particular case of the high priest, this eventuality is nowhere made clearer than in Ex. 28:36–38:

> And you shall make a plate of pure gold, and engrave on it, like the engraving of a signet, "Holy to Yahweh." And you shall fasten it on the turban by a lace of blue; it shall be on the front of the turban. It shall be upon Aaron's forehead, and Aaron shall take upon himself any guilt *('āwôn)* incurred in the holy offering which the people of Israel hallow as their holy gifts; it shall always be upon his forehead, that they may be accepted before Yahweh.

And Num. 18:1 is similarly clear:

> So Yahweh said to Aaron, "You and your sons and your fathers' house with you shall bear iniquity in connection with the sanctuary; and you and your sons with you shall bear iniquity *('āwôn)* in connection with your priesthood."

The latter text expands the areas in which the priests, especially the high priest, bear guilt. Whereas in Exodus such *'āwôn* was understood to derive just from the offering of gifts by the people, in Numbers *'āwôn* could derive from things generally having to do with the sanctuary, including, presumably, its destruction and desecration.

In both texts, however, it is clearly stated that the high priest does bear the *'āwôn* of others, and the Exodus instructions explain how he is able to perform this feat. It is accomplished by dint of his official regalia, in particular the gold plate on the turban. Needless to say, the priest must be in a state of ritual purity to bear the *'āwôn* of others, a situation that moves us back to the case of Joshua, the high priest. Here is an individual born in an unclean land, who has lived in an unclean land, has become priest in an unclean land, and is now clothed in unclean garments. The accuser, and other people in the community, could properly question the ability of this "unclean" high priest, to remove the people's *'āwôn* when he himself is contaminated as a result of the exilic experience. No doubt, such was the gist of the satan's indictment of Joshua. This particular vision presents a way in which such an objection may be met. The exilic experience, a punishment by fire, is understood at least potentially as an experience of purification, just as it is of contamination. Further, Joshua's *'āwôn* is localized in his clothes. It is not understood as adhering to his person, otherwise the expected lustration rites would have been performed.[14]

The high priest, as high priest, bears *'āwôn*, the *'āwôn* of the people.[15] Since the *'āwôn* is directly symbolized by Joshua's clothes, and since the filthiness of the clothes is to be associated with the punishing/purifying fire of the exile, it is not legitimate to assume that the *'āwôn* is the result of Joshua's action. It is a guilt that involves the entire community. And yet, because of the radical character of this *'āwôn*—it results in part from a destroyed and desecrated temple—the high priest is unable to rid himself of it as he might have been able to do if the temple purificatory system were in order. Hence a special act of purification was necessary. The *'āwôn* was not so severe that a direct act of Yahweh was necessary (cf. II Sam. 24 and Job 7:21, instances in which Yahweh was sought to remove *'āwôn*). Nevertheless, it was guilt that could not be removed by normal purificatory rituals. Hence the *mal'āk*, acting in Yahweh's stead, had to remove the *'āwôn* by issuing a command for a change of clothes. Further, lustration rites were not necessary as one might expect. (See Lev. 22 on the importance of washing rites in the process of purification.)

Without much ado then, the *mal'āk* is able to continue with the reclothing of Joshua. In this promise, "I will clothe you with stately robes," the term rendered "stately robes" is rather general. Its use in Isa. 3:22 as part of a list of luxury products would suggest opulent clothing, though not necessarily official priestly regalia. The immediate contrast envisioned in the Zechariah text is, then, not between clean and unclean in the technical priestly sense, but between dirty, ordinary clothing and rich, ornate robes. Since the noun is plural, it may refer to an entire costume and not simply to one particular cloak. This plurality of clothing elements would then allow v. 5 to follow naturally, with the specification of one particular item of Joshua's priestly costume.

[5] Scholars have traditionally been mystified by the mention of only one item of the high-priestly regalia, the turban, in Zech. 3:5. The singularity of the *ṣānîp* (not the usual word for the high priest's

---

[14] On the trenchant issue of purity and contamination, cf. Hag. 2:10–15. The prominence of this issue in both these short prophetic books indicates the serious problem the contamination of exile presented to Israel as it attempted to revivify its older traditions.

[15] On the purity of the Zadokites, cf. Ezek. 44.

turban), as well as the first-person verb initiating the verse, stand as equally problematic elements. We must deal with each of these problems in turn.

Who is speaking? The first-person singular verb would suggest that the visionary, Zechariah, is himself now participating in the conciliar action. The strongest case for Zechariah's participating in the action, i.e., the strongest defense of the MT reading, has been made by N. Tidwell, who maintains that this vision has pronounced parallels with other Old Testament texts, all of which comprise a genre, "a narrative of events in the divine council on an occasion when that council is gathered to make some fateful decision concerning the affairs of men."[16] The strongest parallel is the participation of Isaiah (Isa. 6:8) as he volunteers within the conciliar setting to serve as a herald of the divine council. Other parallels remain problematic. For example, Isa. 40:6 has traditionally been translated, "And I said, 'What shall I cry?' " Elsewhere I have maintained that this verse should be translated, "And she said, what shall I cry?"[17] In the Deutero-Isaiah case, the text-critical issue is directly connected to form-critical considerations. Similarly, in Zech. 3:5 the form-critical issue is linked with a text-critical judgment. There is strong evidence for reading *wayyō'mer*, a third-person masculine singular verb, and not a first-person form of the verb. In order to side with MT and in order to accept Tidwell's thesis, we must know what purpose is served by having Zechariah act in the conciliar setting. In Isa. 6, the importance of Isaiah's appearance is clear: he becomes a viceroy of the council to the human community. In Zech. 3, however, there is nothing to be gained from having Zechariah issue the command concerning the reclothing of Joshua. Furthermore, given the logic of the visionary world, Zechariah has no authority to issue such a command in that setting. It is one thing to volunteer for duty as did Isaiah in Isa. 6; it is quite another to speak with the authority of the deity or his designated representative. We have no reason to think that Zechariah had such authority. I would therefore maintain that LXX and V offer the best reading and that we should translate: "and he said." The *mal'āk* continues speaking in his role as Yahweh's designated convener of the divine council.

As for the turban, it is important to note that the writer has employed a word different from the usual technical term for the high-priestly turban, i.e., he has used *ṣānîp* instead of *miṣnepet*.

---

[16] N. Tidwell, *"Wā'ōmar* (Zech. 3:5) and the Genre of Zechariah's Fourth Vision" (I Kings 22; Isa. 6; 40; Job 1; 2; Zech. 1; 3; 6)," *JBL* 94, 1975, 352.

[17] See D. Petersen, *Late Israelite Prophecy*, 1977, 20–21.

Interestingly, this term, along with the word for stately robes, has been drawn from the list of finery contained in Isa. 3:18–23. Surely this is more than coincidence. The author must have known of this list or something very much like it. The list in Isa. 3 was composed, or perhaps better, included in that book to show what would be lost on the fearful day of Yahweh. "Yahweh will take away the finery," and instead there will be rottenness, baldness, sackcloth. Writing from the perspective of the defeat and exile, the author of Zechariah could maintain that such a day has already occurred (cf. Isa. 3:25–26). People had fallen in battle; lamentation and mourning have overtaken Israel. Our writer appears to maintain that it is, at least for Joshua, time to revert to the period of luxury and finery. It is time to move from sackcloth to gowns. The issue is therefore more than just a return to proper priestly regalia, though that is of course included. These allusions to finery in Isa. 3 indicate that what is happening to Joshua signals the end of a period of exile and lamentation and an end to attendant miseries.

What else may be said about this item of clothing? The specific noun that occurs in this text, *ṣanîp*, occurs three times in MT. Other than in the Zechariah text, it occurs in Job 29:14 within a simile to characterize Job's moral worth: "My justice was like a robe and a turban." And it is used symbolically in Isa. 62:3 of Zion's future elevated status:

> You shall be a crown of beauty in the hand of Yahweh,
>   and a royal turban *(ṣᵉnîp mᵉlûkāh)* in the hand of your God.

Clearly, the Job and Trito-Isaiah usages suggest that this headdress is one of splendor. It may even indicate royal status.

Furthermore, the turban that is placed on Joshua's head is clean, not impure or dirty. The adjective used here, *ṭāhôr*, is less restricted than is its potential antonym, *ṣô'îm*, since *ṭāhôr* can indicate ritual cleanliness as well as physical and moral purity. In this particular context, the divine council, there is every reason to think that the turban is both physically clean and ceremonially pure.

One may well ask why this term, *ṣānîp*, was used instead of the usual term for the high-priestly turban, *miṣnepet*. I think it is facile to maintain that any different headdress is in fact intended here. The technical term *miṣnepet* entailed flexibility too. It could also refer to the royal turban (Ezek. 21:31). One may suggest two reasons for this particular usage. (1) The use of *ṣānîp* gives royal overtones to this scene. Clearly, the prerogatives of Joshua were noteworthy, especially now that there was no invested king on the throne. (2) Moreover, the use of the nontechnical term for "turban" avoids giving the sense of an official investiture. Clearly Joshua was already high priest. The use of ṣānîp indicates that we have here a scene of postexilic cleansing and restitution, not an ordination of the high priest.

The other garments that were put on Joshua are not detailed for us. They were probably the high priest's costume, though one cannot be certain.

Zechariah 3:5, and the visual part of the description, terminates with the seemingly awkward statement that the *mal'āk* of Yahweh was standing (there). This comment, which many commentators have sought to excise, does function importantly. It serves again to indicate both Yahweh's absence and yet his control of the situation through a divinely designated agent. Yahweh is *deus absconditus,* and yet a plan is working itself out.

By the end of the vision, we have been allowed to glimpse one part of the proceedings in the divine council. Joshua has been accused and has been found innocent. *'āwôn* has been removed from him and he has been clothed in elegant and pure garments. Since a turban is mentioned, noted explicitly, there is reason to think that Joshua's new costume was, in fact, the regalia of the high priest. However, there is little warrant for thinking that the scene is one of ordination to that office. The scene entails the purification of an unclean high priest, one who does not have the option of normal purification rituals and this for at least two reasons: The temple purification system is not yet functioning, and the radical impurity of birth in an unclean land requires radical purification—purification in the divine realm. With his iniquity removed and with his high-priestly garments pure by the end of the vision, Joshua is ready to assume the official office of high priest.

By way of further understanding the particularities of this vision, further consideration of the high-priestly clothes and turban are requisite. One question which seems inescapable is that of the significance of the clothes and the changing of clothes and the particular items which Joshua puts on. Are these actions or items of clothing related to some specific ceremony attested elsewhere?

Changing of clothes by the high priest is known to have transpired in at least two different contexts: in the ceremony of investiture (see Ex. 29; Lev. 8), and on the Day of Atonement (Lev. 16). Both these situations entail certain similarities to the Zech. 3 description and therefore require some comment.

As for the ordination of the high priest, the official regalia of the high priest are listed in Ex. 28–29; 31; and in Lev. 8 within the instructions for and description of the investiture of the head priest. The regalia listed include: coat, girdle, robe of the ephod, ephod, breast piece, and turban and holy crown (see Lev. 8:7; Ex. 28:4; 29:5). The ritual itself includes the following events: the washing of the high priest's head, and then a sacrifice. As a part of the last-mentioned rite, oil and blood are put on the person and clothes of the candidate (and upon other priests as well); see Ex. 29:21, 29–30. Clearly the issues of purification and of new, clean clothes, which include a headpiece, are present both in the high-priestly investiture ceremonies and in the action in Zech. 3. However, despite these similarities, there are important differences between these two descriptions. In Zechariah, unlike the descriptions in Leviticus and Exodus, there are: (1) no washing rites, (2) no detailed list of a costume, and (3) no sacrifices. One cannot imagine an official investiture within the Israelite tradition without the first and third elements. These differences between the Zech. 3 scene and that in the other texts strongly suggest that whatever is being described in Zech. 3, it is not the installation of Joshua as high priest. High-priestly clothes and purity are also an issue on the Day of Atonement (Lev. 16:4). Again, specific items of clothing are mentioned, a set different from the garments for ordination. In this context, the high priest is to wash himself and then put on the linen coat, linen breeches, linen girdle, and linen turban.[18] As the description of the clothes makes clear, this particular costume is different from the one used in the ordination ritual. The garments for the Day of Atonement are also to be left in the temple. After going into the holy place, the high priest is to take these garments off, wash, and then put on other garments (Lev. 16:23–24).

In both ceremonies, ordination and Day of Atonement, clothes are put on, an entire costume is mandated. And in both instances, the clothing ritual is preceded by ablution rites and is accompanied by sacrifices. In Zechariah, however, a full costume is not described in detail. Only the turban is mentioned explicitly, and this in addition to the more general "stately robes." Further, in Zech. 3 there are neither ablution rites nor attendant sacrifices. Finally, and strikingly, of the four major pieces of clothing expressly restricted to the high priest,[19] none are mentioned explicitly in Zech. 3. There is therefore no warrant for maintaining that the action described in

---

[18] On the specific character of this cloth, see M. Haran, *Temple and Temple Service,* 1978, 174.

[19] Ibid., 166–169.

Zech. 3:1–5 comprises either a rite of ordination or a ritual portion of the Day of Atonement ceremonies.

Coming to this negative conclusion, however, should not prevent us from building upon the singular emphasis that does occur in the Zechariah text. Nowhere in descriptions of the ritual priestly garments does the turban, whether *ṣānîp* or *miṣnepet*, stand out as more important than other elements of the regalia. Such, however, is the case in Zech. 3. Why? To answer this question, it is important to know two things about the high-priestly turban. First, this head covering was distinct from that worn by other priests. They wore caps, *migbā'ôt* (Ex. 28:39–40; 39:28). Haran maintains, no doubt correctly, that the high-priestly headdress indicated special prestige within the priestly class.[20] Second, when one examines the descriptions of the high priest's turban, it soon becomes clear that the turban was inextricably linked with another object, one that, like the turban, only the high priest could wear, the plate of pure gold upon which were engraved the words "Holy to Yahweh."

This plate was fastened to the turban by a blue lace, i.e., it was a permanent part of the turban, as Ex. 28:38 indicates: "It shall always be upon his forehead, that they may be accepted before Yahweh."[21] "They," of course, refers to the entire Israelite community. The purpose of the gold plate is clearly stated: "It shall be upon Aaron's forehead, and Aaron shall take upon himself any guilt incurred in the holy offering which the people of Israel hallow as their holy gifts." What makes this statement of purpose so important is that the *ṣîṣ* (plate of gold) allows the high priest to bear the *'āwôn* of the people (the same term as used in 3:4). The ability of the high priest to bear the *'āwôn* of the people, and in so doing to enable the people to be acceptable before Yahweh, is central to his ritual role and also central to the issues raised in the book of Zechariah.

Zechariah's concerns here involve meta-ritual. How can the whole temple ritual system be set in motion again if everyone is unclean? The high priest cannot bear anyone's guilt since he, or at least his clothing, is soiled. What happens in this vision of Zechariah makes the restoration of the ritual system possible, and this by means of an ad hoc cleansing ritual in the divine council. The normal purification rituals are impossible and are therefore not invoked.[22]

[20] Ibid., 170.
[21] See Ex. 28:38 and Lev. 8:9 for the notion of the turban as a crown.
[22] As noted earlier, there are similarities between this text and Isa. 6, another text that

This vision, like several of the other visions, serves to correct an erroneous presupposition, namely, the notion that Joshua is somehow worthy of indictment by the satan (Yahweh's prosecuting attorney) or by anyone else. Joshua's clothes may need cleansing, but Joshua is worthy neither of indictment nor of punishment.

This issue of correction extends beyond the identity of Joshua to the issue of the high-priestly office itself. As we have had occasion to see in the Introduction, there is an alternate way of construing the rebuilding of the Israelite community, that of Ezek. 40–48. And here, interestingly, there is considerable talk of priests. The Zadokites are to have authority and pride of place in the new order. The Levites, by contrast, are declassed. However, there is no special role allocated for a high priest. This is all the more striking since the *nāśî '*, the prince, does have a prominent role, even in ritual matters (Ezek. 44:3) The Zechariah visions seem to provide a corrective to the perspective of Ezekiel. This vision stresses the importance of the high priest in the polity of the restored priesthood, a role ignored in Ezek. 40–48. The vision in Zech. 3 then describes action in the visionary world that serves to cleanse Joshua's clothes and to remove the *'āwôn* he is bearing. Such action enables the high priest to perform again his duties on behalf of the Yahwistic community.

The Responses (3:6–10)

After the fourth vision concludes and the possibility of proper ritual purity is reestablished, two oracular responses and one deuteroprophetic response follow. It is my position that, in all likelihood, neither oracle belonged originally with the vision. In any case, each oracle promulgates a very specific implication of the vision, and the implications stand at loggerheads with each other. The first response (3:6–7, 9) attempts to routinize Joshua's access to the divine council, whereas the second oracular response (3:8) attempts to correct an apparent tilt toward Joshua in the previous vision by pointing to the importance of Zerubbabel. The two oracles offer, as it were, competing claims and interpretations of the fourth vision. A final verse (3:10) builds upon one of the oracular responses and provides a final, paradisal perspective for the future.

[6–7] Rather than observing Yahweh's presence in the divine

---

describes purification in the divine council. By comparison, it is easier to cleanse Joshua, as one need only change his clothes. For Isaiah's cleansing, his body needed to be touched, and this with an object taken from the active practice of the temple cult, an action therefore unavailable for Zechariah's cleansing.

council, we hear his words in a block of oracular material immediately following the conclusion of the vision. The legal imagery of the divine council proceedings are maintained in the opening clause: The *mal'āk* admonishes Joshua. The idiom *'wd b* is particularly at home in the legal context. The phrase can mean "testify against" (Deut. 4:26; 30:19; 31:28), or more generally (as here), "admonish, warn, or enjoin." Such legal language serves to establish a direct linkage between the oracular material and the just completed vision. Both vision and oracle are set in the legal assembly, the divine council.

Just as in Zech. 1:14, the *mal'āk* is here privy to Yahweh's intentions and words. Hence he proceeds with a full form of the so-called messenger formula, "Thus says Yahweh of Hosts," to introduce the first oracle. He admonishes Joshua, solemnly exhorts him to a particular course of action. And in so doing, he appears to perform the role of the prophet.

The oracle itself is something of a problem and this because of syntactic ambiguity. The speech begins with two clauses which are introduced by the standard conditional particle *'im:*

> If you walk according to my ways,
> and if you keep my charge . . .

Each of the next two clauses are introduced by the particle *wᵉgam*. Normally this word functions as an adverb meaning "in addition, moreover." It does not regularly occur at the beginning of the apodosis of a conditional clause, i.e., indicating the "then" clause in an "if . . . then" construction. The problem in a nutshell is whether the *wᵉgam* . . . *wᵉgam* clauses belong in the protasis or the apodosis of this conditional blessing, as Beuken puts it.[1] Does it continue the "if" clause or begin the "then"? The decision is an important one. If the ambiguous clauses belong in the protasis, then the strength of the admonition is greater. Joshua would receive four admonitions instead of two. Further, he would have fewer ritual/political prerogatives than if ruling the house and guarding the court were not conditional. If, on the other hand, these two clauses belong in the apodosis, then Joshua's authority in the society is stronger; he is weighted with less moral constraint.

Careful attention to the specific language in the theme clauses is helpful as we attempt to reach a decision about the syntactic matter. The first two clauses present language that may be constructed as very general: "If you walk according to my ways, and if you keep my

---

[1] Beuken, 290.

charge." The first clause is particularly prominent in the deuteronomistic corpus, e.g., Deut. 8:6.[2] The second clause is much less
prominent in deuteronomistic literature[3] and does occur elsewhere.
The term *mišmeret* can be used to refer to a general obligation (Gen.
26:5), a general prohibition (Lev. 18:30), or even a purely secular duty
(Isa. 21:8; Hab. 2:1). The notion of keeping Yahweh's charge can have
a very general admonitory force (see Mal. 3:14). It can also have a
more specialized meaning. The noun *mišmeret*, here translated as
"charge," is used nine times in Num. 3.[4] Specifically, the term
indicates a form of priestly service. However, when it has this
particular nuance in Num. 3, it usually stands in construct with another
noun, e.g., "charge of the entire congregation" (Num. 3:7). The
precise form of *mišmeret* used in Zech. 3:7 does not, therefore, allow
us to conclude that the more specific meaning—priestly service—is
intended in the text. What is perhaps most instructive about the
significance of *mišmeret* is its use in Ezek. 40–48, a text with which we
have often seen the visions of Zechariah to be in dialogue. In Ezek. 44,
the author is concerned about identifying those who are to have access
to the rededicated temple: "Mark well those who may be admitted to
the temple and all those who are to be excluded from the sanctuary"
(Ezek. 44:5). He goes on to charge Israel with the duty of keeping
foreigners out of the sanctuary. By allowing foreigners into the temple,
Israel had not kept Yahweh's "charge" (Ezek. 44:8). And then, by
way of positive injunction, we learn who is to keep Yahweh's
"charge": the Levites. They shall not serve as fully enfranchised
priests (Ezek. 44:11, 16); nevertheless they shall keep Yahweh's
"charge in the temple" (Ezek. 44:14). Such phraseology means,
among other things, that for this exilic writer, keeping Yahweh's
charge could be distinguished from functioning as a priest. And yet,
since the Levites could do "all that is to be done in it [the temple]"
(Ezek. 44:14), it is difficult to know exactly what is forbidden to them.

   In contrast to this Ezekielian perspective stands our Zechariah text,
a text that relates "keeping the charge" to the high priest. It is not, as in
Ezekiel, a carte blanche blessing upon a group, but rather a
conditional blessing upon one priest's (presumably a Zadokite's)
activity.[5]

   [2] C. Jeremias, *Nachtgesichte*, 213 n. 41; M. Weinfeld, *Deuteronomy and the
Deuteronomic School*, 1972, 333.
   [3] See Deut. 11:1 and Weinfeld, *Deuteronomy and the Deuteronomic School*, 75 n. 4.
   [4] See Baldwin, 115; C. Jeremias, *Nachtgesichte*, 213.
   [5] See J. Levenson, *Theology of the Program of Restoration of Ezekiel 40–48*, 1976,
146–147.

In the next clauses, which stand in the aforementioned ambiguous syntactic construction, two places are mentioned—in the phrases "administer my *house*" and "oversee my *courts*." Although the referent of the first noun, house, is ambiguous—it could refer either to the house of Yahweh as temple (see Zech. 1:16; 4:9; 5:11; 7:3; 8:9) or to the house of Judah/Israel (see Zech. 8:13, 15, 19), since the house stands in parallelism with "my courts"—the most probable reference is the temple compound. Moreover, when Yahweh is understood to speak of "my house," that expression refers consistently to the temple in Jerusalem.

The interior syntax of the third poetic colon in v. 7 is itself problematic. The object of the verb *dîn* ("to judge") is regularly a person or a group of people, not a place. Hence one standard lexicon (BDB, 192) is forced to list this particular attestation of the word as having a separate meaning, "govern." Most commentators[6] are constrained to provide some sort of figurative translation for *dîn* or to insert a preposition preceding *bêt* (i.e., "judge concerning my house"). Rather than worry at the outset about the best way to juxtapose "judge" and "my house," it is perhaps preferable to raise the issue of what is at stake in this activity. In Zechariah, Joshua the high priest is admonished to judge "at (or concerning) the temple." Is this admonition or prerogative consonant with other Israelite perceptions about who shall perform that function? The major points for comparison are available in Deut. 17 and Ezek. 44. In Deut. 17, the issue of judging is raised. Responsibility for judging lies with Mosaically authorized Levitical priests and the judge (Deut. 17:9). The rhetoric of the description, "they" in vs. 10–11, strongly suggests that the Levitical priests are the primary judicial authority in this context. Further, the text makes clear that they are to judge "at the place which Yahweh your God will choose," a place which after the time of Josiah was none other than Jerusalem. There can be little doubt that if the Levitical priests are understood to function as judges in Jerusalem, they are doing this at the temple. Not dissimilarly in Ezek. 44, in a section devoted to outlining the duties and responsibilities of the Levitical priests, this same group is associated with judging. "In a controversy they shall act as judges" (Ezek. 44:24), again presumably at the temple compound. The claim in Zech. 3:7 is different.[7] It concentrates responsibility for judging at the temple, not on a class of priests (the Levitical priests), but rather on the high priest himself. Zechariah's claim is, therefore, rather innovative. From his

---

[6] E.g., C. Jeremias, *Nachtgesichte*, 215.
[7] Cf. ibid., 219–221, on the relation of Zech. 3 to Ezekiel.

perspective, greater responsibility devolves on the high priest in the judicial arena.

In the second colon, responsibility for keeping charge of the courts is articulated. The term for "courtyard," *ḥāṣēr,* is not fully understood, since the system of inner and outer courtyards of the Jerusalemite temple is itself imperfectly known. I Kings 6:36 attests an inner courtyard, and I Kings 7:12 an outer courtyard. However, the precise range of activities undertaken in the inner as opposed to the outer courtyard is unclear. Sacrifices could be made and vows could be paid in Yahweh's courts (Isa. 1:12; 62:9; Pss. 96:8; 116:19; 135:2). And improper ritual action could take place there. So Manasseh is remembered as having erected improper cultic apparatus in the courtyard (II Kings 21:5). And Ezekiel attests improper worship in the inner court, Ezek. 8:7–13. Clearly the courtyards were important as a place of Israelite ritual activity, whether orthodox or heterodox. As far as historical development goes, the inner courtyard was apparently expanded at the expense of the great court.[8] Weinfeld contends that two separate courts developed "about the time of Ahaz or of Hezekiah, a situation that obtained into the Second Temple Period."[9] Zechariah seems interested in having the high priest exercise control not only over the temple proper but over the temple compound as well.

What is interesting in this regard is to note again the claim of Zechariah as that compares with the perspective preserved in Ezekiel's temple vision. The temple courtyard is the subject of considerable attention in that literature (see Ezek. 40:17–47). And the so-called Zadokite stratum in that temple vision makes clear that Zadokite Levites are in charge of at least the inner court, so Ezek. 44:17. What in Ezekiel is given into the hands of a group of priests is, in Zechariah, made the specific responsibility of one individual, the high priest.

At this point it is appropriate to attempt a resolution of the syntactic problem. Since all four cola in Zech. 3:7 raise the issue of responsibility over areas of action (areas that might be assigned differently, since all can be construed to entail responsibility over the temple complex, and since Beuken and others have shown that the *weˤgam . . . weˤgam* sequence may be translated as part of an apodosis), it makes sense to read all four clauses as part of the conditional charge to Joshua:

> *If* you walk according to my ways,
> and if you keep my charge,
> if you administer my house,
> and if you oversee my courts, then . . .

[8] See R. de Vaux, *Ancient Israel,* Vol. 2, *Religious Institutions,* 1965, 317.
[9] Weinfeld, *Deuteronomy and the Deuteronomic School,* 192–194.

Joshua is challenged to accept responsibility as high priest for activity that might otherwise (Ezek. 40–48) devolve on a group of priests, a group without an explicitly defined authority structure.[10]

The apodosis provides the reward to Joshua should he accept this responsibility. He is to receive a new sort of access to the deity: "I will let you move around among those standing here." Unfortunately, the word regularly translated "right of access" or the like is problematic. If *mahlᵉkîm* is related to the singular noun *mahᵃlāk*, the MT consonants would need to be repointed as *mahlākîm*. This singular noun *mahᵃlā* occurs three times in its absolute form and means "passageway" or "journey" (Ezek. 42:4; Jonah 3:3, 4; cf. Neh. 2:6). On the other hand, if one accepts the MT form, one must hypothesize a singular form *mahlēk* meaning "entrance" or "access."[11] In either case, it is possible to translate the word present in the Hebrew text as "entrance" or "access."[12]

To what is Joshua given access? Who are those "standing here"? It seems clear that those standing here are the *bᵉnê hā'ᵉlōhîm*, the lesser deities who comprise the divine council. The setting is none other than the divine council. Joshua is promised access to this august gathering, and apparently on a continuing basis. He is to have regular access to this group only if he performs the role of high priest by taking authority over other priests and over the temple compound as a whole.

What specific advantage this access to the divine council will yield is not made clear. We may, however, infer its importance by recalling others who have had access to the divine council. One role in ancient Israel was understood as having its authority derive from access to the divine council. Michaiah ben Imlah participated in and knew about the action of the council (I Kings 22). Isaiah volunteered for service within the context of the council (Isa. 6). And Jeremiah claims the authority of the council:

> For who among them has stood in the council of Yahweh,
> to perceive and hear his word,
> or who has given heed to his word and listened?
>
> (Jer. 23:18)

---

[10] Cf. C. Jeremias, *Nachtgesichte*, 216, who sees this as an allocation of royal authority over the temple—cf. the preexilic situation—to the high priest in a time when there was no longer a king.

[11] Thus Rudolph, 93.

[12] See also Mitchell, 160, who discusses alternative grammatical possibilities; Beuken, 293–295, who translates the word as referring to individuals, "I give you men who go . . ."; and R. Kutscher, who argues that the noun is an Aramaism ("*mahlᵉkîm* and the like"; *Leshonenu* 26, 1961/62, 93–96).

Needless to say, all these individuals performed as prophets. And interestingly, the imagery of standing in the council denotes participation in the council's activities and provides authority for prophetic activity (e.g., Jer. 23:18, 22).

From this perspective, the advantage to Joshua in complying with this admonition is clearer. If he so performs, he will have prophet-like authority.[13] He will know what is going on in the cosmic as well as the earthly realm, just as did Micaiah. And he might even be entrusted with a definitive word for a particular situation, as were the prophets. As high priest, he is offered the chance for a new kind of authority, something more than the typical routinized access to Yahweh indicated by the phrase *qārab 'el,* as in Ezek. 44:15 and its preexilic precursors.

The first oracular response, then, serves to highlight the notion of high priesthood. In particular it indicates the arena of responsibility in which the high priest should be active, and it indicates the special prerogative which will be his if he accepts that responsibility. As such, the oracle also serves as something of a corrective to the picture of priestly responsibility in Ezekiel: what was there the provenance of all priests is here focused on the role of one priest. Though conditional, this response serves to highlight the prominence of the high-priestly role in the postexilic polity.

[8] In the second oracular response, in v. 8, the situation is markedly different. Unconditional rather than conditional promises are made. Further, the promises appear to devolve on the Branch, not on Joshua. What do these differences suggest? This question can be answered only after a detailed analysis of the second oracle.

The oracle commences with what form critics have termed the "call to attention": "Now listen." The presence of this formula suggests strongly that v. 8 begins a new unit rather than continues an earlier speech. The addressees of this call to attention are Joshua and his cohorts: "your colleagues who sit before you." The use of the second-person pronominal suffix, *lᵉpāneykā,* as well as the third-person reference to the group, "They are men of good portent," indicates that Joshua, rather than a group, remains the primary subject of this oracle.

Despite this focus on Joshua, one does wonder about the identity of those sitting before Joshua. Many commentators suggest that they comprise a group of priests.[14] Unfortunately, there is little warrant for

---

[13] Cf. C. Jeremias, *Nachtgesichte,* 218, who associates such access with royal prerogatives.

[14] Baldwin, 116; Rudolph, 99.

this assertion. The texts proffered in its defense, II Kings 4:38 and 6:1, do not yield evidence of a priestly assembly with a high priest at its head. Nor does the syntax of the clause itself ("your friends/colleagues sitting before you") require a formal deliberative setting, though it does suggest that the high priest has a higher status (cf. the idiom "sit before" in Gen. 43:33). Those addressed and referred to could equally well be important members of the newly revivified society in and around Jerusalem, quite possibly those who had recently returned from Babylon. Some of those included in the lists preserved in Ezra 2 and Neh. 7 might be candidates for membership in this group.

Following the call-to-attention formula, *šᵉmaʿ nāʾ*, and the designation of those addressed, three clauses introduced by the particle *kî* occur. Such a syntactic sequence is peculiar and therefore difficult to translate. The particle *kî* is often used in the Hebrew Bible as a causative particle. Hence the first clause can, theoretically, be translated *"For* these men are a sign," and then the second *kî* can serve as a subordinating conjunction: *"that* I am bringing my servant." However, *kî* can also function as an emphatic particle, which may or may not be translated. So one might translate, "Indeed, they are men of portent." It is probably best to see this first clause as an aside serving to explain the significance of this group which has just been mentioned, and therefore to understand the first *kî* as a *kî affirmativum*.[15]

There is a further reason for understanding this first *kî* clause as an emphatic parenthesis to the preceding colon. When the second-person masculine singular imperative of *šmʿ* is used and *hinnēh* follows it, the *hinnēh* introduces the message. None of the message occurs prior to the *hinnēh*. So in Isa. 39:5; Jer. 34:4; and Ezek. 21:3, the only elements that occur between *šmʿ* and *hinnēh* are a designation of the audience or a designation in general terms of what is to be heard, e.g., the word of Yahweh. *Hinnēh* serves to introduce the actual oracle. This regularity of usage strongly suggests that the first *kî* clause comprises an emphatic parenthesis.

Whoever these individuals are, they are called, in this emphatic parenthesis, men of portent. This is an odd phrase. What sort of sign or portent they are, or are to be, is not indicated. However, on the basis of the way in which this phrase is used elsewhere (Isa. 8:18; Ezek. 12:6; 24:24, 27), for Yahweh to declare that they are a sign means we must conclude that Yahweh himself has designated them as a sign.[16] If the

---

[15] Rudolph, 98.
[16] See esp. Ezek. 12:6, "I have made you a sign . . ." and Isa. 8:18, "I and the children whom Yahweh has given me as signs and portents."

referent of these men of portent is as general as those who have returned from exile, then the significance might simply be that Jerusalem/Judah/Israel has a future. And that is a significant statement for the late sixth century B.C.E.

In the second *kî* clause, the *kî* also serves as an emphatic. However, here the actual message is introduced as indicated in the *hinnēh*. *Kî* serves to highlight the significance of the message that is introduced by the standard initiatory particle *hinnēh*. Joshua and others are apprised of the specific form of Yahweh's action. Joshua is told that Yahweh is bringing an individual, "my servant"; and then the metaphoric language of the oracles, introduced by the phrase "men of portent," continues. This individual servant is termed a branch, *ṣemaḥ*. To designate some person or place as a plant growth seems at first glance unusual, though such a metaphor is used by several of Israel's prophets. Ezekiel employed this term to describe Jerusalem (Ezek. 16:7). Further, the notion of a Davidic ruler in the future is explored by plant imagery, though not using this particular term for plant: "There shall come forth a shoot from the stump of Jesse, and a branch *(nēṣer)* shall grow out of his roots" (Isa. 11:1). This same notion, of a member of the Davidic line as large plant, also appears in the book of Jeremiah. And there the term *ṣemaḥ* is used to refer specifically to the Davidic ruler.

"Behold, the days are coming, says Yahweh, when I will raise up for David a righteous Branch *(ṣemaḥ)*, and he shall reign as king and deal wisely, and shall execute justice and righteousness in the land" (Jer. 23:5).[17] There can be little doubt that Zechariah and others knew oracles of this sort, i.e., ones in which future weal is linked to the prosperity of the Davidic line conceived of as a growing plant, as *ṣemaḥ*. This picture of weal could be invoked simply by mentioning *ṣemaḥ*, which is precisely what the Zechariah oracle accomplishes. No more need be said. The image of a just and beneficent ruler is called up by the metaphor. Restored royal government at Yahweh's instigation will redound to the welfare of Judah and Israel.

In Zechariah's time, hopes for the culmination of such a promise rested with one person, the returned Davidic heir, Zerubbabel. This sentiment is also attested in Hag. 2:23, a text that emphasizes the political future of the Davidic scion. If we are correct in suggesting that the men of portent are those who had returned from Babylon, then those men would have known Zerubbabel; he had accompanied them

[17] This text appears in a prose version in Jer. 33:14–16. On the relationship of the two Jeremiah texts, see E. Nicholson, *Preaching to the Exiles*, 1970, 89ff.

on their journey to Syria-Palestine. The oracle, therefore, serves to announce weal and, equally important, serves to make that weal focus not on Joshua but on Zerubbabel.[18] Such an announcement serves as a challenge to the immediately preceding oracular response, one that describes the power to rule—albeit in the temple compound—as residing with Joshua. The oracle, i.e, v. 8, short as it is, serves as something of a rejoinder to the sentiment expressed in v. 7.

[9] The sequence of *kî hinnî* in 8d followed by *kî hinnēh* in v. 9 raises serious questions about the connection between vs. 8 and 9. We would expect the one *kî hinnēh* construction to introduce the crucial element in the oracle. To have two such constructions is anomalous. Further, the content and imagery of v. 9 do not continue that begun in v. 7, all the more strange since pride of place in v. 9 shifts back to Joshua.[19] Given this thesis, v. 8 would be an oracular response formulated in dialogue both with the vision and with the prior response of vs. 7 and 9. Zechariah 3:8 would be a response designed to buttress the position of Zerubbabel over against that of Joshua.

As for the continuation of the first oracle in Zech. 3:9, debate has swirled over the identity of the stone. What sort of stone is intended? Is it in fact a stone, or is it a metaphor for a person? If a stone, is it one to be used in the reconstruction of the temple, a ritual cornerstone?[20] Or is it a stone designed for ritual usage? The plethora of earlier interpretations leaves little room for ingenious alternatives. In my judgment, the explanation offered many years ago by Mitchell remains the most satisfactory, and this despite the more recent proposal of Petitjean. Mitchell maintained that one element of the high-priestly regalia, an item indirectly referred to in the vision itself, was intended.[21] It is the metallic plate, the gold plaque that is part of the high priest's headdress as described in Ex. 28:36–38. This object is the probable referent of the Zech. 3:9 stone, since:

1. It is available only to the high priest. Zechariah 3:9 clearly states that the stone functions in conjunction with Joshua: "I have set before Joshua."

2. It is engraved. Exodus 28:36 states, "You shall . . . engrave on it, like the engraving of a signet, 'Holy to Yahweh.' " Zechariah 3:9 states, "I will engrave its inscription."

3. The stone, according to Zech. 3:9, is to have seven "eyes" or

---

[18] Cf. Rudolph, 100.
[19] Rudolph, ibid., argues that 8b is an insertion interrupting the flow of 8a–9.
[20] On this thesis see Petitjean, *Oracles*, 179.
[21] Mitchell, 157–158.

facets. The inscription on the Exodus plaque, "Holy to Yahweh," can be construed as having seven consonants: *qdš lyhw*.

4. The plaque is instrumental in the removal of *ʿāwôn* (sin/guilt) in Israelite ritual. Exodus 28:38 reads, "It shall be upon Aaron's forehead, and Aaron shall take upon himself any guilt incurred in the holy offering which the people of Israel hallow as their holy gifts." So too, the stone in Zech. 3:9 is linked with the bearing and removal of guilt. Just after stating that he will engrave the stone, the deity pronounces, "I will remove the guilt of this land in a single day."

If this identification is correct, then the identity of the stone is no longer a problem. We know what its purpose was and we know what the inscription is to be. And yet, Zech. 3:9 does not provide simply a recapitulation of the metal plaque and of its function when employed by the Aaronite high priest (*"You* shall make . . . *you* shall engrave . . . and *Aaron* shall take upon himself . . ."; Ex. 28:36–38). The major actor is different in Zech. 3:9. In this oracular response to the vision, Yahweh, not Israel, is the primary agent (*"I* have set, *I* will engrave, *I* will remove"). What Israelites and the high priest were to do from the perspective of Ex. 28 is, from the perspective of this writer, to be undertaken by Yahweh. And the claim is actually stronger than that. What Aaron was to bear *(nśʾ)*, Yahweh will remove *(mwš)*. Yahweh will do that which no human could accomplish, even if he were the high priest.

This oracular response is fully consistent with the divine impetus already elucidated in the vision. There Yahweh's agents purified and clothed Joshua. Here Yahweh will act to enable to proper completion of the high priestly regalia. In so acting, he will make it possible for the *ʿāwôn* (the same term used in 3:4) to be removed in a single day. The power of such divine activity resonates with the power of divine activity on another *yôm ʾeḥād*, another single day, that of Gen. 1:5. Yahweh and the purified high priest cooperate to engender a newly purified community. And the impetus for such cleansing action rests essentially with divine, not with human, initiative.

[10] Zechariah 3:10 completes this redactional unit, which comprises all of ch. 3. As is typical of such additions, it is introduced by the adverbial connector. "On that day," here followed by the formula "says Yahweh of Hosts." Two *Stichwörter* make the connection seem less than artificial. The term *rʿh* is present both in v. 10 and in the intrusive oracular addition, v. 8. In addition, the word *yôm* occurred at the end of v. 9, just before the inceptive formula present in v. 10. The connection between v. 10 and the foregoing is stronger than just catchwords. This verse serves to explore thematically one metaphor

included in that same intrusive oracular addition. Verse 10 picks up on
the vegetative imagery introduced in v. 8: "Behold, I am bringing my
servant, the Branch." The word *ṣemaḥ* ("branch") in v. 8 is not only
used in a symbolic way (there it is a clear metaphoric reference to the
Davidic line). This word can also be used to refer to plant material, as
in Gen. 19:25. The use of the term in a complex allegory in Ezek. 17:9
demonstrates that it can also refer to luxuriant plant growth,
suggesting that a vine might bring forth branches, bear fruit, and
become a noble vine. It is this sense of noble and luxuriant growth
which the writer of Zech. 3:10 apparently intended to convey by his use
of the term *gepen*. Here the author depicts a great vine, one under
which people could sit. That notion, suggested in the earlier text by
ṣemaḥ, enabled the author to borrow a formulaic expression of weal
used elsewhere in the Hebrew Bible. I Kings 5:5 [4:25E] reads, "And
Judah and Israel dwelt in safety, from Dan even to Beersheba, every
man under his vine and under his fig tree, all the days of Solomon."
And Micah 4:4 also includes this notion: "They shall sit every man
under his vine and his fig tree, and none shall make them afraid."[22] In
the first of these two examples, the source of weal is Davidic rule—that
of Solomon; whereas in the second, the source of weal is Yahweh's rule
"on that day." This particular expression of good fortune, sitting
under fig tree and vine, was appropriate for describing the effects of
rule by either a divine or a human king. This same notion of royal weal
would appear to be in the Zechariah text as well, since the source of the
plant imagery, the use of *ṣemaḥ*, is directly connected with the Davidic
line. A further important feature of this verse is the scope of the
forthcoming weal. All Israelites will experience this time of peace and
fertility. Such universality is also present in the other expressions of
this formula, e.g., I Kings 5:5 and Micah 4:4. The authors there
describe those who will experience this beneficence as "Judah and
Israel" and "many peoples." This motif of cosmic peace is fully
consistent with the notion "all the earth" which pervades Zechariah's
visions.

  This addition in Zech. 3:10 not only builds upon the vision and the
primary oracular response, both of which focus on purification and the
role of the high-priestly headdress; it also builds upon the secondary or
intrusive oracular response, one that highlights the royal personage
and in so doing allows for reflection on royal, here probably divinely
royal, dominion.[23] Further, v. 10 builds upon notions of present

---

[22] See also the Rabshakeh's speech in II Kings 18:31.
[23] See Rudolph, 103.

purification, setting the society religiously right, and pushes into the future, where the purification will result in peaceful social relationships that benefit society as a whole (cf. Micah 4:4).

In sum, Zech. 3 has tackled an immense and difficult problem for the postexilic community. How may the serious contamination of destruction and exile be cleansed? The vision (vs. 1–5) suggests that the cleansing of the improperly accused Joshua will be accomplished in the divine council, but not by the deity himself. In the first oracular response (vs. 6–7, 9), Joshua is offered significant prerogatives if he accepts responsibility over the temple compound. However, he is penultimately important because Yahweh, by means of recreating the gold plaque, will remove Israel's guilt "in one day." With the high priest cleansed (vs. 1–5) and with the guilt of the people removed (v. 9), the new community could begin to function again. The second oracular response (v. 8) appears designed to balance the prior emphasis on Joshua by pointing to the importance of the Davidic branch in the forthcoming restoration. Verse 10 concludes the section by uniting themes and words present in both oracular reponses and by pointing toward a period of social peace which will result from divine and human royal dominion.

Zechariah 4:1–6a, 10b–14

I see a lampstand, all of it is gold

1 The messenger who spoke with me returned and roused me as when one is awakened.
2 And he said to me,
      "What do you see?"
    And I said,[a]
      "I see a lampstand,
        all of it is gold.
      A bowl[b] is on its top,
        and seven are its lamps.
      There are seven spouts[c]
        for the lamps upon its top.
3 There are two olive trees above it,[d]
        one to the right of the bowl
        and one to its left."
4 I responded to the messenger who spoke with me,
      "What are these, my lord?"

5   Then the messenger who had spoken with me said,
       "Do you not know what these things are?"
     And I said, "No, my lord."
6a   Then he responded to me,
10b   "These seven are the eyes of Yahweh;
          they range about over all the earth."
11   Then I asked him, "What are those two olive trees
       at the right and the left of the lampstand?"
12   And then a second time I asked him,
       "What are the two streams of olive oil
          which empty out through the gold spouts upon them?"ᵉ
13   And he said to me,
       "Do you not know what these are?"
     And I said, "No, my lord."
14   And he said,
       "These are the two sons of oil
       who stand before the Lord of the entire earth."

a. Reading with Qere. Ketib preserves a 3 masc. sg. converted imperfect.

b. Read *gullāh* without mappiq, which is surely present in MT as a dittography from the preceding word.

c. MT *mûṣāqôt* is problematic. Some take the root to be *yṣq* and theorize a nominal form, **mûṣeqet*, "pipe" (e.g., JPS). Others (e.g., Rudolph, 107) take the root to be *ṣwq*, "be narrow," and argue for a noun *mûṣāq*, "a pinch." See also K. Möhlenbrink, "Der Leuchter im fünften Nachtgesicht des Propheten Sacharja," *ZDPV* 52, 1929, 285.

d. There is ambiguity as a result of the preposition *'āleyhā*. One expects, literally, "above it" or "over it," though many translate "by it" (e.g., RSV). See the commentary for discussion.

e. Verse 12 is abysmally hard to translate. The difficulty may well result from a redactor who wanted to cloud the meaning of the previous verses.

The Fifth Vision

[1] The fifth vision commences in an unusual way. We are told that the *mal'āk* returns and that Zechariah is roused. In the fourth vision, in ch. 3, we observed that the usual dialogue between Zechariah and the *mal'āk* is absent. The reason for this lack of communication between the two is that the *mal'āk* was fully involved in the divine conciliar activity. In the fourth vision he was functioning at a remove from the prophet. Now he has returned to his accustomed role as interlocutor and interpreter.

Also important in 4:1 is the view that the prophet has lasped into a state similar to sleep. The return of the *mal'āk* signals the "reawakening" of the prophet. One must, however, wonder if the author intended us to think that Zechariah had actually fallen asleep. In my judgment, such a contention is unlikely. Otherwise the following simile, "as when one is awakened," would be redundant. From the writer's perspective, Zechariah may have been deep in thought, or perhaps in a state of trance possession, but he was not actually asleep. Such a contention is fully corroborated by the actual language used in the clause describing the *mal'āk*'s action toward Zechariah. The verb *'wr* in the hiphil conjugation is used not only to mean "awaken" but also to mean "stir up, rouse to action" (cf. Joel 4:9 [3:9E], "Stir up the mighty men for war"; see also Dan. 11:2, 25).

[2] In the visions up to this point, Zechariah has reported seeing an object or scene at the very beginning of the vision report: "I saw a man mounted on a bay horse (1:8); "I saw four horns'" (2:1 [1:18E]); "I saw a man holding a measuring line" (2:5 [1E]); "He showed me Joshua, the high priest" (3:1). However, in the fifth vision, the pattern of which is approximated by the seventh vision, the *mal'āk* begins the interrogation before Zechariah reports seeing anything. We first hear "What do you see?"—a question that when used in the sixth vision follows Zechariah's report of ocular experience. The format of this fifth vision suggests that the *mal'āk* is prodding Zechariah to continue with his visionary activity. The *mal'āk* seems to be saying, "Just because things seem to be going properly," in accordance with the messages of the first four visions, "do not think that the world has been set fully right." This is at least one way of interpreting the basic thrust of the *mal'āk*'s opening words to Zechariah. Only after having been prodded by the initial question does Zechariah again report seeing an object, this time a gold lampstand of rather specific design. In sum, both the notion of being roused and the unusual sequence of question and then statement of object work together to indicate that a new visionary sequence has commenced. Yahweh's work of weal, as that reached a preliminary climax in the restoration of the high-priestly figure, has not yet been completed. More work remains to be done.

After Zechariah is prodded to visionary activity, he does report seeing several objects. Specific though these descriptions of the objects are, a gold lampstand and two olive trees, their exact configuration and physical relation to each other have remained a difficult problem. The reasons for this difficulty are several:

1. The specific Hebrew terms included in the description—*mᵉnôrāh* (lampstand), *gullāh* (bowl), *rō'šāh* (top), *šib'āh nērôt* (seven lamps), *šib'āh mûṣāqôt* (seven pipes or indentations)—as well as *šᵉnê ṣantᵉrôt hazzāhāb* (the two gold spouts), if one includes v. 12—are difficult to combine into one integrated ritual object.

2. The term *mᵉnôrāh* has, for millennia, signified a well-known object in Jewish ritual practice, a seven-light candelabrum. It is difficult to read the term *mᵉnôrāh* and not have that object come immediately to mind.

3. Two other biblical texts (Ex. 25:31–40; 37:17–24) describe a gold lampstand or *mᵉnôrāh*, a lamp to be placed near the tabernacle. It is not at all clear what relationship this clearly described lampstand has to the menorah envisioned by Zechariah.

4. Archaeologists have, during the past century, discovered a number of lamps and lampstands, some of which appear to be quite similar to that described in Zechariah's fifth vision.

5. The placement of the olive trees in relation to the lampstand is not absolutely clear. They flank it, but the preposition used to describe their relationship to the lamp may indicate that they are above and not simply next to the lamp.

For these reasons at least, we must ask afresh, what might Zechariah have in fact seen? At the same time we must remember that this issue of what he saw is, analytically speaking, different from the question of what those objects signified from the perspective of the angelic interpreter.

The term *mᵉnôrāh* is (with the sole exception of II Kings 4:10) in the Hebrew Bible always used to refer to lampstands created for ritual usage. In the ritual contexts apart from Zech. 4, the term is used in two quite different ways. On the one hand, it is used in the plural *(mᵉnôrôt)* to refer to lampstands that were created for Solomon's temple. These lampstands were understood to derive from Phoenician tradition. Hiram of Tyre, the imported artisan, fashioned them, along with other metallic objects, for temple use (I Kings 7:49). We are told that there were ten such lamps (I Kings 7:49; II Chron. 4:7), "five on the south side and five on the north side." And in Jer. 52:19 we learn that "the lampstands" were among the plunder that the Babylonians captured in 587. These historical sources suggest, from beginning to end, that there were ten gold lampstands in the Jerusalem temple. They were manufactured during the united monarchy and were lost at the defeat of Jerusalem. In these same texts, the notion of a single lampstand, the *mᵉnôrāh*, is lacking.

On the other hand, the singular noun *mᵉnôrāh* occurs primarily in the Tetrateuch.[1] Furthermore, the object referred to is always the so-called tabernacle *mᵉnôrāh*. This same notion of a singular *mᵉnôrāh* also occurs in II Chron. 13:11.

All references to multiple lampstands stem from descriptions that refer to the preexilic temple and that, in all likelihood, were written in the preexilic or early exilic period. And all references to a singular *mᵉnôrāh* derive from literature that probably was written in the postexilic period. This situation is striking evidence about the ritual history of lampstands. There is little or no evidence for a singularly significant lampstand prior to the period of the exile. That lampstands were used in the preexilic period is not to be gainsaid. That one lampstand was peculiarly significant, whether as tree of life or symbol of Yahweh's presence, is difficult indeed to affirm. Zechariah's vision of a gold lampstand may well be the first time one *mᵉnôrāh* is singled out as especially significant. On traditio-historical grounds alone, it is unlikely that what Zechariah "saw" is what the priestly writers meant by their *mᵉnôrāh*, the so-called tabernacle *mᵉnôrāh*.

The first descriptive element that Zechariah includes in his vision has to do with the composition of the *mᵉnôrāh*. It is made entirely of gold. Interestingly, the other two *mᵉnôrāh* traditions—the Solomonic lampstands and the tabernacle lampstand—each include mention of gold as well. And yet, in each case, the description of the gold is different. The priestly lampstand is to be made out of "pure gold," *mᵉnôrat zāhāb ṭāhôr* (Ex. 25:31 et passim). The term "pure" *(ṭāhôr)*, when applied to metal within a priestly context, is ambiguous. Nonmetallic objects, when ritually clean, are pure (e.g., Lev. 11, on various types of clean versus unclean animals; Lev. 13, on various types of clean versus unclean persons). However, when the term "pure" is applied to metallic objects, it could refer to metals that appear in their natural state, e.g., native gold or silver, and yet that have been refined to remove minor impurities; or it could perhaps refer to native gold that has fewer impurities than other, less pure forms of native gold.[2] Meyers comments, "Though the usual priestly use of *ṭāhôr* expresses matters of ritual or cultic purity, the likelihood is strong that when it refers to gold it also conveys a technical meaning relating to methods for procuring pure

---

[1] Ex. 25:31–35; 31:8; 35:14; 37:17–20; 39:37; 40:24; Lev. 24:4; Num. 3:31; 4:9; 8:2–4. All of these texts are regularly assigned either to the priestly hand or to the hand of a priestly redactor (see M. Noth, *A History of Pentateuchal Traditions*, 1972, 268–273).

[2] According to C. Meyers, *The Tabernacle Menorah*, 1976, 55 n. 133, the technology for refining impurities out of gold is unlikely to have been in use prior to the fifth century B.C.E.

gold by 'washing.' "[3] In my judgment it is more likely that the term *ṭāhôr*, if it has a more technical, nonritual connotation, refers to the quality of the gold rather than the method by which it is mined, i.e., washed from the surrounding matrix. Despite the ambiguity this term entails, we may be sure that the priestly writer thought that the tabernacle *mᵉnôrāh* was to be made of the best quality gold and that it was to be ritually pure.

When the gold lampstands placed in Solomon's temple are described, the gold is described as *sāgûr*. Biblical Hebrew usage would suggest that this term refers to beaten gold (I Kings 6:20, 21), and perhaps to solid gold (I Kings 7:49, "the lampstands of pure gold"—though here the reference could be to an object overlaid with gold veneer).[4] The term *sāgûr* is quite clearly cognate to Akkadian *sagru, sakru,* and the phrase *zāhāb sāgûr* is cognate with Akkadian *ḫurāṣu sakru,* though unfortunately the precise meaning of this Akkadian phrase is not clear.[5] Since one text (I Kings 6:20, 21) clearly refers to a form of gold that is used to overlay a part of the temple, the use of the phrase *zāhāb sāgûr* is probably not a reference to the purity of gold but rather to the form in which it is used, a type of gold overlay. Thus it is possible that the gold lampstands in the Solomonic temple were not solid gold but rather gold overlay.

When we return to the description of the gold lampstand in Zechariah's vision, we discover that Zechariah's claim is neither that of the priestly writer nor that of the narrative preserved in Kings. He does not claim that the gold is pure, either ritually pure or metallurgically untainted, nor does he maintain that it is gold overlay, *zāhāb sāgûr*. He states that the *mᵉnôrāh* he sees is solid gold, a claim different from that which is presented explicitly in either of the other *mᵉnôrāh* traditions—though of course there is nothing in the priestly tradition which would lead one to think that the tabernacle *mᵉnôrāh* was not solid gold.

After the general statement "I see a lampstand, all of it is gold," Zechariah provides a more detailed description of its construction. We are told three things: It has a bowl on its top; there are seven lights on its top; and there are seven indentations for the lights, which are also on the top of the bowl. Each of these elements requires comment.

---

[3] Ibid., 29–30.

[4] Cf. also II Chron. 9:20; 4:20, 22; Job 28:15. J. Gray translates the term in I Kings as refined gold, adducing Arabic *sajara* ("heat an oven") as evidence for refining activity (*I & II Kings,* OTL, 1974, 170).

[5] See Meyers, *The Tabernacle Menorah,* 30, 52 n. 100.

1. The term *gullāh* means basin, bowl, or pool (see Eccl. 12:6; Josh. 15:19).[6] Clearly a rounded container or installation suitable for holding or storing some sort of liquid—whether water, oil, or wine—is intended by such a term. Fortunately, there is considerable artifactual evidence for both lamps and lampstands which have a bowl that serves as a reservoir for the oil which the lamp burns. Such lamps or lampstands clearly fit this first part of Zechariah's description. (See Figure 1.)

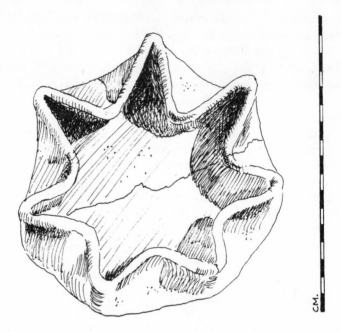

Figure 1. *Seven-spouted lamp from Dothan Tomb 1, Late Bronze–Iron I*

2. Zechariah reports that seven lights are on the lampstand; more specifically, these lights are on "its" top. The referent for the pronoun "its" must be a noun of the feminine gender. Unfortunately, both the word for "lampstand" and the word for "bowl" are feminine. Hence the reference is ambiguous. The strictest construction of the syntax would require the referent to be the lampstand, since reference to the

[6] Cf. the use of the term *gullāh* to describe one element of the capitals on columns in the Jerusalem temple (I Kings 7:41–42).

lampstand occurs most immediately, on the suffix of *rō'š*, and before the preposition in question. Interestingly, many of the lamps and lampstands discovered by archaeologists have pinches on the clay rims that allow more than one wick to be placed in a given lamp. Put another way, one lamp may have several, even seven or more lights, as in Figure 1. Both artifactual and textual evidence allow for a number of lights, i.e., wicks, on one lampstand (cf. Ex. 39:37; 40:25).

3. Most problematic are the *mûṣāqôt*, the spouts or indentations (see the textual note). The only other apparent usage of this term in biblical Hebrew comes in II Chron. 4:3, a text difficult in its own right. The Chronicles passage parallels one in I Kings 7:24, a verse that describes the design of the bronze "sea" placed in the temple compound. According to I Kings 7:24, the sea has gourd-shaped objects (*p^eqā'îm*) under its rim. They were cast of a piece with the sea itself (*y^eṣuqîm bîṣuqātô*) and were aligned in two rows (*š^enê ṭûrîm happ^eqā'îm*). The Chronicles passage appears to be a corrupt version of this earlier description. II Chronicles 4:3 starts out by referring to the image of oxen (*ûd^emût b^eqārîm*) that proceed for ten cubits. Then oxen are described as below the "sea" and *y^eṣûqîm b^emuṣaqtô*, literally, cast with its spouts/niches. However, when this phrase is compared with its parallel in Kings, it would appear that the Chronicles version is a corruption, based on the accidental introduction of *mem* into *bîṣuqātô*. Put another way, the theorized noun **mûṣeqet* does not occur in II Chron. 4:3. If Möhlenbrink's proposal for the etymology of *mûṣāqôt* in Zech. 4:2 is correct, as deriving from *ṣwq*, "be in straits," then there is no Hebrew noun **mûṣeqet* which derives from *yṣq*.

Following Möhlenbrink's proposal, which has been accepted by North, among others, we may construe the term *mûṣāqôt* in Zech. 4:2 to refer to a pinched lip on a lamp rim, a place in which the wick might be placed so as to drape down into the round reservoir of oil.[7] From a structural perspective, then, Zechariah's lampstand apparently entails stand, bowl, lights, and indentations for a wick. Quite fortuitously, excavations at Tel Dan in 1969 yielded a lampstand, dated by the excavator to the early Iron Age, which has all the essential features of the lampstand that Zechariah describes. (See Figure 2.) This particular lampstand is similar to one found earlier at Taanach, which has been dated ca. 1300 B.C.E.

In sum, the lampstand seen by Zechariah bears strong structural similarity to a lampstand ceramic tradition attested in Syria-Palestine in the Late Bronze and Iron Ages. All of the specific features in the

[7] R. North, "Zechariah: Seven Spout Lampstand," *Bib* 51, 1970, 183–206.

descriptions of the lampstand in 4:2—the bowl, a stand, multiple lights, and pinches in the clay rim—are explicable on the basis of lampstands discovered in the Levant and dating to the monarchic period and earlier. On the basis of this evidence, we have a reasonably good idea of what Zechariah probably saw.[8] From this perspective, what is unusual about Zechariah's lampstand is not its configuration. What is unusual is its composition—totally of gold.

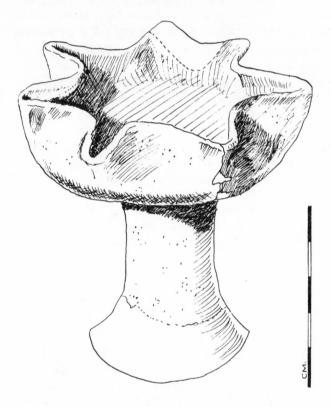

Figure 2. *Seven-spouted lamp on stand from Dan, Iron I*

If Zechariah's lampstand appears to be similar to those attested archaeologically, what is its relation to the lampstand described in Ex. 25, the so-called tabernacle lampstand? That lampstand is provided

[8] We need not depend upon Galling's reconstruction now that the Dan lampstand is available (see *IDB* III, 66).

with a considerably more detailed description than what is given in Zech. 4. It is to have a base, a shaft, and six branches, three stemming from each side. Each of the branches is to terminate in "three cups made like almonds, each with capital and flower" (Ex. 25:33). On the central shaft, there are apparently to be four cups made like almonds, with their capitals and flowers. The lampstand is to bear seven lights so oriented that they "give light upon the space in front of it." Though many scholars have thought that the seven lights were to be distributed each to a branch and one on the central stem, this is never explicitly stated in the text. Since the termination of the stem is larger than the terminations of the individual branches, it is possible that all the wicks were placed on the central structure.[9] The lampstand is to be fashioned out of gold, "the whole of it one piece of hammered work of pure gold."

It is extremely difficult to proffer any reconstruction of that ritual lampstand, the more so since the first artifactual evidence for a lampstand with branches, the sort of menorah used in Jewish tradition, is first attested in the Roman period in the coinage of the Maccabees and on the Arch of Titus in Rome.[10] What one may say about this lampstand is that it is markedly different from that described in Zech. 4. (1) Explicit mention of a separate base and shaft, found in Ex. 25, is lacking in Zech. 4. (2) There is no mention of branches in the Zechariah lampstand, and these elements are constitutive for the description in Ex. 25. (3) There is no mention of elaborate terminations in the lampstand envisioned by Zechariah. (4) Explicit reference to floral or agricultural motifs (branches, almonds, flowers), which predominates in Ex. 25, is totally missing in Zech. 4. Clearly, the differences between these two lampstands outweigh the similarities, e.g., the presence of seven lights, or the composition out of gold. Hence, it is unwarranted to assume that Zechariah's lampstand bears significant resemblance to the lampstand described by the priestly writer in Ex. 25. And it is equally inappropriate to infer that whatever significance the Exodus lampstand entails may also apply to the lampstand which Zechariah saw. That lampstand bears strong resemblance to lamps excavated in Syria-Palestine which predate his activity, and not to lampstands excavated and iconographically attested which significantly postdate his activity (e.g., the branched menorah).

[3] We may therefore be reasonably certain of the form of the menorah in the tableau. The scene continues in v. 3. Zechariah sees two olive trees. Given the well-known configuration of the olive tree

---

[9] See Meyers, *IDB Supp*, 586–587.
[10] See *IDB* III, 65.

and the distinctive luster of its leaves, there can be little doubt about the identity of these objects. The placement of these two olive trees in the tableau is quite another matter. The text apparently locates the trees with reference to the lampstand, i.e., the pronominal suffix on the preposition '*al* presumably refers to the lampstand. The trees are listed as '*āleyhā,* by or above it. The preposition is itself ambiguous. Most translators choose the former option, by or beside the lampstand. This interpretation places the trees with their bases on the same horizontal plane as the one on which the base of the lampstand rests. There is, however, warrant for considering the other option, since the trees are located in relationship to one specific element of the lampstand. They flank the bowl, the text states, "one on the right of the bowl and one on its left." Because the bowl is the uppermost part of the lampstand, it is appropriate to view the trees as having an elevated position in the vision. The trees may be understood to float in the upper register of the scene, flanking the bowl of this brilliant gold lampstand.

[4–6a] Clear though the scene is, Zechariah is apparently puzzled. He asks the messenger, "What are these?" A strict construction of the grammar requires that "these" refers not to the lights on the lampstand but rather to the olive trees, since they are the elements most recently mentioned. Then for the first time in the visionary sequence, Zechariah receives something of a reprimand from the *mal'āk.* The heavenly messenger responds, "Do you not know what these things are?" Perhaps we are to think that the *mal'āk's* counterquestion includes reference to all that Zechariah has just seen, i.e., the lamp as well as the olive trees. In any case, he seems to suggest that Zechariah should have understood the significance of the objects this time, something that has not been the case in earlier visions and something that will not be repeated in the subsequent visions. Whatever the reason for the *mal'āk's* counterquestion, it stands as a rebuff to the prophet. And it gains the admission by Zechariah: "No, my lord [I do not know what they signify]."

Immediately after Zechariah's admission of ignorance, we are told that the *mal'āk* speaks again. Verse 6a reads, "And he responded to me . . ." What follows this introduction is an oracle dealing with quite another issue, the status of Zerubbabel in temple-building ceremonies and what that means for the postexilic polity. The oracle, Zech. 4:6b–10a, is, as most commentators have maintained, a poetic intrusion into the interpretation of the vision.[11]

___

[11] See the standard commentaries and Beuken's quite different assessment.

[10b] After this intrusive word from the deity, which I will consider below, the interpretation of the *mal'āk* which was introduced in 6a continues in 10b. We hear "these" spoken of again, and yet "these" now has a referent other than the one apparent in Zechariah's question. Zechariah was speaking either about the trees or about all the objects in the vision together. The *mal'āk*, however, speaks of a more discrete set, seven things: "These seven are the eyes of Yahweh, they range over all the earth." As one looks back to the description of Zechariah, it is possible that this number seven can refer to two nouns, either lights or indentations. And yet since the indentations provide for the wicks that create the lights, the referents are, in fact, indistinguishable. The *mal'āk* is referring to the seven indentations as they allow for or create the lights. Put another way, the *mal'āk* is focusing Zechariah's attention on one element in the vision, the lights of the lampstand. And he relates these lights to active eyes of the deity: "the eyes of Yahweh, they range about over all the earth." What does the *mal'āk* intend by such an interpretation?

The notion of the eye or eyes of Yahweh is well attested in the biblical material, so well attested that the frequency of usage has generated a rather complex notion. Surprisingly, this anthropomorphism has not been the subject of comprehensive study.[12] In my judgment, one may describe the concept of the eye(s) of Yahweh in the following ways:

1. There is a usage which suggests that Yahweh's eyes encompass the earth. Nothing is hidden from him. (Cf. Prov. 15:3, "The eyes of the Lord are in every place, keeping watch on the evil and the good"; see also Ps. 66:7.)

2. Given this fact, no one—man, woman, nation—should think it possible to hide from Yahweh's eyes. (Cf. Job 34:21, "For his eyes are upon the ways of a man, and he sees all his steps.") His vantage is such that he can see everything. (Cf. Psalm 14:2, "Yahweh looks down from heaven upon the children of men"; see also Ps. 113:5ff.)

3. When God "eyes," he will be able to determine whether an individual or group is following his dictates to act properly. So Ps. 14:2 continues: ". . . to see if there are any that act wisely, that seek after God." A text in Jeremiah is similar in providing a logical corollary. The deity, with his eyes open to all the ways of men, will reward everyone according to the fruit of his doings (Jer. 32:19).

---

[12] A. Oppenheim's essay, "The Eyes of the Lord," *JAOS* 88, 1968, 173–180, is of great value. More typical, however, are statements such as those of Beuken, 265, that Yahweh's eyes are a symbol for his all-knowing character, a facet of his character that can work itself out in either a judgmental or a beneficent way.

4. To this extent, Yahweh can be understood as "setting his eye for good or for evil." In his fifth vision, Amos sees and hears Yahweh say, "Though they go into captivity before their enemies, there I will command the sword, and it shall slay them; and I will set my eyes upon them for evil and not for good" (Amos 9:4). Ezekiel's formulaic expression "My eye will not spare, I will have no pity" is an expression of this same motif (Ezek. 5:11; 7:4, 9; 8:18; 9:10). Jeremiah uses this same basic vocabulary—the verb *śām (śym)* and the preposition *'al*—to describe Yahweh's restorative action toward those who have been exiled: "I will set my eyes upon them for good (Jer. 24:6; cf. Ezek. 20:17).

5. Other texts describe Yahweh's eyes as on or upon those who fear him. Israel receives a beneficent gaze as a sign of favor or protection: "I will instruct you and teach you the way you should go; I will counsel you with my eye upon you" (Ps. 32:8); "Behold, the eye of the Lord is on those who fear him, on those who hope in his steadfast love" (Ps. 33:18); "He does not withdraw his eyes from the righteous" (Job 36:7); "But upon the house of Judah I will open my eyes, when I strike every horse of the peoples with blindness" (Zech. 12:4).

Interestingly, the eyes of God can be construed as the beneficent side of the deity, and this in contradistinction to his face, which is one figure of speech for that aspect of the deity which is directed against evildoers: "The eyes of Yahweh are toward the righteous, and his ears toward their cry. The face of Yahweh is against evildoers, to cut off the remembrance of them from the earth" (Ps. 34:15–16).

Such is the biblical usage of the phrase "the eyes of Yahweh." In an important article, Oppenheim has argued that "the eyes of the Lord" is an expression that receives much of its significance from the notion of the eye(s) of the king as that expression is preserved in ancient Near Eastern sources. There the phrase refers to "informers, accusers, internal spies, censors, secret agents and their like."[13] Oppenheim makes a strong case that such activity is reflected in biblical traditions about such figures as the satan, the couching demon *(rābiṣum)* mentioned in Gen. 4:7.[14] It is clear that some biblical texts concerning the omnipresent eyes of Yahweh may reflect this usage derived from human political agency. However, not all notions of the deity are so easily reduced to their putative human prototype.

The closest parallel to the notion of the eyes of Yahweh, as that is found in Zech. 4:10b, is presented neither in extrabiblical nor in

---

13 Oppenheim, "The Eyes of the Lord," 180.
14 See E. Speiser, *Genesis,* Anchor Bible, 1964, 33.

biblical texts that reflect Oppenheim's notion of royal eyes. Rather, in II Chron. 16:9 we encounter exactly the phrase that occurs in the Zechariah vision interpretation, "The eyes of Yahweh range over the entire earth." In order to understand fully the significance of this phrase, it is necessary to assess its use in the Chronicles passage, a text that has often been misunderstood. In this text, Asa, king of Judah, is being criticized by the prophet Hanani for having enlisted Syrian aid in order to defeat the Northern Kingdom. Hanani has just stated—in the form of a rhetorical question—that Asa had earlier defeated a large political force: "Were not the Ethiopians and the Libyans a huge army with exceedingly many chariots and horsemen? Yet because you relied on Yahweh he gave them into your hand." Clearly, Asa had, at an earlier moment, acted properly by avoiding foreign entanglements that would have insulted Yahweh. After this statement, there follows a clause that includes the phrase relevant to this discussion. This clause functions as an explanation of how Asa was able to defeat such a large coalition. Introduced by a causative *kî*, it reads: "For Yahweh's eyes range about over the entire earth to show his might on behalf of those whose heart is blameless toward him." After this explanation of earlier weal, the topic shifts to Asa's more recent disobedience: "But you have acted foolishly concerning this [more recent matter]. Indeed, from now on you shall have wars" (II Chron. 16:9b). It is important to note, contra Oppenheim, that Yahweh's eyes have nothing to do with observing or punishing Asa's current, and errant, behavior. Rather, this phrase indicates the divine presence acting beneficently toward those who obey his precepts. This use of the phrase "the eyes of Yahweh" is very similar to that in Ezra 5:5: "But the eye of their God was upon the elders of the Jews, and they did not stop them [from their building activity] till a report should reach Darius." In both Chronicles and Ezra, two postexilic texts, the eyes of Yahweh signify benevolent divine presence.

Such a positive interpretation of this image fits well within the context of Zechariah's visions as well. Zechariah's visions and their interpretations uniformly offer words of weal to the revivified Judahite community. That Yahweh's eyes will be covering the earth would be, as in II Chron. 16:9; Ezra 5:5, and elsewhere, a symbol of divine beneficence to the Judahites of the late sixth century.

One implication of the interpretation of the lights as Yahweh's eyes has yet to be broached. The lights of the lamp symbolize the deity's eyes, and by inference the lampstand itself symbolizes the deity. This is, of course, not stated explicitly. Israel's aniconic tradition was and remained strong. And yet, this implication of the lampstand's function in the vision is difficult to gainsay.[15]

In the case of Zechariah's lampstand, we are probably dealing with a standard religious motif, that of light as symbolizing the presence of the deity. Surprisingly, this motif is not particularly prominent in the Hebrew Bible. And yet, another anthropomorphism connected with the deity's head, the face, is connected with the light motif: "May Yahweh give the light of his face upon you" (Num. 6:25); "Lift up the light of your face upon us, O Yahweh" (Ps. 4:7 [6E]). (See also Pss. 31:17 [16E]; 44:4 [3E]; 80:7; 90:8.) Equally interesting, the notion of having the light from Yahweh's face on someone usually means restoration, salvation—the same sort of motif that we have discovered concerning the postexilic usage of the "Yahweh's eyes" motif. Put another way, the lampstand as a source of light is analogous to Yahweh's face, just as the lights themselves symbolize Yahweh's eyes. In both instances, such symbolism entails good news for the Judahites.[16]

We may not stop by suggesting that the eyes of Yahweh symbolize a beneficent gaze. The angelic interpreter is more specific: These seven are the eyes of Yahweh. What does this specificity mean? It has been a commonplace, since the time of Gunkel, to suggest that the eyes of the deity refer to the seven planets (so Horst and other commentaries). This interpretation is attested as early as Philo and Josephus. However, it is important to know that there is little evidence for such a notion in either Mesopotamia or the Levant prior to the Greco-Roman period.[17] One might further add that the so-called astral explanation hardly suffices as an interpretation by the *mal'āk*. To point outside the vision, when there are already seven lights mentioned, does little by way of explaining these eyes of Yahweh. Further, we have already seen that there is a notion of the eyes of Yahweh in the Hebrew Bible, a notion which, especially in the postexilic texts, conveys a distinct message of weal. To say that the seven lights represent the eyes of Yahweh, so understood, is to have offered a comprehensive and

---

[15] Interesting in this regard is the claim of Meyers that the tabernacle menorah becomes, in Israel, a symbol of the deity's presence. This case, however, depends upon the notion of symbolism markedly absent from the lampstand described in Zechariah's vision, the arborescent motif. Assertions about the tabernacle menorah as symbolizing the divine presence should not be used to argue for the thesis that Zechariah's lampstand entails such presence.

[16] Cf. C. Jeremias, *Nachtgesichte*, 180–182, who also maintains, on the basis of Neo-Babylonian seal evidence, that the lampstand symbolizes Yahweh's presence.

[17] Ibid., 185.

meaningful explanation of the envisioned object. Appeal to the seven planets serves only to create a further ambiguous situation. If the *mal'āk* had intended to refer to the planets by including the number seven in his interpretation, what would that have meant? No convincing answer is forthcoming. Rather, it suffices to say that the seven lamps are the eyes of Yahweh. That, in and of itself, is a message of good news for the newly reinstituted community. And, as Jeremias rightly emphasizes, the texts say, "These seven are the eyes of Yahweh," and not, "These are the seven eyes of Yahweh" (and this in contrast to the emphasis on the two olive trees as signifying two sons of oil, 4:14). In this latter instance, the number two is more important in the interpretation than is the number seven in the interpretation of the eyes.[18]

[11, 13–14] After Zechariah learns what the lights symbolize, he asks another question: "What are those two olive trees which are at the right and the left of the lampstand?" Leaving aside for the moment v. 12 (which is almost certainly a later addition to the text), we see that the *mal'āk* again expresses surprise, and perhaps dismay, at Zechariah's ignorance. Zechariah 4:5b ("Do you not know what these things are?") is virtually repeated. And again, Zechariah must admit that he does not know. Whereupon the *mal'āk* functions again as an exegete. The interpreter states that the two trees are the sons of (the) oil who stand next to the Lord of the entire earth. At the outset, one is impressed by the repetition of the phrase, *kol-hā'āreṣ*, "the entire earth," a phrase and motif that recurs in virtually all of Zechariah's visions. Twice in the interpretation of this vision alone, the phrase specifies the scope of Yahweh's activity. Despite the fact that the two trees become symbols for something other than Yahweh, the interpretation ends up pointing not to the sons of oil but rather to the deity which they flank.

What does this symbolism mean? This more general question may be broken down into several subqueries: (1) What is it to symbolize a person with an olive tree? (2) What does this particular word for oil

---

[18] One problem has received particular attention: the potential correspondence between the *šib'āh 'ênāyim* in 3:9 and the fact that the seven lamps are referred to as the *'ênê yhwh* (see Petitjean, *Oracles*, 183). It seems to me, however, inescapable that the number seven in 3:9 refers to a particular number of inscribed consonants, *qdš lyhw*, whereas the number seven in 4:2 and 4:10b refers to the number of wick niches in a lamp bowl. The pervasiveness or holiness of the number seven is not at stake. To recognize the special significance of the number seven is not, however, to say that the referent of the numerical adjective must always be the same or that the number must express the same basic notion.

connote? (3) What is it to term someone a "son of oil"? (4) Does this description have anything to do with the ritual of anointing? (5) What is the connection between the two elements in the vision—the olive tree and the lamp? These questions provide the substance for the following analysis.

The interpreting angel makes clear that the trees are to be understood as persons, the sons of oil. What does such imagery signify (olive trees as persons)? Olive trees are used as personifications in the Hebrew Bible at least six times. In the Jotham fable, the tree speaks: "Shall I leave my fatness by which gods and men are honored . . ." (Judg. 9:9). And Israel/Judah are personified by this motif in Hos. 14:6, "His beauty shall be like the olive," and Jer. 11:16, "Yahweh once called you, 'A green olive tree, fair with goodly fruit.' " Similarly, individuals could be thought of as olive trees: "But I am like a green olive tree in the house of God" (Ps. 52:10 [8E]); "Your children will be like olive shoots around your table" (Ps. 128:3); "He will shake off his unripe grape, like the vine, and cast off his blossom, like the olive tree" (Job 15:33). With the exception of the last-cited passage (a text in which the olive tree's discarding of its blossom prematurely is understood to symbolize the fate of the wicked man), these references signify a positive image of the person or group so symbolized. And in Job, only an unnatural event, early loss of blossom, enables the olive tree to be thought of negatively. The naturally developing and harvested olive tree provides a positive symbol. To speak of a person using the image of the olive tree is, therefore, to view him or her as beautiful, productive, and important.

What, then, is to be gained from designating someone as a son of oil? In answering this question, one must be sensitive to the particular term for oil used in the Zechariah text. The noun *yiṣhār* is never used to describe, literally, olive oil; i.e., the phrase *zayit yiṣhār*, olive oil, never occurs.[19] Instead, this particular noun is regularly used in a stereotypic list ("grain, wine, oil") to indicate the natural and bountiful harvest of Syria-Palestine. Certain references indicate clearly that the oil comes from a tree, i.e., that *yiṣhār* is indeed olive oil. The primary connotation of the noun remains, however, fertility. The following texts indicate well this essential character: "And she did not know that it was I who gave her the grain, the wine, and the oil" (Hos. 2:10 [8E]); "Yahweh answered and said to his people, 'Behold, I am sending to you grain wine, and oil, and you will be satisfied' " (Joel 2:19); "The threshing floors shall be full of grain, the vats shall

---

[19] The term *šemen*, oil, is used in such constructions.

overflow with wine and oil" (Joel 2:24); "They shall come and sing aloud on the height of Zion, and they shall be radiant over the goodness of Yahweh, over the grain, the wine, and the oil, and over the young of the flock and the herd; their life shall be like a watered garden, and they shall languish no more" (Jer. 31:11 [12E]); "He will love you, bless you, and multiply you; he will also bless the fruit of your body and the fruit of your ground, your grain and your wine and your oil, the increase of your cattle and the young of your flock, in the land which he swore to your fathers to give you" (Deut. 7:13). The listing of such passages could go on. Clearly, the noun *yiṣhār* is indicative of agricultural blessing; it is always linked with at least one other agricultural product, wine, and almost always with grain as well.

Apart from cultic gifts, no specific use is offered for *yiṣhār*, oil. It is, therefore, a term that indicates Yahweh's beneficent action and yet that entails little by way of specific application. It is a word open to the specific imagery of the context in which it is used.

Furthermore, the noun for oil used in Zech. 4:14 is never used within the context of an anointing ceremony. The term for oil used in that context is *šemen* (I Sam. 10:1; 16:1, 13; II Kings 9:3, 6; Lev. 8:30). One may speak of an oil of anointing, *šemen hammišḥāh*, but not of an oil of anointing using the noun *yiṣhār*. The vocabulary of Zech. 4:14 does not, therefore, lead one to think that the individuals so personified have been or are being anointed. Furthermore, as I have shown earlier, the author of these visions has been concerned throughout to keep his proposals and discussions at the meta-level. One would not, in principle, expect him to propose the anointing of a political leader. This fact has made it problematic especially for those interpreters who have translated "sons of oil" as "anointed ones." As one such interpreter has written, "It is doubtful whether Zerubbabel would ever have undergone the ceremony of anointing."[20] It is therefore difficult to understand what sense it makes to equate the "oil" status of Zerubbabel and Joshua, if the reference of oil is to anointing. Clearly, Joshua as high priest was already anointed. And equally as clear, Zerubbabel as appointee of the Persian government would not have been anointed into his role as governor. Hence, though it would appear to be the case that Joshua and Zerubbabel are symbolized in this vision and its interpretation, there is little warrant for understanding the phrase "sons of oil" to designate them as anointed.[21]

---

[20] Baldwin, 127.
[21] Contra (among others) Rudolph, 107–108; C. Jeremias, *Nachtgesichte*, 184; R. Mason, 48; Baldwin, 124.

What is at stake if not the anointing of Joshua and Zerubbabel? The specific phraseology of the text provides an answer. First, the text here (v. 14) focuses on the number two differently from the way the number seven was handled earlier (v. 10). Here we are told that these are the two sons of oil, whereas in the earlier verse we read that "these seven are the eyes of the Lord." Not only are the sons definite here ("the sons") but the number two becomes part of the interpretation as it did not earlier. The formulation here emphasizes the "twoness" of the persons. It is a given, a fundamental feature of the vision. As Jeremias has observed, this "twoness" works itself out in symmetric and heraldic fashion. One may envision two trees or individuals on either side of the deity. Rudolph refines this notion by suggesting that the scene is that of a seated deity flanked by his aides.[22] Such an interpretation is justified by the particular description in v. 14, two sons of oil positioned next to *(hā'ōm'dîm 'al)* the deity. In Isa. 6:1–2 we read, "I saw Yahweh sitting upon his throne, high and lifted up; . . . above him stood *('ōm'dîm mimma'al lô)* the seraphim." And in I Kings 22:19 we read, "I saw Yahweh sitting on his throne, and all the host of heaven standing beside him *('ōmēd 'ālāyw)* on his right hand and on his left." (Cf. also Gen. 18:8b; Judg. 3:19b.) In both texts, when the deity is flanked by persons, he is seated. The latter text is particularly significant since the notion of disposition explicitly on the right and on the left hand is shared by the description in Zechariah. Corroborating Rudolph's notion is our interpretation of the primary vision itself—that of two trees elevated above the lampstand. The interpreted persons have the same heraldic position as did the uninterpreted trees.

It is also clear that such flanked divine presence normally takes place in the divine council and/or its earthly counterpart, the temple. Furthermore, we must integrate what we have learned from another of the Zechariah visions, Zech. 3:7, with what is revealed in Zech. 4. In 3:7, clearly a divine council scene, we are told of those who stand here *(hā'ōm'dîm hā'ēlleh)*, the inhabitants of the divine council. In that vision, Joshua the high priest is apparently promised access to the divine council. In Zech. 4, we now hear of two persons who apparently have access to the divine council, who will flank the seated deity. And as we have shown earlier, the number two is emphasized in the vision's interpretation. If Joshua has specific significance vis-à-vis the deity in Zech. 3, that place is clearly modified in Zech. 4. The interpretation of this fifth vision clearly prohibits any notion of one figure alone having

[22] Rudolph, 107.

special access to or prerogatives with the deity. And if, as many have suggested, Joshua and Zerubbabel are the "sons of oil," then this vision appears to emphasize the diarchic character of the postexilic polity. There are two important positions vis-à-vis the deity.

Also important in attempting to discern the precise meaning of this vision is the noun "son." This word does, of course, have the sense of denoting a member of a class; i.e., a *ben-'ādām* is a human, not a deity. And a *ben-yiśrā'ēl* is an Israelite, not a Canaanite. However, when one takes seriously the fact that Zerubbabel and Joshua are being described with this noun, one must also remember that language of sonship has been used earlier in Israel to describe the relationship of the community's leader to the community's deity. In Ps. 2:7, we hear the deity pronounce, presumably on the day of an Israelite king's coronation, "You are my son, today I have begotten you." The notion of the king as an adopted or "reborn" son of Yahweh is elsewhere attested in the Hebrew Bible. (See II Sam. 7:14, "I will be his father, and he shall be my son"; see also I Chron. 28:6; Ps. 89:26.) The notion of the king as being in a filial relationship to the deity is a standard way of speaking about kingship in ancient Israel.

What seems significant about the Zechariah vision is its emphasis on two sons of oil. Earlier one could only speak of one significant son, the king. The import of Zechariah's vision is that two sons may now be spoken of. One senses that this pluralism, or at least dualism, entails a significant restructuring of the Judahite/Jerusalemite polity. Such imagery indicates a situation in which the community is to expect more than one divinely designated agent. And given the inherent imagery of *yiṣhār*, oil, such dualism is good as is the bounty of Israel's harvest.

The specific elements included in this vision are especially intriguing, namely, the tree and the lamps. Explicitly filial language has been introduced: "sons of oil." Just as Yahweh can beget a son (i.e., in the coronation ceremony), so too he is the granter of fertility to Israel. Hosea writes, "She did not know that it was I who gave her the grain, the wine, and the oil" (Hos. 2:10 [8E]). Yahweh can beget sons, and he can grant fertility. These two generative and beneficent acts have been symbolized by the phrase "the two sons of oil."

Following this line of argument, we are now able to broach explicitly the question of the relationship of the two primary images in the visionary tableau, i.e., the relationship of the trees to the lamp. The tableau is clearly heraldic: there is a tree on either side of the lampstand. Further, it is altogether likely that the trees are located spatially above as well as on either side of the lampstand. It takes little imagination to observe that olive trees located above a lampstand, which has a bowl normally filled with olive oil, might entail the notion of consubstantiality. Olive trees provide the substance by means of which the lamps burn.[23] The lights of the lamp are only able to burn when the bowl contains oil. The lamp functions properly only as the result of the bounty of the olive trees, bounty that in turn is the result of the deity's beneficence. And similarly, the trees need light, sunlight—itself a creation of the deity—in order to produce their crop. The lampstand depends upon *yiṣhār* for its operation and at the same time provides an appropriate use for that agricultural commodity.

If the lampstand somehow symbolizes the divine presence and the two trees symbolize the two ruling functionaries of the postexilic community, does this scene entail symbiosis at the level of divine-human relations? One may, I think, answer in the affirmative. Just as the lamp needs oil to function, so the deity needs—in order to have a community that venerates him—leaders, both civil and religious. And just as the trees need light to generate produce, so the newly reinstituted community's leaders need the support of the deity, the beneficent gaze of the deity's eyes, in order to carry out their work. The logic of lamplight enables the author to reflect upon complementary roles in the postexilic community.

Such a view of the vision's significance carries several important messages. First, the polity of the new community is to be diarchic rather than monarchic, its leadership comprising two individuals of equal status. Second, the relationship between the deity and the community's leadership is more of a two-way street than it was under the earlier system. As before, the community requires divine support, but now the deity is understood as in need of the people, or at least of the people's leaders. A human-divine political symbiosis is constitutive for the postexilic community. Third, the leaders of the community are close to Yahweh, not isolated from him.

[12] Verse 12 is, by almost universal agreement, understood to be an addition to the original vision and its interpretation.[24] Not only is a second question without parallel in the other visions, it separates the answer, which is provided in vs. 13–14, from the question concerning the identity of the two olive trees. Furthermore, v. 12 adds to the detail

---

[23] Baldwin, 123, began to explore this tack but apparently felt that such a notion was theologically inappropriate.

[24] See Ackroyd, *Exile and Restoration*, 192; Rudolph, 109; Mason, 47–48, who attributes it to the editor of Haggai; Mitchell, 164; cf. Rignell, *Nachtgesichte*, 168ff., who maintains that v. 12 is a clarification of v. 11. Beuken, 270–274, views 4:11–14 as a late addition to the earlier interpretation of 4:8–10a.

of the tableau; it requests information about the significance of "the two streams," features that had not heretofore been mentioned. This procedure of entering new information about the primary vision within the interpretive scheme has no parallels in the other visions. Finally, there is no answer provided to this question. Verse 14 is not a plausible response to vs. 11–12. In sum, there is every reason to construe v. 12 as an addition to the primary text.

What was the point of this addition? This is a difficult question to answer because of the ambiguity of the language in v. 12. The initial element in the question picks up on the number two as well as on the olive trees and yet introduces a new factor, the noun *šibbᵃlê* in construct with the olive trees. The problem with this descriptive term is that there are two Biblical Hebrew nouns, both spelled *šibbōlet*, meaning two quite different things: *šibbōlet* I, cognate with Akk. *šûbultu*, Aram. *šubaltā'*, means "ear of grain"; whereas *šibbōlet* II signifies "flowing or deep liquid" (Ps. 69:3, 16 [2, 15E]; Isa. 27:12). Since *šibbōlet* I is the more frequently attested noun, and since it refers to an agricultural entity, one struggles to relate it to the olive tree.[25] Such struggle is, however, unsuccessful; it is difficult indeed to think of individual olives scattered through an olive tree as analogous to ears of grain at the end of a stalk. And yet translators work diligently to make the grain imagery fit the olive tree (JPS—"What are the two tops of the olive trees"; RSV—"What are these two branches of the olive tree? NAB—"What are the two olive tufts?"). Since olives do not grow in clusters, and since there is no special significance to individual branches in the total configuration of the tree, and since in any case the branches would probably have been described as *ᵃlēh zayit* (Gen. 8:11), it is extremely difficult to render *šibbōlet* as the actual processible fruit of the tree in the way in which it refers to the harvestable ear of grain. And the expression should, by analogy, refer to the fruit of the tree, not to its branches.

This difficulty of utilizing *šibbōlet* I in Zech. 4:12 forces one to consider the alternative, *šibbōlet* II, translating *šibbᵃlê* as a liquid: "What are the two streams of/for the olive trees?" However, given the expression "olive's oil" *(šemen zayit),* as found in Ex. 27:20; 30:24; Lev. 24:2 as an expression for the processed oil, we would expect *šibbᵃlê zayit* rather than *šibbᵃlê hazzêtîm.* Compounding the ambiguity is the ensuing clause: "which are next to the gold pipes which pour out

---

[25] In all texts that use, apparently, *šibbōlet* I, the noun refers to ears of grain as they grow or are harvested (Job 24:24; Gen. 41:5; Isa. 17:5; Ruth 2:2; one text, Judg. 12:6, allows for no conclusion in this regard).

the golden [oil] from them." Various emendations have been proposed to clarify this more than likely corrupt formulation.[26] Again, there are virtually insurmountable problems as one seeks a convincing translation. The noun *ṣant'rôt*, "pipes," occurs only once in biblical texts and is usually associated with the noun *ṣinnôr (II Sam. 5:8, "water shafts"; Ps. 42:8 [7E], "[water] spouts") and construed as a noun construction with infixed taw.* If one follows the notion of *šibbōlet* II, then one could translate, "What are the two streams of olive oil which empty out through the gold spouts upon them?"[27] This proposal has the advantage of minimal correction to the text and of sustaining the notion of oil being poured out in all parts of this late addition.

Interestingly, most commentators are quick to admit that though Zech. 4:12 remains ambiguous, the general sense of the author is clear. Mitchell writes, "Now the object [of the interpreter who wrote v. 12] was to connect the lights with the olive trees."[28] Ackroyd similarly suggests that "the additional interpretive element in verse 12 introduces, apparently, a picture of some kind of connection between the leaders, represented by olive trees, or here as olive shoots, and the lamp which they supply with oil. . . . It may be that the meaning of verse 12 is intended to be an elaboration of the leader's function in relation to the people, rather than the mediating of life to the lamp which symbolizes the presence of God. . . . The obvious interpretation of verse 12 is that it refers to the supplying of the lamp, but perhaps it is really intended to make a more general comment on the mediating of blessing, since in fact the text does not precisely state that the oil flows into the bowl of the lamp."[29] However, Rudolph maintains, in opposition to the foregoing position, that such an interpretation would constitute blasphemy. Rather, the interpolator found the interpretation of the trees as men unsatisfactory and proposed to formulate another perspective on the two olive trees.

The fact that two interpreters can come up with quite different senses of the basic, though ambiguous, meaning of the text would seem to suggest that attempts to seek clear meaning in unclear words and syntax is a dubious approach.

I propose the following alternate solution. Verse 12 may well have been designed to obfuscate the quite clear and potentially "blasphemous" picture created by the interpreted vision. Any number of

---

[26] Rudolph, 104; Mitchell, 167–168.

[27] Reading *'ᵃlêhem* instead of *mē'ᵃlêhem*, the *mem* being a dittography from the plural morpheme of *hamrîqîm*.

[28] Mitchell, 168.   [29] Ackroyd, *Exile and Restoration*, 193.

commentators have noted that one might think that trees are present in order to provide oil for the lamp, and yet they do not pursue such a tack because it would suggest divine dependence on nondivine elements (so Baldwin, Rudolph). However, as I have indicated earlier, the symbiosis implied in the vision—a certain consanguinity between Yahweh and the community that venerates him—provides a forceful way of understanding the new relationship between Yahweh and his people embodied in the postexilic community. And yet, from a religiously more orthodox position, such a notion of the basis for the new community may have seemed offensive. Hence, someone may have wanted to cloud what was a rather clear picture of divine dependence. What better way of obfuscation than to introduce extraneous detail in a new question? The very thing which is implied in v. 14—the connection of oil between the two trees/men and the lamp/deity—is challenged indirectly by v. 12, a verse in which the "two" are elaborated and yet a verse in which the lampstand is pointedly ignored. Only ingenious and thoroughgoing textual emendations provide this missing element. I am forced to suggest that v. 12 is difficult to translate because it was intended to be unclear. Some pious commentator took offense at the rather clear motif of divine-human interdependence and obfuscated that picture by the introduction of puzzling detail and cryptic syntax.

Now we are in a position to consider the other interpolation in Zech. 4, this time a block of oracular material, vs. 6b to 10a.[30]

Zechariah 4:6b–10a

Not by might, not by power

6b This is the word of Yahweh to Zerubbabel:
"Not by might,
not by power,
but by my spirit,"
    says Yahweh of Hosts.
7 "What are you?
A great mountain?[a]
Alongside Zerubbabel,
    you are a plain.
He will bring out the former stone.

---

[30] Cf. NEB for a fundamentally different division of the text.

(There will be) shouts of
'Grace! Grace!' for him."[b]

8 And the word of Yahweh came to me:
9 "The hands of Zerubbabel founded this house;
his hands will complete it,
in order that you[c] may know that
Yahweh of Hosts has sent me to you.
10a For whoever despised the day of small things
will rejoice when they see the tin tablet
in the hand of Zerubbabel."

a. Reading *har gādôl*. The *h* prefixing *gādôl* in MT is probably a dittographic addition from the *h* in *har*.

b. Reading *lô* instead of *lāh*.

c. Reading *wîda'tem* with Syr, Targ, V instead of MT *wᵉyāda'tā*. Cf. Zech. 2:13; 6:15; Petitjean, *Oracles*.

As noted earlier, the fifth vision has been interrupted by an interpolation. The answer to the question presented in 4:5 occurs in 4:10b, i.e., it occurs after an oracle comprising 4:6b–10a.[1] Before we may address the redaction-critical question as to why an editor inserted the oracle at this place in the vision narrative, we need to determine the

---

[1] Mention should have been made of Beuken's and Petitjean's interpretations of Zech. 4:6–10. (1) Instead of interpreting 4:6aβ–10a as a later interpolation, Beuken, 260ff., argues that the core of the original night vision included part of what was traditionally thought to have been secondary. According to his analysis, 4:1–3, 4–5; 6aα, 10b, and 6aβ–7 comprise the original vision and word of Yahweh. Vs. 11, 13, 14, and later v. 12, comprise a secondary and allegorical explanation of an original parable. Beuken's basic presupposition is that no author would have accorded Joshua equal status with Zerubbabel ca. 520 B.C.E. However, there is every reason to think that just such claims were being made against the status of Zerubbabel, and that Joshua is a likely figure as an opponent. (2) Petitjean's approach is more akin to the one proposed in this study. He points to many parallels between ancient Near Eastern building practices and the Zechariah pericopes. Thus: *(a)* The importance of the royal hands in 4:9a is reflected in Akkadian building inscriptions (*Oracles*, 229–230). *(b)* The metal stone of 4:10a reflects the metal tablet of the Assyrian building deposits (p. 236). *(c)* And 4:7b refers to the old foundations, the *ašru*, or foundation stone (pp. 249–251). *(d)* The *har-haggādôl* in 4:7 refers to the ruins of the temple and the power of Enlil, the *šadû rabû*, and thereby offers a denigration of Babylonian power, since the "rough places" (Isa. 40:3–5; 42:14–17) are to be made low. Some of these arguments, as we have seen, are more impressive than others. However, Petitjean's theory about the homogeneous character of the pericope depends little on the parallels he has adduced. On the basis of this theory, he reorganizes the pericope around the building foundation theme into one original whole, the basic content of which was Zech. 4:8, 6aβ–7, 9, 10a (p. 267). To my mind, no convincing proof is given for this reorganization.

meaning of the oracles that have been inserted into the vision report. Content and formulary characteristics suggest that this oracular material is not homogeneous. The introductory statement of address has a literary quality, a formula that we might expect to find introducing a series of statements. And we have, I think, two subsequent oracles, vs. 6aβ–7 and vs. 8–10a.[2] If we may presuppose a collection of Zechariah's prophetic statements, some of which concerned Zerubbabel, material like Zech. 4:6aβ–10a would have originally been a part of that collection. The continuity of subject matter—the rebuilding of the temple—and the presence of building-deposit imagery—stone and tin tablet—in both pericopes strengthen this assumption.[3]

[6b] The first oracle does not begin on an irenic note. Of the first four words, two are the negative particle *lō'*. A position of some sort is being challenged. The issue, although initially murky, has to do with what authorizes a certain action. The poem emphasizes that whatever will or is taking place will not be accomplished by might *(ḥayil)* or by power *(kōaḥ)*. Rather, it will occur because of "my spirit."[4] The presence of the pronominal suffix "my" is of critical importance. It tells us not only that the spirit is Yahweh's but also that "might" and "power" are presumed, in this instance, to be human and not divine qualities. Put another way, 4:6 emphasizes that the action being described is under divine and not human control. Nevertheless, at the end of 4:6, we are not at all clear what activity is being discussed.[5]

[7] Zechariah 4:7 begins to clarify the matter, since two individuals are introduced, one of whom is named. Zerubbabel receives an endorsement. He is a mountain when compared to the "you," who is labeled "a plain." Zerubbabel will receive shouts of approbation, whereas the "you" is not mentioned in this regard. There is every reason to connect the "you" with the words "not by might," "not by power," and to connect Zerubbabel with "by my spirit."

Verse 7 contrasts Zerubbabel with another person, the "you" to whom the oracle is addressed. Seen in this light, the addressee would have to be someone of authority, someone whom we might expect to challenge Zerubbabel's initiative in temple reconstruction. The most obvious figure is Joshua, the high priest, who is here being warned to

---

[2] Cf. Amsler, 92–95. He perceives three oracles: 6aβb, 7, 8–10a.

[3] Thus, e.g., O. Eissfeldt, *The Old Testament: An Introduction*, 1965, 431ff.

[4] Cf. Hag. 2:5.

[5] Cf. Petitjean, who understands the "spirit of Yahweh'" to be a divinely authorized wind which parallels Mesopotamian notions of a wind that clears away the ruins of a destroyed temple (*Oracles*, 258).

leave matters of reconstruction to the royal house. The imagery in v. 7 is that of contrast: Zerubbabel, the mountain, versus someone else, the plain. If the other party was in fact the high priest, the *har-haggādôl* is a deft play on *hakkōhēn haggādôl*. The identification of the adversary as the high priest is tentative. It is possible that the regional administrator from Samaria, Tattenai, with his cohorts, was the object of this polemic.[6] More certain is the admonishing character of the oracle; Yahweh's spirit is on the side of Zerubbabel, and no might nor power will be able to overpower or interfere with his efforts.

That Zechariah thought the initiative for rebuilding lay with Zerubbabel is not difficult to ascertain. Zechariah 4:8–10 and 6:12–13 make this point quite plain. That Zechariah cautioned Joshua in other places is, of course, extraordinarily difficult to show, since a pro-Priestly or Chronistic redaction has probably leveled such objections.[7] Zechariah 3:8–10 emphasizes Yahweh's action in such a way as to deemphasize the power and initiative of Joshua (or Tattenai).

These pericopes reflect Zerubbabel's royal responsibility for temple reconstruction. As Davidic prince, he was proleptic king. That the king was at least titular temple builder, and many times participant in the actual construction, has been demonstrated by Kapelrud, Ellis, and Halpern.[8] In the ancient Near East, a king often acted symbolically in the construction of a temple. For example, Gudea of Lagash entered the temple, made a mud brick, raised it before the people, and with that brick laid the foundation *(uš)* of the temple.[9]

A close examination of the enigmatic *hā'eben hārō'šāh* in 4:7 suggests that the scene described is consistent with ancient Near Eastern building rites, rites in which the royal figure participated in temple construction.[10] Ellis' work on Mesopotamian building practices yields a very interesting cognate. It seems that when a temple was to be rebuilt or renovated, a brick or stone—the *libitu maḫrītu*, "the first (or former) brick" (a semantic parallel to *hā'eben hārō'šāh*)—was

[6] Thus Rudolph, 113.

[7] Beuken, passim.

[8] A. Kapelrud, "Temple Building, A Task for Gods and Men," *Or* 32, 1962, 56–62; R. Ellis, *Foundation Deposits in Ancient Mesopotamia*, 1968, 20ff.; B. Halpern, "The Ritual Background of Zechariah's Temple Sons," *CBQ* 40, 1978, 167–180.

[9] Thus R. Ellis, *Foundation Deposits*, 20–26; 170–172.

[10] See A. Petitjean, "La mission de Zorubabel et la reconstruction du temple, Zach 3:8–10," *EThL* 42, 1966, 40–71; D. Petersen, "Zerubbabel and Jerusalem Temple Reconstruction," *CBQ* 36, 1974, 366–372.

removed from the earlier ruin or edifice by the cultic singer or *kalû*.[11] Ellis comments:

> The usual function of the *kalû* was to placate the gods; in this case the essential part of the ritual was the removal of the brick from the old temple. The brick was set aside, offerings were made and lamentations were sung before it, while the temple was being demolished, until the foundations of the new temple were laid. The purpose of this ritual was apparently to bridge the gap between the existence of the old and new temples.[12]

A Seleucid ritual text from Warka records the practice:

> When the wall of a temple falls into ruin, in order to demolish it and refound the temple, the diviner shall investigate (?) its site. . . . The builder of that temple shall put on clean clothes and put a tin bracelet on his arm; he shall take an axe of lead, remove the first brick, and put it in a restricted place. You set up an offering table in front of the brick for the god of foundations, and you offer sacrifices.[13]

One must be circumspect in drawing comparisons using the *libitu maḫrītu,* since the meaning of *maḫrītu* is ambiguous. Ellis has proposed a revision in the traditional translation of *maḫrītu* as "first," and has suggested the meaning "former" brick.[14]

In an attempt to define the importance of this "former brick," Ellis says:

> What does show clearly in these texts is the peculiar symbolic significance of the brick. The success of Gudea's brick-molding was an omen of the happy outcome of the entire construction. The veneration of the old brick prescribed by the *kalû* ritual probably had the purpose of preserving the continuity of worship. The single brick embodied the essence of the god's home and bridged the gap between the destruction of the old building and the founding of the new.[15]

By analogy, the *hā'eben hārō'šāh* in Zech. 4:7 is probably a building deposit which signified continuity with the earlier temple. Such a "former brick" emphasized sacral continuity.

That a ceremony not unlike the *kalû* ritual accompanied the reconstruction of the second temple seems most probable. As corroborating evidence we need only turn back to the oracles of Haggai. In Hag. 2:15–19, the prophet is drawing a contrast—between

---

[11] Thus Ellis, *Foundation Deposits,* 26–29. Cf. E. Lipiński, "Recherches sur le livre de Zacharie," *VT* 20, 1970, 30–33.

[12] Ellis, *Foundation Deposits,* 13.

[13] Ibid., 184.

[14] Ibid., 27 n. 120. Cf. Petitjean, *Oracles,* 249–251.

[15] Ellis, *Foundation Deposits,* 29.

the days in which agricultural productivity was meager, the days before the temple was restored, and the days in which the earth will yield bountifully, the days after "stone was placed upon stone in the temple of Yahweh" (v. 15). This vision of high crop yield was closely tied (either by Haggai himself or by the Chronistic redactor) to a specific day: "from this day onward" (v. 15); "from this day onward, from the twenty-fourth day of the ninth month" (v. 18); "From this day on, I will bless you" (v. 19). This picture of beneficence corresponds directly with the weal expected from temple-building rituals.[16] Such an appeal to future bounty is, after all, the heart of Haggai's argument: once the temple was rebuilt, benefits would accrue to the people. The turning point, the day when one should begin to expect those benefits, would most naturally be the day of ritual dedication, the day in which the continuity between the old and the new temple was ritually declared. Hence the rededication probably occurred on "this day"—the twenty-fourth day of the ninth month (Hag. 2:18), or November-December 520 B.C.E.[17]

From a broader perspective, this first oracle, Zech. 4:6b–7, emphasizes Zerubbabel's prerogatives in the early postexilic community by pointing to his participation in the temple restoration ritual. A legitimate inference from this conclusion is that the prophet viewed the Davidide, Zerubbabel, as a royal figure, whether or not he had been invested as king.

The final element of this first oracle corroborates our interpretation of it as a favorable word to the royal figure, Zerubbabel. There were to be shouts of acclamation: *ḥēn, ḥēn!* This is a word that can mean "beautiful in appearance," "acceptable," even "acceptable in the eyes of the deity." Not surprisingly, the king, in a royal psalm, is described with such language:

> You are the fairest of the sons of men;
>   grace is poured upon your lips;
>   therefore God has blessed you for ever.
>   (Ps. 45:3)

The situation in Zech. 4:7 is similar. The language of acclamation is such as befits a king or, at least in this case, a member of the Davidic line.

---

[16] In many ancient Near Eastern mythic texts, a manifestation of fertility follows the enthronement of the god in his temple. For example, in the Baal-Anath cycle, once Baal's temple was built and once he had been avenged by Anath, it was recorded that "the heavens rain oil, the valleys flow with honey" (*CTA* 6. III. 6–7).

[17] Ezra 3:10–13 is probably a late reflection on this ritual with the typical Chronistic deemphasis of the royal figure's function after the fall of the Judahite state.

[8-10a] The second oracle, 4:8–10a, is more straightforward. It is introduced by the same formula that we find in 6:9; 7:4, 8:1, 18. The prophet emphasizes that Zerubbabel will finish what he started—the reconstruction of the temple.[18] How v. 10a functions as a part of this promise is the puzzling feature of this oracle. The beginnings of restoration were of no comparison in grandeur to what had gone before. This we may also infer from the account in Ezra 3:12. Somehow, the significance of the *hā'eben habbᵉdîl* was supposed to assuage previous times of inferiority. If this phrase denotes a tin plummet, as LXX and many commentators suggest, it is difficult to understand how the presence of a building implement guarantees the overcoming of "the days of small things."

Scholars have often conjectured about the meaning of this heretofore obscure phrase *hā'eben habbᵉdîl*.[19] The two most common proposals have been (1) to read *hā'eben bᵉdōlaḥ,* instead of MT, as a reference to some royally symbolic signet stone (on *bᵉdōlaḥ,* cf. Num. 11:7; Gen. 2:12); and (2) to follow the interpretation of LXX, which sees MT as a tin plummet in the hand of Zerubbabel and not in the hand of someone else, i.e., Joshua or any other usurper. As an alternative to these options, I prefer to read with MT and see a reference to a tin or metallic tablet, a building deposit.[20]

Reference may be made again to Ellis' work, where he has discussed the tablets, not only stone but metallic, that were described in building texts and found in archaeological excavations. For example, in the palace of Sargon II at Khorsabad, the following inscription was found written upon tablets of gold, silver, and magnesite: "I wrote my name on tablets of gold, silver, copper, tin, lapis lazuli, and alabaster, and I deposited (them) in (several places) in the foundations."[21]

The historical distribution of this metallic tablet usage is particularly interesting. Such tablets were widely used in the Middle Babylonian period and for some reason died out in Neo-Babylonian times. The Achaemenid period, however, saw a renaissance of this practice, as tablets from the time of Darius II and Xerxes attest, though these latter tablets often did not carry inscriptions.[22] (We are not told of an

[18] See Petitjean, *Oracles,* 229–230; B. Halpern, "The Ritual Background of Zechariah's Temple Sons," *CBQ* 40, 1978, 171, on the significance of the royal hands in temple-building.

[19] For other possibilities, see E. Sellin, *Das Zwölfprophetenbuch übersetzt und erklärt,* 1930, 504–505; Petitjean, *Oracles,* 230–234.

[20] See, similarly, Petitjean, *Oracles,* 236.

[21] As translated in Ellis, *Foundation Deposits,* 101–102.

[22] Ibid., 104.

inscription on the tin tablet in Zech. 4:10.) Such a use of this metallic tablet by Zerubbabel would clearly fit with contemporary building practices to the east.

The presence of such metallic objects helps to explain how Zechariah meant to contrast the reconstruction of the temple to "the days of small things." As Ellis notes:

> Much of the reason for the deposits of valuables is probably to be seen in a desire to enhance the value of the building and the validity of the ceremonies connected with its construction, by the use of impressive and costly substances. To found a building on gold, silver, and precious stones, gives a theoretical sumptuousness pleasing to the builder and hopefully, his gods.[23]

The presence of such a building deposit, a tin tablet, was evidence, at least in Zechariah's eyes, that the second temple was no paltry sanctuary.

In this second oracle, the prophet is concerned to emphasize the task of temple reconstruction by the royal figure. The pericope underlines the presence of the Davidic heir in almost an *Erweiswort* form (v. 9b). That is, the prophet's words will be authenticated—considered valid in opposition to anyone else—when the task is done. And the task can be done legitimately only by Zerubbabel.

Having discerned the meaning of these oracles—how they serve to enhance the status of Zerubbabel as temple builder, and this in opposition to Joshua, the high priest—we are now in a position to reflect on the rationale for the place of this material within the fifth vision. That vision has as one of its essential purposes the articulation of the relationship between the two officials—the religious and civil leaders—in the early postexilic community, as well as the relationship of these two officials to the deity. One point of the vision is that the two human officials are fundamentally equal in significance. This egalitarian sentiment was not shared by the person responsible for the oracles preserved as 4:6b–10a. The author of these oracles clearly argues on behalf of a superior status for Zerubbabel. It is he, by dint of Yahweh's authorizing spirit, who is a "great mountain," who will receive acclamation by shouts of "Grace! Grace!" and who will be remembered as temple builder, a new Solomon. Hence it was highly appropriate for the author or conservator of this material to insert it in this vision. The editorial process tips the scales in favor of Zerubbabel, the more so since Joshua had apparently received special mention in the fourth vision.[24]

---

[23] Ibid., 140.

[24] For a different redaction-critical proposal, see Rudolph, 115.

Zechariah 5:1–4

I looked up and saw a flying scroll

1 Again I looked up and saw a flying scroll.
2 He asked, "What do you see?"
   And I said, "A flying scroll,
      twenty cubits long and ten cubits wide."
3 He said to me:
   "This is the curse which is going out over all the earth;
   for all who steal have remained up till now unpunished,
   and all who swear (falsely) have remained up till now
      unpunished."[a]
4 "I have sent it out," says Yahweh of Hosts.
   "It will enter the house of the thief
      and the house of the one who swears falsely by my name.
   It will lodge in the midst of his house,
      and it will annihilate its timber and stones."

a. Verse 3b is not to be translated in the future tense. The verb *niqqāh* is a 3 masc. sg. perfect. Moreover, the curse is being sent out because people now remain unpunished. Cf. similarly JPS.

The Sixth Vision

[1–2] If the fifth vision inaugurated a new visionary sequence which treats of the new political-religious leadership configuration, the sixth vision focuses on the character of social relationships in that new order. Moreover, Zechariah is now caught up in the visionary experience. The formal language of vision report is brief: "Again, I looked up and saw . . . ," a formula repeated in Zech. 6:1. Only in these two visions does the language point explicitly to the repetitive nature of the experience ("again").

Zechariah had just seen two objects in static configuration, though with dynamic meaning, two olive trees which symbolized the new political and religious polity of Judah. Now he sees only one object moving in the air, a flying scroll. The term *mᵉgillāh* clearly refers to a scroll, not a codex or book.[1] The term is probably a shortened version

[1] The codex gradually became prominent in the late Greco-Roman period (*IDB* IV, 920–921).

of the phrase "rolled book" (as Ps. 40:8 [7E]; Ezek. 2:9; cf. Isa. 34:4).[2] A length of about 30 feet seems to have been the upper limit for such a scroll.[3] In this regard, it is interesting to observe that the Qumran Isaiah scroll (1QIsa[a]) is a little more than 24 feet long and almost 11 inches wide. And, of course, Isaiah is a rather long book.[4]

To see a scroll was, therefore, for a Judahite in the Persian period, not an impossible thing. To see it floating up in the air was quite another matter. Scrolls are normally in someone's hands, lying on a table, placed in storage jars or the like. They are always touching something. The scroll that Zechariah sees is touching nothing; it is between heaven and earth, disconnected from scribe or lector. This is the first unusual feature of Zechariah's sixth vision.

The second unusual feature is revealed only as the dialogue between the prophet and the messenger develops. After Zechariah reports that he has seen a soaring scroll, the *mal'āk* asks him, "What did you see?" This question is highly unusual. The *mal'āk* asked this same question in Zech. 4:2. And yet, in that earlier text, Zechariah had not reported any visionary experience. Hence in ch. 4, after having been asked this question, Zechariah could provide a visionary description. Here in ch. 5, however, Zechariah has reported the basic visionary object before the *mal'āk* asks him, "What do you see?" The effect of this reversal of the expected patter of question and answer is to heighten the unbelievability of the envisioned object. One might translate the question to mean, "I can't believe what you just said. Let's try it again. What do you see?" Whereupon Zechariah repeats the initial description and expands upon it. He sees a soaring scroll, twenty cubits long and ten cubits wide. And here the second unusual element of this vision unfolds. The scroll is out of all proportion. Scrolls are normally much longer than they are wide; the Qumran Isaiah scroll represents a length to width ratio of approximately 30:1. However, the soaring scroll that Zechariah sees, apparently unrolled, entails a ratio of 2:1.

---

[2] Despite the fact that we know scrolls were used at the time Zechariah was written (cf. Jer. 36), we are unable to judge whether leather or papyrus was the more frequently used material. Papyrus pieces datable to the eighth-seventh centuries have been found at Wadi *Murabba'ât,* and some of the Dead Sea scrolls were written on leather. M. Haran argues that the transition from papyrus to leather took place earlier in the postexilic period as part of a more general Aramaization of the ancient Near East ("Bible Scrolls in the Early Second Temple Period—The Transition from Papyrus to Skins," *EI* 19, 1982, 86–92).

[3] *IDB* IV, 920.

[4] See E. Würthwein, *The Text of the Old Testament,* 1957, 8, who attests that the longest surviving papyrus scroll is 40 meters long. Greek papyrus scrolls tend to average 6–10 meters in length.

And thirdly, the scroll is obviously unrolled, otherwise Zechariah could not comment on its dimensions. The scroll which Zechariah sees is, therefore, triply difficult: it soars, it is out of proportion, and it is unrolled without anyone holding on to it.[5] It is difficult to deny that the dimension of the temple porch corresponds exactly to that of the scroll. However, it is equally difficult to explain what meaning that might have for the vision, the more so since the temple plays virtually no role in Zechariah's vision.

[3] Because of the peculiar character of this object, the *mal'āk* does not even bother asking Zechariah what the object signifies. After all, the *mal'āk* himself apparently had a difficult time believing that such an object existed. However, once the object is described, he is immediately able to provide an interpretation of its significance: "This is the curse which is going out over the earth . . . ," and this interpretation is followed by a *kî* clause explaining why it was necessary for such action to be undertaken.

The first problem we confront is the definition of the word *'ālāh,* "curse." At the outset, I should note that this noun provides something of a wordplay with the word for scroll, *mᵉgillāh.* Two of the three consonants (*l* and *h*), are identical in these two words. Because of the similarity in the sound of these two words, their correlation in Zech. 5:2–3 is enhanced. However, much more than phonetic similarity is at stake.

The *mal'āk* informs Zechariah that this scroll is *the* curse, the one that proceeds out over the entire land. What is such a curse? Fortunately, the term *'ālāh* is used elsewhere in the Hebrew Bible. There are at least three distinct uses of this term.[6] First, the *'ālāh* may be used against an unknown perpetrator of a crime. Judges 17:2 is paradigmatic in this regard. Someone had stolen 1,100 pieces of silver from an Ephraimite woman. Since the identity of the criminal was unknown, the woman uttered a curse against him in order to gain some sort of legal leverage on the perpetrator. The curse caused the woman's son to own up to the crime, whereupon she blessed the son and apparently in so doing removed the curse from him. This use of the *'ālāh* refers to the public making of a curse upon someone of unknown identity (cf. Lev. 5:1; Prov. 29:24).

---

[5] Some interpreters have proposed that the irregular ratio of the scroll reflects the dimensions of the temple porch, a section of the temple twenty cubits long and ten cubits wide (I Kings 6:3). See Mitchell, 169; Baldwin, 126; Mason, 57; B. Halpern, "The Ritual Background of Zechariah's Temple Song," *CBQ* 40, 1978, 178–179; cf. C. Jeremias, *Nachtgesichte,* 189 n. 4.

[6] For a good overview, see J. Scharbert, "*'ālāh,*" *TWAT* I, 279–285.

The second form of *'ālāh* is quite different. Here someone has been accused of a legal infraction, and yet the accusation cannot be proven. Num. 5:21–28 provides an ideal example. If a woman is accused of adultery, and yet the case can not be proven, she must drink "the water of bitterness that brings the curse." The woman "takes the oath of the curse" (Num. 5:21). If guilty, she will suffer bodily affliction; if not, she "shall be free and shall conceive children" (Num. 5:28). Initially we are told that "the priest shall write these curses in a book," just before the water of bitterness is ingested. This use of the *'ālāh* is dependent on having the curses recorded in a formal, inscriptive manner (cf. also I Kings 8:31), and deals with a known person.

A third major type of *'ālāh* has to do with treaties. When Abimelech and Isaac came together, Abimelech and his cohort said, "Let there be an *'ālāh* between you and us, and let us make a covenant with you" (Gen. 26:28). Similar in its linking of covenant and *'ālāh* is Ezek. 17:13, "And he took one of the seed royal and made a covenant with him, putting him under oath" (*'ālāh*). Both texts indicate that the contracting of a treaty could entail the operation of a curse.

What, precisely, is an *'ālāh* within the context of a treaty? The use of this term in Deut. 29 helps us answer the question. The noun *'ālāh* is used nine times. In vs. 11, 13, and 18 [12, 14, 19E], it clearly refers to or modifies directly the word "covenant" itself.

> . . .that you may enter into this covenant of Yahweh your God and into its *'ālāh* which Yahweh your God has made with you this day.[7] (Deut. 29:11 [12E])

> And it is not with you alone that I have made this covenant and this *'ālāh*. (Deut. 29:13 [14E])

> ". . . and one who when he hears the words of this *'ālāh*." (Deut. 29:18 [19E])

In the next two verses, the usage is more discrete. Deuteronomy 29:19 [20E] refers to curses in this book: "All the curses written in this book will settle against him, so that Yahweh will blot out his name from under heaven." And similarly, v. 20 [21E] reads, "Yahweh would single him out from all the tribes of Israel for calamity, in accordance with all the curses of the covenant written in this book of the law."

These latter two texts use *'ālāh* to refer to the so-called covenant curses, i.e., specific maledictions bringing affliction upon a person or a

---

[7] The words *bᵉrît* and *'ālāh* are often understood as a case of hendiadys: "sworn covenant" (Scharbert, 283).

society that violates the stipulations contained in a covenant such as the one which provides the substance of the book of Deuteronomy. Maledictions of this sort are, of course, listed in a terse and formulaic way in Deut. 28. For example: "Cursed shall you be in the city, and cursed shall you be in the field. Cursed shall be your basket and your kneading-trough" (vs. 16–17). Similar curse material appears in an expanded way in Deut. 28:20–68. Moreover, the issue of houses, as that occurs in Zech. 5:4, is included in these more general curses (Deut. 28:30b, "You shall build a house, and you shall not dwell in it").

This same notion of curses that are written down and that will go into effect when the covenant is broken is reflected also in two postexilic texts:

I will bring upon this place . . . all the çurses that are written in this book. (II Chron. 34:24)

. . . and the curse and the oath which are written in the law of Moses. (Dan. 9:11)

Quite clearly, the covenant contracted between Israel and Yahweh entailed curses that were thought to be written down, presumably upon normal writing material, i.e., a scroll. Therefore, to see a flying scroll and to label it as an *'ālāh* is to enter the realm of covenant ideology.

[4] The curse that Zechariah sees is understood to be sent over "all the earth." The phrase *kol-hā'āreṣ* is, as we have seen, something of a *leitmotiv* in Zechariah's visions. Earlier, this phrase had referred to the entire earth (Zech. 1:11; 4:10b; and later, 6:5). Since the Israelite covenant with Yahweh seems to be the controlling idea in the sixth vision, many have thought that the phrase "all the earth" in this vision must refer only to the land of Judah (i.e., at this time the territory immediately adjacent to Jerusalem), since Yahweh's claims would have been accepted only in that area. Were Zechariah's attention focused exclusively on the area of Syria-Palestine, one might be forced to decide in favor of the more localized interpretation of this phrase. Since, however, Zechariah—outside the visions—addresses Judahites who live in Babylon (see, e.g., 2:10 [6E]), one need not assume that Zechariah's discourse or visions are limited to Syria-Palestine, the more so because of the cosmic scale of his visions. In sum, it is preferable to think literally of all the earth, and yet to recognize that it is a curse of the Israelite covenant which is in force. Put another way, the curse may be sent out against Judahites both in Syria-Palestine and in the diaspora.

Why was it necessary for the curse to be sent out? The *mal'āk* provides Zechariah with an answer. The legal-covenantal system, the normative ethos of Israel, was not working. There were people who stole and yet remained unpunished; and there were those who "swore" and remained unpunished.[8]

Two sorts of infractions are involved here, infractions related directly to the prohibitions of the Decalogue. First, as becomes clear in the poetic oracle in Zech. 5:4, one party is indicted for swearing improperly by Yahweh's name. Interestingly, the language appears to be a conflation of the formulations of two commandments. Both Ex. 20:7 and 20:16 appear to be involved. Exodus 20:7 speaks of raising up *(nś')* the name of Yahweh in vain *(laššāw')*. Zechariah picks up on the notion of Yahweh's name and yet uses the language of making an oath, *hannišbā'*, which is lacking in the Decalogue. Furthermore, in Zech. 5:4, those who remained unpunished are described as swearing falsely, *laššāqer,* again language drawn from the Decalogue, "You shall not commit perjury *('ēd šāqer)* against your neighbor" (Ex. 20:16).

There are two sorts of infractions and yet the two infractions represent language drawn from at least three of the stipulations in the Decalogue. Put another way, Zechariah is doing something more than just quoting two of the commandments. He is utilizing Decalogue material to create the notion of serious infractions that remain unpunished.[9]

One might contend that Zech. 5:3 provides an explanation sufficient to understand this peculiar flying object. Zechariah and the reader now know the problem, unpunished evil deeds, and they also know that the *'ālāh* is designed to punish those offenders. There is, however, more to be said. Zechariah does not know the source of this flying curse, nor does he know how it will take effect. This information is provided, appropriately, in an oracle from the deity. After already learning that "this is the curse which goes out . . . ," we are now told that Yahweh himself sent out the curse. It is not the result of some freak accident—an unidentified flying object—nor is it a meaningless illusion, a freak fragment of Zechariah's dreams. Zechariah learns that the scroll has been sent by none other than Yahweh.[10]

That Yahweh has sent the curse scroll is explained quickly. Against whom it is sent and how it will work takes longer to elucidate. Clearly,

[8] Cf. Deut. 5:11 where *nqh,* "swear," is used in a similar context.
[9] The actual source of the "swearing falsely" language may in fact be Lev. 19:12.
[10] One senses here a resonance with the tetrateuchal traditions in which Yahweh is understood to have written the two tablets of testimony, "tables of stone, written by the finger of God" (Ex. 31:18).

the scroll has been sent and yet the curses have not taken effect. But they will.[11] A whole new image is introduced here, and yet it probably derives from the Decalogue material which the author has been mining. The curse will work itself out against the house(s) of the thief and the "swearer." In the first two cola of Zech. 5:4 the character of the swearer is fleshed out, when compared with the one-word description in 5:3. He is "one who swears falsely by my name," a mixing of language from two of the Ten Commandments. Then we learn that *'ālāh* will enter the respective houses of the thief and the "false swearer." And it will work its effect not only by destroying the house but also by destroying as well the materials out of which the house was constructed, wood and stone.

The destruction of a house is attested as punishment in both biblical and extrabiblical texts. Jeremias has surveyed this material and notes that destruction of a person's house as punishment for theft or lack of loyalty is attested in Hab. 3:13b; Dan. 2:5; 3:29; and Ezra 6:11.[12] The last text mentioned is significant since it refers to punishment for those who violate Cyrus' edict enabling the reconstruction of the Jerusalem temple: "Also I make a decree that if any one alters this edict, a beam shall be pulled out of his home, and he shall be impaled upon it and his house shall be made a dunghill." Similar language is attested in curses present in ancient Near Eastern treaties; thus *Sefîre* I, C 21–23: "So may the gods overturn that man and his house and all that is in it and may they make its lower part its upper part." On the basis of this data, we may affirm that Zechariah is using standard curse traditions. And yet he appears to be using a rather mild form of these traditions. There is not in Zech. 5, as in many of the other "house" curses, explicit reference to the demise of the person against whom the malediction is directed. The Zechariah curse is directed at the house and not at the person.

What is left out of the curse's effect is, perhaps, as significant as what is included. One might expect a specific threat against the person, or even to the third or fourth generation of his or her descendants (as in Ex. 20:5–6). There is, however, no such language. The curse is effective against the domicile of the unknown perpetrator of evil and is not directed at the person of the perpetrator.

It is now necessary to draw back and ask two basic questions: (1) Do the infractions itemized in the curse refer to specific problems that Judahites were experiencing during this time, or do they represent

---

[11] The verbs in Zech. 5:4b, d, e are converted perfects.

[12] C. Jeremias, *Nachtgesichte*, 193.

more generally the basic legal traditions of ancient Israel? (2) What is the significance of this vision? The first of these questions must be answered before a satisfactory response may be given to the second. Some scholars have maintained that theft was a serious issue during the period 530–520 B.C.E.[13] As Ezek. 11:15 and other texts suggest, those who remained in the land apparently appropriated landholdings of those who were taken into exile. That such was a problem fifty years later, i.e., during the time of Zechariah, is a matter of conjecture. More to the point is, however, the fact that land ownership was a public matter. If someone laid claim to a particular tract of land, one that was owned by someone else, there were two distinct parties, and litigation could be undertaken. Put another way, the *'ālāh* as legal procedure would be inappropriate for the improper acquisition of land. The better case in which to expect the *'ālāh* is the loss of movable property, the case attested in Judg. 17:2. Apart from this postulated case, it is difficult to determine what problems might have made these two issues, swearing and stealing, particularly relevant to the period around 520 B.C.E.

And if these two issues are not uniquely relevant to the society in which Zechariah lived, they may perhaps simply represent the sort of material in which they belong—i.e., legal, or more specifically, Decalogue stipulations. These two forms of infractions, reformulated as they seem to have been by Zechariah, represent the major parts of the Decalogue; swearing falsely by Yahweh's name counts as a violation against the deity, whereas stealing represents a violation of the social order. These two cases are significant because they represent the two basic forms of infraction included in the Decalogue, crimes against Yahweh and crimes against humanity.

What we appear to have in this text is a melding of the legal and covenant traditions. The legal tradition entails maledictions against parties unknown in a society. Clearly, the evildoers of Zech. 5:1–4 are unknown, listed only as those who engage in improper actions x and y. The *'ālāh* is designed to ferret out and punish those who have done wrong and yet who, because they remain unidentified, are unpunished. All this works, as did the curse in Judg. 17:2. There is, however, a difference. In Zech. 5, a particular punishment is mentioned—the destruction of the house of the person so cursed. As Jeremias and others have argued, and as the curses of Deut. 28 suggest, such language is most easily understood as a curse that would go into force automatically at the disobedience of treaty stipulations.

[13] Ibid., 190–191; Horst, 235.

What then may be said about the significance of this vision and its interpretation by Yahweh's messenger? I have argued that the *'ālāh* and its articulation represent legal and treaty conventions of ancient Israel. Further, the specific formulations for error depend upon but are not direct copies of language found in the Decalogue. The covenant and Decalogue traditions represent the normative traditions of Israel. One point of the vision seems to be that the newly restored community will continue the same ideology and value structures that were present prior to the destruction of 587 B.C.E..

Such a radical contention is not without significance, especially after the preceding vision. A new polity had just been inaugurated, a diarchy instead of the earlier monarchy. Such a structure could be understood as a significant change from the norms of earlier Israel. This new polity raised real questions about the extent to which those in Israel stood in continuity with the past. Creative use of decalogue, curse, and legal traditions demonstrate, in this sixth vision, that the old ethos is still normative, even though the structure of governance is new.

The vision establishes continuity with Israel's earlier normative traditions. It also indicates that the social norms of Israel are not, at the moment, in proper working order. And it further suggests that proper enforcement of those norms will not be easily accomplished by the newly authorized civil and religious authority figures. Rather, the norms and their administration are understood to derive from Yahweh. Since theft and false swearing stand in violation of norms that were understood to have been given by Yahweh, the prosecution of the violators of these norms was also understood to be, ultimately, Yahweh's responsibility.

The significance of this vision can also be explored from the perspective of the group that Yahweh is addressing. In Zech. 4, the points of attention are the leaders of the community. In Zech. 5, the focus has shifted to the community as a whole. The references to the Decalogue are, in a very real way, references to the social contract that provides the sense of social cohesion and identity for Israel. Yahweh first addressed the civil and religious leaders and then, with the articulation of those roles, moved to consider the society as a whole, as well as its basic norms. Important and concrete though these issues of polity and social norms are, they are treated in a way fully consistent with the other visions of Zechariah, i.e., the curse is viewed as hovering in an intermediate realm, between heaven and earth. To be sure, it will, when the occasion demands, "enter the house of the thief." But to be effective, it must exist in an intermediate, almost transcendent way, so that it can, when appropriate, enforce the traditional social norms. Yahweh's intentionality for the new community is not, therefore, fully routinized within the new human structures. The curse has a meta-societal status. It exists above, and beyond the control of, the civil and religious leaders. Yahweh, rather than these authorities, has primary responsibility for the articulation and defense of Israel's social contract and norms.

Zechariah 5:5–11

This is wickedness

5 The divine messenger who spoke with me came forward and said
   to me,
   "Lift up your eyes and look!
   What is this which is approaching?"[a]
6 I responded, "What is it?"
   He said, "This is the ephah which approaches."
   And he continued, "This is their guilt[b] throughout all the earth."
7 Behold, a disk of lead was raised,
   and there[c] was a woman sitting in the ephah.
8 He said, "This is wickedness"; whereupon
   he pushed her down into the middle of the ephah
   and put the leaden weight on its opening.
9 Then I lifted up my eyes and looked.
   Two women were coming forth:
   wind was in their wings,
   their wings were like the wings of a stork.
   They lifted up the ephah between earth and sky.
10 I said to the messenger who spoke with me,
   "Where are they taking the ephah?"
11 And he said to me,
   "To build for it a new home in the land of Shinar.
   It shall be firmly set there upon its stand."

---

a. *māh*, "what," is regularly a direct interrogative particle.
b. Reading *ᵃwônām* with LXX, Syr.
c. On the deictic use of *zō't*, see Rudolph, 118.

The Seventh Vision

[5–6] Zechariah is instructed to lift up his eyes, and he apparently obeys, because he immediately says, "What is it?" Here in the seventh vision we seem to be in a situation similar to that of the second vision. After "seeing," the visionary must ask a question about the identity of that which he has just seen. And yet this vision is different from the second one. In Zech. 2:1 [1:18E] we know that Zechariah recognizes what he sees: he sees four horns and remains puzzled by them. But in 5:6 we have no reason to think that Zechariah knows what the object is. In v. 5 the object was described only as something which was approaching. In v. 6 the identity of the object is revealed only by the discourse of the *mal'āk*. He reports that it is an *'êphāh* (a unit of dry measure, here a container, approximately two thirds of a bushel). Out of what such a measure was made, we cannot be sure. Perhaps the container was ceramic, perhaps textile, perhaps metal. It was, at least, appropriate for holding grain, flour, and the like.

Immediately after the object is identified, it is interpreted: "This (the *'êphāh*) is their guilt in all the land." What are we to make of the significance of this object as well as of its interpretation?[1] First, the *'êphāh* itself. The term is used numerous times in the Hebrew Bible. It is, in its most neutral usages, a simple unit of measure—approximately 36.5 liters. It was used to measure, e.g., harvested barley (Ruth 2:17); sacrificial flour (Lev. 5:11); and parched grain (I Sam. 17:17). It could hold various commodities, such as wheat, barley, and flour. For the *'êphāh* to function as a container and a measure of a commodity, it had to contain an agreed-upon amount. That is, the *'êphāh* had to be standarized, and it had to be "just." It is surprising how many times the term *'êphāh* occurs in texts that entail a demand or an admonition that a "just *'êphāh*" be used (e.g., Deut. 25:14, 15; Amos 8:5: Prov. 20:10; Lev. 19:36; Ezek. 45:10; Micah 6:11). Just as when seeing an *'êphāh*, one might ask what it contains, so also one might ask whether it is an accurate or a just measure. The numerous admonitions calling for a just *'êphāh* clearly indicate that an unjust or nonstandard *'êphāh* was used in Israelite society. Hence when Zechariah hears that the object envisioned is an *'êphāh*, he might naturally harbor concern not only

---

[1] Cf. S. Marenof, "Note Concerning the Meaning of the Word *'Ephah'* in Zechariah 5:5–11," *American Journal of Semitic Languages and Literatures* 48, 1931/32, 246–267. Marenof proposed to understand *'êphāh* on the basis of *e-pa*, which was used to describe the ziggurat at Lagash and which may have entered Hebrew as a loanword in a fashion similar to *e-gal (hêkāl)*. Ingenious though this suggestion was, it has not found general acceptance.

about its contents but also about whether it was a just *'êphāh*. The interpretations as well as the remainder of the vision suggest that precisely these two connotations and the attendant issues are, in fact, important for the writer.

The interpretation of the *'êphāh* as a single object seems bound up with the second of the aforementioned connotations. It is defined as "their guilt throughout all the earth." In assessing the significance of the fourth vision, we confronted this same term (*'āwôn*, "guilt") in 3:4 and discovered that it often meant sin guilt, i.e., objectified and transferable guilt. It is the result of transgression and yet does not necessarily adhere to the transgressor. So, for example, the high priest could bear the transgression of the people. According to 3:4, Yahweh removed the taint of transgression from the high priest, contamination which, in all likelihood, was engendered by the sins of the Israelite community.

This notion of *'āwôn*, as something that may be removed from the transgressor and transferred to another party, also appears in the seventh vision. In fact, one might even argue that the *'āwôn* symbolized by the *'êphāh* is the *'āwôn* generated by the people, by their defeat and exile, borne by the high priest, and removed from the high priest in Zech. 3:4. Despite the purification of the high priest, however, the *'āwôn* remains in the land. Furthermore, the specific wording of this text is important in defining the character of the *'āwôn*. According to 5:6, the *'êphāh* is "their *'āwôn*." The text does not state that the *'êphāh* contains *'āwôn*. And this notion is consistent with the use of the term *'êphāh* in the Israelite tradition. The *'êphāh*, given the numerous references to the irregular or unjust *'êphāh*, can, without reference to what it contains, carry a negative meaning. The writer of this text builds on this sense of the term *'êphāh* and identifies the *'êphāh* with the radical guilt generated by the people. The *'êphāh* is itself, in this vision, a symbol of radical guilt and contamination, similar to the clothes of the high priest in 3:4.

[7–8] This object and its interpretation do not conclude the vision. Far from it. Rather, in v. 7 we are immediately given more detail about the scene. We are informed that a roundel of lead, presumably functioning as a lid for the *'êphāh*, was raised, and that a woman was sitting in the *'êphāh*. The total image is bizarre: An *'êphāh* appears, a rather small unit of measure, in which a person sits, and above which a round piece of lead is raised. To the best of our knowledge, lead lids were not used in antiquity for such purposes. Further, the standard capacity of an *'êphāh* could not accommodate a normal human individual, whether male or female. The picture is, simply, incongruous. Hence, we should not be surprised that what follows immediately is yet another interpretation.

First we learned that the *'êphāh* signified radical guilt. Now we are informed that the woman denotes (the) evil. The use of the Hebrew term *riš'āh* ("evil") suggests that we are not to think the visionary is simply restating an earlier point. Rather, a new issue is being articulated. This noun regularly occurs as an antonym of the noun *ṣedeq* and may refer to improper action within the social ambit. The noun is used once with obvious reference to religious, though not necessarily cultic, impropriety in Mal. 3:18: "Then once more you shall distinguish between the righteous and the wicked, between one who serves God and one who does not serve him."[2] The noun *riš'āh* is used often in very general, almost formulaic ways (e.g., Deut. 9:4; Prov. 13:6). In Ezek. 33:12, 19, we learn that *riš'āh* may designate "not restoring the pledge and robbery," as well as the more general "not walking in the statutes of life." If *riš'āh* can be used to describe the improper act, then *'āwôn* refers to the sin guilt incurred by such action. The *'êphāh* with the woman inside, as guilt with sin inside it, represents the total package of error: the act and its consequences. These objects allow the interpreter to visualize the totality of an errant act and to conceive a way in which it might be physically moved from one place to another. The objects, like the garments of the high priest in 3:3–4, serve to objectify evil and its contamination. Further, when evil is thus objectified, it becomes possible to see how such evil and guilt might be removed.

One does wonder why a woman was thought appropriate as a symbol for evil. I have already suggested that the *'êphāh* was an appropriate object to symbolize *'āwôn*, because of the problem of the unjust *'êphāh*. Why, then, might a woman, and for that matter a lead roundel, function in a similar regard? A likely answer points to the popular understanding of the narrative tradition preserved in Gen. 3.[3] One hesitates to say that this story provided a tradition about the feminine as evil, but later religious texts which regard Gen. 3 as authoritative suggest that just such a notion was implicit in the story.[4]

---

[2] Some scholars have maintained that idolatry, i.e., cultic error, is indicated by *riš'āh*. See, among others, Ackroyd, *Exile and Restoration*, 204; Mitchell, 173–174; C. Jeremias, *Nachtgesichte*, 195–196. However, this contention is not warranted on the basis of the biblical usage of the term. Further, just because this *'êphāh* is to be venerated in Babylon, the land of Shinar, does not mean it was venerated in Syria-Palestine. To suggest that "social" evil would become a venerable object in Babylon provides an even stronger polemic against Babylon than simply to suggest that those in the land of Shinar would venerate an idol imported from Syria-Palestine.

[3] Without foundation, in my judgment, is the theory that the woman in the *'êphāh* represents cult prostitution (Mitchell, 173–174). Further, one is hard pressed to discover Mitchell's reason for thinking that the woman is "a very active figure."

[4] Thus I Tim. 2:13–14.

Perhaps one is forced to connect this image in Zechariah to the image
of Eve as perpetrator of error as that is expressed in Greco-Roman
texts. In this regard, it is important to note that this seventh vision has
other contacts with the primeval history, e.g., the plain of Shinar.
Perhaps this reference to the primeval period provides the wherewithal to discuss the character of human error. One might also mention the
text in Gen. 6:1–4, since the daughters of man were thought to have
been contaminated by contact with the sons of the gods. Perhaps Gen.
3 and 6 jointly provide the sort of background that allows the female to
serve as an image of *riš'āh,* just as the *'êphāh* was able to serve as a
symbol of *'āwôn.* There is reason to think that these two elements,
'êphāh and woman, included the potential within the dominant
traditions for expressing *riš'āh* and *'āwôn* respectively.

Immediately after the report about the existence of this woman and
about her significance, a new element occurs. There is action in what
had heretofore been a rather static report. The *mal'āk* thrusts the
woman down into the *'êphāh* and places the lead weight on the opening
of the *'êphāh.* The *'êphāh* is apparently intended to contain the evil,
and until this moment, the lid had not been closed. With this action,
the *mal'āk* has prevented the woman from leaving and in so doing has
encapsulated evil.

One detail in this action report requires elucidation. The piece of
lead is not this time designated as a roundel but rather as an *'eben,* a
stone or weight. That *'eben* can mean a weight is made clear by such
texts as Prov. 11:1; 16:11; 20:23; II Sam. 14:26. Especially important in
this regard are several texts in which the terms *'êphāh* and *'eben*
(meaning "weight") are conjoined:

> You shall have just balances, just weights, a just ephah, and a just hin.
> (Lev. 19:36)

> A full and just weight you shall have, a full and just ephah you shall have.
> (Deut. 25:15)

> > Diverse weights and diverse measures
> > are both alike an abomination to Yahweh.
> > (Prov. 20:10)

> Shall I forget the treasures won by wickedness,
>   and the despicable use of an ephah that is too small?
> Shall I approve anyone with false scales,
>   with cheating weights in his pouch?
> (Micah 6:10–11)[5]

---

[5] J. Mays, *Micah,* OTL, 1976, 143.

In all these texts, the nouns *'êphāh* and *'eben* occur together and mean "measure" and "weight" respectively. Further, and of great importance in all these texts, the focus is on unjust measures and weights. And interestingly, in the last-cited text, Micah 6:10–11, another term, *reša'*, the root of which appears in Zech. 5:8 in the noun *riš'āh*, also appears. In this text, those who accumulate treasure by means of unjust weights and measures are understood to be "wicked." One therefore does well to construe this lead roundel as a lead weight. Archaeologists have discovered both metallic and stone weights in the ancient Near East.[6] Further, the lead weight, along with the *'êphāh*, serves to create the image of injustice, improper social practice, even evil, as the expression "an abomination to Yahweh" suggests.

The lead roundel serves both a pragmatic and social function. It serves to contain evil, and at the same time, and along with the *'êphāh*, to symbolize improper social practice which creates *'āwôn*. The *'êphāh* and the lead weight provide a powerful and complex image. They symbolize evil and, at the same time, contain evil as it is personified by the woman. Because the *'êphāh* and lid symbolize *'āwôn* and because they contain *riš'āh*, they must be removed. It is not enough for the *'êphāh* simply to contain the evil, since the *'êphāh* is itself evil.

[9] In 5:9, after we hear that evil and its effect, guilt, have been localized, we encounter the formulaic language of vision inception: "I lifted up my eyes and looked" (cf. 2:1, 5 [1:18; 2:1E]; 5:1, 5). After the formula, we hear Zechariah report that in this new vision he sees two women approaching. They are approaching, not walking or running, but soaring with the wind in their stork-like wings. And they proceed to lift up the *'êphāh*. Just as the lid was lifted up in 5:7 *(niśśē't)*, so now the entire *'êphāh* is lifted up *(wattiśśe'nāh)* and soars between heaven and earth. We are now in an intermediate realm, a territory important to other visions of Zechariah. In this arena, the evil does not contaminate the heavens, the abode of the deity, nor does it contaminate the human sphere. Nevertheless, this intermediate realm, though it is not the heavens, remains under the control of the deity. The women are not pictured as flying, i.e., actively moving their wings. Rather they appear to soar on the wind, Yahweh's agency of movement. Yahweh could not touch the evil and sin-guilt, but he could provide the power for its removal.[7]

[10–11] After the new creatures and their action are described, the visionary, as elsewhere in the visions, asks a question. He does not ask

---

[6] See "Weights and Measures," *IDB* IV, 830–833.
[7] On the wind as Yahweh's agent, see Gen. 8:1; Ex. 15:10; Jer. 10:13; Num. 11:31.

about the identity of the newly envisioned creatures. They and their purpose are apparently clear. He is, however, concerned about the destination of the *'êphāh*. The *mal'āk* answers this concern and adds even more information. It is almost as if he is answering the question, what are they going to do with the *'êphāh*? We are told that it will be taken to the land of Shinar. A "house" will be built and the *'êphāh*, with its contents apparently intact, will be permanently situated there upon a stand.

The questions raised by this vision are numerous. What does the removal signify? Why are flying creatures, part female and part bird, chosen for the task of removal? Why is the land of Shinar chosen as the place for disposal? Why is a structure built to serve as an architectural setting for the *'êphāh*?

The vision demonstrates that evil, *riš'āh*, and its *'āwôn*, i.e., that which contaminates, can be isolated. Further, we have discovered that the *'êphāh*, the lead weight, and the woman were thought appropriate to signify evil and impurity. From the perspective of 5:1–4, we may say that evil has now been harvested, collected in the *'êphāh* as grain is placed in an *'êphāh*. It has been harvested as the result of active curses outlined in the previous vision, curses that had also been "sent out." Because *'êphāh*, lid, and woman are harvested and isolatable, they are also removable.

But they must be removed by someone or something. I have already suggested that it was important for the removal to occur in the intermediate realm, between the heavens and the earth. Hence, some entities which could travel in this realm were necessary. In this vision, they are winged women. Why women? Jeremias has argued convincingly that the visionary here simply adopts an iconographic tradition and notion well known throughout the ancient Near East, that of a creature which is half animal, half human; more particularly of a female with wings, or one who can fly.[8] Therefore the choice of a woman here may not be unusual. What is unusual is the simile used to describe the wings: "like the wings of a stork." The image created by references to the Levantine stork is at least twofold. The stork could fly high (Jer. 8:7). It could perform the function of removing the *'êphāh* within the realm between heaven and earth. And yet it was an unclean bird (Lev. 11:19; Deut. 14:18). It was a bird uniquely suited for this particular purpose.[9] In sum, a land and society that were being

---

[8] C. Jeremias, *Nachtgesichte*, 199 n. 19.

[9] Eagles too were unclean and could fly high, but they were understood as noble creatures and were therefore inappropriate for this particular task (Prov. 23:5; Isa. 4:31). Cf. C. Jeremias, *Nachtgesichte*, 200.

restored were in need of purification, the removal of '*āwôn*, just as was the case in Zech. 3.

"Removal from" implies "removal to." The land of Shinar, the destination of the '*êphāh*, is—as other biblical texts indicate (Gen. 10:10; 11:2; Dan. 1:2; Isa. 11:11; Josh. 7:21)—Mesopotamia. Isaiah 11:11 understands the land of Shinar to be a place of exile, and a place from which exiles will return to Israel.

One must of course ask why the phrase "in the land of Shinar," rather than "in the land of Babylon," was used by the visionary.[10] One senses that the name Shinar not only indicates Babylon as a place of exile but also refers to a place in which error was perpetrated and in which the deity was provoked to action of significant scale—the dispersal of humanity in Gen. 11. It is perhaps not accidental that in this Genesis narrative people are sent out of a territory and that in Zech. 5:5–11 the same action, sending out—but this time removal of error—is involved.

If people are leaving Babylon and returning to Israel, as Zechariah hopes, then there is an upset in the cosmic balance. This imbalance may be righted by the removal of people—here personified collectively as a woman—from Israel to Babylon.[11] This balance of mass, i.e., of populations, is more than simply a demographic issue. The sending of evil to Babylon also serves to purify Israel and to contaminate Babylon. From this perspective it becomes easier to understand why evil is personified. The logic of the restoration and of the visionary world requires a transfer of people: Judahites from Babylon to Israel and evil person(s) from Israel to Babylon. With this transfer, a demographic equilibrium of movement is achieved. Furthermore, a purification of sorts is accomplished by the removal of sin and guilt, a purification in many respects analogous to the one carried out in Zech. 3. Both were undertaken at the behest of the deity, and yet an agent other than the deity accomplished the actual removal of '*āwôn*. The *mal'āk* removes the garments and the women carry off the evil—'*êphāh*, lid, and woman. Both demographic and ethical-ritual homeostasis are effected by this removal of the '*êphāh* and concomitant return of people from exile.

Once homeostasis has been achieved, it must be preserved. To this end, the *mal'āk* uses an assemblage of language that emphasizes the fixity of the '*êphāh* in Shinar: "build for it a home [i.e., temple]";

[10] Interestingly, LXX, S, T, all read "Babel" instead of "Shinar." See Rudolph, 118.

[11] For the positive use of a collective image, cf. "Zion" in Deutero-Isaiah (e.g., Isa. 40:9).

"firmly set there [established] upon its stand." The double use of the root *kwn* emphasizes this fixity. Further, the specific noun *mᵉkônāh* points to a likely cultic function for an object such as the *'êphāh* in Babylon. The term *mᵉkônāh* is used to designate the stand for sacral objects, e.g., the stand for the lavers in the Solomonic temple in I Kings 7:27ff., and the stand for the altar of the second temple in Ezra 3:3—the latter being a text which, like Zech. 5:11, uses the verb *kwn* and the noun *mᵉkônāh* after the preposition *'al*. One has the impression that the writer is maintaining that the Babylonians will fix and venerate this new cultic object. It will be installed in a "house," the word for house, *bêt*, having here the obvious sense of "temple" (cf. *bêt yhwh*).

One further piece of evidence is important in this regard. The Babylonians were remembered as having dismantled the bronze stands, *mᵉkōnôt*, from the Solomonic temple and as having carried them off to Babylon (II Kings 23:13, 16; cf. Jer. 27:19). Given this tradition, it was possible for Zechariah to think that bases (or at least the material out of which appropriate bases could be made) were already in Babylon, defiled to be sure, but available as a place of rest for the *'êphāh* when it arrived in Shinar. If this cultic character is present in Zech. 5:11, then the vision and its interpretation serve not only to generate equilibrium after the effects of deportation, to create purity in Israel; they also serve to establish a negative image of Shinar, Babylon, the conqueror and plunderer of Jerusalem. That which Babylon plundered enables it to become a place in which evil and error will be cultically installed and venerated. Such a negative image addresses significantly the lack of justice as that is explored in the first vision of the cycle.

This penultimate vision, despite its bizarre imagery, works importantly in the restoration scenario. By means of the *'êphāh*, the lid, and the woman, evil and guilt are conceived as containable and movable. Such imagery presumes that the unknown perpetrator of the sixth vision has been identified. The curses have worked. Now that the evil and impurity have been collected, they must be removed from the land. To this end, the *'êphāh* is carried off by winged women and fixed in Babylon, there apparently to be venerated by the Babylonians. The removal of evil also establishes equilibrium. With people moving from Babylon to Israel, imbalance had been initiated. With someone (the woman here as a collective entity) moving in the other direction, homeostasis was achieved. Once this had happened, the world could be conceived as "at rest," and now properly so. The vision provides a way in which real equilibrium, the world at rest, would be achieved.

Hence, despite the negativity of much of the imagery in the vision, the ultimate impact of the visionary symbolism and action is positive for Israel.

Zechariah 6:1–8

Go out, range over the earth

1 Again I lifted up my eyes and beheld:
  Four chariots were setting out from between two mountains.
  The two mountains were of bronze.
2 The horses of the first chariot were bay,
  the horses of the second chariot were black,
3 the horses of the third chariot were white,
  and the horses of the fourth chariot were dappled.[a]
4 Then I responded to the messenger who had spoken with me,
  "What are these, my Lord?"
5 The messenger responded and said to me,
  "These are the four winds of heaven
    which go out after having presented themselves
    before the Lord of all the earth.
6 As for (the chariot) with the bay horses, they are going out to the east,
    the black horses are going out to northland,
      the white are going out to the west,
    and the dappled are going out to the southland.[b]
7 The strong ones are setting out,[c] intent
  on ranging over the earth."
And he gave the command:
  "Go out, range over the earth."
And they ranged over the earth.
8 Then he shouted out to me and said,
  "See the ones who are proceeding to the northland:
    They have put my spirit at rest in the northland!"

a. Deleting *'ᵃmuṣṣîm*, which has been introduced here as a color because it appears to function as a fourth kind of steed in 6:7. With the restoration proposed in 6:6, it is clear that *'ᵃmuṣṣîm* in 6:7 is resumptive, referring to a quality possessed by all the horses.
  b. Verse 6 is problematic on several counts. It commences with a relative clause, apparently referring to a noun or noun clause which has been lost from

the original Hebrew text. Of the bay, black, white, and dappled color sequence presented in 6:2–3, 6:6 includes only the black, white, and dappled colors. The first color—bay—is missing. Finally, on the basis of 6:5, one expects to have reference to all four points of the compass. In 6:6, the east is missing. The verse appears, on grammatical grounds, to have a lacuna at its beginning; the first color in the sequence is missing; and the direction east is missing; it is therefore probable that a clause stating something like "The bay horses are going out to the east" is to be restored. (For this basic argument, see Rudolph, 122 n. 6, as well as other, older commentaries.) The Jerusalem Bible has included the beginning of the relative clause, *'ᵃšer bāh*, in its translation: "The red horses are going out to the country of the East; the black horses are going out to the country of the North; the white are going out to the country of the West and the piebald are going out to the country of the South."

The verb sequence in 6:6 also presents difficulties. According to the reconstruction of this verse postulated above, the first verb is not extant in the MT but is presumed to be either *yāṣ'û* or *yōṣ'îm*, on the basis of the verbs occurring later in the verse. Even more attractive is the option of pointing these consonants as an imperfect form, *yēṣ'û*. Apart from the problem of the missing first verb, if one follows strictly the verb forms as they occur in the MT (i.e., perfect tense), the text presents us with a situation in which some of the steeds have already been sent out—those to the west and those to the south—whereas those to the north are about to be sent out. I prefer to repoint the MT forms as *yēṣ'û*. (Cf. Rudolph, 122 n. 6 [c]; cf. Mitchell, 182.)

Finally, the phrase *'el 'aḥᵃrêhem* as a direction in which the white horses are heading is puzzling. Literally, the phrase means "after them." One would be forced to think of the white horses heading north after the black horses. Given the four points of the compass mentioned in 6:5, it is unlikely that one or more of the directions would be ignored in the articulation of the vision, the more so since the point of the vision seems to communicate that the world is properly at rest. Hence, on prima facie grounds one expects a direction in place of this phrase. Some commentators have proposed *'el-'ereṣ hayyām*, though it is admittedly difficult to see how such a textual error could have occurred. Ehrlich proposes, more cogently, *'el-'aḥar hayyām*, which is at least close to the preserved consonantal text; *'ḥrhym* to MT *'ḥryhm*. I follow Ehrlich's reconstruction and translate "to the west" (i.e., toward the Mediterranean). Alternatively, one might argue along radically different lines that, despite the fact that the four cardinal directions are implied in Zech. 6:5, only two directions, north and south, are mentioned explicitly in v. 6. And these directions are, after all, the crucial ones if, as seems certain, north refers to the land of exile and south is the direction in which the exiles are returning. If the vision is focused essentially on this bilateral movement, Judahites returning south and *'êphāh*/person moving north, then it is not absolutely necessary to seek all four directions in this vision. (Cf. Mason, 60.)

    c. Reading *yēṣ'û* instead of MT *yāṣ'û*.

The Eighth Vision

[1] The eighth and final vision receives no special introduction. The first five words of the Hebrew text are identical to those introducing the sixth vision in 5:1. But whereas the sixth vision commenced with an initial two-word vision report, the final vision begins with a report that extends without interruption through the end of v. 3. Various objects and colors, as well as geographic detail, provide the substance of this relatively lengthy report. Despite the length of the total visionary description, the report included in v. 1 itself comprises the essential information. Verses 2 and 3 constitute explication of the basic data provided in the first verse.

In the first verse, Zechariah reports seeing four chariots proceeding out from between two mountains, mountains of bronze. Since the moving objects are later interpreted (in 6:5) as the four winds of the heavens, the meaning of the vision is not finally to be gained by appeal to extended reflection on the nature of chariots in the abstract. And yet, it remains important to know what connotations chariots bore in the ancient Near East, and, as well, whether this collocation of images—chariots coming out from between two mountains—has special significance.

Zechariah reports seeing chariots. Of that he is certain. A brief overview of the term "chariot" in ancient Israelite literature suggests that the use of this mode of transportation was limited to kings and persons of high estate (II Sam. 15:1; II Kings 5:21; 9:27; 10:15; II Chron. 35:24). Also, the chariot, though it was obviously of importance as a military vehicle, was also significant as a commodity. Israel apparently held a position of importance in the chariot trade.[1] Furthermore, the chariot was important in a ritual context (I Chron. 28:18; II Kings 23:11) and served, more abstractly, as a symbol for Yahweh's martial presence. Either a chariot (Hab. 3:8) or chariots (Isa. 66:15; Jer. 4:13) could serve as such a symbol. The latter two texts are particularly interesting since they both include the phrase "his chariots like the storm wind/whirlwind," *kassûpāh mark^ebōtāw*. And in this final vision, both chariots and winds are important.

> For behold, Yahweh will come in fire,
>   and his chariots like the stormwind,
> to render his anger in fury,
>   and his rebuke with flames of fire.

[1] Thus J. Bright, *A History of Israel*, 1981³, 216–217.

> For by fire will Yahweh execute judgment,
> and by his sword, upon all flesh;
> and those slain by Yahweh shall be many.
>   (Isa. 66:15-16)

At that time it will be said to this people and to Jerusalem, "A hot wind from the bare heights in the desert toward the daughter of my people, not to winnow or cleanse, a wind too full for this comes for me. Now it is I who speak in judgment upon them."

> Behold, he comes up like clouds,
> his chariots like the whirlwind;
> his horses are swifter than eagles—
> woe to us, for we are ruined!
>   (Jer. 4:11-13)

In both texts, the chariots are likened to storm winds. In Isa. 66, one senses the imagery of the thunderstorm, with lightning as fire; whereas in Jer. 4, the hot dry wind from the desert is the obvious source of the punishing wind. In each case, however, chariots symbolize the attacking presence of the deity, a god approaching from preternatural heights.

The background of such a notion, the deity present in chariots and associated with the winds, is not difficult to discern. Ba'al was known as the rider of the clouds, *rkb 'rpt*, and was understood to be a deity "driving the clouds as a war chariot." And clearly, Yahweh exercised a similar function (Deut. 33:26; Isa. 19:1; Hab. 3:8; Ps. 104:3-4). Psalm 68 is particularly significant, as P. Miller[2] points out:

> The chariots of Yahweh were two myriad.
> A thousand the warriors/archers of the Lord
> When he came from Sinai with the holy ones.
>   (Ps. 68:18 [17E])

Here the march of Yahweh and his hosts into battle is unmistakable. "Chariots" can hardly refer to Israel's army at any early stage in its history; it is obviously the divine army here which marches forth to fight for Israel.[3] Given this religio-historical background, when Zechariah reports that he sees chariots coming from between mountains, the military connotations of the divinely authorized chariots are difficult to avoid. Following the imagery of Ps. 68:18

---

[2] Cf. P. Miller, *The Divine Warrior in Ancient Israel*, 1973, 105.
[3] Cf. ibid., 108-109.

[17E], the chariots are most probably thought to be driven by the divine charioteers, the minor deities known as the sons of the gods. If such is the case, then the chariots are, per se, not iconic representations of the deity. Rather, they signify, in standard Northwest Semitic traditions, the deity's military forces.

The notion of coming from between the mountains is a twist on the standard Northwest Semitic traditions, a twist that appears to betray Zechariah's dependence on Mesopotamian notions. Yahweh is often understood as coming from a mountain, as in Ps. 68:18 [17E], "when he came from Sinai." However, the notion of the deity proceeding from between two mountains is not attested in the biblical material. The idea of two mountains as related to a deity is not unknown in the Northwest Semitic environs. Mot's dwelling is described in the following text, a text that comprises a command of Ba'al to his heralds:

> Then set your face
> Toward Mount Trgzz
> Toward Mount Trmg
> Toward the two hills that stop up the underworld.[4]

Apart from the explicit statement of two mountains, however, this notion does not seem similar to that of Zechariah, since here the dwelling, or at least the realm to which the two mountains provide access, is that of the heavenly or supernal deity, not the god of death and the underworld.

Closer in detail to the Zechariah imagery are usages that reflect the sun-god and his cult. On the basis of II Kings 23:11, we know that chariots and horses were used in Judah as icons for the worship of the sun: "And he removed the horses that the kings of Judah had dedicated to the sun, at the entrance to the house of the Lord, by the chamber of Nathan-melech the chamberlain, which was in the precincts; and he burned the chariots of the sun with fire."[5]

The Mesopotamian sun-god, Šamaš, was often represented in glyptic art. One of the best-known motifs in this material is the depiction of Šamaš appearing between two mountains, which are themselves placed inside two opened doors of the heavenly realm. This scene, of course, depicts graphically the rising sun.[6] However, in none

---

[4] R. Clifford, *The Cosmic Mountain in Canaan and the Old Testament*, 1972, 79.

[5] On this text, see J. Gray, *I & II Kings*, OTL, 1970², 736–737. See also Ezek. 8:16–18 for explicit condemnation of solar worship in an early sixth-century Jerusalemite context.

[6] See esp. the seals #219, 220 in A. Moortgat, *Vorderasiatische Rollsiegel*, 1966, as well as p. 23 of that work. This same basic scene could also occur with the deity appearing

of these depictions is the sun-god portrayed riding in or accompanied by a chariot. Put another way, these several seals which depict Šamaš as the rising sun help explicate the geographic significance of the two mountains that appear in Zechariah's vision. They do not, however, help explain the notion of four chariots at this place.[7]

Also requiring comment is the specification of the mountains as consisting of bronze. It has been commonplace for commentators to relate these two mountains to the two bronze pillars placed before the temple (I Kings 7:15–22). However, what such a connection might mean has yet to be convincingly explained. In my judgment, it is perhaps better to appeal to the iconography of the glyptic evidence just adduced and to build upon the fact that the "doors of heaven" can serve as the setting for Šamaš, quite apart from the heavenly mountains. The doors may well be overlaid with metal, as were, for example, the doors of the Jerusalem temple (so I Kings 6:32). The bronze of the doors may have been transferred to the perceived bronze character of the mountains in Zechariah's vision. Bronze doors qua mountains would convey the impression of strength and permanence.[8]

The details of the vision thus create the following impression. Zechariah sees the edge of the human domain, the gates of heaven at the boundary of the perceptible world. The two mountains were the points at which Šamaš, in the Mesopotamian traditions, becomes visible to humankind. At the entry point to this world, we do not, however, see the sun rising, but rather we see four chariots. Such chariots, given Northwest Semitic notions of chariotry, convey a martial connotation. They were about to set out, and Zechariah might well have expected them to undertake military duty. The visionary, on the basis of the colors of the horses, is able to note that there are four such chariots.

[2–3] What follows in vs. 2–3 individuates the chariots. Geography, the mountains and their composition, no longer plays a role in the visions. Each of the four chariots is defined on the basis of the colors of its horses. About the existence of charioteers, or the number of them, we hear nothing, nor are we privy to the direction in which any of the chariots is heading. The horses of the first chariot are bay; those of the second, black; those of the third, white; and those of the fourth,

---

between two metallic-appearing doors, i.e., without the mountains. See O. Keel, *The Symbolism of the Biblical World*, 1978, 22–24; *ANEP* #683–685. These scenes are most frequent in the late third millennium.

[7] Cf. *ANEP* #689 for the weather god in a chariot, and Moortgat, op. cit., #240, 563, for chariots included in the glyptic material.

[8] Cf. Jer. 1:18; 15:20 for the imagery of bronze walls.

dappled. Only two of these four colors, bay and white, occurred in the description of the horses in 1:8.

Much ink has been devoted to a comparison of the first and last of Zechariah's visions, since they both include detailed descriptions of horse colors. Most instructive, however, are the contrasts within this similarity. In the first vision, there are an indefinite number of horses of each color. In the final vision, there are almost certainly eight horses, two per chariot. In the first vision one horse has a rider. In the final vision the horses all belong with chariots. In the first vision we see the horses at rest in the divine corral; in the final vision we see the horses at an opening that leads into the domain of human affairs. In the first vision the horses have just come from surveying the cosmos, whereas in the second they are about to set out to roam over the earth. In the first vision the colors seem to have no rationale, i.e., there are three colors, two of which are almost identical. In the final vision there are four distinct colors and/or patterns, which, so the interpretation goes, point to the four major points of the compass. The distinctive colors provide the basis for the interpretation of the final vision. Such was not the case in the initial vision.

Perhaps the most comprehensive explanation of the colors of the horses is that used most recently by von Rad, Horst, Baldwin, and others.[9] They maintain that the colors of the first vision are those of the sunset, those of the end of a period, and that those of the eighth vision are those of the early morning, those of a new dawn and day. Intriguing and apt as this suggestion is, it is difficult to see how the "dappled" designation is more appropriate for dawn than sunset. Further, I suspect that though this suggestion might explain the origin of the colors, i.e., signifying the temporal frame of Zechariah's night vision, it does not function importantly as a statement about the interpreted significance of the visions.

[4-5] After seeing the collection of chariots at one specific point, and after seeing explicitly the four chariots and the colors of their respective equine accompaniment, the visionary breaks the silence and directs a question to the *mal'āk* (the typical question, see 1:9; 2:2; 4:4): "What are these?" The *mal'āk* responds immediately: "These are the four heavenly winds."[10] From this statement alone, it seems reasonable to conclude that the chariots and not the horses are being defined. In the first vision, "these" could refer to the horses, an

[9] Cf. G. von Rad, *Old Testament Theology* II, 1962, 287; Horst, 218, 236; Baldwin, 130.

[10] Not so the RSV and other versions that read, "They are going to the four winds of heaven."

indeterminate number of horses functioning as the source of the vision's meaning. However, here in the final vision the key factor is the number four, the number of the chariots and not the number of the horses, which presumably would be at least eight. The four chariots signify the four primary winds of the sky, which are now about to proceed forth, after having presented themselves to the deity. We have just missed a divine council scene and are now privy to the imminent enactment of its decisions.

The notion of the heavenly winds or four winds is attested elsewhere in the Hebrew Bible (Jer. 49:36; Ezek. 37:9; Zech. 2:10 [6E]; Dan. 8:8; 11:4). The motif is complex. It seems to entail vast geographic extent, i.e., it is an appropriate way to depict the breadth of total destruction (Jer. 49:36; Dan. 11:4; Zech. 2:10 [6E]). It can also refer to the totality of the heavenly domain (Dan. 8:8; Ezek. 37:9). And, without explicit use of the number "four" or the noun "heaven," "the winds" can be understood as the deity's messengers. Psalm 104:4 is an excellent example of this notion: "You make the winds your messengers, fire and flame your ministers." This particular text seems to reflect a usage similar to that of Zech. 6:5, i.e., that of the winds as direct agents of the deity, though they are presented in a way different from the winds in Psalm 104. For as we return to Zech. 6:5, we note that they have just "presented themselves" before the deity. This is, of course, specialized language, reflecting the appearance of Yahweh's agent before him in the divine council (thus Job 1:6; 2:1).[11]

The picture given by this identification of the four chariots with the four winds of heaven is one that creates confidence in the world order. The four chariots—or their unidentified riders—have just been present with Yahweh in the conciliar setting. And they have, presumably, been given a mission. The image of the mission is symbolized by the four major directions of the compass, signifying totality, and is reinforced by the explicit mention of Yahweh as lord of the entire earth. Though we do not know at this point in the interpretation of the vision what the mission is, we do know that it will be orderly and comprehensive.

[6] On the basis of the reconstruction proposed in the textual notes, the *mal'āk* goes on in v. 6 to specify in which direction each of the four winds will depart. Each chariot will be drawn by horses of distinctive colors: red to the east, black to the north, white to the west, and dappled to the south. Some commentators have proposed that the color black is especially appropriate as a color of judgment directed

---

[11] The idiom is the hithpael use of *yṣb.*

against the north, the direction which points to Mesopotamia, the land of punishment and exile. However, unless all colors seem significant, it is difficult to maintain that only one has symbolic meaning. Hence it is not appropriate to assert that the color black is especially significant when none of the other colors seems related to their respective points of the compass.

[7] The *mal'āk* continues in v. 7 with his description of the scene and now turns his attention away from the four chariots and to the powerful steeds themselves. Using a rare word, rare at least as a noun, he describes the horses as "the strong ones" who are about to set out, intent on ranging over the earth. This notion of surveying the earth (*hlk* in the hithpael + *bā'āreṣ*) had of course occurred in the first vision (1:10–11), though there the horses had just returned. Here such a mission is about to take place, one pursued with strength and vigor.

Not only do we know that such a mission will be undertaken, we actually hear the command which initiates the action, a command made by the *mal'āk:* "Go out, range over the earth." The reader is informed that the chariots and horses are going out to perform this reconnaissance.

[8] Appropriately, the entire vision sequence concludes with a command to see or look. The visionary is directed to look at those who are going out—presumably the chariots, riders, and horses, with primary emphasis on the horses, since the gender of "horses" agrees with the word for "those who go out," and such is not the case with the gender for "chariots." Furthermore, since the visionary could not observe horses going out simultaneously in four different directions, he is told to look at the horses heading toward the north country, the land of exile, punishment, and imprisonment. And, as an accompaniment to this command, he is informed that these steeds are effecting the purpose of the deity that his spirit/wind/anger be assuaged in this region.[12]

The wordplay on *rûaḥ* is significant. Not only is there cosmic order—the four winds of heaven are explicitly mentioned—but also the deity's *rûaḥ* is properly at rest. The peaceful state of the cosmos, which also was mentioned in the first vision, was, in that prior context, a source for lamentation. Now the universe is ordered, if not fully peaceful: surging steeds are on the move. Furthermore, the deity's anger has been assuaged. International injustice has been corrected.

This vision, as the last in the sequence, picks up motifs included in earlier visions. I have already mentioned the strong similarity to the

---

[12] See Rudolph, 125, for *rûaḥ* as anger here.

first vision as exemplified by attention to horses and their colors. Also, the phrase *kol-hā'āreṣ*, the mention of wind in the previous vision (5:9), and the explicit presence of metal in the last two visions serves to link this vision with those before it. The most pronounced link, however, is achieved by the use of the verb *yṣ'* ("proceed"). This particular term has been prominent in both the sixth and seventh visions. And in the eighth and final vision, this root occurs no less than seven times (Zech. 6:1, 5, 6, 7, 8). It is difficult to ignore the probable reason for the prominence of such language. If a curse is going out, if the *'êphāh* is going forth, if two creatures are setting out, and if the steeds and chariots are sallying forth, surely this sort of action is designed to elicit another exit, that of the return of those in the north country to their homeland. The cosmos has been set right for restoration. Now is the time to return, to begin the concrete work of restoration.

With this sense of conclusion as well as movement, the vision sequence ends. The deity and his agents have done what was necessary, and they have done that which only they could do. Now it is time for the human agents to act. The intermediate realm in which so much of the visionary action has taken place symbolizes the transition from divine to human action. The deity has held council, the patrol has been sent out over the earth. Now the earth can respond to the deity's initiatives.

Zechariah 6:9–15

The crowns will be a memorial

9 Then the word of Yahweh came to me:
10 "Take from those returned from exile,
from Heldai, Tobijah, and Jedaiah,
  who have come from Babylon,
and proceed on that very day
  to the house of Josiah son of Zephaniah.
11 Take silver and gold and make crowns,[a]
  and set (one) on the head of Joshua son of Jehozadak,
  the high priest.
12 Say to him:
'Thus says Yahweh of Hosts,
  Behold, a man—
    his name is Branch—
  shall flourish from his place,
    and he will build the temple of Yahweh.

13 He will, indeed, build the temple of Yahweh.
   He, indeed, will acquire majesty.
   As ruler[b] he will sit upon his throne.
   Beside his throne there will be a priest.
   Peaceable counsel will exist between the two of them.'
14 The crowns[c] will be a memorial in the temple of Yahweh
   for Helem, Tobijah, Jedaiah, and Josiah son of Zephaniah.[d]
15 Those who are distant shall arrive and build
   at the temple of Yahweh."
   Then you will know that Yahweh of Hosts has sent me to you,
   if you truly obey Yahweh your God.

   a. LXX, S, T read *ʿateret*, "crown," as opposed to MT *ʿatārôt*, "crowns." See the commentary for discussion of this issue. Cf. Petitjean, *Oracles*, 280–283, and the standard commentaries.
   b. Cf. similarly JB and NAB.
   c. LXX, S, T read *hāʿateret* as in v. 11, a reading all the more attractive since the following verb is a 3 fem. sg. imperfect. I prefer to follow MT and avoid the harmonizing reading of LXX.
   d. On the variation in the names between vs. 10 and 14, see the commentary.

We have already observed that the writer/editor of Zechariah 1–8 is an accomplished literary architect. In ch. 4, an oracle concerning the role of Zerubbabel in the reconstruction of the temple was enclosed in an envelope comprising the lampstand vision. The effect of this technique was to minimize the authority of Zerubbabel in the final literary product. The situation in Zech. 6:9–15 is not wholly dissimilar. We are presented with one oracle concerning the gathering of precious metals for use in the fabrication of some crowns, precious metals donated by those returning from exile in Babylon. This oracle, comprising 6:10–11, 14, includes specific mention of the high priest's crown. A second oracle, 6:12–13, which refers to the role of the Davidide Zerubbabel in temple reconstruction, is included in the middle of the "crown" oracle.[1] There is a striking similarity between the basic literary technique (the envelope) and the topics treated (the role of Zerubbabel in temple reconstruction and the relative placement of Josiah and Zerubbabel) in both 4:1–14 and 6:9–15.

[9–10] After the standard word-reception formula, v. 9, we encounter imperative discourse directed, presumably, to the prophet.

---

[1] For other divisions of this material, see Ringnell, *Nachtgesichte*, 240–242; Petitjean, *Oracles*, 270–303.

We have an infinitive absolute functioning as an imperative: "Take from those who have returned from exile . . ." What is unusual here is the lack of an object. Take what? It does, however, seem clear that what Zechariah was to receive is specified in v. 11: gold and silver. The inceptive verse of the oracle, by not mentioning what is to be taken, emphasizes from whom it is to be taken, namely, those returning from exile. In good fund-raising fashion, we learn immediately the names of those who are to offer up material wealth: Heldai, Tobijah, and Jedaiah. They, as the donors or at least bearers of such wealth, receive primary attention. The oracle then continues in the imperative mood. Zechariah is to take what he is given and proceed to the home of Josiah, son of Zephaniah. Such movement is to be immediate, as the use of the phrase "on that very day" indicates. We may not be certain that the author intended eschatological overtones, i.e., that this phrase carries, as in Zech. 12–14, a virtual apocalyptic tenor. However, given the prominence of the phrase "on that day" in apocalyptic collections, it is difficult to view this action as simply mundane.[2]

We know little about the four individuals mentioned in this oracle. Perhaps it is significant that of the four names, three are theophoric, containing the name Yahweh. Such usage serves to identify the "orthodox" character of those returning from exile and to legitimate whatever wealth they contribute to the rebuilding efforts.[3] Such a notion is further justified by the fact that Zephaniah, father of Josiah, may well have been an important functionary, the "second priest" referred to in II Kings 25:18, who was taken into exile.[4] If, on the other hand, there was a Zephaniah who remained in Jerusalem, then this act of Zechariah, of carrying the precious metal to Josiah's house, would be something of an act of integration, uniting the efforts of two distinct groups, those who had remained in Judah and those who had been in Babylon.

[11] In v. 11 we learn not only what Zechariah is to receive but also what is to be done with it. Gold and silver are to be gathered from those who had just come from exile. It is possible that this gold and silver was being provided at the behest of the Persian government, and that those named were simply entrusted with its safe transport to Syria-Palestine. This interpretation is, however, unlikely, given the fact that the objects, which were to be made out of gold and silver, would serve as

[2] This is the case especially since gold and silver in Hag. 2:8 function as marks of Yahweh's decisive action on behalf of Israel.

[3] On the single non-theophoric name, Heldai, see Ackroyd, *Exile and Restoration,* 194–195 n. 81; Petitjean, *Oracles,* 274–277.

[4] See also Jer. 29:25, 29.

memorials to those particular individuals. One should therefore think of the gold and silver as donations from those coming from exile. That some Israelites had done well and continued to prosper in their new home we know from other texts. Hence it was only appropriate, at least from the perspective of those attempting to rebuild Jerusalem, that those in exile or recently returned from exile assist in the rebuilding of Judahite society.

Zechariah is commanded to take gold and silver and to make crowns. Other ancient texts read "crown." This singular reading is, in all likelihood, an attempt to reconcile the crown of only one individual, the high priest, with the apparently embarrassing fact of the construction of two crowns. Since the plural form creates the more serious problems for the narrator, the principle of *lectio difficilior* requires that the MT reading be preserved. Moreover, the diarchic situation envisioned in 4:1–5, 10b–14 is consistent with the creation of two crowns.

After the command to make crowns is given, the piling up of verbs and action continues. The third verb occurs as the seventh word of the sentence. "(You shall) set (one) upon the head of Joshua, the high priest." The action contained here most probably does not refer to an actual investiture of a high priest. Anointing and the attendant ceremony were the means by which kings and high priests were inducted into office. Crowns were, of course, appropriate for persons who had been ritually invested. However, the act of placing a crown on someone's head did not in itself signify the actual conferral of kingship or high priesthood. Such a deed was honorific and not performative in ancient Israel.

If these verses do not function to confer the high priesthood on Joshua, what is their purpose? Clearly, they seem to point to an enhanced position for the high priest. As we have already seen in Zech. 4, there was apparently some dispute about the role of the high priest vis-à-vis the Davidide. The oracle in 4:6–10 stresses the importance of Zerubbabel. The mention of a crown for Joshua in 6:11 represents a tilt in another direction, toward the high priest. The reasons for this tendency or response are contained in the oracle that occurs in the next two verses.

[12–13] If v. 9 introduced a private oracle, one directed to Zechariah alone, then v. 12 introduces an oracle which, if we take seriously the so-called messenger formula and the command "Say to him," is to be pronounced publicly. Just as the rhetorical situation distinguishes 6:9–11, 14–15 from 6:12–13, so too the subject matter in 6:12–13 is also different. With vs. 12–13, talk of crowns ceases and we return to an issue broached earlier in another apparently public oracle, 4:6–10a, that of the reconstruction of the temple. In that oracle we discovered that pride of place is to be given to Zerubbabel as he participates in a ritual similar to the ancient Near Eastern *kalû* ceremony. So too in 6:12–13, the focus is on an individual important in the rebuilding of the temple. And interestingly, the matrix for both these oracles deemphasizes the role of Zerubbabel.

The oracle opens with a striking image, a person symbolized by a branch and even named as Branch, *"ṣemaḥ."* As we have seen earlier, in 3:8, this title is best understood as an appellation for a future Davidic ruler (see also Jer. 23:5; 33:15). Given the political context of Zechariah 1–8, there can be little doubt that this symbol refers to Zerubbabel.[5] And, given the olive-tree imagery in the interpretation of the lampstand vision in ch. 4, the notion of branch here is even more concrete than it was in 3:8. The oracle impels us to think of this branch as flourishing "from its place." Precisely what "from its place" means is obscure. Interestingly, the cognate accusative *ṣmḥ-yiṣmḥ* (literally, "branch branching") also occurs in Jer. 33:15, though there the reason for the flourishing growth is linked explicitly to Yahweh: "I will cause a righteous branch to flourish out of David." Given this statement, the phrase "out of/for David" is syntactically parallel to "from/out of his place." The formulations of Zech. 6:12 are therefore distinctly paralleled in Jer. 33:15. Hence we should expect Yahweh to be the source of the luxuriant growth of the branch as that is described, albeit enigmatically, in 6:12.

What follows may seem to be a non sequitur: "and he will build the temple of Yahweh." However, the verb "he will flourish" is linked to "build" with a *waw* conversive. The notions are syntactically related. And the image of upbuilding is present in both cola—the flourishing of a branch and the construction of a building. The logical connection is implicit rather than explicit. Just as branch/wood is instrumental for construction, so *the* Branch is instrumental for the rebuilding of Yahweh's house. And such statements, as we know from 4:6–10, are implicitly negative as well: if someone is building the temple, someone else is not building the temple. The position of the Davidide is here being enhanced in distinction to other potentially significant functionaries, especially the high priest. This emphasis on the rebuilding of the temple is obviously of critical importance, since it is reiterated in v. 13. However, in v. 13, the personal pronoun "he" is written separately. It could have simply been included in the inflected

[5] See Ackroyd, *Exile and Restoration,* 174 n. 12.

verb form. That it is written separately indicates that the stress is not so much on the actual construction of the temple as upon the person responsible for such construction.

That same personal pronoun "he" recurs in the second colon of v. 13. And here the focus switches away from the temple to the status and role of the Branch, the Davidide: "He will acquire majesty." There are numerous instances in which the divine king, Yahweh, is understood as having majesty (e.g., Ps. 104:1). However, earthly kings may also have such glory:

> In your majesty ride forth victoriously.
> (Ps. 45:4)

> His glory is great through your help;
> splendor and majesty you have granted him.
> (Ps. 21:6 [5E])

Kings regularly are thought to have majesty, *hôd*. Such an expectation fits the situation in Zech. 6:12–13, where the Davidide Zerubbabel is the one to whom the image of "Branch" may be presumed to refer. "As ruler he will sit upon his throne." This clause, like the previous one, points to only one role in ancient Israel, that of king (e.g., I Kings 1:46; 16:11). To sit on the throne and to bear majesty are the prerogatives and responsibilities of the king.

After such pronounced emphasis on the status and work of Zerubbabel as a royal figure in the reconstruction of the second temple, our gaze is directed to another figure, that of a priest. We are not told that he is the great or high priest, but we should probably infer that he is. "Beside his [the Branch's] throne there will be a priest." We may, I think, appreciate this image only by contrasting it with what is present in the *mᵉnôrāh* vision and in its interpretation. There Yahweh, symbolized as light, is flanked by the priest and the king respectively. The image is of equal status for king and priest. Such is not the case in the oracle that occurs in the middle of the lampstand vision. There Zerubbabel is construed as temple builder, a mountain in contrast to Joshua, who is a plain. So also, the surrounding oracular material in Zech. 6 emphasizes the prominence of Joshua. He is to have a crown upon his head. But in the interior oracle, as was the case in 4:6–10, Zerubbabel as a royal figure has a status higher than that of Joshua. The image of someone standing over or by the throne is clearly that of an attendant or someone of importance, though of lesser status.[6] The high priest is, therefore, implicitly given a status lower than that of the Davidide.

---

[6] Cf. I Kings 2:19.

This oracle does, however, conclude on an ironic note. The interaction between priest and Davidide will be characterized by *ʿaṣat šālôm*, "peaceable counsel." This is a peculiar phrase. The term *ʿēṣāh* is not used elsewhere in the Hebrew Bible to refer to a joint situation or to a relationship.[7] Usually one hears of the counsel of a person or a deity. The peculiarity of this usage is that the emphasis is in all likelihood on *šālôm*, on the peaceable character of the relationship between these two functionaries. There shall be *šālôm* despite the fact that one party, the Davidide, is elevated above the other, the priest.

In sum, 6:12-13 is a carefully constructed oracle. It serves to enhance the status of the royal figure, Zerubbabel, and at the same time to explain the relative positioning of the two figures, Davidide and priest. Both explicitly and implicitly the Davidic scion achieves pride of place.

[14] Introducing the second part of the oracular envelope, v. 14 jolts the reader back to the issue of crowns. The word order is unusual since the sentence begins with a noun, "crowns," rather than having the more typical verb-first word order. Both syntactically and topically we are moved beyond the range of issues in vs. 12-13.

As was the case in v. 10, the issue of crowns is related to specific people. In v. 10, Zechariah was supposed to receive gold and silver from Heldai, Tobijah, and Jedaiah and take it to the house of Josiah. In v. 14 we hear about crowns as a memorial for Helem, Tobijah, Jedaiah, and Josiah/Hen. Two of the four names present are different from v. 10. Moreover, Josiah/Hen is now listed as having the same status as the three initial "contributors." Since in both variations, the names become shorter, it is possible to construe Helem and Hen as acceptable nicknames, perhaps those of friends, rather than as inexplicable textual errors.[8]

More important than the variation in proper names is the

---

[7] See II Sam. 15:31, 34. These particular texts are instructive because they present us with the king or the pretender receiving advice from an apparent member of the court: David from Hushai and Absalom from Ahitophel. Further, for someone to be providing counsel to the king indicates both an important position and also an element of subordination. The king may or may not take a counselor's advice. The role of counselor has less autonomy than that of priest. The use of *ʿēṣāh* is therefore a nuanced one, because it, too, serves subtly to relate the counselor to the king in a subordinate way.

[8] Cf. Rudolph, 127; Petitjean, *Oracles*, 297-298. A. Demsky, "The Temple Steward Josiah ben Zephaniah," *IEJ* 31, 1981, 100-102, has recently argued convincingly that the Akkadian title which is used in neo-Assyrian texts, *laḫḫinu* (and also its Aramaic cognate, *lᵉḥēn*), refers to an official in the court or the temple who is responsible for handling assets such as gold or silver. This hypothesis appears altogether likely as an explanation for the labeling of Josiah as *lᵉḥēn*.

importance that the crowns will have. Despite the fact that one of the crowns is to be placed on the head of the priest (v. 11), the crowns are to bear significance as memorials in the temple and not finally as headpieces for either king or high priest.

This notion of something becoming a memorial does occur elsewhere in the biblical material (Ex. 30:16; Num. 10:9–10).[9] In Num. 10:9–10, sacrifices—burnt offerings and peace offerings—are understood to function as memorials for the people before God. In Ex. 30:16, the parallel to Zech. 6 is even stronger, since in both texts permanent assets are involved. Money, "atonement money," garnered by the census, is to be used for the "service of the tent of meeting; that it may bring the people of Israel to remembrance before Yahweh" (Ex. 30:16). As was the case in Num. 10, all Israel is achieving the memorial through the presentation of these monies.

The situation in Zechariah is different from these other two memorial texts only in one essential way: several individuals and not all Israel will be memorialized. What all these texts (Ex. 30; Num. 10; and Zech. 6) do have in common is that the memorial objects occur in the ritual ambit: sacrifices, money for the temple, and crowns to be deposited in the temple. And to this extent, the Zechariah text presents a not unusual notion of memorial.[10]

[15] Things change markedly in 6:15. Not only does the issue of temple reconstuction appear again, as in the oracles inserted into ch. 4, but attention is also devoted to those not on the scene, to those far off (cf. 2:10 [6E]). Clearly the situation was otherwise in 6:9–11, 14. There Zechariah was concerned to respond to the potential for assistance provided by those who had just returned from Babylon, apparently as fund-raisers. And as any fund-raiser knows, if funds come from a specific source, one attempts to discover other individuals from that context who might also provide help. Zechariah has just encountered those who are near and who had been at a distance. Hence he now hopes that others who are at a distance will return to Judah so that even more asse ts might be garnered for the reconstruction efforts.

The term *rāḥôq*, "distant," in both singular and plural forms, is often used in conjunction with *qārôb* to signify "the near and the far."[11] This conjunction of particular terms does not occur in Zechariah. However, as I have suggested above, the oracle in 6:9–11,

---

[9] On the general idea of a memorial, *zikkārôn*, see B. Childs, *Memory and Tradition*, 1962, 66–70.

[10] The fact that the objects become a memorial should dissuade us from construing Zechariah's action here as a mere symbolic action; thus Petitjean, *Oracles*, 303.

[11] Thus Ezek. 6:12; 22:5; Isa. 33:13; 57:19; Jer.25:26; Dan. 9:7; Esth. 9:20.

14 has as an essential feature those who are near: Heldai, Tobijah, and Jedaiah. The movement from those with whom Zechariah can have close contact to those who are at a distance is, structurally, typical for texts in which the term *rāḥôq*, when it refers to people, is used.

The expectation expressed here is not simply that those who are far off will return. Even as those who had just returned—Heldai, Tobijah, and Jedaiah—contributed to the temple apparatus by providing gold, so too Zechariah looks forward to help in temple reconstruction from those who will return in the future. That they are to help in the rebuilding process is indicated by the idiom *bnh b*, "build at," an idiom used in only one other passage in the biblical material (Neh. 4:4, 11 [10, 17E]). Those who return in the future are expected also to take part in the reconstruction of the temple.

Following this statement of expectation is a formula that occurred earlier, in the oracular material of the book: "Then you will know that Yahweh of Hosts has sent me" (Zech. 2:13, 15 [9, 11E]; 4:9b). In the last-mentioned example, the formula occurs immediately following the statement that Zerubbabel is to lay the foundation of the temple and that he will complete it. Interestingly, explicit mention of the temple rebuilding occurs immediately before all uses of this formula. Further, the identity of those responsible for the reconstruction of the temple is mentioned in both texts. In both instances the people are those returning from Babylon. Zechariah or an editor seems to be saying that as the temple is rebuilt by those who have been in exile—and not by those who remained in Syria-Palestine—the authenticity of his prophetic activity and message will be recognized. It is difficult to avoid the inference that Zechariah has particular sympathies with those who have been in exile.

When we add to the discussion the other two uses of the formula "You shall know that Yahweh of Hosts has sent me" (2:13, 15 [9, 11E]), we have a good idea of the situation that Zechariah or a traditionist thinks will verify his vision for the future: proper treatment of Israel's enemies (2:13 [9E]); a new relationship between Yahweh and Israel (2:15 [11E]); and a temple rebuilt by the appropriate leadership (4:9b; 6:15).

Unlike other instances in which this verification formula is used, in ch. 6 it is followed by a conditional clause. In the final instance in which there is a possibility of corroborating the prophet's task, the text refers not only to the return of those in exile, not only to their participation in the construction of the temple, but also to the recognition of the validity of Zechariah's own work as contingent upon the obedience of the populace to the voice of Yahweh. It is not accidental that obedience is here described in terms of obeying the voice of Yahweh. From the perspective of prophetic tradition, the prophets were those individuals who communicated the deity's words to the populace. Thus, to obey the voice of Yahweh is to heed that which Zechariah and others proclaim.

Zechariah 7:1–3

Shall I weep and fast?

1 In the fourth year of King Darius' reign, the word of Yahweh came to Zechariah, in the ninth month, Chislev, on the fourth day.

2 Bethelsarezer and Regemmelek,[a] and their men, sent to seek help from Yahweh

3 through the priests who are at the temple of Yahweh of Hosts and through the prophets, saying, "Shall I weep and fast in the fifth month as I have done these past years?"

a. LXX, S, and T understood MT Bethelsarezer to comprise a person's name, Sarezer, and the name of the place, Bethel, to which the persons were sent. Rudolph, 135–136, treats Bethel as the place-name but reads it as the subject of the sentence: "Bethel sent Elsarezer and Regemmelech . . ." I follow the proposal, originally made by Wellhausen, that Bethelsarezer is one name. Cf. Ackroyd, who reads, "Then Bethelsarezer the Rab-mag of the king . . . ," i.e., taking the first but not the second as one name (*Exile and Restoration,* 207). To seek more by plumbing the meaning of individual elements in these names is unwarranted.

MT reads, literally, "his men." In all likelihood, this form represents a singular suffix referring to a plural entity; i.e., one should translate, "their men." Cf. GK §145m.

[1] Chapter 7 commences with the third and final date formula in the book of Zechariah 1–8. It points to a time almost one year after the visions were received and almost two years since the beginning of Zechariah's prophetic activity. The language is stereotypic and yet it differs from the date formula in Zech. 1:1 and those in Hag. 1:15b; 2:10; and 2:20 in at least two ways. First, not only in the month enumerated but also its name is given. To this extent the formula is similar to that in Zech. 1:7, a text in which the eleventh month is defined as *šᵉbāṭ*. Only in these two texts is the month named. Second, in Zech. 7:1 Darius is designated explicitly as *hammelek,* the king.

Although Darius is mentioned by name in Zech. 1:1, 7, he is termed *hammelek* in only one other place in the prophetic corpus, in Hag. 1:1—the first date formula for this block of literature deriving from the late sixth century. The presence of this designation in the first and last date formulae in Haggai-Zechariah 1–8 serves to unify this material in a subtle way. Without being heavy-handed, the redactor has made it clear that his readers live in a new historical-political era, one in which *the* king is not a Davidide but is rather a foreigner. Such a circumstance required a major restructuring of Israel's thought about its own internal organization and its relation to Yahweh, a move away from the national religion of monarchic Yahweh to a religious configuration less oriented to territory and state. And yet, in order not to diminish hopes for restoration of something not radically dissimilar from Israel's earlier political norms, i.e., monarchic Israel, the editor has not included Darius as "the king" at every opportunity, but only in the first and the last of his chronological markers.

It would be improper to focus on the date formulae to the exclusion of the controlling clause in this text, a clause that appears in conjunction with all the other date formulae except one, Hag. 1:15b. We now learn that the word of Yahweh came to the prophet on that specific day. Further, in Zech. 7:1 we are dealing with an editorial statement that controls the rest of Zech. 7. All the individual oracles comprise the *d'bar yhwh,* the word of Yahweh, which comes to Zechariah. And as shown by the first example, 7:2–3, something need not be an explicit word from Yahweh to be included within this group of sayings otherwise construed as *d'bar yhwh.*

[2–3] After these introductory words, the writer includes a report of a question that was directed to priests at the temple of Yahweh of Hosts and to prophets. Two individuals have sent a request—whether in person or not is impossible to say—for help from Yahweh. The phrase *ḥlh* + *p'nê yhwh* is regularly used to describe the seeking of assistance in the face of severe difficulty (Ex. 32:11; I Kings 13:6; II Kings 13:4; Jer. 26:19; Dan. 9:13; Ps. 119:58). Some translations (e.g, RSV) use language that softens the character of the request. However, the specific Hebrew phraseology, such as that used by Moses as he interceded on behalf of the people when Yahweh (Ex. 32:11) was threatening their total destruction, suggests dire straits. Bethelsarezer and Regemmelek present a question of moment, and one that serves to introduce a concern and an issue which inaugurates the final block of material in Zechariah 1–8.

Hebrew Bible references to such pleas often reflect the seeking of help by the leader of the Israelite community, the king (I Kings 13:6; II

Kings 13:4; Jer. 26:19). And once, in I Kings 13:6, an author makes clear that the monarch uses the good offices of a prophet when seeking help. Such is the case in Zech. 7:1–3. Not only is the request directed to "prophets" (Zechariah and his followers?) but it also is designated for priests at the temple. Whether the priests received the request (in addition to Zechariah), we do not know. But we are certain that it was directed to Zechariah. And we receive his response, at least as conceived by the editor of the book, in 7:4–8:23.

The entreaty is couched in the first-person singular: "Shall I weep and fast in the fifth month as I have done in past years?" Bethelsarezer and Regemmelek may be speaking on behalf of an unidentified superior. Or they may be presenting their query with a single voice. In either case, a rite of lamentation has been celebrated in Bethel and someone wants to know if the rite should continue during a time of restoration.

What did such a rite celebrate? A look at the reports of the destruction of Jerusalem provide the necessary information. The rite was celebrated in the fifth month. And it was in the fifth month of the year that Nebuchadnezzar's troops burned the temple, the palace, "and all the houses of Jerusalem" (II Kings 25:9; see also Jer. 52:12ff.). The fifth month was *the* month in which the temple and all Jerusalem was destroyed. Surely the lamentation referred to in the question is a lamentation commemorating this calamitous moment in Judah's history. There is no other fifth month of equally lamentable significance.

Of what this ceremony consisted we are not told. And it probably does not matter, since the question does not have to do with the nature of the rite but rather with the question of whether or not the rite should continue at all. Put another way, the petitioner wants to know if the lamentable period of destruction, punishment, and exile is over. What sort of rites and attitudes are appropriate for a time in which the community and temple are being rebuilt, and yet a time in which Jerusalem and Israel barely exist and certainly are not gloriously restored? Is it a time of continued grief or a time for hope and celebration?

Zechariah's responses are varied (7:4–7, 8–14; 8:1–23) and in their present form are probably as much the product of editorial work as of Zechariah himself.[1]

---

[1] This material has been divided up in varying ways. Cf. Beuken, 118–156; Petitjean, *Oracles,* 304–362; and Rudolph, 135–146. The latter is an approach similar to the one followed here.

Zechariah 7:4–7

Do you not eat and drink for yourselves?

4   The word of Yahweh of Hosts came to me:
5   "Speak to all the people of the land
    and to the priests:
  'When you fasted and mourned
    in the fifth and seventh months,
  this seventy-year period,
  did you indeed fast for me?
6   When you eat and drink,
    do you not eat for yourselves
    and drink for yourselves?
7   Are not these the words which Yahweh proclaimed
    through the earlier prophets,
  when Jerusalem and its cities were inhabited
    and at peace,
  when the Negeb and the Shephelah were populated?'"

[4] In this, the first of several responses to the question presented in
v. 3, the prophet himself provides questions, three in all. The first two
questions are couched as direct words of the deity, whereas the final
question, since it refers to Yahweh in the third person, may be
construed as a question promulgated by the prophet himself.

The first question, in v. 5, is introduced by clauses that direct the
prophet to address two different groups. Since the question in v. 3
specifies two groups, such specification is wholly appropriate. What is
slightly unusual is that the two groups are not identical. The question
of Bethelsarezer and Regemmelek in v. 3 is directed to the priests and
the prophets. Since Zechariah is presumably one of the prophets
mentioned in v. 3, it would be inappropriate for "the prophets" to be
included as the addressee of Zechariah's question. Hence the audience
for these words is enlarged to include the *'am hā'āreṣ,* the "people of
the land." This phrase, though unusual significance has been imputed
to it, in all likelihood refers here (as in Hag. 2:4) to the inhabitants of
the Judahite territory as that was recognized about 520 B.C.E.[1] By means

---

[1] See, e.g., E. Würthwein, *Der 'am ha'arez im AT,* 1936. See also Beuken, op. cit.,
and Petitjean, *Oracles,* 307.

of this audience designation, the author/redactor has been able to move the discourse from a question limited to a small audience to a discussion that involved the entire Yahwistic community residing in the land in and around Jerusalem.

[5] The oracle itself continues to expand upon the original question in v. 3. Not only the audience but the days of the fast are greater. In v. 3 we are told about a fast in the fifth month. Now, in v. 5, there is reference to a fast in the fifth and seventh months. As Rudolph suggests, a fast in the seventh month most probably commemorates the death of Gedaliah, the governor appointed by the Babylonians (Jer. 41:1–3; II Kings 25:25).[2] The seventy years, as Zech. 1:12 suggests, refers to the time of subjugation, roughly 590–520 B.C.E.[3]

After this temporal language—fifth month, seventh month, seventy years—we focus on the nature of the first critical question. Zechariah has reformulated the language of ritual. In 7:3, it was weep *(bkh)* and fast *(nzr),* and now it is fast *(ṣwm)* and mourn *(spd).* Why this change? The reason is not obvious. One may suggest that the language of the original section, *bkh* and *nzr,* is rather general—e.g., *bkh* is not limited to the ritual ambit. Zechariah's discourse in v. 5 tightens the discourse. The verb *ṣwm* is limited to ritual abstention from food and *spd* is used especially with reference to lamenting. Zechariah's new vocabulary makes clear that the weeping and fasting focus on rites of lamentation for destruction and death, as suggested also by the fifth and seventh months, periods that commemorate the destruction of Jerusalem and the death of Gedaliah, respectively. Further, Zechariah's redefinition specifies the character of the rite. It was shedding tears plus the ritual denial of food.

Once this redefinition has been accomplished, Zechariah can then state the critical question: Did you indeed fast for me? This has been viewed by many interpreters as a rhetorical question, i.e., as a question which has an obvious answer, which requires no response, and which has been addressed to stimulate further reflection.[4] And normally, the answer has been understood as a negative: No, you have not fasted concerning me. And this answer has, in turn, been understood as an indictment of the sort of ritual practice that has just been mentioned. One does need to ask, however, whether proper fast days were normally understood as directed toward Yahweh.

Fasting did, of course, involve abstention from food, but in David's

---

[2] Rudolph, 144.
[3] See C. Jeremias, *Nachtgesichte,* 131–132.
[4] Cf. Beuken, 147–152.

case (II Sam. 12:15b–23) it was part of a rite in which David "besought God for the child" (II Sam. 12:16a). Similarly, Saul fasted as part of an attempt to communicate with the deity (I Sam. 28:23). This same motif is attested in Jer. 14:12: "Though they fast, I will not hear their cry." Fasting was not simply a way of working out one's grief. It was normally understood to be part of a way in which communication with the deity was achieved.

When this communication was not present, condemnation of the sort preserved in an early postexilic text was trenchant:

> Fasting like yours this day
>   will not make your voice to be heard on high.
> Is such the fast that I choose,
>   a day for a man to humble himself?
> Is it to bow down his head like a rush,
>   and to spread sackcloth and ashes under him?
> Will you call this a fast,
>   and a day acceptable to Yahweh?
>   (Isa. 58:4b–5)

And yet fasting remained a viable religious rite in the postexilic period:

> "Yet even now," says Yahweh,
>   "return to me with all your heart,
> with fasting *(ṣwm)*, with weeping *(spd)*, and with mourning *(bkh)*;
>   and rend your hearts and not your garments."[5]
>   (Joel 2:12–13a)

The critical question is, to use the language of Isa. 58:4, have these fasts—the ones in the fifth and seventh months—enabled the voices of those making them to be heard on high? The presumed answer is no, they have not; and yet no reason is offered.[6]

[6] With this implied negative answer provided by the first question, Zechariah offers yet another question, one that by implication clarifies the ambiguity of the previous query: "When you eat and when you drink, do you not eat for yourselves and drink for yourselves?

One searches in vain for a special meaning in this verse. There is rather a simple, irrefutable point involved. People eat and drink for their own nourishment; and that is acceptable.[7] If one eats for nourishment, the natural case, one expects that not eating would point

---

[5] See also Ezra 8:23, "So we fasted and besought our God for this, and he listened to our entreaty." Cf. Neh. 1:4.

[6] Cf. Beuken's form-critical argument, op. cit., 147–153.

[7] The reference here is not, in my judgment, to meals consumed as part of a cultic act; cf. Rudolph, 144 n. 6, and Petitjean, *Oracles,* 314.

away from oneself, and to someone or something else, in this case Yahweh. And yet the negative answer to the first question would suggest that such fasting has, like eating and drinking, normally been done in the self-interest of the people.

This word of Yahweh, in the form of two pointed questions concerning fasting and eating, as well as the theology of both activities, reflects, as we have seen, issues also addressed by a contemporary of Zechariah's, Trito-Isaiah (Isa. 58). These particular sentiments about fasting are not shared in any obvious way by preexilic prophets.[8] Hence there is reason for Zechariah to establish the authority for his apparent claim that both eating and fasting are likely to focus on the individual and not on Yahweh, and that fasting is therefore inherently problematic. For this reason, Zechariah makes an appeal to the authority of earlier prophets in order to justify his claim based on an almost purely logical analysis of fasting. Consistent with the interrogative style of this section, the author formulates his claim in the form of a question.

[7] Verse 7 confirms the notion that Zechariah is answering a question—one addressed to both priests and prophets. He is answering from what he takes to be a normative prophetic stance. Put another way, the questions articulated in Zech. 7:5–6 are regarded as the sort of things said by the earlier prophets. And then Zechariah specifies the conditions under which earlier prophets spoke. It was a time of peace and significant population. This comment suggests that lack of population was, at least by Zechariah, thought to be one of the critical curses of the era in which he was living. And it reinforces the strength of the discourse presented elsewhere in the book, e.g., "Flee from the land of the north" (2:10 [6E]), and "Jerusalem shall be inhabited . . ." (2:8 [4E]). Further, this reference to the earlier prophets not only reveals a critical issue, the lack of population; it also suggests that those prophets were correct—and by inference it suggests that Zechariah, who is also a prophet, is correct. Jerusalem had, at an earlier time, been populated and at peace. It had been ringed with cities. The Negeb as well as the Shephelah had also been inhabited. Such changes in fortune—population to depopulation, peace to war, city to non-city—were remembered as foretold by Israel's prophets. Thus Jer. 22:21 reads: "I spoke to you in your prosperity, but you said, 'I will not listen.' " Similarly the notion of depopulation appears not infrequently in prophetic texts predicting future punishment.[9] Israel's

---

[8] Cf. Beuken, 148–150.
[9] See Isa. 6:11; Jer. 4:7.

prophets were the ones who had foreseen such a catastrophe. By recalling the accuracy of earlier prophetic words, Zechariah, as prophet, buttresses his own rhetoric, here presented in the form of incisive questions concerning the character of eating and that of fasting.

In this brief section, the author replies to one question, that presented in 7:3, with three other questions. It is therefore difficult to be certain about the manner in which the original question is answered by these responses. The logic of Zechariah's counter-questions suggest a certain distrust of eating-fasting rituals. Is it possible that the author is suggesting that unregulated fasting rites, especially as they seem to have developed in response to the destruction of 587 B.C.E., are not wise and that the earlier standardized rituals, i.e., burnt offerings and the like, are those appropriate for the age in which the temple is being restored? More cannot be said.

Zechariah 7:8–14

Then I blew them away with a storm

8 The word of Yahweh came to Zechariah:
9 "Thus says Yahweh of Hosts:
    Execute true judgment;
        act loyally and benevolently with each other.
10 Do not wrong the widow or the orphan,
        the alien or the poor.
    Do not plot malevolently
        against each other."
11 But they refused to listen.
    They turned their rebellious backs
        and kept their ears from hearing.
12 They made their hearts like stone
        against hearing the words of instruction[a]
    which Yahweh of Hosts had sent
        through his spirit by means of the earlier prophets.
    Then great wrath came from Yahweh of Hosts.
13 "Thus it was, when I called,[b]
        they did not listen.
    So when they called,
        I would not listen," says Yahweh of Hosts.

14 "Then I blew them away with a storm[c]
throughout all the nations which they had not known.
And the land which they left was made desolate
so that no one traversed it.
They caused a pleasant land to become desolate."

a. Literally, "the torah and the words." The phrase is an obvious case of hendiadys.
b. Reading *qārā'tî* with S instead of MT *qārā*.
c. On *wᵉ'ēsā'ᵃrēm*, see GK §§23h, 52n.

[8] The final question in the series of questions that comprise 7:4–7 alerts us to a stratagem of the person who wrote this material. The author has, in v. 7, identified the issues raised by the question of Bethelsarezer and Regemmelek and has connected that inquiry with the discourse of earlier prophets. They too spoke about the matters of proper and improper fasting and about the tendency for self-centered behavior. Now, in 7:8–14, after the standard formula of introduction in 7:8, "The word of Yahweh came to Zechariah," the writer presents us with the sorts of things said by the earlier prophets. We are given an oracle that is followed by an assessment of the people's response to this sort of prophetic proclamation.

[9–10] The oracle begins with a stereotypic formula of introduction. Then follow a series of imperatives, a grammatical feature that has led some interpreters to label this unit an oracle of admonition conditioned by wisdom perspectives.[1] Richter, in delineating this form, which occurs with some frequency in the prophetic literature, points to a number of texts. Of these, Jer. 22:3 provides an excellent parallel to the Zechariah passage:

> Thus says Yahweh:
> Do justice and righteousness,
> and deliver from the hand of the oppressor
> him who has been robbed.
> And do no wrong or violence to the alien, the orphan,
> and the widow,
> nor shed innocent blood in this place.

In both Zech. 7:9–10 and Jer. 22:3, the oracles are introduced by the messenger formula. This is followed by positive admonitions and prohibitive injunctions. The admonitions are general and speak of

[1] Thus W. Richter, *Recht und Ethos*, 1966, 41–67, esp. p. 59 on Zech. 7:9–10. Richter is followed in this regard by Beuken, 123–124.

acting justly—whereas in the negative mode specific groups needing protection are mentioned. This format is typical for the wisdom admonition. All this suggests that Zechariah is utilizing material found elsewhere in the prophetic corpus, i.e., he is including the standard prophetic style of speech. With the very first word of the oracle, we encounter language similar or identical to that used elsewhere in the preexilic prophetic literature. It is difficult to determine whether the author of this section of Zech. 7 is including an oracle which he knew or whether he is composing a message based on prophetic models.[2] The language and ideas are typical of Israel's classic prophets. Thus, for example, the notion of acting loyally, or out of loyalty *(ḥesed)*, is also present in Jer. 9:23; that of acting justly with one another, in Jer. 7:5; that of not oppressing the alien, the orphan, or widow, in Jer. 7:5–6; and that of not plotting malevolently, in Jer. 48:2. It is interesting that so many parallels to this rhetoric appear in the book of Jeremiah, and more particularly in the so-called Jeremianic prose. Nevertheless, it remains difficult to argue that Jeremiah was uniquely significant for the writer of Zechariah.

The similarities between Zech. 7:9–10 and Jer. 7:5–6 are significant, almost as much so as the parallels between Jer. 22:3 and other Zechariah oracles.

> For if you truly amend your ways and your doings, if you truly execute justice with one another, if you do not oppress the alien, the orphan or the widow, or shed innocent blood in this place, and if you do not go after other gods to your own hurt, then I will let you dwell in this place, in the land that I gave of old to your fathers for ever. (Jer. 7:5–6)[3]

Since this text is almost certainly a late element in the composition of the book of Jeremiah, it is difficult to argue for literary dependence of Zechariah on Jeremiah. It is preferable to speak of thematic commonality: justice and oppression as they relate to the possession of the land and as they are expressed in rather stereotypic language, i.e., that of widow, alien, and orphan.[4] Formally, this is often the stuff of prophetic discourse.

The oracle consists of two admonitory styles: one positive, the other negative. On the one hand, a certain style of mutual behavior, loyal and loving, is commanded. And on the other hand, economically

---

[2] Beuken, 124, maintains that the oracle is an authentic oracle of Zechariah.

[3] Petitjean, *Oracles,* 333–336, perceives this text as something of a Jeremianic code that served as a model for the Zechariah composition.

[4] Note the regular use of these classes in Deuteronomy, e.g., Deut. 14:29; 24:19–21.

oppressive action and secretive chicanery are proscribed. Interestingly, the positive behavior is directed to a general entity, "one another." The language is inclusive, i.e., extending throughout all sectors of the Israelite community. However, the negative behavior, though it too in Zech. 7:10c includes the idea of mutuality, focuses on a subsection of that community, those economically and socially disadvantaged: the widow, the orphan, and the alien. The oracle almost implies that the powerful can (and no doubt will) continue to plot against each other.[5] However, such plotting should not be used to gain advantage over the socially deprived.

This oracle was included by the editor because it is so typical. We should not expect anything unusual, and we do not find anything unusual. The author has capably introduced words that might have been spoken by any number of Israel's prophets, even Zechariah himself, and which interestingly seem to mirror most directly the words of one of those prophets, Jeremiah, who was active before and after the defeat of Jerusalem.

And yet, as one examines carefully this example of prophetic discourse, one discovers that it is not without its own unique coloring. Beuken has observed that nowhere else in the Old Testament is the word *ḥšb* ("plot") used in the context of warning.[6] Further, he contends that the specific phraseology in Zech. 7:9–10, *'îš 'et 'āḥîw* (see also 8:16–17), introduces a note of individuation not common in similar formulations. Petitjean also observes innovative elements, e.g., the inclusion of the poor in the stereotypic description of disadvantaged groups in ancient Israel, and the use of *ḥesed,* unusual when compared with similar texts in Jeremiah.[7] Thus, what appears on the surface to be typical prophetic language is, on closer examination, language that betrays the hand of a creative author. Rather than providing a pale copy of prophetic speech, he has provided vigorous prophetic discourse.

[11] With the conclusion of the oracle, the writer shifts from the language of prophetic performance to the language of the historian. The writer's concern is what happened as a result of such prophetic proclamation. And it is not a disinterested question, since the writer understands himself to be exercising a prophetic function in responding to the question raised by Zechariah. He therefore has an interest in how individuals are likely to respond to his words, especially

5 Cf. Petitjean, *Oracles,* 337–341, who perceives a reference to the judicial system.
6 Beuken, 125.
7 Petitjean, *Oracles,* 335.

since the matter of public response to prophetic words has been problematic in the past.

In assessing the response of Israel to earlier prophetic words, the writer does not for long use neutral language. After stating the obvious, that they refused to pay attention, he introduces a series of images that portray the character of Israel's refusal to hear. He first describes body language: turning a rebellious back, keeping ears from hearing.[8] The image is of self-conscious manipulation of one's body to prevent response to Yahweh. The oracle, from this perspective of the response, was actively disobeyed. Such language is used elsewhere in the Hebrew Bible, e.g., Neh. 9:29. Interestingly, this statement is, like Zech. 7:9–10, a historical essay, specifically stating the character of the people's disobedience which resulted in their total destruction.

[12] A second image is provided in v. 12, that of hardening one's heart. However, here, rather than simply saying what was said about Pharaoh in Ex. 7:14 *et passim*, that he hardened his heart, *kbd + lēb*, a more graphic image is used. "They made hearts like stone."[9] It should be remembered that in the psychology of ancient Israel, the heart was thought of as the source of the will and moral sensibility and not, as is more common today, the seat of courage.[10]

Finally, Yahweh's will is described in no uncertain terms as *tôrāh/d'bārîm*, words of instruction which Yahweh had communicated through the earlier prophets. The implications of such a statement are profound. One might imagine someone from another sector of Israelite society suggesting that the words of instruction were present in the book of the covenant and that it was incumbent upon all Israelites to know and obey those dicta. Such is not the case here. Rather, following the basic notion of the prophets, neither the priests, the Levites, the wisdom teachers, nor the elders in the gate were those entrusted with the words of instruction. And it was these prophets who had been ignored by the preexilic Israelites.

Especially interesting here is the notion of the authority of the prophets. They are sent by Yahweh and inspired by "his spirit." This is unusual language.[11] Some have maintained that the expression "his spirit" is an editorial insertion. Compare the similar formulation in

[8] Cf. Baldwin's assessment on turning the shoulder and yoke imagery, op. cit., 147.
[9] Emery or diamond could also be offered as a translation for *šāmîr;* see also Jer. 17:1; Ezek. 3:9.
[10] *IDB* II, 549–550. Cf. Isa. 6:10 on the ears and heart within the prophetic process of communication.
[11] S. Mowinckel, "The Spirit and the Word," in the article "Reforming Prophets," *JBL* 53, 1934, 199–227.

Neh. 9:30: "Many years you bore with them, and warned them by your spirit through the prophets; yet they would not give ear." And yet, though unusual, this expression, along with the formulation of Neh. 9:30, enables the writer to reflect upon the function and authority of the prophets. They were, from this perspective, agents inspired by Yahweh's words to the people. Rather than putting distance between Yahweh and other people, as Mitchell maintains, this notion of "spirit" enables the prophets to be viewed as direct agents of the deity. To reject them is to reject the deity.

When the obduracy of the Israelites to whom the earlier prophet spoke has been defined, the writer is able to move on to a description of the result, what happens when prophetic words of instruction are resolutely ignored. The author then describes Yahweh's judgment. Thus when the prophets were rejected, Yahweh became angry.

The specific term used for "anger" occurs without an adjective, is not part of the typical deuteronomistic sequence (Deut. 29:27; Jer. 21:5; 32:37; 50:13), and is without an equally powerful verb (cf. Num. 17:11 [16:46E], "wrath has gone out"). The result is understated and yet powerful: Yahweh's anger happened! One senses a certain automatic quality to the action. His anger had to come into play when his agents were so firmly rejected. So runs the interpretation of past events from one prophet's perspective.

[13] In v. 13 both text and grammar are problematic. What we are apparently presented with is another view of the catastrophe that Israel has suffered. We already have one such view from the perspective of the people's lack of response to the prophets. Now we hear the same basic story without specific mention of the prophets and in a first-person divine oracle. It is the same basic story since it entails a description of both Israel's disobedience (Yahweh calling and Israel not hearing) and Israel's punishment (the people calling and Yahweh not responding).

This vocabulary appears elsewhere in the Hebrew Bible. In Proverbs we hear Dame Wisdom proclaim, "Then they will call upon me, but I will not answer" (Prov. 1:28).[12] Similar expressions are also to be found in early sixth-century prophetic literature.

Though they cry in my ears with a loud voice, I will not hear them. (Ezek. 8:18b)

Though they cry to me, I will not listen to them. (Jer. 11:11b)

[12] On this basic issue, see Petitjean, *Oracles*, 353–354; Beuken, 129–132.

On the basis of these parallels, it is clear that the author of Zech. 7 is utilizing a way of speaking that had been formulated earlier.

Beuken maintains that this verse represents the combination of two different forms, that of the priestly oracle of salvation and that of the covenant formula.[13] He further contends that this verse derives from the Levitical milieu, which also lies behind Jer. 11:11. One needs to respond, however, that since the same expression occurs in Ezekiel and in Proverbs, the provenance of such language is broader than that of one priestly group. Beuken is, I think, on the right track by pointing to the covenant connection in this material, i.e., that the immediate relationship articulated in the expression "I will be your God and you will be my people" is reflected in the language of Zech. 7:13. And this is, after all, the point behind Zechariah's retelling of the disaster from the covenant perspective: Israel was related intimately to an agent whose words it regularly ignored and who therefore had every right to ignore its pleas for help when it was punished.

[14] With v. 14 we come to the final retrospective statement of this woeful history, the characterization of the punishment that Yahweh meted out to Israel. It continues the first-person discourse initiated in v. 13, literally, "I stormed them away." The storm wind *(sa'ar* or *s⁽ārāh)* is an image often used to symbolize Yahweh's wrathful action (for *sa'ar,* see Jer. 23:19; 25:32; 30:23; Ps. 83:16; for *s⁽ārāh,* see Isa. 29:6; 40:24; 41:16; Jer. 23:19; 30:23). Zechariah 7:14 is the only text in which the piel form of the verb occurs. Nevertheless, several other prophetic speeches use the root *s'r* in a similar way. Compare Hab. 3:14 ("who came like a whirlwind to scatter me"); Isa. 40:24 ("Scarcely are they planted, scarcely sown, scarcely has their stem taken root in the earth, when he blows upon them, and they wither, and the tempest [*s⁽ārāh*] carries them off like stubble"); and Isa. 41:16 ("You shall winnow them and the wind shall carry them away, and the tempest [*s⁽ārāh*] shall scatter them"). This image, at least for Deutero-Isaiah, is clearly that of seeds and grain being scattered over the ground. The image serves to explain the use of the preposition '*al* ("over" or "upon") rather than *b* ("throughout"). And again, it is interesting to note that the storm imagery is particularly prominent in the book of Deuteronomy.

The people of Israel have been scattered like seed upon ground with which they are unfamiliar—"nations which they did not know." This expression, "which they did not know," is particularly prominent in

¹³ Beuken, 129–132.

the deuteronomistic corpus.[14] It can refer to gods (Jer. 7:9; Deut. 13:3 [2E]), people (Deut. 28:33), or a land which they did not know (Jer. 15:14; 16:13; 17:4; 22:28). However, in no case is this phrase used in the dtr. literature with the more neutral *gôy*.

More to the point, what does it mean to live among those whom one does not "know"? The phrase is used so often in the Hebrew Bible and especially in the dtr. corpus that it must have some cutting edge. Fortunately, we know that "to know" *(yd')* can mean to stand in covenant relationship.[15] Hence, to be introduced into a society in which one is not known is to exist in a situation without social status, without protection. One is at the mercy of the host country. Israel could become acquainted with those in whose midst it dwelt in exile. But it could not know them in this technical sense of the word.

One part of the punishment of Yahweh was understood to have a social dimension, namely, the dispersal of people like so many individual grains of wheat into places in which they would have no protection, in which they were liable to fall prey to those among whom they live.[16]

In a disjunctive clause introduced by *w^ehā'āreṣ* we learn that not only were the people scattered but the land, the soil of Israel, was itself eroded away. This destruction of the land is also described in "people" language. It was so desolate that no one even walked back and forth over it. The image is stronger than the destruction of cities or the removal of population. The land was so thoroughly ruined that it was not even productive for the itinerant sheepherder.

Such images of depopulation and total ruin of land are apparently at home in the language of covenant curses, especially as these have been incorporated into the rhetoric of the prophets.[17] However, it is difficult to suggest, as does Beuken, that this language has as its home the communal lament. Rather, this is language formed by the covenant idiom and explicitly refined by the language of covenant curses. That it appears prominently in Ezekiel and Jeremiah should be no surprise, since these are the two prophets who proclaimed the demise of the Judahite state.

The final part of v. 14 is succinct in the same way as v. 11. Verse 11 encapsulates the errant ways of the Israelites. In v. 14, what has been said rather expansively earlier is now summarized in three words, words that have a wistful tone. The land that had been pleasant is now

---

[14] See ibid., 132.

[15] H. Huffmon, "The Treaty Background of Hebrew Yāda‘," *BASOR* 181, 1966, 31–37.

[16] Cf. the covenant curses in Deut. 28:63–68.

[17] E.g., Ezek. 36:33–36 and Jer. 9:9–11. Cf. Beuken, 134–135.

desolate. The verb combination *śym l*e*śammāh* is, as Beuken has observed, particularly prominent in the Jeremianic literature (Jer. 4:7; 18:16; 19:8; 25:9; 51:29). And the phrase *'ereṣ ḥemdāh* also is used in Jer. 3:19: "I thought how I would set you among my sons, and give you a pleasant land, a heritage most beauteous among the nations." (Cf. Ps. 106:24, "Then they despised the pleasant land.") This final clause, succinct as it is, appears to be created using language known elsewhere in the Israelite ambit.

Verse 14, which concludes the tale of woe in Zech. 7:8–14, is a pastiche. It includes the image of the storm wind, prominent in earlier prophetic discourse. It utilizes phrases common to the dtr. tradition: "whom you do/did not know." The language of desolation harks back to covenant curse formulations. And the final reference to the pleasant land echoes earlier Jeremianic formulations.

What we have in Zech. 7:8–14 is an integrated historical essay, exploring the demise of the Judahite state. And the material presented represents the actual historical sequence of events: the giving of a prophetic oracle (8–10), which is disobeyed (11–12a). Hence, Yahweh's punishment had to come (13–14).

Why has this essay been placed here in the book? There is an implicit *Stichwort* connection between 7:7 and 7:8. Verse 7 refers to earlier prophetic words. Verses 9–10 comprise just such prophetic words. And since 8:1ff. constitutes a message of weal, the words of woe in 7:8–14 make an appropriate transition between the probing questions concerning fasting and the definitive response to that question as it appears in Zech. 8.[18]

Zechariah 8:1–17

Thus says Yahweh of Hosts

1 Then the word of Yahweh of Hosts came to me:
2 "Thus says Yahweh of Hosts:
I feel a great jealousy for Zion;
I feel a fierce jealousy for her."

[1] Chapter 8 commences, as did the major block of material in 7:4–14, with the so-called "word occurrence" formula: "Then the

---

[18] Cf. Beuken, who views this section as a Levitical sermon, and Petitjean, who sees 7:7–14 as a composition reflecting the ruin and desolation present in communal laments after 587.

word . . . came to me." And just as was the case with the earlier
material, this formula introduces a series of integrated though
disparate oracles—in 8:2–17. The same formula occurs again in 8:18
and is in turn followed by the messenger formula in 8:19.

A variety of proposals have been offered to explain the overall
composition of Zech. 8, made up as it is of a number of different
oracles. Petitjean suggests that vs. 1–8 and 9–13 comprise literary
compositions; vs. 14–17 an oracle of salvation; and vs. 18–23 another
literary composition.[1] Beuken, on the other hand, argues that vs. 1–6
are a series of originally distinct oracles; vs. 7–8 a late addition to that
small collection; vs. 9–13 a Levitical sermon; and vs. 14–15 and 16–17
two additional oracles.[2] I am inclined to move in the direction
suggested by Rudolph, i.e., by viewing 7:4–8:23 as an entire block of
heterogeneous material roughly divided into three major blocks
(7:4–14; 8:1–17, 18–23) and then subdivided on formulaic grounds into
discrete units which were, in all likelihood, separate utterances of
Zechariah or some prophetic traditionalist.[3]

[2] In 8:2, the oracular bicolon is introduced by the standard
messenger formula. The oracle is made up of highly charged
language, that of jealousy.[4] Since Yahweh was often construed as a
male deity, and since Zion/Jerusalem was female in gender and open
to personification (cf. Isa. 40:6–11), sexual symbolism when
jealousy is mentioned is distinctly possible. Such jealousy on the part
of a male was not unknown in Israel (cf. Prov. 6:34, "For jealousy
makes a man furious, and he will not spare when he takes
revenge").[5] Such was the power of jealousy that certain rituals
became necessary for its resolution, the *tôrat haqqᵉnā'ōt* (Num.
5:29). Further, such language has martial implications. So the exilic
poet wrote, "Yahweh goes out like a mighty man, like a man of war
he stirs up jealousy" (Isa. 42:13). And his tradent, Trito-Isaiah,
wrote similarly, "He wrapped himself in jealousy as a mantle" (Isa.
59:17).

The language of human emotion is used in Zech. 8:2 for a specific
purpose. This oracle represents *the* place in chs. 7–8 in which the
language of woe changes to that of weal. Zechariah 7:4–17 has detailed

---

[1] Petitjean, *Oracles*, 363–438.

[2] Beuken, 156–183.

[3] Rudolph, 142–152.

[4] See Petitjean, *Oracles*, 267–368, and Beuken, 175–177. Beuken follows Brongers in
arguing for a nonsexual connotation to this discourse (H. Brongers, "Der Eifer des
Herrn Zebaoth," *VT* 13, 1963, 269–284).

[5] Cf. Prov. 27:4; Song of Songs 8:6b.

the reason for Israel's destruction. Now, in ch. 8, the oracles address the future and what its likely configuration is to be.

This language of jealousy had occurred earlier in the book, in 1:14. There it was part of the response to an oracle of a lament, a response necessitated by the lament of the *mal'āk* on behalf of the people. However, in Zech. 8:2, the language of jealousy occurs as a spontaneous outburst, Yahweh's response to the description of a pleasant land made desolate.[6]

The use of the modifier *ḥēmāh* enforces the violent, even uncontrolled aspect of this powerful emotion. The conjunction of *ḥmh* and *qn'* occurred earlier in Ezekiel and referred to the fate of Judah:

> Thus says Yahweh:
> Behold, I speak in my jealous wrath,
> because you have suffered the reproach of the nations.
> (Ezek. 36:6b)

This language, both in Ezek. 36 and in Zech. 8, highlights the intensity and the violence of Yahweh's feeling for Jerusalem/Zion. Given the strength of Yahweh's emotion, it is impossible for the history of woe to continue. A change is about to occur.

3   Thus says Yahweh:
     "I am returning to Zion.
     I will dwell in Jerusalem's midst,
     so that Jerusalem will be called
        the city of faithfulness;
     the mount of Yahweh of Hosts will be
        the mount of holiness."

[3] Just as 8:2 shares language and ideology with 1:14, so 8:3 resonates with 1:16.[1] In 1:16 we read, "I am returning *(šabtî)* to Jerusalem with compassion." And in 8:3, the following phrase occurs: "I am returning *(šabtî)* to Zion." Then, in the second colon of 1:16, there is explicit reference to the temple, "my house being built in her." In Zech. 8:3, the notion of temple reconstruction is less specific: "I will dwell in the midst of Jerusalem." The verb *škn* in 8:3, is, of course, used to depict Yahweh's indwelling presence as was the case in 2:14 [10E]: "I will come and dwell in your midst." There can be little doubt

---

[6] On the difference between Zech. 1:14 and 8:2, cf. Rudolph, 147.

[1] Petitjean argues that these verses are related to Zech. 2:14–15 [10–11E] as well (*Oracles*, 370–371).

about the "temple" focus of such language, and this in contrast to the non-temple language of the visions themselves (cf. 2:8–9 [4–5E]).[2] Syntactically, this verse comprises a main clause followed by a result clause. The result clause sounds rather like a pastiche of prophetic discourse. The notion of an *'îr hā'emet* is remarkably similar to the *'îr haṣṣedeq* of Isa. 1:26. Perhaps the presence of *'emet* and not *ṣedeq* here is conditioned by its occurrence in Zech. 7:9; 8:16. In any case, Yahweh's presence is understood as resulting in a particular quality for the city, faithfulness. And interestingly, in Isa. 1:26, Yahweh's action, too, is necessary for there to be a city of righteousness.

As for the notion of a holy mountain, the similarity to expressions in Joel 3:17 and Isa. 52:1 is pronounced, i.e., a holy city coupled with the hope that there will be no more violation by impious strangers.[3]

From a redaction-critical perspective, it is important to observe what has been achieved by juxtaposing Zech. 8:3 to 8:2. The former verse raises the issue of violent, even uncontrolled emotion, the strength of which could have palpably negative results. The presence of 8:3 suggests that the deity has channeled this emotion in a positive direction, i.e., that he will return to Jerusalem and reside there, and that the city will benefit in concrete ways as a result of his presence. Both religious (holiness) and ethical (faithfulness) vocabularies are appropriate for describing the qualities of this new city.

A final point. The emphasis in Zech. 8:3, and in fact 8:1–3, is upon Yahweh's return and the benefits that the city will receive from his presence. Divine initiative—rather than particular human efforts—seems critical to this author's view of postexilic restoration. And it is divine initiative within an urban, i.e., Jerusalem-oriented, context.[4]

4   Thus says Yahweh of Hosts:
     "Old men and women shall again
        rest in the plazas of Jerusalem,
     each with staff in hand
        because of their great age.
5   Also, the plazas of the city will be filled
        with boys and girls,
     laughter filling its plazas."

---

[2] For *škn b*, see Joel 4:17, 21; Isa. 8:18; Ps. 135:21.
[3] On this issue, cf. Ezek. 20:40–44.
[4] On renaming of the city, see Ackroyd, *Exile and Restoration*, 212, and Ezek. 48:35.

[4–5] Zechariah's words of weal continue in this next brief oracular unit. Interestingly, the context for reflection about good times remains urban reality. In 8:3 we were told about the faithful city. Now we hear about old men and women in plazas in the city. Clearly, Zechariah is centrally concerned with Jerusalem and its immediate environs as the setting in which renewal will take place.

The character of the city as a site of holiness and faithfulness was articulated in 8:3. Now the specific issue broached in ch. 7, the depopulation of Jerusalem and its status as an inhospitable region, is addressed. Jerusalem will now have a significant population. The author of this oracle uses a literary technique of mentioning two polar extremes, young and old, and thereby indicating the totality of the group.[1] To refer to many old people and many young people is a graphic way of referring to the totality of a population. Further, the activities described—resting, laughing—suggest a pleasant existence, life in which the citizens of the city are not always pressed by concerns for finding food, shelter, and clothing.

The motifs of this brief and well-written oracle, those of a city rebuilt, of many people, and of children playing, are shared by Jer. 30:18–21.[2] But Zechariah's oracle is sharpened to treat just the issues of quality of life, the city plan, i.e., the open spaces, and the significant repopulation that will occur.[3] Moreover, the prophet thinks that what will happen has existed before, as the presence of '*ōd* in the oracle suggests.[4] Put another way, what is depicted in Zech. 8:4–5 is understood as a former way of life for Israel and not a kind of urban existence that has never before existed.

Sexual complementarity is also stressed in this future condition. We do not hear of old men, but rather old men and old women. And similarly, we are told of boys and girls, not just children. This vision is one of completeness, the two sexes coexisting in harmony.

Moreover, Petitjean argues convincing that the specific location mentioned twice in this oracle, the *rᵉḥōbôt* ("plazas"), is especially apt since it was in these open places that the earlier prophets understood death and destruction to have occurred (Amos 5:16; Jer. 9:20; Lam. 2:11, 12).[5] The role of the plazas signals the changing role of urban

[1] Cf. Isa. 65:20 for a similar use of infants and old men.

[2] See also Mason, 69.

[3] It is stretching the point to suggest a paradisal existence, i.e., children making noise by laughing and yet not disturbing the older citizens. For discussions of the repopulation motif, see Petitjean, *Oracles,* 373–374, and cf. Jer. 30:18–21; 31:2–6, 23–30; 33:1–13.

[4] See Beuken, 176–177, on the formal characteristics of the so-called '*ōd* promise. Beuken maintains that Zechariah took over this linguistic feature from the book of Jeremiah.

[5] Petitjean, *Oracles,* 372–373.

entities for Judahite experience in the sixth century. What was earlier a symbol for national degradation and defeat becomes a sign of hope. The young and the old are united by the focus of their activities in public space.

6 Thus says Yahweh of Hosts:
"Even though it seems miraculous
in the eyes of the remnant of this people
(in these days),[a]
should it also seem miraculous in my eyes?"
says Yahweh of Hosts.

a. Omit *bayyāmîm hāhēm;* thus Ackroyd, *Exile and Restoration*, 213 n. 137. On grounds of syntax alone, it should be clear that we are in the midst of a series of originally unrelated utterances that have now been placed in a meaningful order. There is no referent in v. 6, i.e., the "it" is—at least internally—not defined. However, the saying now functions to refer to the restoration of Jerusalem, which has just been broached in vs. 1–5.

[6] The key word in 8:6 is, of course, "miraculous." That Yahweh could act in a mighty way, doing miraculous things, is well attested in the Old Testament. Such descriptions are particularly at home in hymnic language (e.g., Ps. 139:14). Put another way, the issue of whether or not Yahweh could, in theory, act in a mighty or miraculous way is not at issue here. That issue is broached with similar phraseology in Gen. 18:14; Jer. 32:17, 27 when the deity asks, "Is anything too miraculous for Yahweh?"[1]
The Zechariah oracle seems concerned, rather, with the problem of assessing the deity's character on the basis of human expectation in this difficult moment. By human standards, the restoration of Jerusalem, as depicted in 8:1–5, lies beyond normal expectations. Furthermore, those who envision such restoration are likely to be few, just as this remnant is modest in number. And a weak people is likely to have difficulty in thinking of a powerful God, the more so if this deity is the god of a defeated people.[2] The point of the utterance seems to be this: "Just because you are a weak remnant of what was earlier a glorious nation, do not infer that your deity is incapable of miraculous activity

[1] Beuken, 177–178, identifies such discourse as *Streitfragen,* "antagonistic questions," and notes that in Jeremiah the question follows an *'ōd* promise as it does in Zech. 8. Cf. Petitjean, *Oracles,* 375–377.
[2] Ackroyd senses a similar point and sees Zechariah here providing a "word of hesitation" that expresses an "undertone of lack of faith" (*Exile and Restoration,* 212).

such as has just been announced." God will not admit such doubts about his abilities.

7   Thus says Yahweh of Hosts,
     "I will save my people
     from the eastern region
     and from the region of the west.
8   I will bring them
     and they will dwell in the midst of Jerusalem.
     They will be my people
     and I will be their God,
     in truth and in sincerity."

[7–8] The oracle in vs. 7–8 is, like the other oracles in ch. 8, introduced with the messenger formula. Here the formula introduces a direct word of the deity, a statement of intention. Yahweh states that he will, literally, "save [his] people from," an idiom that regularly indicates those from whom, or a region from which, a group is being rescued.[1] Such sentiments, i.e., "saving from" within the context of the Babylonian exile, are expressed elsewhere in sixth-century literature.

   For lo, I will save you from afar,
       and your offspring from the land of their captivity. . . .
   For I am with you to save you,
       says Yahweh. (Jer. 30:10–11//46:27–28)

Similar also, at least in its reference to compass directions of the Israelite diaspora, is Isa. 43:5–6:

   Fear not, for I am with you;
       I will bring your offspring from the east, . . .
       and from the west I will gather you;
   I will say to the north, Give up,
       and to the south, Do not withhold.

However, the Zechariah text oddly mentions only east and west, whereas north is the common direction for reference to the location of exile (e.g., Zech. 2:10 [2:6E]; Jer. 31:8).[2]
   Yahweh will save because those dispersed are "my people" (*'ammî*). That expression is reiterated in the more technical covenant

---

[1] See Petitjean for a discussion of *hôšia'*, *Oracles*, 379–380.

[2] Cf. Rudolph, 178, who suggests that the east-west axis parallels the direction of the sun. Ackroyd, *Exile and Restoration*, 213, sees this as referring to the directions of two Near Eastern powers, Babylon and Egypt.

formulary in v. 8, "They will be my people *(lî l*ʿ*ām)* and I will be their God."[3] Yahweh will save this people because they are related to him in a legal contract. The particular phraseology of this oracle suggests that the covenant of old still obtains. Contrary to appearances, they are God's people now (v. 7), and they will continue to be God's people in the future (v. 8). No new covenant is promised.[4] Rather, the old ordinances (see Zech. 7:9; 8:16) remain in force, and the old mutual responsibility between deity and people is still intact.

Further suggestive in this text is the continued urban character of the restoration. Earlier oracles in Zech. 8 (vs. 2, 3, 4–5) included this focus on Yahweh's chosen city. It should hardly be surprising, then, that in vs. 7–8 the people are being brought back to dwell in Jerusalem.[5]

The final two words are not regularly found in the covenant formula expression. Perhaps it is best to understand the presence of *be'ᵉmet* in 8:8 as forming an *inclusio* with *'ᵉmet* in 8:3. What is in v. 3 a quality of the new city is also in v. 8 a quality of the covenant relationship. A similar formulation occurs in Hos. 2:20–21 [19–20E], i.e., one finds such qualities prefixed with the preposition *b*. Here the language is that of marital rite: I will betroth you to me in righteousness and in justice, in steadfast love and in mercy. I will betroth you to me in faithfulness.

The connotations of this marriage-rite language may well carry over into Zech. 8:8 and in so doing may stress the personalized character of the covenant relationship between Yahweh and Israel, a relationship that remains in force.

9　Thus says Yahweh of Hosts,
"Let your hands be strong,
　　you who in these days have been hearing these words
　　　from the mouths of the prophets,
　　since the day on which the foundations
　　　of the temple of Yahweh of Hosts were dedicated
　　　for reconstruction.
10　Indeed, before those days
　　there was no wage for human or for beast,
　　nor was there security from enemies
　　　for the person who traveled about,
　　because everywhere I set neighbor against neighbor.

---

[3] For similar uses, see Hos. 1:9; Jer. 7:23.
[4] Cf. Petitjean, *Oracles*, 380, who perceives this as the promise of a new covenant.
[5] The emphasis on the whole land as a context for restoration in Deutero-Isaiah provides a marked contrast (see Isa. 44:3–4).

11 But now
   I will not (act)[a] toward the remnant of this people
      as I did formerly,"
         says Yahweh of Hosts.
12 "Indeed, there shall be a sowing of peace;[b]
      the vine will yield its fruit,
      the earth will yield its produce,
      the heavens will yield their dew.
   I will bestow upon the remnant of this people all these things.
13 Just as you have been a reproach among the nations,
      O house of Judah and house of Israel,
   so now I will rescue you
      and you will become a blessing.
   Do not fear!
      Let your hands be strong!"

a. There is no verb in this clause.
b. For alternative interpretations, cf. Ackroyd, *Exile and Restoration*, 214 n. 141 ("For the seed shall prosper"); Mitchell, 214; Petitjean, *Oracles*, 397–398.

If the major historical retrospective in 7:8–14 serves to explain how it is that Israel suffered national degradation, the subunits in 8:9–13, another historical retrospective, contrast the time and conditions of punishment with those of the hoped-for restoration. Also, both passages use admonitory language. In Zech. 7, the admonitions were fundamentally ethical in their import, e.g., "Do not oppress the widow" (7:9–10). In Zech. 8, the language is less specific and more encouraging: "Do not fear" (v. 13); "Let your hands be strong" (vs. 9, 13).

[9] Indeed, the oracle commences with just this sort of hortatory language. After the messenger formula, we confront the first of two citations of the clause "Let your hands be strong." This formulation occurs at both beginning and end of the oracle and thereby creates an effective *inclusio*. Such language, along with the "Do not fear" formula (v. 13), is used with great frequency in martial contexts, e.g., Judg. 7:11. Beuken has described this imperative rhetoric as a formula of encouragement *(Ermutigungsformel)*.[1] He maintains that such language occurs in the Hebrew Bible in its original setting only in Judg. 7:11, in the context of holy war. This formula has an inextricable

[1] Beuken, 158–161.

connection to the oracle of salvation, as it does in Zech. 8:9–13. Moreover, Beuken argues that such usage is markedly similar to that of II Chron. 15:5, 7, a text which, along with Zech. 8:9–13, he labels as a Levitical sermon. Perceptive though Beuken's comments are in this regard, it is difficult to argue for a correlation between these two texts on the basis of one formulaic occurrence, the more so since the formula does occur rather frequently in the Hebrew Bible.

More critical to an interpretation of this pericope than putative parallel texts is the identification of the audience. In this verse the hearers are identified in two quite distinct ways: they are people who have heard something, and they are people who have heard something at a particular time. A proper understanding of this oracle requires attention to these two emphases. First, the people are defined as those who have heard these words from the mouths of prophets. Again, there are two salient features. If, as I maintain, 8:9–13 is a self-contained composition, then we need to search for evidence of such words inside the unit and not elsewhere in the book of Zechariah. Since 8:10ff. sounds like the language one expects from a prophet and since just such language does appear in Hag. 1:6, it is altogether likely that the prophets being referred to here are Haggai and Zechariah. They were, after all, remembered as the instigators of the rebuilding campaign and were remembered as having been among those who rebuilt the temple (Ezra 5:1; 6:14). If this reference is indeed to Haggai and Zechariah, then the composition is of necessity biographical, i.e., an addition to the prophet's own compendium of vision reports.

If the prophets referred to are Haggai and Zechariah, then what is the day since which they have been speaking? There can be little doubt that *the* day to which this text refers is the ritual rededication of the temple, the Israelite equivalent of the *kalû* ritual. It was on this day that the temple once more became sacrosanct and the proper rebuilding of the temple could go forward. That such a singular day had occurred is made clear by Hag. 2:15.

If our reconstruction of the background of this verse is correct, the author, in mentioning prophets, is probably referring at least to Haggai. In so doing, he is advocating the completion of the temple soon after its ritual rededication. The period of time to which this unit refers is about 520—the date of rededication—and before 515, when the temple was actually finished. The date included in Zech. 7:1 could therefore apply to the period to which such language was addressed. This reconstruction enables us to learn that the people were being urged to continue with the work of reconstructing the temple, or perhaps better, an editor's idea of how they should have been urged.

[10] With 8:10, we hear an example of the words that the prophets had spoken to the people. The time before the temple was rededicated is described in two ways, and is viewed as under Yahweh's aegis. First, there is economic language. No wages were paid for either human or animal work. The former case, wages for humans, had also been cited by Haggai as an example of woe prior to the rebuilding of the temple. In Haggai, it was a matter of inability to retain one's wages (Hag. 1:6). In Zechariah, the case is more severe. There were no wages. Further, there were wages for neither human nor beast. Even though a person had animals, he or she could not count on letting out an animal for hire or selling it for a profit.[2] The situation depicted is radical unemployment.

By way of offering a partial explanation for such a situation, the author indicates next that violence was rampant. Trade was impossible because of attacks. And without trade, the economy of Syria-Palestine was jeopardized. The author makes it clear that such a situation was not the result of divinely caused crop failure, as Haggai had explained it (Hag. 1:7–11). Rather, the problem was social strife—again, as with Haggai, caused by the deity.[3]

[11] The divine oracle continues in 8:11 with the use of a temporal particle, *wᵉ'attāh*, to indicate a turnabout on the part of the deity.[4] Since there is only a remnant left (cf. the same term *šᵉ'ērît* in v. 6 and in Hag. 1:12, 14), Yahweh declares that he will not continue to act toward them as he has in the past. The emphasis here is on the deity's initiative and not, at first, on what he will provide in the future.

The saying in 8:11 is remarkably brief. There is not even a verb. Literally, the deity says, "I will not toward the remnant of this people as I [did] formerly." Beuken—correctly, I think—hears intimations of the so-called covenant formulary which has been included explicitly in Zech. 8,[5] especially since covenant language continues in vs. 12–13. Again, as was the case earlier, there is no reason to think of a new covenant. Rather, Yahweh will honor the old formulary now that the suffering of the people has worked itself out. The turnabout is concluded by the terminative formula "says Yahweh of Hosts."

[12] Beginning with an asseverative *k,* the next section of the discourse, v. 12, outlines the nature of Yahweh's regenerative activity toward this remnant of a people. The outline of the character of this

---

[2] Ex. 22:14 [15E] indicates directly that animals were in fact rented out.
[3] Beuken, 162–163, argues that Zech. 8:10 is remarkably similar to II Chron. 5:5–7.
[4] H. Brongers, "Bemerkungen zum Gebrauch des adverbialen *wᵉ'attāh* im A.T.," *VT* 15, 1965, 289–299 (cited in Beuken, 163 n. 2).
[5] Beuken, 164.

new action is profoundly different from the descriptions of woeful existence in v. 10. Earlier we heard about individuated existence, a lack of earnings for either human or beast, the conflict of neighbor against neighbor. Now the rhetoric involves not so much particular cases as universal action. Not even the particular deity, Yahweh, is mentioned. Rather, though Yahweh's sovereignty is presumed, we hear about a nonspecific "sowing of peace." And here an antithesis is set up with the period of nonpeace mentioned in v. 10.

This general expectation of weal is established by means of agricultural language. There will be a "sowing of peace." The metaphor suggests that it will happen slowly and require patience, just as does the maturation of seeds in a field.[6] And agents to accomplish this agricultural weal are mentioned: vine, earth, and heavens.

This perception of the future in agricultural terms is, of course, shared by oracles in Haggai: Hag. 1:10–11; 2:19. Interestingly, Hag. 1:10 parallels closely the language of Zech. 8:12, though in Haggai the heavens are withholding their dew and the ground is withholding its produce—because the people have not rebuilt the temple as quickly as they ought.

That this change in fertility, according to Zech. 8:12, will happen is not open to question. What is open to question is who will reap the benefits. And here Yahweh states clearly, "I will bestow all these on this remnant." This language of inheritance picks up the promises, especially those of the deuteronomist, made to Israel as it entered the land. Israel is to take possession of the land and all its fertility.[7] Just as Israel once took possession of the land, so now Israel, or a remnant thereof, is to take possession of the fertility of a land in which it already resides. The situation is different from that in the promises of Deut. 6:10ff.; 8:7–10.[8] There the land was fertile and Israel was entering the land. Now Israel is already in the land, and the land has not been fertile. But it will, in the future, return to its ideal image of land "flowing with milk and honey." The old-style promises could not be used, since Israel had been experiencing devastated, nonproductive land, and not a rich land "full of all good things, cisterns hewn out, vineyards, olive orchards and fruit trees in abundance" (Neh. 9:25).

[13] As if to make clear the character of the future blissful state, the oracle continues with a brief contrast of reproach versus blessings. It is

---

[6] Here there is a significant contrast between Zechariah's expectation of immediate change and that of Haggai. The view expressed in this verse is more in line with the process articulated in Zechariah's visions.

[7] Deut. 1:38; 3:28 [29E]; 12:10; 19:3; 31:7; Josh. 1:6.

[8] Here contra Beuken, 167.

important to know precisely what a *q^elālāh* is. Israel had not become a curse upon the nations.[9] Rather, Israel had become the source of curse language, i.e., could be used as an example of cursed existence by all other nations.[10]

In order to change the people's status as accursed, Yahweh will rescue them, so that the people will become a source for language of divinely blessed existence (Zech. 8:7). And again, this is discourse particularly at home in the dtr. corpus, as in Deut. 28.

This oracle also serves to indicate a major shift in the character of Israel's status. Earlier (v. 11) the people could be described as a remnant. Now—in v. 13—the nation-state language of Israel and Judah is appropriate. It is also interesting that the language of the covenant as found in Deuteronomy is used by this writer. Yahweh appears to bestow blessings of a nonconditional sort. And yet the covenant context from which this language is drawn is certainly that of a conditional covenant.

In completing this section, in v. 13c the author appropriates formulaic language, "Do not fear," from the priestly oracles of salvation, especially as those are preserved in holy-war contexts. Also present is the formula with which this section opened, "Let your hands be strong." This *inclusio* suggests strongly that Zech. 8:9–13 is an integrated whole, a strong statement of restoration. It affirms communal identity and, more particularly, agricultural well-being. And it admonishes the people to act in the process of restoration.

14   For thus says Yahweh of Hosts,
      "Just as I devised evil for you
            when your fathers angered me,
            and I did not relent," says Yahweh of Hosts,[a]
15   "Now I have again made plans, in these days,
            to act benevolently toward Jerusalem
            and toward the house of Judah.
      Do not fear!
16   These are the things which you must do:
      Speak truthfully to one another,[b]
            deliver true and just decisions in your gates.
17   Do not plot malevolently against each other,
            do not honor a false oath;
      for all these are things which I hate," says Yahweh.

---

[9] See Beuken, 168–169, and the standard commentaries.
[10] Such language is particularly common in dtr. and in Jeremianic prose.

a. Note the reverse order of the MT formula with *nihāmᵉtî*.
b. Deleting *ᵉmet* at the beginning of the third colon in v. 16, as LXX.

[14–15] Immediately after the lengthy piece outlining the imminent change from a cursed to a blessed existence for Israel, a new unit commences, one introduced by the messenger formula. And it too sets up the contrast between a past and present time of woe and a future time of weal, in vs. 14–15. Further, the presence of the "Do not fear" formula in vs. 13 and 15 serves to link these two distinct units.[1]

If there is a basic theme that pervades the first two verses of this block, it is that of divine intentionality, as evidenced by the double occurrence of the root *zmm*. Interestingly, this word is used, outside of these two occurrences, to refer only to Yahweh's intentional action in punishment—e.g., in Jer. 4:28, "For this earth shall mourn, and the heavens above be black; for I have spoken, I have purposed *(zammōtî);* I have not relented *(nihamtî)* nor will I turn back."[2] Hence, when Zechariah introduces the root *zmm,* he establishes an expectation of woe, only later, in 8:15, to shift that expectation to hope—hope of a new time "in these days."

The writer thought it necessary to give a rationale for Yahweh's intentionality for evil. To do this he appropriates language similar to that used elsewhere in the book. The notion of "fathers" as responsible for the current generation's plight is affirmed in the first oracle, Zech. 1:1–6. And the language of Yahweh's wrath *(qṣp)* is attested in Zech. 7:12. This explanation, that an earlier generation had offended Yahweh and thereby aroused his wrath, is the standard one for Zechariah.

Moreover, this same language of divine wrath is prominent in Jer. 10:10 (poetry); 21:5 (prose); 32:37 (prose); and 50:13 (poetry). This is significant because the juxtaposition of the two verbs in Zech. 8:14 also occurs in Jer. 51:11–12. One senses that Jeremiah's rhetoric has been carried into and interpreted for a new generation by one of Zechariah's tradents.

That Yahweh had not relented from his earlier intentions would not preclude the possibility of his changing his plans in the future. Such is the thrust of Zech. 8:15. Yahweh will again make plans, but this time for a different effect, for good. This is, as I indicated earlier, a remarkable use of the term *zmm,* the only time in the Hebrew Bible that it refers to benevolent intention. Moreover, the source of such an

---

[1] See Petitjean, *Oracles,* 413, and Baldwin, 154, for comment on two positive and then two negative statements.
[2] See similarly Jer. 51:12; Lam. 2:17; Zech. 1:6.

intention is different. Yahweh had been angry with Israel's fathers. Now he will intend good for entities described in physical rather than personal language: Jerusalem, house of Judah. Perhaps this difference in vocabulary enables Yahweh to change his mind without seeming inconsistency, i.e., moving from talk of fathers to talk of place. It is interesting that future weal focuses on a city and an area, if that is what "house of Judah" means.[3] Also interesting is the fact that no reason is given for Yahweh's change of mind. And by way of contrast, we are told why he intended punishment for Israel. Perhaps the notion of Jerusalem as a city in which Yahweh is understood to reside serves to explain why he must change his mind. Yahweh was constrained, in the final analysis, to act benevolently toward Jerusalem. This prediction of a change of fortune ends with the "Do not fear" formula.

[16] Without any transitional formula, the oracle shifts to an apparently unrelated topic, the obligations that Israel must undertake. There is a change from indicative to imperative discourse; from language about what Yahweh will do to language about what Israel must do. Introducing this section is a general imperative, stating in a comprehensive manner that Israel must do certain things. This use of the noun *dābār* to refer to commandments is well attested (see, e.g., Ex. 24:3).[4] As we have seen earlier, there is little reason to think that Zechariah contemplates the enactment of a new covenant. Hence, it is licit to maintain that the obligations to which he refers belong to the covenant of old, that this is an admonition based upon earlier precepts. It is therefore no accident that Zech. 7:9 includes phraseology similar to that in 8:16: "Execute true justice" (JPS). The formulation in 8:16 makes more specific the application of such justice. It refers to the legal institution of judging in the gate (see, e.g., Deut. 21:19; Ruth 4:1–11). However, the imperatives immediately preceding and following this reference to the administration of justice in the city gate are much more general in their import. The admonition "Speak truthfully" may be construed as similar in import to the Ninth Commandment, "You shall not bear false witness against your neighbor" (Ex. 20:16). However, this term, *'emet*, has been used as something of a subtheme in ch. 8 (vs. 3, 8, 19).[5] As one might expect, such language does occur in other prophetic texts, e.g., Jer. 9:4 and Ps. 15:2–3, the latter example being particularly significant since it

---

[3] The latter phrase could, of course, refer to the Davidic dynasty, though I do not think it does in this particular verse.

[4] See also M. Weinfeld, *Deuteronomy and the Deuteronomic School*, 1972, 65, 152, 261, 304, 336.

[5] On this issue, cf. Petitjean, *Oracles*, 413.

includes a formula of reciprocity ("against his neighbor") as do the formulations in Zech. 8:16–17.

[17] The language of Zech. 8:17a parallels, or better, is virtually identical to that of Zech. 7:10b. As noted in the commentary on the earlier section, the use of *ḥšb* in admonitory language is highly unusual. These uses (7:10b and 8:17a) appear to constitute language of the prophet rather than stereotypic usage. Petitjean stresses, I think correctly, that the particular formulation in 7:10b and 8:17a emphasizes "interiority" and not only reciprocity. The use of *bilbabkem* in both texts broaches the matter of human intentionality, just as the verb *zmm*, earlier in this unit, broaches the matter of divine intentionality. A change in Yahweh's intentions for Zion signals a call for proper human intentions in the house of Israel.[6]

The next colon, "Do not honor a false oath," is puzzling, at least at the literal level. What is a false oath? Is the issue that of perjury, as in Ex. 20:16? Unfortunately, the phrase *šĕbuʿat šeqer* occurs only in this text. The word *šĕbûʿāh* is understood as something that may or may not be kept (e.g., the oath of Yahweh mentioned in Jer. 11:5). On the basis of this text, and on the basis of the legal imagery elsewhere in this unit, it seems reasonable to conclude that an oath based on lying is prohibited. For example, in the case of Ex. 22:8ff., if a neighbor has indeed been responsible for the death, injury, or removal of an animal, and he swears that he is not so responsible, then the oath could be described using the vocabulary of Zech. 8:17. It is a false oath. To love, much less honor, such oaths would jeopardize the entire legal system. Hence, such action is prohibited.

The final clause of this oracle provides a reason for compliance. Yahweh hates all these things: speaking untruthfully, not providing justice in the gates, malevolent plotting, and making improper oaths. Some of the admonitions remind one of the formulations in the Decalogue. In one of the motivation clauses, in Ex. 20:5b–6, Yahweh states that he will punish those who hate him. In Zechariah, the language of hating is different. Here Yahweh is the hater, not of people, but of actions. The notion of Yahweh as hater is attested in Deuteronomy as well as in a number of prophetic texts, e.g., Deut. 12:31; Isa. 1:14; Jer. 12:8.[7]

This oracle concludes on a negative note, even though its primary

---

[6] On the connections between Zechariah and Levitical formulations (esp. Lev. 19:11–12), see Petitjean, *Oracles*, 416–417.

[7] Cf. Petitjean, *Oracles*, 418. In all these instances, Petitjean maintains that the object of Yahweh's antipathy is improper cultic action (cf. Pss. 5:6; 11:5).

purpose is that of an oracle of salvation (v. 15). It begins by citing Yahweh's "evil" intentions and it ends with references to his hatred. Surely such a rhetorical tactic is designed to garner adherence to the principles articulated in vs. 16–17. What was an oracle of salvation now functions as an oracle of admonition.[8]

Zechariah 8:18–23

The fasts shall become happy assemblies

18 And the word of Yahweh of Hosts came to me:
19 "Thus says Yahweh of Hosts,
    The fast of the fourth month,
    the fast of the fifth month,
        the fast of the seventh month,
        and the fast of the tenth month
shall become for the house of Judah
    joyful and celebrative,[a]
        happy assemblies;
But you must love truth and peace."[b]

a. Compare the various translations.
b. With JPS, viewing the final clause as adversative.

[**18–19**] Several oracles have intervened since Sharezer and Regemmelek addressed a question concerning fasting practices (7:3); the editor now sees fit to introduce Zechariah's response. Whether or not the response originally followed immediately after the question, we cannot know. What we do know in retrospect is that an editor thought it necessary to provide (1) a number of oracles by way of response to the question; (2) oracles from Yahweh; (3) oracles of promise conditioned by words of admonition; and (4) some reflection about the nature of ritual action, especially that of eating and fasting. Once these issues had been brought up, the redactor judged that an answer to the specific question could now be given.

The response is, not surprisingly, introduced by the messenger formula. Just as with the prolegomenon to the response, so now the response itself is structured as a divine oracle. The answer is Yahweh's and not just that of the prophet. And yet at the same time, the

[8] Cf. Beuken, 173.

inceptive statement "The word of Yahweh came to me" indicates that the divine response was made through Zechariah and not through another party, i.e., not to the priests who were also consulted on this matter (Zech. 7:3).

Zechariah's response is rhetorically brilliant. He begins by enumerating fasts, not only the fasts about which a question had been raised, those in the fifth and seventh months, but fasts in the fourth and tenth months as well. One almost senses that Zechariah is about to lay on even more vigorous fasting requirements, the more so since the previous oracles had been filled with admonitory language.

In commenting on 7:3, we determined that the fast in the fifth month most probably commemorated the fall of Jerusalem, in particular the destruction of the temple in 587 B.C.E. Also it seemed likely that the seventh-month fast mentioned in Zech. 7:5 referred to the death of Gedaliah, provisional governor of the occupied territory. What then is the significance of the fasts just mentioned, those in the fourth and tenth months? Many commentators have argued that the fourth month was remembered as that in which the city was successfully attacked (Jer. 39:2)—and that it was during the tenth month that Nebuchadnezzar laid seige to Jerusalem (Jer. 39:1; II Kings 25:1–2).[1]

By saving mention of these last two fasts until this moment in the discourse, Zechariah is able to pull out all the stops in creating a picture of absolute doom. He does this by highlighting all the critical moments in Judah's demise: siege, destruction of city wall and temple, and the death of a temporary governor. Not only is the author painting here a picture of the fullest gloom, but he is also successful in having Zechariah control the discussion. Those from Bethel have asked about one fast. Zechariah has expanded the discussion to include all the fasts that derive from the period of Judah's defeat. The first two cola of this oracle therefore serve to remind the listeners of the total defeat and the response of lament, as well as to establish Zechariah's authority to answer the question.

The second bicolon, which is of course part of the sentence begun in 8:19a, provides the surprise. Those days, known as fasts, shall become for the house of Judah—that entity to which weal has been promised in 8:15—joyful and celebrative occasions, happy assemblies. The language here is carefully chosen. These times are still intended to function in a ritual context. Zechariah's rhetoric does not downplay

[1] So Baldwin, 143; Petitjean, *Oracles,* 422; Rudolph, 151. Cf. Ackroyd, *Exile and Restoration,* 207 n. 122.

the importance of collective religious behavior. The switch is from ritual deprivation, fasting, to ritual celebration, feasting.

What sort of expectation do these particular terms for celebration bring? There are three terms: *śāśôn, śimḥāh, mō'ªdîm ṭôbîm.* The first of these terms is particularly significant: *śāśôn* connotes social mirth, happiness similar to that of a wedding celebration, e.g., Jer. 7:34; 16:9; 25:10; 33:11. More importantly, it points to social joy associated with eating (Isa. 22:13). It is a word associated with promises of restoration to Zion (Isa. 51:3). Perhaps more important, it is, in postexilic usage, associated with other words to refer to celebrative banquets (Esth. 8:16–17). This term was undoubtedly used by Zechariah because it provided such a stark contrast to the notion of fasting, the topic under discussion. While *śāśôn* could mean joy, in many places (and no doubt here) it means joyful meals. Zechariah's first description of what the fasts shall become refers to a specialized form of joy associated with people and fasting.

The second noun, *śimḥāh,* reinforces the notion of joy introduced by *śāśôn,* and does so in an alliterative fashion. It has a general import of gladness or happiness, as does *śāśôn,* and it is often associated with social festivities (e.g., Gen. 31:27; I Kings 1:40; I Sam. 18:6; Isa. 9:2 [3E]; Esth. 9:17, 18, 22).

The final phrase, "happy assemblies," though it does not occur elsewhere in this particular form, implies a ritual connotation for these feasts. They are not to be thought of as one-time drinking bouts or haphazard meals. They are, rather, the feasts that comprise the official cultus of Yahweh. And since this response is directed to the house of Judah, one is led to think that such feasting will occur in Jerusalem, as the expectation articulated in Isa. 33:20 suggests: "Look upon Zion, the city of our appointed feasts." To have such feasts was to celebrate the renewal of a ritual place and the renewal of the ritual order.

Using these three terms, Zechariah is able to respond to the question that had been raised by fasting. Some scholars have debated the extent to which Zechariah's answer is a "direct" answer. This debate is rather beside the point since Zechariah does answer the question. The prophet has maintained that the time for fasting is over and the time for feasting is imminent.

This proclamation does not, however, terminate the discourse (despite some proposals to strike the last clause of 8:19). Consistent with the block of oracles between the question in 7:3 and the response in 8:18–19 (i.e., material full of admonitions), this response, which functions not unlike an oracle of promise, concludes on a hortatory

note: "But you must love truth and peace." This is strange and yet
makes good sense. In the previous oracle there was talk of Yahweh
hating: That which Yahweh hates must not be done. Rather, Judahites
should love what Yahweh loves—truth and peace. Interestingly, one
of these qualities, truth, was prominent in the formulation of 8:14–17.
Truth is both a specific quality mandated for judicial proceedings
(8:16–17) and also a request for proper human interaction in the
general social order.

A final problem. Love is commanded here. This is, from our
perspective, odd. We do not usually think of love, or more generally
beneficence, as something which can be commanded. To be sure,
there is similar language elsewhere in the Hebrew Bible. Perhaps the
most famous example is found in Deut. 6:4–5: "Hear, O Israel:
Yahweh is our God, Yahweh alone. And you shall love Yahweh your
God with all your heart, and with all your soul, and with all your
might." In Deut. 6, love is required as an element of covenant
loyalty. And yet, interestingly, the form of the verb "to love" is in
the indicative, *wᵉʾāhabtā*, whereas in Zech. 8:19 it occurs in the
masculine plural imperative, *ʾᵉhābû*. Such occurrences of the verb
ʾhb in the imperative mood are extremely limited: Hos. 3:1; Prov.
4:6; Ps. 31:24 [23E]; Amos 5:15; and Zech. 8:19. A glance at these
texts suggests that Zechariah's language most closely approximates
that of Amos, i.e., it is an admonition to seek or love a particular
quality (Amos 5:15, "Hate evil, and love good, and establish justice
in the gate"). It is active language consistent with the new activity of
feasting.

Zechariah's response to the question asked by those in Bethel could
be briefly described as contingent blessing. Things will be better, but
Israel is still required to act in certain ways. Zechariah has by the
specific language in this section emphasized specific action, i.e.,
eating, as well as active pursuit of certain moral qualities, truth and
social well-being.[2]

20 Thus says Yahweh of Hosts,
    "Yet again,[a] peoples[b] will come,
      many city dwellers;
21 the inhabitants of one city will go to another:
    'Let us go to seek help from Yahweh,
      to find Yahweh of Hosts.'
    'Let me go as well.'

---

[2] On the occurrences of *šlm* and *ʾmt* in Zechariah, see Petitjean, *Oracles*, 424–425.

22 Many peoples will come
    and a vast number of nations
    to find Yahweh of Hosts in Jerusalem,
    to seek help from Yahweh."

a. See commentary for discussion of the phrase '*ōd '*ašer*.
b. Cf. LXX for the reading '*ammîm rabbîm*, "many peoples." This is no doubt a harmonizing reading, predicated on *rabbôt* in the second colon of Zech. 8:20, and perhaps on Isa. 2:3.

[20–22] The penultimate oracle in Zech. 8, like many others in this chapter, is introduced by the formula "Thus says Yahweh of Hosts." The first colon, however, includes a problematic phrase, '*ōd '*ašer*.[1] There are two separate problems. (1) Does '*ōd*, with which this discourse commences, signify "yet," "still," or "again"? (2) What is the function of '*ašer*? The first problem is more severe than the second. Does the particle mean that something is expected which has not happened before, i.e., "Peoples will sometime (in the future) arrive"? Or does it signify that peoples will come as they have in the past, i.e., "Peoples will arrive again"? Much here depends on the interpretation of the entire oracle.

The majority of commentators understand this oracle to be part of a larger tradition, the pilgrimage of nations to Jerusalem.[2] This is a tradition preserved in other postexilic texts (Isa. 2:2–4; 60:1–3; 66:18–21). Nevertheless, it is also possible to argue that the particle '*ōd* has a special significance here which depends on its placement in the book of Zechariah. In Zech. 7:3–8:19, the author has presented a series of events in which individuals come from a city to seek help from Yahweh. In 8:20 we hear, not of individuals from one city, but rather "peoples" from many cities. They are coming "to seek help from Yahweh," exactly the same phrase used in Zech. 7:2. The term '*ōd* makes considerable sense given this typological relationship between the seeking in Zech. 7:2 and that in 8:20–21.

In all probability, both the tradition of the pilgrimage of the nations and the reference to the seeking of the Bethelites establish the context for this particular oracle. Hence, it is quite reasonable to translate this phrase as "yet again."

The second issue is raised by the presence of the particle '*ašer*. It is difficult to understand how this word could function here in its typical

[1] For a discussion, see E. Lipiński, "Recherches sur livre de Zacharie," *VT* 20, 1970, 42–46; Petitjean, *Oracles*, 425–426.
[2] See Beuken, 179; Rudolph, 152.

role as a general relative particle. It is, however, possible to maintain that it serves as an introduction to direct discourse and must here be out of place, i.e., it belongs before and not after the *'ōd*. It is this solution I prefer.

The divine oracle begins with a prediction of future action. Nations will come. These same two words occur together in another oracle that articulates a vision of future weal, Isa. 2:1–4. There too the vision is of "nations//peoples," "flowing//going" to Jerusalem because Yahweh is there. And there one party is quoted as saying something very similar to that which is found in Zech. 8:21, "Come, let us go up."

$$l^ekû \ w^ena^{'a}leh \ (Isa. \ 2:3b)$$

$$nēl^ekāh \ hālôk \ (Zech. \ 8:21)$$

The unit in Isa. 2:1–4 is, however, longer. More is said about the reason for which nations are going to Jerusalem. In Zech. 8, all we know is that nations are proceeding to Zion in order to seek Yahweh. No more is said. Perhaps the beneficent peace expressed in Isa. 2:1–4 is implied, perhaps not. What is emphasized in Zech. 8 is mutual interaction, the discourse that produces movement of people. When one person expresses a sentiment in favor of movement toward Jerusalem, another party will join in the movement.

What lies beyond such movement is left unsaid. But the motif probably is that of pilgrimage per se, of seeking Yahweh's presence in a particular place.[3] Seeking Yahweh, going to be near him, is what is at stake.[4]

In some ways this oracle seems repetitive. There is an almost dogged emphasis upon national entities seeking Yahweh. And yet the matter is expressed with literary skill. The verbs *ḥlh* and *bqš* are used in chiastic fashion: *ḥlh-bqš* in v. 21 and *bqš-ḥlh* in v. 22. One senses the writer has said what he wants to say with precision.

Only one implication of the poem remains to be examined, that of the character of the entities approaching Yahweh. We hear talk of nations and peoples in v. 22. This is a stereotypic word pair which also appears in Isa. 2 and Micah 4. What is not stereotypic in Zech. 8:22 is the way in which the pilgrims are described, as inhabitants of cities. This is powerful language, speaking of city dwellers risking movement from one place to another. Further, it is language that has special

---

[3] It is interesting that neither the temple nor Zion is mentioned here, as it is in Isa. 2:1–4.

[4] For a profound assessment of the pilgrimage motif, see V. Turner, *Image and Pilgrimage in Christian Culture*, 1978.

import: Judah had just gone through a period in which many of its towns were destroyed and left uninhabited. For Judahites to look forward to a time at which other city dwellers would travel to Judah, presumably to the city of Jerusalem itself, comprises a radical change of fortune for this scattered people. It is this radical message which the author quietly introduces with the more typical language of nations seeking Yahweh.

23 Thus says Yahweh of Hosts,
  "In those days,
    ten men from every nation,
      of every language,
    will seize, will grasp the cloak
      of each Judahite and say,
    'Let us go with you,
      for we have heard that God is with you.'"

[23] In this final oracle of Zechariah 1–8, the theme of future weal continues.[1] Moreover, particular ties link the foregoing oracle with this final piece. In Zech. 8:20–22 and 8:23, there is mention of multiple national units. More particularly, the term *gôyîm* is present in vs. 22 and 23. Furthermore, both final oracles contain direct discourse from non-Israelites. And both final units entail the pilgrimage motif within the direct speech of the nations. One may infer that these last two oracles comprise something of a thematic if not formal unity, a commentary on the situation by non-Israelites, or perhaps more precisely, statements indicating not only the activity of Israelites but that of non-Israelites as well.

The first words of Zech. 8:23 do, however, serve to set it apart from the previous oracle in one distinctive way. What will occur is projected into the indefinite future, "in those days," the plural form of the eschatological terminus technicus "on that day."[2]

If the notion of seeking Yahweh is the key idea in Zech. 8:20–22, the idea of seizing or grasping is the key motif in Zech. 8:23. The verb *ḥzq*, "grasp," occurs twice in this one verse.

Several obvious questions arise in the interpretation of Zech. 8:23. What is it to grab someone's garments? The particular term used is

---

[1] On this unit, cf. E. Lipiński, "Recherches sur le livre de Zacharie," *VT* 20, 1970, 42–46. His analysis of Zech. 8:20–23 does not distinguish two separate units, each with a distinctive theme.

[2] See Petitjean, *Oracles*, 434–435, on this issue.

"corner," presumably the corner of the cloak. Interestingly, the term is prominent in the book of Haggai as well (Hag. 2:12). Further, it was to the corners of such cloaks that tassels were to be attached, so Num. 15:38. Given the priestly legislation contained in Num. 15, to mention the corners of a Judahite's garment is to refer to a potentially definitive Judahite characterisitc. A non-Judahite who might see a garment with tassels attached to its corners would know immediately the religious identity of its wearer. Such language was used in the book of Haggai to refer to matters of ritual purity. For Zechariah, the skirt, though it signifies religious particularism, serves as a motif that makes a national pluralism possible, and enables the *gôyîm* to walk with Judahites.[3]

The term *yᵉhûdî*, "each Judahite," used to describe each individual who venerates Yahweh, is interesting. Many interpreters have pointed to the fact that this phrase occurs elsewhere in the Bible only in Esther (Esth. 2:5), a book which in all likelihood postdates Zech. 8. However, since the singular gentilic is present in Jer. 34:9 and the plural form appears in Jer. 52:28, 30, it seems inappropriate to argue on the basis of linguistic evidence alone that this oracle is not an integral part of the collection. The phrase *yᵉhûdî* seems important here because it confers individual identity on those who venerate Yahweh, and enables one such venerator to serve as an attraction for ten individuals of different linguistic groups.

It is interesting, and suggestive of the utopian character of this oracle, that immediately after we hear that these ten speak foreign tongues, they begin speaking to the individual Judahites. Such a vision strongly adds to the high view of the Judahite expressed in this oracle. Not only does he wear a distinctive cloak, not only does he act as something of a magnet, but he also has phenomenal linguistic competence. Each of the Judahites will be able to understand the myriad of tongues in which they are to be addressed. Even though the Judahites are passive, allowing themselves to be touched, they are described in a very honorable manner.

The discourse of foreigners (and it is striking that the collection of Zechariah 1–8 concludes with the speech of one of the *gôyîm*) begins with exactly the same word as in Zech. 8:21b, *nēlᵉkāh*, "let us go." However, here the similarity ends. What had earlier (vs. 21–22) been a dialogue between members of different nations now becomes a dialogue between members of the nations and Israel. Furthermore,

[3] Cf. Petitjean, *Oracles*, 435ff. He bases his analysis on Ezek. 16:8; Ruth 3:9; I Sam. 15:27.

what had earlier been quite typical pilgrimage language, "seek the face of Yahweh," presumably in Jerusalem, now is less definite. The image conveyed is that of accompanying someone on an indefinite journey rather than proceeding immediately to a definite place. The fact that the phrase "in those days" precedes the oracle suggests that this journey is not that of the Yahwists returning to Jerusalem after the exile, but a mere archetypical pilgrimage.

Even though a pilgrimage site is not mentioned, the pilgrimage experience of communities still remains at the root of this oracle. As Turner has shown, a salient characteristic of pilgrimage is the sense of community which it engenders among pilgrims of various backgrounds. The journey and its experiences are what count, and less so, in this particular oracle, the ultimate or geographic goal of the pilgrimage.

The *gôyîm* offer a reason for their desire to walk with Judahites. They are a people who have God with them. The unstated presumption of the *gôyîm* is that if they, the *gôyîm,* walk with or attach themselves to the Israelites, then God (*'elōhîm*) will also be with the non-Judahites.

What precisely is meant by having *'elōhîm* with Israel is not wholly clear. Some have suggested that Isa. 7:14 ("God is with us") lies behind this formulation.[4] Perhaps Isa. 45:14; I Sam. 17:46; II Kings 1:16; Isa. 41:10, or even covenant texts may lie behind this expression. In my judgment, it is unlikely that any particular tradition, covenant or otherwise, lies behind this formulation in Zech. 8:23. The best case could be made for the promises of Deutero-Isaiah and their reverberations in this next generation of Judahites. In any case, what is affirmed here is Yahweh's integral relationship with Israel. Yahweh is Israel's God. The hope is expressed, however, that Yahweh (identified as *'elōhîm,* a more general divine name) will be the god of the nations as they walk with the Judahites.

A final note. Given the specific language of this oracle, someone must have been saying that *'elōhîm* was with Israel. The *gôyîm* report that they have heard such things reported. Put another way, there is implied dialogue here just as there was explicit dialogue in the previous oracle. The *gôyîm* have been provoked to speech and movement by an expression of religious particularism, not by some universal cultural appeal. And it is on this particularist and yet pluralistic note that Zechariah 1–8 concludes.

4 Thus Petitjean, *Oracles,* 437; cf. Isa. 8:8, 10.